The Use of Commercial Arbitration Rules in Investment Treaty Disputes

International Litigation in Practice

General Editors

Loretta Malintoppi
N. Jansen Calamita

Advisory Board

VOLUME 11

The titles published in this series are listed at *brill.com/inli*

The Use of Commercial Arbitration Rules in Investment Treaty Disputes

Domestic Courts, Commercial Arbitration Institutions and Tribunal Jurisdiction

By

Joel Dahlquist

BRILL
NIJHOFF

LEIDEN | BOSTON

Library of Congress Cataloging-in-Publication Data

Names: Dahlquist, Joel, 1987- author.
Title: The use of commercial arbitration rules in investment treaty disputes : domestic courts, commercial arbitration institutions and tribunal jurisdiction / by Joel Dahlquist.
Description: Leiden, The Netherlands : Koninklijke Brill NV, [2021] | Series: International litigation in practice, 1874-0502 ; volume 11 | Based on author's thesis (doctoral - Uppsala universitet, 2019) issued under title: The use of "non-ICSID" arbitration rules in investment treaty disputes : domestic courts, commercial arbitration institutions and arbitral tribunal jurisdiction. | Includes bibliographical references.
Identifiers: LCCN 2020057317 (print) | LCCN 2020057318 (ebook) | ISBN 9789004413672 (paperback) | ISBN 9789004413689 (ebook)
Subjects: LCSH: Investments, Foreign–Law and legislation. | International commercial arbitration. | International and municipal law.
Classification: LCC K3830 .D34 2021 (print) | LCC K3830 (ebook) | DDC 346/.0926–dc23
LC record available at https://lccn.loc.gov/2020057317
LC ebook record available at https://lccn.loc.gov/2020057318

Typeface for the Latin, Greek, and Cyrillic scripts: "Brill". See and download: brill.com/brill-typeface.

ISSN 1874-0502
ISBN 978-90-04-41367-2 (hardback)
ISBN 978-90-04-41368-9 (e-book)

This book is printed on acid-free paper and produced in a sustainable manner.

For Tollered, where I started, and for Lara, where I arrived

Contents

Acknowledgements

This book builds on my doctoral dissertation, successfully defended at Uppsala University in March 2019. The original manuscript contains a lengthy acknowledgement of the various people and institutions to whom I am grateful for assistance, resistance and inspiration. In revising that manuscript, I have been ably assisted in the finalization of this book by Jan Kunstyr.

London, September 2020

Figures

Abbreviations

BIT	Bilateral investment treaty
CETA	EU-Canada Comprehensive Economic and Trade Agreement
EA	Emergency arbitrator
ECT	Energy Charter Treaty
ICAA	International Commercial Arbitration Act (Canada)
ICC	International Chamber of Commerce (Court of Arbitration)
ICC Rules	Arbitration Rules of the International Chamber of Commerce
ICSID	International Centre for the Settlement of Investment Disputes
ICSID AF Rules	ICSID Additional Facility Rules
ICSID Convention	Convention on the Settlement of Investment Disputes between States and Nationals of Other States (1965)
OECD	Organization for Economic Co-Operation and Development
NAFTA	North American Free Trade Agreement
PCA	Permanent Court of Arbitration
PILA	Swiss Federal Act on Private International Law
SAA	Swedish Arbitration Act
SCC	(Arbitration Institute of) the Stockholm Chamber of Commerce
SCC Rules	Arbitration Rules of the Arbitration Institute of the Stockholm Chamber of Commerce
UNCITRAL	United Nations Commission for International Trade Law
VCLT	Vienna Convention on the Law of Treaties (1969)

Introduction

On 5 February 2018, an emergency arbitrator legally seated in Stockholm ordered the state of Mongolia to allow an imprisoned foreign investor access to local and international legal counsel.[1] The claim was brought under the Energy Charter Treaty (ECT), a multilateral investment treaty which allows investors to bring arbitrations directly against states. The investor, Mr. Munshi, is a dual national of the United Kingdom and Australia and had initiated the emergency claim under the Arbitration Rules of the Arbitration Institute of the Stockholm Chamber of Commerce (SCC Rules), which is one of the four sets of arbitration rules available to foreign investors protected under the ECT.

Emergency arbitration allows a claimant in an arbitration to access interim measures prior to the constitution of a full tribunal. It was introduced by the SCC in the 2010 version of the SCC Rules, and provides for the resolution of the request for interim measures within five days. Furthermore, although the ECT entered into force in 1998 (in 2000 for Mongolia), the emergency arbitration provisions in the SCC Rules are structured so that they apply if the arbitration is initiated after 2010, meaning that Mongolia's accession to the ECT now also encompasses consent to emergency arbitration. Subsequent to the emergency proceeding, Mr. Munshi reportedly requested arbitration against Mongolia, under both the ECT and a bilateral investment treaty.[2] It is likely that the emergency order will be at issue in that still-pending arbitration. Around the same time, and in the same jurisdiction, the Svea Court of Appeal in Stockholm was faced with challenges against two separate treaty-based arbitral awards. Similar to the emergency arbitrator in *Munshi v. Mongolia*, the two tribunals had been legally seated in Stockholm and derived their jurisdiction from an investment treaty: in *PL Holdings v. Poland*[3] *it was a bilateral investment treaty between two* EU *states, while in Novenergia v. Spain*[4] it was the ECT. Furthermore, both cases were administered by the SCC, and arbitrated under the SCC Rules.

---

1 *Mohammed Munshi v. Mongolia*, SCC Case No. 2018/007, Award on Emergency Measures, 5 February 2018.

2 J Hepburn and L E Peterson, *Emergency Arbitrator Bernardo Cremades Orders Mongolian State to Ensure Businessman Has "Reasonable Access" to Counsel, but Declines to Order State to Free Him from Prison*, 3 April 2018, https://www.iareporter.com/articles/emergency-arbitrator-bernardo-cremades-orders-state-to-ensure-businessman-has-reasonable-access-to-counsel-but-declines-to-order-state-to-free-him-from-prison/, visited 4 July 2020.

3 *PL Holdings S.a.r.l. v. Poland*, SCC Case No. 2014/163, Partial Award 28 June 2017.

4 *Novenergia II - Energy & Environment (SCA) (Grand Duchy of Luxembourg), SICAR v. The Kingdom of Spain*, SCC Case No. 2015/063, Final Award, 15 February 2018.

 | DOI:10.1163/9789004413689_001

After the two states lost their respective arbitrations, they both moved to challenge the awards in the court of the seat of the arbitration – Stockholm – which had been designated by the SCC during the arbitrations.[5] Both states rely on the Court of Justice of the European Union's ("the CJEU") decision in the *Achmea* case[6] to argue that the arbitral tribunals did not have jurisdiction to hear the cases. In the *Achmea* case, rendered on March 6, 2018, the CJEU held that arbitrations based on investment treaties between two EU member states were not in conformity with EU law. Both the *PL Holdings* tribunal and the *Novenergia* tribunal, however, had rejected that EU law had any relevance for their jurisdiction, and proceeded to render final awards. The court challenges mean that at the time of writing, Swedish courts must determine the much-discussed issue of the *Achmea* judgment's effect on arbitral jurisdiction under international treaties between EU member states: the *Novenergia* challenge is pending before the Svea Court of Appeal, whereas the *PL Holdings* challenge is before the Swedish Supreme Court (which has turned to the CJEU with a request for a preliminary reference).

Also in early 2018, another SCC award was partially set aside by the United Kingdom's High Court of Justice.[7] Unlike the *Munshi, Novenergia* and *PL Holdings* tribunals – which were all legally seated in Stockholm – the *Griffin Group* tribunal was seated in London, providing the UK High Court jurisdiction to hear any challenge against the award.[8] The *Griffin Group* tribunal had rendered a partial award, finding that it lacked jurisdiction over most of the claims brought by the investor. The tribunal's reading of the underlying bilateral investment treaty's arbitration clause only permitted claims for judicial expropriation, and the investor moved to challenge this decision. The UK High Court stated that a jurisdictional challenge under the English Arbitration Act is a "re-hearing,"[9] and therefore proceeded to make its own interpretation of the treaty's arbitration clause. Ultimately, the court read the treaty provision more broadly than the tribunal, and found that also other claims were covered, including claims based on creeping expropriation and certain violations of the

5 Under Article 25(1) of the SCC Rules, if the parties do not agree to a seat, the SCC Board designates one. The same applies under Article 18(1) of the ICC Rules. This is discussed further at 4.3.2.

6 *Slovak Republic v. Achmea B.V.* (Case C-284/16).

7 GPF GP S.à.r.l v. The Republic of Poland. UK High Court of Justice, [2018] EWHC 409 (Comm), Judgement, 2 March 2018. The award is unpublished, but discussed by the UK High Court.

8 *GPF GP S.à.r.l v. Republic of Poland*, SCC Case No. V 2014/168, Award on Jurisdiction, 1 February 2017. As the award is not in the public domain, it is not clear how London was decided to be the place of arbitration.

9 Griffin v. Poland, UK High Court, para. 64.

fair and equitable treatment standard.[10] The High Court therefore set aside those parts of the partial award that rejected jurisdiction over these claims, and instead "substituted" them with the court's own finding that the tribunal *did* have jurisdiction.[11] The court also instructed the tribunal to "take the necessary steps for the continuation of the proceedings towards the liability phase dealing with the measures identified."[12] At the time of writing, the arbitration is still pending and it is unclear how the tribunal has proceeded with the case.

In yet another development in a domestic court in the spring of 2018, the French Court of Cassation rendered its judgment on the validity of another treaty-based award. The dispute in *Energoalians v. Moldova*[13] had been based on the ECT, and challenged by the losing state on the ground that the arbitral tribunal lacked jurisdiction under the ECT, because Energoalians had held a contractual right in Moldova, which was not sufficient to establish a protected "investment" under the treaty. The state was initially successful in its challenge at the Paris Court of Appeal, which interpreted the ECT as not affording protection for contractual rights.[14] This decision was appealed to the Court of Cassation, which came to the opposite conclusion and, in a decision on 28 March 2018, found that the ECT's definition *did* cover contractual rights, thus upholding the *Energoalians* award.[15]

These four cases are all recent developments, but they have more in common than the fact that they took place during the span of a few months in early 2018. Together these cases, which were all heard under commercial arbitration rules, demonstrate how similar issues are adjudicated under different treaties, in front of different bodies applying different types of norms. The arbitrations in *Munshi*, *Novenergia* and *Energoalians* were based on the multilateral ECT, whereas *PL Holdings* and *Griffin Group* were based on bilateral treaties. All but *Energoalians*[16] *were administered by commercial arbitration institutions, and all cases are governed by a domestic lex loci arbitri* and (different) domestic courts overseeing the arbitration.

10 Ibid., paras. 86–108; paras. 112–131.
11 Para. 144.
12 Ibid.
13 *Energoalians TOB v. Republic of Moldova*, UNCITRAL, Award, 23 October 2013.
14 Moldova v. Energoalians, Paris Court of Appeal.
15 French Court of Cassation, 16–16568, Judgement, 28 March 2018.
16 Although seated in Paris, the *Energoalians* case was an *ad hoc* arbitration heard under the UNCITRAL Rules. However, it seems that the ICC Court was designated as appointing authority, but never had any reason to be involved in the arbitration, *Energoalians TOB v. Republic of Moldova*, UNCITRAL, Award, 23 October 2013, para. 9.

The cases also share another important feature, which is the primary focus of this text: they all raise questions with respect to arbitral tribunal jurisdiction. The emergency arbitrator in *Munshi* was competent to hear the claim against Mongolia by virtue of the SCC introducing emergency arbitration in its 2010 arbitration rules, with application to treaty-based arbitration generally, including in cases where the state's consent to arbitration predates 2010. Thus, when Mongolia ratified the ECT, the treaty did not provide for emergency arbitration, which is a subsequent creation by the SCC, but in 2018 the *Munshi* emergency arbitrator found that it did. Furthermore, as part of the same institution's administration of the *PL Holdings* and *Novenergia* arbitrations, it had designated Stockholm as the legal place of arbitration in both disputes. One consequence of this decision is that the Stockholm court is now faced with the jurisdictional consequences of the *Achmea* decision in two different scenarios: one based on a bilateral investment treaty and one based on the ECT. In *Griffin Group*, the place of arbitration was instead London, meaning that the challenge was brought not to the Svea Court of Appeal, but to the UK High Court, which found that under its own domestic law it was entitled to "re-hear" any jurisdictional issue. In doing so, the court pronounced itself on a jurisdictional matter which is frequently litigated in investment treaty arbitration, i.e. the scope of an arbitration clause limiting tribunal jurisdiction to certain aspects of an alleged expropriation. Similarly, the French Court of Cassation determined the extent to which a contractual right can be understood as an "investment" under the ECT, a familiar question in investment arbitration. Its finding was in conformity with that of the tribunal's majority, but came after a lower French court had first reached the opposite conclusion.

While these four cases are either still pending or were finally decided just prior to the completion of the present text, they are but a few of many examples of cases where rules initially drafted for commercial arbitration govern investment treaty disputes. There have been hundreds of such investment treaty arbitrations, and many are still pending or waiting to be initiated under the numerous investment treaties that allow for the application of traditionally commercial arbitration rules. The following text examines this application, focusing on if and how the scope of arbitral tribunals' mandate is shaped by the use of these rules, which regularly involves decision-making by both domestic courts and commercial arbitration institutions in a manner that may have consequences for the jurisdiction of arbitral tribunals. Domestic courts are often tasked with reviewing whether an arbitral award should stand or be set aside. As part of this review, courts have been asked to interpret the scope of the arbitral tribunal's jurisdiction. Commercial arbitration institutions, on the other hand, develop the arbitration rules which apply to the disputes.

These rules are then managed and interpreted by the institutions, as part of their administration of arbitrations.

This book addresses questions based on issues such as the ones highlighted in the four cases above: how have domestic courts approached problems of treaty-based jurisdiction? Has the application of commercial arbitration rules, as administered by traditionally commercial institutions, affected the jurisdictional scope in treaty-based cases? And, more broadly, how, if at all, have these two types of actors influenced our understanding of arbitration tribunal jurisdiction in investment arbitration?

CHAPTER 1

The Research Focus and Its Context

1.1 Introduction

There are a number of arbitration rules with the potential of being applied to disputes in an investment treaty context. Of these, only the ICSID Convention and its annexed ICSID Arbitration Rules originated with investor-state disputes in mind. A majority of the known investor-state arbitrations filed between 1987 and 2017 were governed by the ICSID Convention, with the remainder being governed by "non-ICSID" Rules.[1] In practice, there are four other sets of rules regularly used by investors:

- The UNCITRAL Arbitration Rules[2]
- The ICC Rules of Arbitration[3]
- The SCC Arbitration Rules[4]
- The ICSID Additional Facility Rules[5]

Given that almost half of all known investment treaty disputes are arbitrated under "non-ICSID" rules, there is limited research on this phenomenon. Partly, this is probably a function of the fact that arbitrations under commercial rules tend to be less publicized, making them less likely targets for research. Regardless of the reason, the fact remains that the use of these rules is under-studied in investment treaty arbitration literature.

If an investor pursues non-ICSID arbitration, this choice presents a number of legal issues that might be fruitful to explore. While the ICSID Convention occupies a specific, "self-contained," single place on the map of international dispute resolution, the non-ICSID category is open, in the sense that a whole range of legal norms and actors might potentially be involved in the adjudication of such a case, shaping procedural aspects that are well-known to seasoned practitioners, such as costs, case administration, and enforcement

1 UNCTAD, *Investor-State Dispute Settlement: Review of Developments in 2017*, 2 June 2018, Issue 2, p. 2.

2 Unless otherwise specified, the following text refers to the 2013 version of the UNCITRAL Rules.

3 Unless otherwise specified, the following text refers to the 2017 version of the ICC Rules.

4 Unless otherwise specified, the following text refers to the 2017 version of the SCC Rules

5 Unless otherwise specified, the following text refers to the 2006 version of the ICSID Additional Facility Rules.

 | DOI:10.1163/9789004413689_002

mechanisms.[6] The present inquiry, however, focuses on another, arguably more fundamental, issue, namely that of arbitral jurisdiction.

All arbitration derives its authority from the consent of the disputing parties.[7] The consent, recorded in an arbitration agreement, is a function of party autonomy: the parties choose arbitration and shape the proceedings according to their preferences. In this respect, arbitration based on treaties does not differ, as a matter of principle, from arbitration based on contracts. Irrespective of one's perspective of the 'hybrid' nature of investment arbitration,[8] it is clear that the parties to *any* arbitration must consent to it; this principle applies equally to both private, contractual arbitration and to public, inter-state arbitration.[9] Nevertheless, investment treaty arbitration differs from other types of arbitration in several ways with respect to the arbitration agreement. For example, investment treaties almost always include objective jurisdictional requirements, such as jurisdiction *ratione materiae*, *ratione personae* and *ratione temporis*. These requirements pose a limitation on the party autonomy (or at least to the autonomy of the potential claimant):[10] the scope of jurisdiction typically excludes claimants who are not investors holding an investment, as defined by an applicable treaty. Most investment treaty disputes involve complex jurisdictional issues such as these. The frequency of jurisdictional issues is reflected also at the stage when an award is challenged: investment arbitration awards are often challenged on jurisdictional grounds, whereas their commercial counterparts more rarely concern such questions.[11]

Another key aspect of investment treaty arbitration is the fact that the contracting parties and the disputing parties are different. Under the conventional understanding of the consent to arbitration, the respondent state gives its consent in an interstate treaty, while the investor gives its consent by subsequently

---

6 See generally *2015 International Arbitration Survey: Improvements and Innovations in International Arbitration*, by Queen Mary University of London and White & Case Law firm.

7 A M Steingruber, *Consent in International Arbitration*, Oxford 2012, p.12 with further references; G Wang, "Consent in Investor-State Arbitration: A Critical Analysis" (2014) 13 Chinese Journal of International Law 335.

8 See generally Z Douglas, "The Hybrid Foundations"; A Roberts, "Clash of Paradigms."

9 C McLachlan, L Shore and M Weininger, *International Investment Arbitration: Substantive Principles*, Oxford University Press, 2007, para. 7.186.; Z Douglas, *The International Law of Investment Claims*, Cambridge University Press, 2009, para. 125.

10 A M Steingruber, p. 2.

11 Cf. K Hobér and N Eliasson, para. 28.162. Furthermore, this is evidenced by the high frequency of bifurcated arbitrations, where jurisdictional issues are dealt with separately see A Carlevaris in C Giorgetti (ed.). 182–183, with further references.

requesting arbitration relying upon the state's treaty "offer."[12] Consequently, there are not always any negotiations between the disputing parties prior to the existence of a formal dispute, and the theoretically asymmetrical arbitration agreement – specific to the dispute that has arisen –[13] is comprised by a combination of the state's offer in the treaty and the investor's consent when it requests arbitration. This has implications for the content and scope of the arbitration agreement, including the applicable arbitration rules. If the treaty only provides for arbitration under the ICSID Convention, the investor can only request ICSID arbitration. If the treaty provides for several *fora* – and thereby, if the respondent state has consented to arbitration pursuant to different potential rules – then the investor may choose between the available options.[14]

These specificities distinguish jurisdiction in treaty-based arbitrations from jurisdiction in contract-based arbitrations. What is more, because these jurisdictional issues are regulated in treaties, arbitral tribunals often have to engage with general international law, as, by extension, do other ancillary actors such as reviewing bodies and administrating institutions. This engagement is the focus of the present text: as non-ICSID arbitration involves more, and different, actors than does ICSID arbitration, what are the consequences of these actors' involvement for how arbitral jurisdiction is understood in international investment law more widely?

The fact that domestic courts play a role in the development of international law is well-known and already studied in other contexts, as discussed below.[15] The manner in which they construe the scope of arbitral tribunals' jurisdiction, however, is largely understudied. Furthermore, compared to

---

12 First explained in J Paulsson, "Arbitration Without Privity." Although the notion that this asymmetry is able to create an arbitration agreement has been questioned, it seems to be widely accepted in practice and will not be discussed further this study. For an overview of public international law critique of this "contractual" approach to understanding the consent to arbitration in investment arbitration, see A M Steingruber, pp. 60–66.

13 Unlike a contractual arbitration agreement, which typically refers to any future dispute under the agreement, see C Schreuer, "Calvo's Grandchildren: The Return of Local Remedies in Investment Arbitration," in The Law and Practice of International Courts and Tribunals 4: 1–17, Brill 2005, p. 10 (citing the ICSID tribunal in SGS v. Philippines).

14 In theory, the disputing parties could agree separately on an arbitration clause when the dispute has arisen, and thereby bypass the asymmetrically construed arbitration agreement based on the above model. This appears to very rare. Instead, the dogmatic approach to the formation of the arbitration agreement – as formed when the claimant-investor accepts the offer from the respondent state, including the limitations and requirements contained therein – has been the basis of the disputing parties' consent in every arbitration subject to this study.

15 See Chapter 3.2

domestic courts, the role of commercial arbitration institutions, it is submitted, is virtually unexplored in international law research so far. If the two types of actors in fact do influence arbitral jurisdiction – and thereby the kinds of disputes that are arbitrated, and how – they might contribute to a degree of internal fragmentation of international investment law, as explained below.

1.2 The Bigger Picture

1.2.1 *Introduction*

This sub-section explains the background against which the research takes place. First, investment treaty arbitration may be said to be characterized by a certain degree of internal fragmentation, as demonstrated by the fact that different types of actors may be involved in the adjudication of similar disputes, potentially leading to different approaches and outcomes. The fact that the actors involved in this decision-making may be actors other than arbitral tribunals has not previously been the subject of much study.

Secondly, investment treaty arbitration as it has been known to date is the subject of broad reform discussions based on a number of perceived concerns with the current system. One of these concerns is that the decision-making is inconsistent and unpredictable. There is thus a connection between the internal fragmentation and the reform discussions, in the sense that a better understanding of the fragmented nature of decision-making may inform the conversation about how the current system ought to be changed.

1.2.2 *Internal Fragmentation*

1.2.2.1 What Is Meant by "Internal Fragmentation"

Investment treaty arbitration is decentralized and characterized by a lack of hierarchy. Furthermore, unlike many other specialist areas of international law, the field lacks a single "deliberative hub."[16] One consequence of this decentralized nature is that a large number of similar treaties are interpreted by *ad hoc* arbitral tribunals, which are not standing bodies but rather authorized to determine a single dispute, after which their mandate is extinguished. However, other actors might also be involved in the adjudication. This is particularly the case in non-ICSID arbitration, which relies on a commercial

16 The term is borrowed from T St John, p. 246, who argues that jurisdictions compete to attract cases, stating that "[c]ompetition without a multilateral place for monitoring makes it more difficult for governments to be informed or exert control."

arbitration framework involving domestic courts and, sometimes, commercial arbitration institutions, as ancillary actors.

The focus of the present text emphasizes this fragmentation *within* the field of investment arbitration – internal fragmentation, in short[17] – by focusing on two distinct types of actors, whose role in investment law is often overlooked. This focus is different from the more general fragmentation discussion on the development towards a multitude of courts and tribunals in the international sphere, which increasingly adjudicate specific areas of international law with a rising degree of specialization.[18] While there are functional similarities between the larger fragmentation discussion in international law and the "intra-investment law" lens employed here, they are two different notions. Rather than looking at the relationship between investment treaty arbitration and general international law, the present book focuses on international investment law's internal fragmentation.[19]

1.2.2.2 The Concerns Associated with Inconsistent Interpretations

A point of departure for this book is that the internal fragmentation of investment treaty arbitration has not previously been fully appreciated, and that by studying non-ICSID arbitration this phenomenon can be better understood. Compared to the "self-enclosed" and convention-based ICSID framework, various actors potentially influence the content of international investment law when disputes are arbitrated in a traditionally "commercial" framework. Has this fact led to different approaches in how these actors shape the scope of arbitral decision-making, and if so, do these different approaches lead to inconsistencies or conflicting decisions? These questions, which are dogmatic in nature, also tie into a more overarching normative idea: is it desirable that investment treaties vest authority in domestic courts and commercial arbitration institutions? Questions such as these are familiar to the fragmentation

17 Cf., S Schill, "W(h)ither Fragmentation," at 887; 905; J Alvarez, "A BIT on Custom" (2009) 42 NYUJ Intl L & Poly 17, at 80; B Simma, "Foreword," in A von Bogdany and I Venzke (eds.), *International Judicial Lawmaking – On Public Authority and Democratic Legitimation in Global Governance*, Springer, 2012, p. XI.

18 See for example ILC Fragmentation Report; UG Blum, "Bilateralism, Multilateralism and the Architecture of International Law," (2008) 49 Harv Int'l LK 32; O K. Fauchald and A Nollkaemper (eds.).

19 This does not exclude that there is fruitful territory to explore concerning the role of investment treaty arbitration in the fragmentation of international law generally. Occasionally in the below study, domestic court judgments are discussed which might be of relevance for general international law. However, such issues are not the focus here. See also generally, for example, C McLachlan, "Investment Treaties and General International Law," The International and Comparative Law Quarterly, Vol. 57, No. 2 (Apr., 2008), pp. 361–401.

debate in international law generally, but translated to the present context it poses questions as to the nature of investment treaty arbitration.

This nature is changing, as concerns mount about inconsistent decision-making. Most prominently, in November 2018, Working Group III of the United Nations Commission on International Trade Law (UNCITRAL) agreed by consensus that it was desirable to develop reforms relating to "unjustifiably inconsistent interpretations of investment treaty provisions and other relevant principles of international law by ISDS tribunals."[20] However, it is possible that not only arbitral tribunals, which seems to be the assumed sole decision-maker, but also courts and institutions contribute to the concerns relating to consistency, coherence and correctness.

1.2.2.3 The Fragmented Architecture of Non-ICSID Arbitration

In investment treaty arbitration, domestic courts and arbitration institutions derive their mandate from treaties, in the sense that their involvement stems from their direct (as is typically the case for commercial arbitration institutions) or indirect (as is typically the case for domestic courts) designation in an investment treaty. Furthermore, they are primarily involved in the scenario where the ICSID Convention is not the governing framework for the dispute. Domestic courts and commercial arbitration institutions apply and interpret two different kinds of supplementary norms (domestic law and commercial arbitration rules, respectively) in determining the scope of arbitral jurisdiction. Domestic courts primarily do this in the context of set-aside proceedings after the award has been rendered, whereas arbitration institutions both draft and interpret the arbitration rules that govern pending arbitrations.

At the stage where the validity of a treaty-based arbitral award is challenged, the matter can be brought either to an international body based on the ICSID Convention, or before any of a number of different domestic courts, depending on what is authorized by the treaty in question. ICSID annulment is conducted within a central, unified institutional framework provided by the ICSID Convention. This means that the challenge against an ICSID award is carried out with application of the exact same, convention-based provisions. The grounds for annulment are listed in Article 52 of the ICSID Convention, a provision which by definition must be addressed, to some degree, by every ICSID *ad hoc* annulment committee. Consequently, there is a considerable body of cases to rely upon for parties and committees. The institutional presence of the ICSID Administrative Council, in which each contracting state is represented, and the ICSID Secretariat also means that reforms can be carried

20 United Nations Doc. A/CN/9/964, para. 40.

out, with consequences for every future annulment proceeding. By contrast, in the non-ICSID scenario, the award must be challenged in domestic court, and the present inquiry studies how different courts, in several different domestic jurisdictions, have approached such challenges. As introduced above, the tribunal's jurisdiction – based on a treaty – is often the subject of these challenge proceedings.

Secondly, whereas ICSID is an international organization with a secretariat of international civil servants that administers every ICSID arbitration, two commercial arbitration institutions also have significant experience of administering treaty-based cases under their own rules – the International Chamber of Commerce International Court of Arbitration (ICC) and the Arbitration Institute of the Stockholm Chamber of Commerce (SCC).[21] These private institutions have developed their arbitration rules primarily in the context of commercial arbitration, although more recently they have started taking treaty-based disputes into account to a certain extent when updating their rules. In addition to setting the framework for the dispute through their arbitration rules, institutions also make decisions – as authorized by their arbitration rules – before and during arbitrations.

Thus, domestic courts and commercial arbitration institutions, while not typically associated with public international law adjudication, are a frequent presence in non-ICSID investment arbitration. This text investigates whether, and if so how, this presence has consequences for the scope of the arbitral tribunal's jurisdiction. Although arbitral tribunals determine their own jurisdiction,[22] these other actors may potentially influence the scope of that jurisdiction, directly or indirectly. Building on a study of (i) domestic court decisions pertaining to the scope of arbitral jurisdiction, and (ii) awards and decisions from treaty-based arbitrations administered by the ICC and the SCC, the following text describes and analyses the experience of both domestic courts and arbitration institutions, with the aim of contributing to a better understanding of if and how these actors may shape the scope of arbitral jurisdiction.

1.2.2.4 Why Understanding the Extent of Internal Fragmentation Matters

One may get the impression that investment arbitration is moving away from its *ad hoc* roots, towards something more consistent, the assumption being that

21 As discussed further below at 2.6.

22 Albeit not finally, under the doctrine of *kompetenz-kompetenz* discussed below at 2.3.

the latter is the functional end-game for any developing legal area.[23] While the premise for the present text does not require a stand as to whether investment treaty arbitration is a "legal system,"[24] nor for that matter that any legal system has to strive to be coherent, it is evident that many states prefer a move in that direction.

This text is not primarily intended as an interjection in this debate, but rather as a contribution to the doctrinal platform upon which it must take place. It is therefore necessary to state at the outset that the focus here is the "present-day" system, and the experience of disputes under investment treaties to date. In the arbitrations forming the basis for the cases studied in this text, the different tribunals were put in place by the disputing parties, with their mandates extinguished at the conclusion of the dispute. The powers and responsibilities vested in the tribunals emanate from the disputing parties, who are the parties to the individual arbitration agreement. This fundamental premise is especially relevant in the non-ICSID context, where the underlying investment treaty refers to arbitration rules, and arbitral institutions, whose main activity is contractual arbitration.[25]

This being said, it is also clear that taken together, these individually separate disputes – and the various associated institutional decisions, as well as court judgments ruling on the validity of the resulting awards – together form something that is larger than a vast number of isolated islands. It does not suffice to assume that individual tribunals have acted in vacuums, while ignoring systemic consequences. The present study exists in the midst of this tension between a focus on specific outcomes and concerns with overarching systemic effects, as it discusses the role of two different kinds of actors, with different functions, in shaping the scope of arbitral tribunal jurisdiction. The very premise for the research questions is that useful knowledge can be derived from the study of formally separate, seemingly isolated disputes.

23 As evidenced by the many concerns raised over the lack of "consistency" or "predictability" inherent in the current framework.

24 In the legal sense, it is difficult to delineate the "regime" or "system" of investment treaty arbitration. In the present text, these terms are used solely for pedagogical purposes. See further J Viñuales, "Sources of International Investment Law: Conceptual Foundations of Unruly Practices," in S Besson and J d'Aspremont (eds.), The Oxford Handbook of the Sources of International Law, Oxford University Press, 2017, p. 1070.

25 When the arbitration is instead governed by the ICSID Convention, a multilateral procedural convention ratified by 162 states, the situation is slightly different and the systemic implications of jurisdictional decisions arguably somewhat more visible; for example, most tribunals have to interact with Article 25 of the ICSID Convention.

This text does not primarily employ a normative lens. Thus, the focus here is not principally whether the involvement of domestic courts and commercial institutions in non-ICSID arbitration, and the associated risks of inconsistent and unpredictable decision-making, is desirable or not. Instead, the focus is primarily to understand and analyse the extent of these activities, which is practically relevant. As mentioned above, one of the main concerns voiced against the present-day system of investment arbitration is the lack of consistency in the decision-making. Consequently, the reform discussions are focused on proposals that are intended to address this perceived shortcoming. Therefore, the questions studied here may be relevant as part of the ongoing reforms.

1.2.3 *Reforms of Investment Arbitration*

As already mentioned, investment treaty arbitration is undergoing reform. Not only are individual states drafting model treaties[26] and entering into bilateral treaties[27] which in various ways change the procedural framework which so far has governed investment arbitrations; there are also multilateral negotiations taking place, most notably in UNCITRAL Working Group III. As part of these reform efforts, more information about how the current system operates has been requested by states.[28] ICSID, as an international organization, is active

26 See for example Model Text for the Indian Bilateral Investment Treaty (available at http://investmentpolicyhub.unctad.org/Download/TreatyFile/3560, visited 5 January 2019); Dutch Model BIT (available at https://www.internetconsultatie.nl/investeringsakkoorden, visited 5 January 2019); Brazilian Cooperation and Facilitation Investment Agreement (discussed by N Bernasconi-Osterwalder & M Brauch, *Comparative commentary to Brazil's cooperation and investment facilitation agreements* (CIFAs) *with Mozambique, Angola, Mexico, and Malawi,* September 2015. Available at http://www.iisd.org/library/comparative-commentary-brazil-cooperation-and-investment-facilitation-agreements-cifas, visited 5 January 2019.

27 Comprehensive Economic and Trade Agreement between the European Union and Canada (CETA); The EU-Singapore Free Trade Agreement (EUSFTA); EU-Vietnam Trade and Investment Agreements.

28 OECD Appointing Authority Paper, para. 21. Furthermore, during the initial stage of the ongoing work in UNCITRAL Working Group III, a delegate from the Russian Federation emphasized the need for data on current practice of investor-state arbitration, in particular as it concerns the experiences of arbitral institutions, see, Archive of Working Group Audio Recordings, U.N. COMM'N ON INT'L TRADE LAW, http://www.uncitral.org/uncitral/audio/meetings.jsp, 28 November 2017, from time 15:09:51. The UNCITRAL Secretariat responded to the Russian delegate that the Secretariat had been in consultation with various stakeholders but not those institutions primarily involved in commercial arbitration, to which the Russian delegate replied that also commercial arbitration institutions administer treaty arbitrations, and that their experience might provide relevant input [to the reform work], from time 15:13:38 in the same audio recording. Following this exchange, several arbitral institutions intervened to announce their presence as observers in the

in reform discussions, most visibly through the proposed changes of the ICSID Arbitration Rules, which are the end-result of an ongoing consultation process involving the member states.[29] While the ICSID Convention has never been changed, its associated arbitration rules are occasionally updated and this recent round of proposed changes is a response to the ongoing reform requests.

1.2.3.1 How the Reform of Non-ICSID Arbitration Is Different from ICSID Arbitration

Compared to the ICSID regime, the more fragmented non-ICSID situation is different in several ways, which may influence the way the rules are utilized in future disputes. Individual states cannot "denounce" the use of these rules, the way the ICSID Convention can be denounced. Furthermore, there is no double-consent requirement in non-ICSID arbitration.[30] Once an investment treaty refers to the UNCITRAL Rules, the ICC Rules or the SCC Rules, individual states have limited means of influencing the content of the rules, save for an amendment or a termination of the investment treaty itself. At the same time, however, these rules – in particular the institutional rules – are arguably more responsive and flexible tools than are international conventions such as the ICSID Convention. The mandate to make use of this flexibility rests solely with the ICC and the SCC, however, both of which currently lack institutionalized channels to formally involve sovereign states in their rule updates. This begs the question how this flexibility has been used by institutions. In theory, the commercial arbitration rules could be used in a way that addresses concerns raised by states about the procedural nature of investment arbitration. Specifically concerning fundamental issues of arbitral jurisdiction – i.e. what types of disputes are possible to adjudicate and in what manner – it is possible that the past experience could provide guidance for future reforms. Similarly, different domestic courts have repeatedly been faced with issues of tribunal jurisdiction, primarily in the context of the dozens of final awards that have been challenged on jurisdictional grounds. In any potential reforms, the nature of a supervisory body, ensuring that only disputes that are properly within the jurisdiction of a future disputes body are adjudicated, is likely to be a major point of contention. What can be learnt from studying past experience of domestic courts in this regard?

Working Group, and in subsequent meetings both the ICC and the SCC have participated as observers with the right to intervene.

29 All documents from the ICSID Rules and Regulation Amendment Process are gathered at https://icsid.worldbank.org/en/amendments, visited 5 January 2019.

30 See 3.4.2.

1.2.3.2 The Need for More Information

Finally, one related contextual element motivating the present study is that the way in which the application of non-ICSID rules affects fundamental aspects of investment dispute resolution was not thoroughly considered when states first allowed for it in their investment treaties. The multitude of potentially applicable norms, be they domestic arbitration statutes or commercial arbitration rules, are the result of a largely bilateral treaty regime, and the consequences of their application do not appear to have been contemplated by the various states that initiated it. Given this, and the many reforms currently being considered, the present inquiry might remedy some of the earlier lack of understanding, so that states might benefit from this study's findings for their future treaty-making.

It is against this background of potential increasing fragmentation within, as well as mounting institutionalized reform of, investment treaty arbitration that the following research questions are asked. The purpose of this book is to use the experience of domestic courts and commercial arbitration institutions to create a map of sorts, explaining the contours of the fragmented decision-making within investment treaty arbitration. What have these ancillary actors done when faced with treaty-based jurisdiction, and how, if at all, does their involvement inform how the scope of jurisdiction evolves? These questions will now be specified.

1.3 First Focus: Domestic Courts' Interpretation of Treaty-Based Arbitral Tribunal Jurisdiction

In international commercial arbitration, there is an intricate normative web that forms the legal boundaries of any individual dispute. This web consists of a number of norms, primarily party agreement, the applicable arbitration rules (if any), and the law at the place of arbitration, which together define the scope of jurisdiction of the arbitral tribunal. Under the well-established principle of *kompetenz-kompetenz,* arbitral tribunals determine their own jurisdiction,[31] as defined by these norms. This principle applies equally in many types of international arbitration.[32] That being said, when arbitrations are conducted under commercial arbitration rules, the tribunal's determination is subject to

31 See for example G Born, p. 200; Redfern and Hunter, p. 347.

32 For a discussion in the state-state context, see *Arbitration between the Republic of Croatia and the Republic of Slovenia, Croatia v Slovenia,* Partial Award, PCA Case No 2012-04, 30 June 2016, Permanent Court of Arbitration.

the control of a domestic court at the place of arbitration. Thus, every treaty-based non-ICSID arbitration requires a domestic place of arbitration, and the courts of that jurisdiction may be asked to review the jurisdiction of the tribunal either during the arbitration, or after the final award has been rendered. The vast majority of domestic courts' interactions with treaty-based arbitral jurisdiction has taken place in the latter scenario,[33] in the form of set-aside applications at the place of arbitration, targeted at the tribunal's jurisdiction.

How have domestic courts approached this task, when a tribunal's jurisdiction under an investment treaty is challenged at the place of arbitration? Does it matter – for purposes such as standard of review and interpretation – that the consent to arbitration originates in a treaty, rather than in a contract as envisioned by domestic arbitration legislation? As for standard of review, to what extent have domestic courts "retried" issues of treaty-based jurisdiction? As for interpretation, how have domestic courts approached the interpretation of jurisdictional clauses: with the aid of rules of interpretation from public international law, or on the contrary with the assistance primarily of domestic principles? Finally, do the approaches taken by one court in a specific case affect how another court, or arbitral tribunal, approach similar issues?

1.4 Second focus: Commercial Arbitration Institutions and Treaty-Based Arbitral Tribunal Jurisdiction

As will be developed further in Chapter 2, many investment treaties refer to commercial arbitration rules. The most common set of rules is the UNCITRAL Rules, followed by the ICSID Additional Facility Rules, the ICC Rules and the SCC Rules. All these rules require a place of arbitration – and thereby also supervisory domestic courts – but the two latter are particularly interesting in the present context, as they are drafted, maintained and interpreted by their respective arbitration institution.[34]

Traditionally, commercial arbitration institutions such as the ICC and the SCC are not understood to play any significant role in public international law. They are private business organizations.[35] Moreover, there is no

33 As discussed further at 3.1, in a small number of cases courts have been involved during pending arbitrations.

34 The UNCITRAL Rules are designed for *ad hoc* arbitration and as such not tied to one institutional body, whereas the ICSID Additional Facility Rules are primarily used by ICSID to administer disputes involving parties that do not come from an ICSID state.

35 For a critique of this proposition, see B Warwas, in particular Chapter 2, who argues that commercial arbitration institutions are increasingly filling a "public" function.

institutionalized input from sovereign states in the drafting of the ICC and SCC Rules. The fact that they are not created by states, but by businesses, arguably excludes them from the widely used definition of an "international organization."[36] The many accounts of how international organizations increasingly develop into autonomous actors, and of how permanent secretariats influence the development and decision-making of international organizations do not address commercial arbitration institutions.[37] The role of commercial arbitration institutions is therefore often missing in public international law studies. Similarly, the many studies of the functioning of arbitral institutions in the context and culture of international commercial arbitration have a commercial focus, meaning that the treaty-based activities of the institutions are either expressly or implicitly left out.[38]

The present text is less concerned with how the ICC and the SCC ought to be categorized, and more with what they actually do. For the present purposes, therefore, it is sufficient to note that the traditional research divide between the spheres of international law and commercial arbitration means that there is a gap; the treaty-based work of these institutions tends to "fall between the cracks" in existing literature.

Arbitral jurisdiction is an apt topic to study in order to connect these otherwise often separated spheres of international (investment) law and commercial arbitration. As will be developed below, the studied arbitration rules are primarily drafted for, and applied to, contractual disputes between entities acting in their private capacities. However, when these rules – as promulgated, administered and interpreted by a private institution – govern treaty-based arbitration, they form part of the arbitration agreement between the investor and the state. In particular before (i.e. when the rules are drafted and amended) and during (i.e. when the dispute is administered) arbitrations, institutions

36 See, for example, J Alvarez, *International Organizations as Law-makers,* Oxford University Press, 2010, pp. 2–5 with further references.

37 See for example M N Barnett and M Finnemore, "The Politics, Power, and Pathologies of International Organizations," International Organization, Vol. 53, No. 4 (Autumn, 1999), 699–732; T Piiparinen, "Secretariats," in J K Cogan, I Hurd and I Johnstone (eds.), The Oxford Handbook of International Organizations, Oxford University Press, 2016; J H H Weiler, "The Rule of Lawyers and the Ethos of Diplomats: Reflections on the Internal and External Legitimacy of WTO Dispute Settlement," Journal of World Trade 35(2):191–207, 2001; A Anghie, "International Financial Institutions," in C Reus-Smit (ed.), *The Politics of International Law,* Cambridge University Press, 2004; I Venzke, *How Interpretation Makes International Law – On Semantic Change and Normative Twists,* Oxford University Press, 2012, pp. 69–71.

38 See for example B Warwas; Stone Sweet and Grisel; J Karton, *The Culture of International Arbitration and the Evolution of Contract Law*, Oxford University Press, 2013.

might affect the scope of the tribunal's mandate, as they both determine the framework for the procedure, and occasionally interpret that framework.

Even if commercial arbitration institutions are not created by states, they are referred to in many investment treaties as the preferred administrators of disputes, and as such presumably given a certain role in international investment law. No previous attempt seems to have been made to study the practice of commercial arbitration institutions in administering treaty-based arbitrations or, in other words, to connect the commercial background of arbitration institutions to their experience administering treaty-based disputes, which often involve elements of public international law.

Moving on to the questions asked here, the conventional understanding of commercial arbitration institutions is that they do not make decisions, but rather administer and facilitate decision-making by others.[39] To the extent that any decision-making in institutional investment arbitration is relevant to study, a traditional perspective would therefore suggest, it is the one performed by arbitral *tribunals*. This text explores to what extent this traditional view rings true in the present context. Do commercial arbitration institutions in fact influence, directly or indirectly, the scope of jurisdiction?

In addition to the administration of pending disputes, the institutions also draft and amend the rules. Has the structure of the ICC Rules and the SCC Rules affected the scope of tribunal decision-making? To what extent have the two institutions taken the specificities of treaty-based consent to arbitration into account in their arbitration rules?

Finally, and more generally, given how frequent and complex jurisdictional issues are in investment treaty arbitration, what does the use of commercial arbitration rules to solve treaty-based disputes tell us about how notions of private dispute resolution, such as party autonomy and contractual interpretation, informs treaty-based jurisdiction?

1.5 Outline

The following text is structured in four parts. First, a background chapter introduces the history of non-ICSID arbitration in investment treaties. The purpose of this introductory chapter is to describe when and where commercial arbitration clauses started to appear in investment treaties, which initially provided only for ICSID arbitration. This background chapter sets the stage for the discussion that follows in the two main chapters, which discuss some of

39 R Gerbay pp. 118–147 and pp. 173–175 with further references.

the consequences of states' inclusion of non-ICSID rules in investment treaties. These two main chapters focus on two different kinds of actors that are regularly involved in non-ICSID investment arbitration: domestic courts and commercial arbitration institutions, respectively.

First, the experience of domestic courts in determining the scope of arbitral jurisdiction is discussed, primarily focusing on the post-award stage where one party challenges the validity of the award on jurisdictional grounds. Then, the penultimate chapter addresses the experience of the ICC and the SCC, with a focus on how these rules – as they have been developed and interpreted – influence the scope of arbitral jurisdiction. Finally, the concluding chapter discusses the findings of the previous chapters, and attempts to answer the questions posed.

The majority of the research for this book was carried out between 2016 and 2018, with some updates in 2019. The historic background chapter is based on information available during this time, primarily the UNCTAD BIT database (supplemented by treaties obtained directly from governments, subsequently submitted to UNCTAD for inclusion in their database. The chapter on domestic courts takes into account challenge proceedings that have been finally determined as of 1 January 2020, with occasional later developments discussed when relevant. The chapter on commercial arbitration institutions builds on on-site research carried out at the ICC and the SCC in 2016 and 2017, with the generous consent of the institutions. Some subsequent material has been taken into account, to the extent that it is in the public domain.

CHAPTER 2

Commercial Arbitration Rules in Investment Treaties – A Historic Background

The purpose of this background chapter is to outline the emergence of commercial arbitration rules in investment treaties. In investment law literature generally, the potential application of commercial arbitration rules in treaty-based disputes is largely taken for granted. It seems the question *why* these rules are applied has never been seriously investigated. This introductory chapter aims at contributing a first step towards answering that question, in a way that helps to contextualize the following chapters.

First, the emergence of investment treaties allowing for investors to bring treaty claims against states – which initially was synonymous with claims under the ICSID Convention – is briefly explained. Then follows a section describing the emergence of the "non-ICSID" arbitration rules in investment treaties, which compared to the ICSID Secretariat's promotion of ICSID arbitration was characterized by a lack of institutional involvement.

An important corollary to the existence of the option to arbitrate under non-ICSID rules is the extent to which this option is utilized in practice. As outlined below, many 20th century treaties allow for both ICSID and at least one additional, alternative forum for arbitration. Although the primary interest here is to discuss when and why states started to consent to certain types of arbitration, it would be relevant to also ascertain the extent to which investors avail themselves of this consent. Such a study is not easily done, however: whereas the ICSID Secretariat publishes both the existence of a dispute, as well as the resulting award, unless the parties object,[1] the default rule under the non-ICSID rules is often the opposite.[2] Consequently, it is notoriously difficult to determine how frequently treaty arbitrations are conducted under non-ICSID rules. That being said, it is possible to obtain at least a general understanding of the magnitude. In a 2013 UNCTAD study of known investment arbitrations, 61% were ICSID cases, roughly one fourth of known cases were arbitrated under the UNCITRAL Rules, while the SCC Rules represented 5% of the known cases and "other rules" 8%.[3] It must be emphasized that

1 ICSID Convention, Article 48(5).

2 See below p. 70.

3 UNCTAD, *Recent Developments in Investor-State Dispute Settlement (ISDS)* (UNCTAD/WEB/DIAE/PCB/2013/3), p. 4.

 | DOI:10.1163/9789004413689_003

these figures are based on the number of *known* cases, a method that naturally favours ICSID arbitration. For example, the "other rules" category in the UNCTAD study includes eight known ICC cases, whereas the material studied for Chapter 4 of this book shows that the number of actual ICC cases at the time was significantly higher.

Although the following text demonstrates that commercial arbitration rules found their way into investment treaties during the 1980s and gained momentum in the 1990s, no overarching explanation for this development is provided here. It must be pointed out that there are no indications that the development was the result of conscious, concerted efforts among states. Instead, the results suggest that various actors made bilateral choices through small and seemingly uncoordinated steps. This finding would be in line with the general development of international investment law, a field which lacks an institutional centre of gravity.[4] Nevertheless, this text provides two possible explanatory factors that may have influenced states' decision to include non-ICSID arbitration rules in investment treaties.

The first such explanation is the Iran-United States Claims Tribunal's (the Tribunal) use of the UNCITRAL Arbitration Rules. Although unique in its circumstances, the Tribunal has provided an important and much-studied jurisprudence on various matters of international law. Its effect on procedural aspects of investment treaty arbitration, however, has not been studied to the same degree. In this Chapter, it is argued that the Tribunal's work with the UNCITRAL Rules, which came at a crucial time in investment treaty practice, demonstrated the Rules' suitability for non-contractual disputes, which may have influenced choices made by states in their investment treaty practice. A second potential explanation given for the rise of non-ICSID Rules is the discontent with the ICSID system that surfaced following the first annulment decisions in the 1980s. Investment treaty practice shows that ICSID lost its monopoly status in treaties' arbitration clauses around this time.

2.1 The (Very) Early Treaty Practice: ICSID Monopoly

The very first generation of bilateral investment treaties, concluded in the late 1950s and 1960s, show a large degree of similarity. These treaties demonstrate the well-known pattern of a capital-exporting country (such as, for example, Belgium, Germany, the Netherlands, Switzerland and Sweden) concluding treaties with countries wishing to attract investment (such as, for example,

4 Discussed further at 5.3.

Chad, Congo, Ecuador, Indonesia and Uganda) and their language shows clear traces of having been proposed by the former and accepted by the latter. This first generation of treaties, starting with the one concluded between Germany and Pakistan in 1959, did not include provisions on dispute resolution between investors and states. At the time, there was no established mode of such international dispute settlement. During the first decade of bilateral treaty practice, the treaties instead focused on substantive protections, presumably relying on existing mechanisms of diplomatic protection to solve potential disputes; state-state arbitration was also frequently included. Similarly, none of the *multilateral* investment treaties concluded prior to 1971 allows for arbitration between investors and states.[5]

The 1966 entry into force of the ICSID Convention was a game-changer in many respects. Even though the Convention was drafted primarily with investment contracts in mind, shortly after its entry into force, states started to include references to the Centre in treaties' dispute resolution provisions.

Compared to later practice, the language of the very first arbitration clauses demonstrates a relatively large degree of variance.[6] This subsequently changed during the 1970s, when most treaties contained similar language, albeit in several different shapes. As discussed below, this convergence in drafting was likely influenced by the ICSID Secretariat's decision to issue model clauses in the late 1960s. It also appears that the second wave-treaties to a large extent

---

5 See The Agreement on Arab Economic Unity, signed on 3 June 1957 (coming into force on 30 April 1964); General Treaty on Central American Economic Integration Between Guatemala, El Salvador, Honduras and Nicaragua signed at Managua on 13 December 1960; The Common Convention on Investments in the States of the Central African Customs and Economic Union, adopted at Yaoundé, Cameroon, by the Council of Heads of State of the Customs and Economic Union of Central Africa (Federal Republic of Cameroon, Central African Republic, Republic of Congo-Brazzaville, Republic of Gabon, Republic of Chad) at its meeting on 14 December 1965; The Andean Subregional Agreement signed on 26 May 1969.

6 Compare for example the operative language in three of the first treaties. The 1970 Belgium – Indonesia BIT states that "each Contracting Party hereby irrevocably and anticipatory gives its consent to submit to conciliation and arbitration any dispute relating to a measure contrary to this Agreement, pursuant to the Convention of Washington of 18 March 1965, at the initiative of a national or legal person of the other Contracting Party, who considers himself to have been affected by such a measure." The 1970 Netherlands – Kenya BIT states that "the Contracting Party in the territory of which a national of the other Contracting Party makes or intends to make an investment, shall give sympathetic consideration to a request on the part of such national to submit for conciliation or arbitration, to the Centre established by the Convention of Washington of 18 March 1965, any dispute that may arise in connection with the investment. The 1973 France – Mauritius BIT, in more indirect language, provides that the treaty "comporteront obligatoirement une clause prévoyant que les differ ends relatifs à ces investissements devrant étre soumis [to ICSID]."

use a "copy paste"-approach, borrowing language from earlier treaties. By contrast, during the first wave of treaties, there were simply very few earlier treaties to copy from.

While the main focus of this study is the emergence of the non-ICSID rules, it is important to understand how investor-state arbitration emerged in the first place. At the early stage, treaty clauses providing for investor-state arbitration referred only to ICSID arbitration; in fact, many of the early treaties' arbitration clauses are located under the headline "Reference to International Centre for Settlement of Investment Disputes" rather than the subsequently more common generic language.[7] Since the first decade-worth of treaties providing for arbitration against host states exclusively refers to ICSID Convention arbitration, the next sub-section provides a short explanation of the creation of ICSID and the organization's early work with investment treaty arbitration promotion, in order to provide a context to better understand the subsequent development of non-ICSID treaty arbitration.

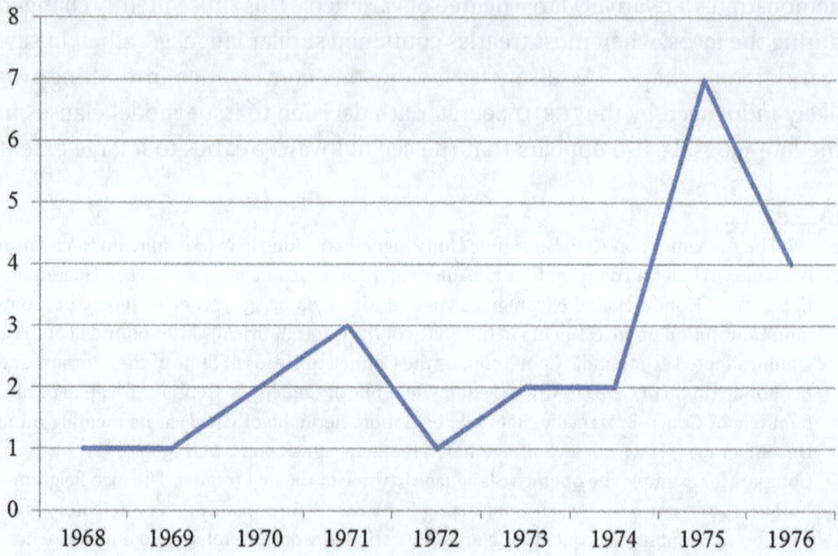

FIGURE 2.1 The early years, ICSID references in treaties
SOURCE: THE AUTHOR

7 See for example Singapore – Sri Lanka BIT (1980); Senegal – United Kingdom BIT (1980); Romania – Sri Lanka BIT (1981); Bangladesh – BLEU (Belgium – Luxembourg Economic Union) BIT (1981).

2.2 The Early Years at ICSID

Unlike the other arbitration rules in this study, ICSID arbitration combines a public international law foundation with a permanent secretariat.[8] The 1965 ICSID Convention established the Center,[9] including the Administrative Council,[10] consisting of state representatives, and the Secretariat, led by a Secretary General.[11] The Convention also authorizes the Administrative Council to adopt various procedural rules, including the arbitration rules.[12]

As described in a study by former ICSID Deputy Secretary-General Antonio Parra[13] and in a monograph by Taylor St John,[14] the ICSID system was largely a creation by the World Bank and in particular by the bank's General Counsel Aron Broches, who was subsequently to be named the first Secretary-General of ICSID.

The World Bank's attempt to establish a multilateral framework for foreign investment came after several unsuccessful attempts in other contexts.[15] In an era of de-colonization and cold war tensions, efforts to regulate global investment flows were easily politicized to the extent that it was hard to agree on any international instrument. The drafters of the ICSID Convention avoided this by focusing exclusively on the procedure, as opposed to substantive investment protection, and by making that procedure available on an opt-in basis.[16] The Convention, in the words of a commentator involved in the drafting, "was to be an arbitration convention, not a convention concerning the international law of investment."[17]

Furthermore, the state representatives working under Broche's leadership on the drafting of the Convention were not policy generalists but rather a

8 Whereas the UNCITRAL Rules are managed and updated by the United Nation Commission on International Trade Law, and thus subject to state participation, the Rules are intended for *ad hoc* arbitration and as such not connected to a permanent administrative body. The SCC and ICC Rules are connected to their respective institutions, which are discussed in Chapter 4.

9 After some discussion in the drafting committees, the ICSID Convention uses the English spelling "Centre," as opposed to the American "Center," see 2 History of the ICSID Convention, p. 749. In this text, the American spelling is maintained for reasons of consistency.

10 ICSID Convention, Articles 4–8.

11 Ibid., Articles 9–11.

12 Ibid., Article 6.

13 A Parra, particularly chapters 2–6.

14 T St John, The Rise of Investor-State Arbitration - Politics, Law and Unintended Consequences, Oxford University Press, 2018.

15 The 1948 Havana Charter and the 1962 OECD Convention.

16 2 History of the ICSID Convention, p. 74.

17 A Lowenfeld, p. 51.

relatively small group of legal experts, participating in the closed-door discussions in a "quasi-personal" capacity.[18] States were encouraged to send persons with legal procedural expertise and thus the drafting group consisted of relatively like-minded specialists, many of whom had previous ties to the World Bank, and who also constituted an early community of investment law practice.[19]

Despite what might appear as a narrow focus on arbitration, the ICSID Convention has had a palpable effect on the development of international investment law. When the ICSID Convention was drafted, however, investor-state arbitration under investment treaties did not yet exist.[20] The phenomenon is not expressly mentioned in the *travaux preparatoires* to the Convention, which instead reflect that the consent to arbitration primarily discussed by the drafters was to be located in contracts directly between state and investors.[21] Therefore, the ICSID Convention and its associated arbitration rules were not originally intended primarily for the treaty arbitration they are now mostly used for.[22] However, the drafters envisioned that references to the ICSID Convention could be included in national investment legislation.[23] In fact Aaron Broches affirmed, when asked during the Convention preparation, that a mutual consent to arbitration could be in the form of a unilateral offer of jurisdiction from a host state, thereafter accepted by the investor.[24] This possibility

18 T St John, p. 138.

19 Ibid, p. 137.

20 Until the first treaty-based ICSID arbitration in 1990, *AAPL v. Sri Lanka* (ICSID Case No. ARB/87/3) consent to ICSID arbitration was primarily located in an investment agreement between the host state and the investor, the sole exception being *SPP v. Egypt* (ICSID Case No. ARB/84/3), where the tribunal's jurisdiction was based on a provision of Egypt's foreign investment legislation, see M Kinnear and F Grob, "Asian Agricultural Products Limited v. Sri Lanka: 25 Years Later," in A Magnusson, U Franke and J Dahlquist, *Arbitrating for Peace*, Kluwer, 2016.; L Poulsen, *Bounded Rationality*, pp.138–139; A Parra, pp. 171–172; J Pauwelyn, At the Edge of Chaos, pp. 397–399, deeming the AAPL case a "silent revolution."

21 Other than in passing, see History of the ICSID Convention, Documents Concerning the Origin and the Formulation of the Convention, Volume II, pp. 274 and 400. See also A Parra, 2nd ed., p. 56.

22 Professor Andreas Lowenfeld from the US delegation claims that "none of the discussion at the consultative meetings [...] addressed the possibility that a host state in a bilateral treaty could give its consent to arbitrate," A Lowefendeld, p. 56.

23 Cf., C Schreuer, "Denunciation of the ICSID Convention and Consent to Arbitration," in Balchin, Chung, et al. (eds), *The Backlash against Investment Arbitration*, Kluwer Law International 2010, p. 357.

24 History of the ICSID Convention, Documents Concerning the Origin and the Formulation of the Convention, Volume II, p. 275.

of "arbitration without privity"[25] – novel at the time – is confirmed by the official commentary to the Convention.[26] Furthermore, as St John shows, both Broches and several other individuals involved in the drafting clearly understood the potential connection between bilateral investment treaties and the ICSID Convention.[27]

It is important to note at this stage that the ICSID Convention, and its associated arbitration rules adopted by the Administrative Council, only sets up a framework on an opt-in basis. It is not enough for states to ratify the Convention; in addition, for the Center to have jurisdiction to administer disputes, a separate agreement to that effect between the disputing parties is required.[28] The most important form for those agreements has over time become investment treaties; in modern times, ICSID's non-treaty caseload is negligible.[29] Below, it is discussed how this development is partly the result of the ICSID Secretariat's active work to that effect.

2.2.1 *The ICSID Secretariat*

The role of Aron Broches in the initiation and creation of ICSID should not be underestimated.[30] In an interview with Broches after he had retired as Secretary-General and General Counsel of the World Bank, the interviewing World Bank historian referred to ICSID as Broches' "baby."[31]

What is more relevant for the present purposes, after the establishment of the Center Broches, as the first Secretary-General, and his small Secretariat[32]

25 A term coined by Jan Paulsson in Arbitration Without Privity.

26 Report of the Executive Directors on the ICSID Convention, para. 24. See also L Poulsen, Bounded Rationality, pp. 136–137.

27 T St John, pp. 150–152.

28 The "double consent" was often used to alleviate concerns from states in the drafting of the ICSID Convention, see T St John, pp. 101–103. See also J Pauwelyn, At the Edge of Chaos, p. 393 with further references and S Puig, Emergence & Dynamism, pp. 540–542.

29 As of 30 June 2018, contractual cases represented 16% of the total ICSID caseload, see ICSID, *The ICSID Caseload – Statistics* (*Issue 2018-2*), p.10.

30 This is one of the main sentiments advanced by T St John. See also A Lowenfeld at 50–52; S Schwebel, "Foreword," in A Broches, *Selected Essays – World Bank, ICSID, and Other Subjects of Public and Private International Law,* Martinus Nijhoff (1995), p. ix.

31 The World Bank/IFC Archives, Transcript of interview with Aron Broches, May 23 1984, p. 35. As an anecdote, in the same interview Broches said that Israel eventually ratified the Convention after he asked the state to do so "as a personal favour" to him, at p. 40.

32 This sub-section largely builds on the extensive research conducted by T St John in her monograph on the early years of ICSID. She uses the term "ICSID Secretariat" interchangeably with "ICSID" and "the Centre" when describing ICSID in the late 1960s and early 1970s. This approach is consistent with ICSID publications from the time and will be used here as well.

took on the task of promoting ICSID arbitration, primarily by virtue of ICSID clauses in both contracts and domestic investment legislation but also, subsequently, in investment treaties. In fact, the dissemination of knowledge about ICSID was identified as an "urgent task" during the early years.[33]

During the creation of ICSID, Broches and other World Bank officials had given the impression of a passive centre, simply administering arbitrations.[34] In her historical study, Taylor St John shines new light over early Secretariat practice and demonstrates how the Secretariat, especially in the early years, actively promoted the use of ICSID arbitration.[35]

General efforts to raise awareness of the new Center and its services were an integral part of this promotion. During the first ten years, ICSID's Annual Reports had a sub-heading titled "Information Activities," where progress was reported on traditional information dissemination such as the distribution of leaflets and the Secretariat's participation in seminars.[36] But the Secretariat also worked more hands-on with specific efforts to ensure that the Center would be utilized. They did so by directly addressing both states and investors.

2.2.1.1 Promoting ICSID to States

In his remarks at the inaugural meeting of the ICSID Administrative Council in 1967, Aron Broches noted that many investment treaties at the time allowed for interstate arbitration, but added: "now that the facilities provided by the Convention [are] available it might be advisable to substitute these procedures, at least on an optional basis, for those provided in these treaties."[37]

Working with national governments came naturally to the ICSID Secretariat; at the same inaugural meeting Broches expressed a hope that the Centre could "count on the governments of the Contracting States" to assist them in their efforts to spread the word.[38] At the time, 28 states had ratified the Convention,[39] but ICSID could also rely on its function as part of the World Bank Group, with Aron Broches acting simultaneously as ICSID Secretary-General

33 ICSID First Ann. Rep. 1966/1967 p.4. Parra also notes that this task "preoccupied" Broches and his Secretariat at this time, p. 132.

34 T St John, p. 189; S Puig, Emergence & Dynamism, p. 540.

35 T St John, Chapter 5.

36 Ibid., p. 139 with further references.

37 ICSID Doc. AC/67/18, Administrative Council Proceedings, First Annual Meeting, 25 September, 1967, para. 11.

38 Ibid.

39 ICSID First Annual Report, 1966/1967, p. 3.

and World Bank General Counsel, to interact with World Bank member states not yet party to the convention.[40]

While the initial promotion of ICSID arbitration focused largely on obtaining states' advance consent in domestic investment legislation, the Secretariat also, in 1969, issued model BIT clauses for easy reference by state parties.[41] In the introduction to these model clauses, it is stated that they are

> designed to facilitate any particular use of the Convention that the parties to bilateral investment treaties might wish to make. They are formulated so that they can be inserted into new agreements of this type, but they could equally constitute the substance of a special protocol concluded in relation to an existing instrument.[42]

An active ICSID Secretariat, offering its assistance to states wishing to include ICSID clauses in their treaties, supported this model language.[43]

When surveying BIT practice, the model language issued by the Secretariat is absent in the early arbitration provisions concluded after 1969; the treaty language, and its variance, instead implies that these early clauses were individually negotiated.[44] Later on, many ICSID references are clearly inspired by the Secretariat's model language,[45] which was the starting point for the spread of ICSID clauses in investment treaties.[46]

During the 1970s, the number of ICSID references grew slowly, with roughly a handful of treaties per year allowing for investors to avail themselves of the Center and its rules. This growth rate remained constant until the middle of the 1980s, when an acceleration in number of treaties can be detected.

---

40 T St John, pp. 190–193; S Puig, Emergence & Dynamism, p. 544.

41 ICSID Doc. ICSID/16, *Model Clauses Relating to the Convention on the Settlement of Investment Disputes Designed for Bilateral Investment Treaties.* Available in International Legal Materials, Vol. 8, No. 6, 1969, pp. 1341–1352.

42 Ibid., p. 3.

43 Address by Aron Broches to the Second Annual Meeting. September 30, 1968; ICSID Sixth Annual Report 1971/1972, p. 4.

44 See for example Netherlands – Kenya BIT (1970); Netherlands – Malaysia BIT (1971); Morocco – Netherlands BIT (1971); Netherlands – Singapore BIT (1972); France – Mauritius BIT (1973); France – Indonesia BIT (1973).

45 See for example Singapore – United Kingdom BIT (1975); Egypt – United Kingdom BIT (1975); Korea, Republic of – United Kingdom BIT (1976); Egypt – Japan BIT (1977).

46 T St John, pp. 205–206.

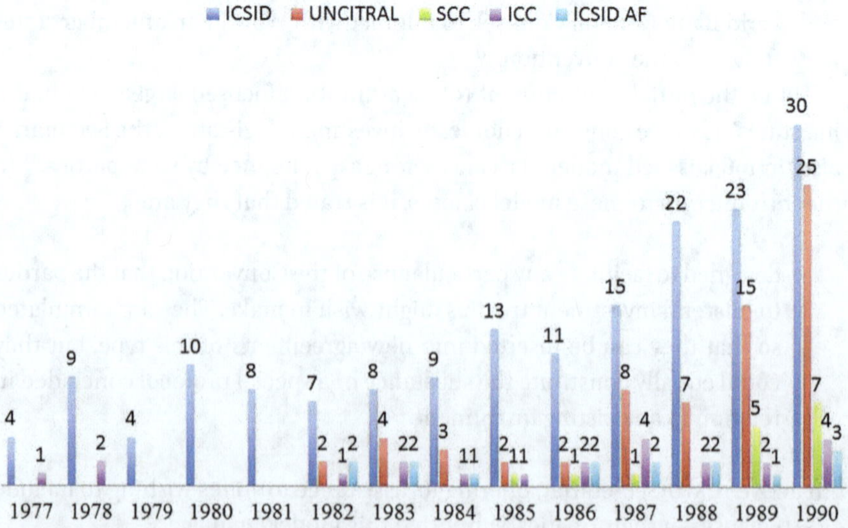

FIGURE 2.2 Acceleration in arbitration consents
SOURCE: THE AUTHOR

Although the number of treaties referring to ICSID arbitration grew steadily, complemented by a growth of signatories to the Convention,[47] the ICSID system was nevertheless faced with a "slow start."[48] By 1988, some 140 treaties allowed for ICSID arbitration but only 23 arbitrations had been initiated pursuant to the Convention.[49] Only one of these was based on a treaty.[50] A former employee at the World Bank's legal department described how ICSID for the first twenty years was "begging for cases [but] cases didn't come" and how other World Bank employees at the time said "ICSID; well you do nothing."[51] It is clear that, at this time, there is an apparent gap between the number of state consents to ICSID arbitration and the number of cases initially launched. Broches himself, in reference to the treaty consents in 1984, stated that ICSID had "an enormous potential clientele" which was yet not fully realized.[52] In part, the initial lack of casework left the ICSID Secretariat ample time to promote both the ICSID Convention and consents to ICSID arbitration in investment treaties.[53]

47 A Parra, p. 122.
48 R Dolzer & C Schreuer, p.224.
49 A Parra, p. 157.
50 AAPL v. Sri Lanka, above footnote 75, was registered in 1987 and the award rendered in 1990.
51 T St John, p. 187.
52 The World Bank/IFC Archives, Transcript of interview with Aron Broches, May 23 1984, p. 45.
53 L Poulsen, Bounded Rationality, p. 57.

2.2.1.2 Promoting ICSID among Investors

The ICSID Secretariat spent its first years devising and implementing a strategy for "information activities" in order to promote consent to ICSID jurisdiction.[54] An important but challenging aspect of this work, it appears, was to raise awareness of ICSID not only among states but also among investors.[55] After all, the number of states giving advance consent to ICSID arbitration would not matter much if foreign investors were not taking up the offer to initiate arbitration.

While it is hard to gather statistics on the extent to which investors inserted ICSID clauses in contracts negotiated directly with state counterparts,[56] the slow uptake in the treaty caseload clearly indicates that investors were not initially as susceptible to ICSID efforts as were some states. There are several possible explanations for this: the futility in bringing together private investors (as opposed to states, which are easily identifiable), as well as the fact that ICSID's inter-governmental origins made the young Center ill-suited to this type of outreach.[57] As a consequence of the difficulties to educate investors about the combined utility of the ICSID Convention and BITS, few investors likely realized the tools available to them, at least prior to *AAPL v. Sri Lanka*.[58]

Nevertheless, the Secretariat seemingly devoted extensive time and effort to address groups of foreign investors, advocating for the value of ICSID arbitration. One way to do this, more in line with the institution's inter-state background, was to approach investors via their capital-exporting governments, for example via domestic investment insurance programs.[59]

It was not until the 1990s and especially the first decade of the 21st century that treaty arbitration clauses started to make marks in the Center's caseload. At least in part, the gap between state consent and actual use of the Center seem to be explained by the failure to convince investors to avail themselves of the advance consents given by states.

2.2.1.3 The ICSID Additional Facility Rules

In 1978, the ICSID Administrative Council adopted a set of arbitration rules with the express intention to allow the Secretariat to administer certain types

54 A Parra, p. 121.

55 T St John, pp. pp. 194–196.

56 In 1986, a commentator noted that "in spite of the relatively few arbitration cases, ICSID has been chosen in many investment contracts," KH Böckstiegel, "States in the International Arbitral Process," 2 ARB.INT'L 22 (1986), p. 31.

57 T St John, p. 194.

58 J Pauwelyn, At the Edge of Chaos, p. 397.

59 ICSID Seventh Annual Report, 1972/1973, p. 3. See also T St John, p. 194.

of disputes that fall outside of the scope of the ICSID Convention. The Additional Facility Rules (the "ICSID AF Rules") were in part a response to the narrowly worded scope of the Centre's competence in Article 1(2) of the ICSID Convention, which restricts the Centre to "provide facilities for the conciliation and arbitration of investment disputes between Contracting States and nationals of other Contracting States in accordance with the provisions of this Convention." In practice, this means that for the Convention to apply, both the respondent state and the investor's home state must be contracting parties. By contrast, the ICSID AF Rules are designed so that they are applicable to proceedings where either the respondent state or the investor's home state is *not* a member of ICSID.[60]

The ICSID AF Rules, originally intended to be temporary,[61] were proposed by Aron Broches in 1976 as a way to expand the Centre's role to administer disputes that would otherwise fall outside of its jurisdiction under the ICSID Convention.[62] In addition to the restrictions on nationality, the AF Rules would also apply to a wider range of subject matters than the "investment" needed to establish jurisdiction under the ICSID Convention.[63] After some discussion, chiefly among the capital-exporting states on the Administrative Council, some of whom felt that opening up the Centre's work to non-signatory states would weaken ICSID and remove incentives to sign the ICSID Convention, the ICSID AF Rules were adopted without any modification of the Convention. This was done on the insistence by Broches, who viewed the AF Rules not as an extension of the Centre's "jurisdiction" (which would likely have required a modified ICSID Convention) but rather of its "activities" (which did not).[64]

The ICSID AF Rules were initially adopted for preliminary period of five years, which ended after Aron Broches had retired. His successor, Heribert Golsong, suggested in 1983 that the Facility, which by then had never been used, should be terminated.[65] Instead, the Administrative Council agreed to wait another year to evaluate the Rules. In 1984, Golsong had been replaced by Ibrahim Shihata, who unlike Golsong issued a report along more positive lines, which likely contributed to the Administrative Council approving the

60 ICSID Additional Facility Rules, Article 2.

61 T St John, p. 243.

62 Tenth Annual Meeting, 7 October, 1976, Administrative Council Doc. AC/76/40A, Annex, Statement by Mr A. Broches.

63 A Parra, pp. 147–148.

64 A Parra, p. 141.

65 ICSID Doc. AC/83/3, Additional Facility: Note of the Secretary-General, 27 July, 1983.

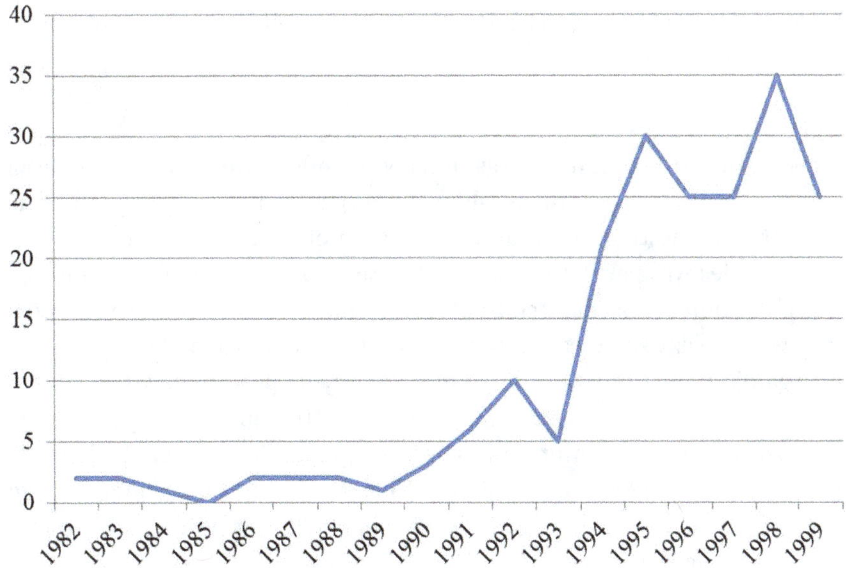

FIGURE 2.3 ICSID Additional facility rules
SOURCE: THE AUTHOR

Rules. As shown in Figure 2.3, by 1984 a few states had also started to include references to the ICSID AF Rules in their investment treaties.

Through the adoption of the ICSID AF Rules, the scope of the Centre's mandate was expanded beyond that provided by the ICSID Convention. In addition to the arbitration rules, the Additional Facility was set up as a way to allow the Secretariat to work outside of the Convention also in other instances: to facilitate fact-finding and provide conciliation services, neither of which has been used to any significant degree.

In terms of the procedural framework provided in the ICSID AF Rules, there are significant similarities with other commercial arbitration rules, especially the UNCITRAL Rules developed around the same time.[66] There are many elements of the ICSID AF Rules which deviate from proceedings under the ICSID Convention: for example, there must be a legal seat (in a state that is a member to the New York Convention)[67] and there is no enforcement available under the ICSID Convention. In subsequent sections of this study, therefore, ICSID AF cases are treated as "non-ICSID cases" when that is relevant, for example

66 A Parra p. 133. See also *Organization of American States Foreign Trade Information System, Guide to Commercial Arbitration and Other Alternative Dispute Resolution Methods,* available at http://www.sice.oas.org/dispute/comarb/icsid/icsid3.asp, visited 5 January 2019.

67 ICSID Additional Facility Arbitration Rules, Article 19.

when such awards are challenged before the courts at the legal seat of arbitration, as discussed in Chapter 5.

2.2.1.4 Summary

While the ICSID Convention was initially intended primarily for arbitration based on investment contracts, although also contemplating unilateral state consent in domestic legislation, the inclusion of ICSID references in investment treaties was partly the result of the Secretariat's later advocacy to that effect. The number of treaty consents to arbitration did not, however, immediately result in any significant number of ICSID cases based on treaties.

Regardless, the ICSID Secretariat in many ways appears to have been instrumental in encouraging investment treaty arbitration in its early years. In the later part of the 20th century, it has been suggested that Ibrahim Shihata carried on with this work, raising Broche's baby "almost from infancy, through adolescence, to its present young, but rapidly maturing, adulthood," promoting ICSID to an even larger degree.[68]

By including advance consent to ICSID arbitration in investment treaties, states took the first step towards modern-day investment treaty arbitration. Starting in the 1970s, the legal foundation for what has subsequently been understood as "arbitration without privity" was laid, largely thanks due to work by the ICSID Secretariat. Less research, however, has been conducted into the somewhat later development – a second step in this drive towards broad advance consent, if you will – when other arbitration rules started to be inserted into investment treaties.[69] These rules lack a unitary driving force resembling the ICSID Secretariat, as well as an express state mandate to facilitate the settlement of disputes between investors and states. The following sub-section explores when these other rules started to appear in investment treaties and also introduces two reasons which might help to understand why this happened.

2.3 The Rise of Non-ICSID Rules

Whereas the first BITS with investor-state arbitration clauses exclusively provided for ICSID as the arbitration regime, at a certain point in time other

68 C Brower, "Ibrahim Shihata and the Resolution of International Investment Disputes: The Masterful Missionary," ICSID Review - Foreign Investment Law Journal, Volume 15, Issue 2, pp. 289 and 293. See also S Puig, Emergence & Dynamism, pp. 547–554.

69 The development, although well-known, is usually mentioned as a side note in historical accounts of the rise of investment arbitration, see for example T St John, pp. 205–206; S Puig, Emergency & Dynamism; pp. 578–580; K Vandevelde, pp. 458–464.

options were included in investment treaties. Little study seems to have been conducted into this practice. In 1995, Rudolf Dolzer and Margrete Stevens devoted a few pages of their early treatise to "Non-ICSID Clauses" and noted "a quite recent trend [...] to set forth several different possible forms of arbitration for investor-State disputes."[70] The text then goes on to list several examples. It is claimed that, in addition to ICSID arbitration, UNCITRAL and ICC references are the most common.[71] In a later study of bilateral investment treaties, conducted after the explosion of investor-state disputes, Kenneth Vandevelde notes the frequent occurrence of non-ICSID rules being included in investment treaties and goes on to give several examples, based on a survey of the treaty practice of several capital-exporting countries with BIT programs.[72]

A more comprehensive study was conducted by the OECD Investment Division in 2012.[73] The study uses a random sample of 1,660 bilateral investment treaties to categorize statistically various aspects of the treaties' dispute resolution clauses. For the purposes of the present study, some of the OECD study's key findings include the result that 96% of the surveyed treaties allow for investors to initiate arbitration[74] and, while there is substantial diversity in the surveyed clauses, 56% of the treaties offer the investor the opportunity to choose from more than one type of arbitration.[75]

2.3.1 *The First References to Non-ICSID Rules*

The first non-ICSID references are a few ICC references in French BITs from 1977 and 1978.[76] A few years later, starting in 1982, non-ICSID arbitration rules regularly start to appear in treaties. The first treaty to give the investor several choices, concluded between the United Kingdom and Belize in 1982, still maintains the option of ICSID arbitration but also gives the investor the choice of the ICSID Additional Facility, UNCITRAL and ICC Rules.[77] This approach of giving the investor a broad spectrum of choices – the so-called "cafeteria

70 R Dolzer & M Stevens, p. 147.

71 Ibid., p. 121.

72 K Vandevelde, pp. 458–464.

73 J Pohl, K Mashigo and A Nohen (2012), *Dispute Settlement Provisions in International Investment Agreements: A Large Sample Survey,* OECD Working Papers on International Investment, 2012/02.

74 Ibid., p.10.

75 Ibid.

76 The France – Syrian Arab Republic BIT (1977), France – Sudan BIT (1978); France – El Salvador BIT (1978) and Morocoo – Gabon BIT (1979) all give the foreign investor the choice between ICSID and ICC arbitration.

77 Belize – United Kingdom BIT (1982).

approach"[78] – was not particularly popular in the 1980s, evidently preferred primarily by the United Kingdom and Belgium/Luxembourg.[79]

Also in 1982, the first treaty referring to investor-state arbitration without referring to ICSID is concluded between France and Panama (which has not signed the ICSID Convention): Article 8 of that treaty provides that, save for any other agreement between the disputing parties, the arbitration shall be conducted under the UNCITRAL Rules.[80] That same year Panama also concluded a BIT with the United States (subsequently replaced by a Free Trade Agreement that entered into force in 2012) which allows for arbitration under the ICSID Additional Facility rules.[81] In the following years, Panama concluded several investment treaties allowing for investors to initiate non-ICSID arbitration.[82] These treaties are the first of many concluded by non-ICSID states that exclusively refer to arbitration outside of the ICSID system.[83]

As demonstrated by the table, ICSID remained the primary choice for states even after the "cafeteria" approach took off in the 1990s. In fact, there was not a year during the 20th century when the main alternative – the UNCITRAL Rules – was referenced in more treaties than ICSID: the smallest gap is in 1997, when 116 treaties with ICSID references were concluded and 113 with UNCITRAL references. In addition, while the SCC Rules are referenced in roughly a handful of treaties per year and the ICC Rules and the ICSID AF Rules to a somewhat larger extent, the numbers of annual ICSID and UNCITRAL references both consistently reach three figures in the 1990s.

In the early 1990s, the single most common type of clause refers to both ICSID and UNCITRAL arbitration, leaving it to the investor's discretion to initiate arbitration under either one. This type of clause still remains the primary

---

78 C McLachlan, L Shore and M Weininger, *International Investment Arbitration: Substantive Principles*, Oxford University Press, 2007, para. 3.33.

79 See for example Saint Lucia – United Kingdom BIT (1983); BLEU (Belgium – Luxembourg Economic Union) – Turkey BIT (1986); Malta – United Kingdom BIT (1986); Dominican Republic – United Kingdom BIT (1987); BLEU (Belgium – Luxembourg Economic Union) – Malta BIT (1987); BLEU (Belgium-Luxembourg Economic Union) – Poland BIT (1987); Antigua and Barbuda – United Kingdom BIT (1987); Grenada – United Kingdom BIT (1988); Bolivia, Plurinational State of – United Kingdom BIT (1988).

80 France – Panama BIT (1982), Article 8.

81 Panama – United States of America BIT (1982), Article VI.

82 Panama – United Kingdom BIT (1983); Panama – Switzerland BIT (1983), which appears to be the first time an UNCITRAL clause is accompanied by an appointing authority (the Permanent Court of Arbitration); Germany – Panama BIT (1983).

83 These include several treaties concluded by Cuba, Haiti, Panama, Poland, Russia, as well as a number of Bulgarian and Chinese treaties from the 1980s.

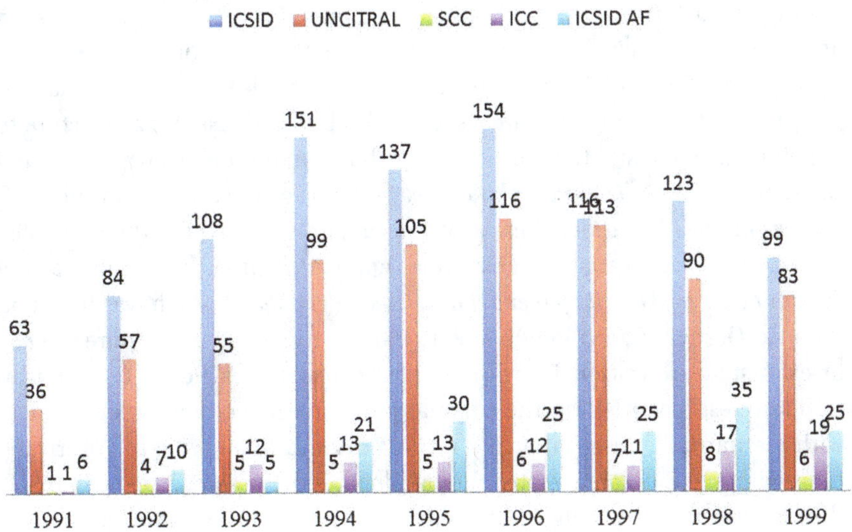

FIGURE 2.4 The 1990s
SOURCE: THE AUTHOR

choice towards the end of the century, possibly to the extent that it can be deemed the "standard" arbitration clause in BITs during the time period.[84]

2.3.1.1 "Pure" *Ad Hoc* Clauses

It is also common for states to consent to *ad hoc* arbitration, with procedural specificities included in the treaty, without necessarily referring to any set of arbitration rules. Some version of such *ad hoc* clauses are modelled on the state-state arbitration clause included in the same treaty,[85] while a tendency can be detected towards the end of the 1980s to provide that the *ad hoc* tribunal shall either apply the UNCITRAL Rules or decide its own rules of procedure "in compliance" with these rules.[86] Similarly, some *ad hoc* clauses also

84 As discussed further in Chapter 7, this combination of ICSID and UNCITRAL also seems to be a common feature in more recent investment treaties.

85 See for example Netherlands – Oman BIT (1987); China – Poland BIT (1988); Switzerland – Uruguay BIT (1988); Germany – Poland BIT (1989); Egypt – Uzbekistan BIT (1992); Cuba – Italy BIT (1993); Cuba – Germany BIT (1996); Oman – Pakistan BIT (1997); Algeria – Niger BIT (1998).

86 See for example BLEU (Belgium-Luxembourg Economic Union) – Czech Republic BIT (1989); Poland – Sweden BIT (1989); Bulgaria – China BIT (1989): Norway – Poland BIT (1990); France – Slovakia BIT (1990); Netherlands – Slovakia BIT (1991); Albania – Greece BIT (1991); Greece – Slovakia BIT (1991); Bulgaria – Switzerland BIT (1991); Greece – Poland BIT (1992); Singapore – Viet Nam BIT (1992); Algeria – France BIT (1993); Bulgaria – Greece BIT (1993); China – Cuba BIT (1995); Germany – India BIT (1995); Belarus – Iran, Islamic Republic of BIT (1995); China – Lebanon BIT (1996); Algeria – Qatar BIT (1996); Algeria – Egypt BIT (1997); Iran, Islamic Republic of – Lebanon BIT (1997); China – Qatar BIT (1999).

refer to the ICSID Arbitration Rules as the guiding procedural rules for such and *ad hoc* tribunal[87] (without expressly consenting to arbitration pursuant to the ICSID Convention) or to the SCC Rules.[88] Such "pure" *ad hoc* clauses, which do not expressly indicate a set of rules but rather set up a structure to appoint a tribunal and then directs that tribunal to decide its own procedural rules, might raise questions as to the exact status of the arbitration rules references in the arbitration. These problems might be overcome when both disputing parties agree that the given rules apply in their entirety. This was the case in *ECE Projektmanagement et al v. Czech Republic*,[89] which was based on the 1990 German-Czech Republic BIT. That treaty provides for "pure" *ad hoc* investor-state arbitration, i.e. without reference to any particular type of arbitration rules. Nevertheless, the tribunal in its first procedural order decided, with the parties' consent that the 1976 UNCITRAL Rules were to govern the proceedings.[90] The same approach was adopted by the *Saar Papier* tribunal,[91] thereby effectively turning these awards into UNCITRAL awards, despite the states providing for "pure" *ad hoc* arbitration in the treaty.

2.3.1.2 Other Referenced Arbitration Rules

The studied treaties also include a number of references to other non-ICSID rules than the four studied in this text. Anecdotal observations from the 2012 OECD survey confirm this result also in more modern treaties.[92] Whereas SCC arbitration is not included in any treaties concluded by the institution's home

87 This approach of "indirect" ICSID arbitration appears particularly common in Chinese treaties concluded before the Chinese ratification of the ICSID Convention in 1993. See for example China – Denmark BIT (1985); China – Singapore BIT (1985); China – Sri Lanka BIT (1986); China – Switzerland BIT (1986); China – New Zealand BIT (1988); China – Hungary BIT (1991); China – Mongolia BIT (1991); Bolivia, Plurinational State of – China BIT (1992); Argentina – China BIT (1992); China – Viet Nam BIT (1992); China – Estonia BIT (1993); China – Slovenia BIT (1993). See also Cambodia – Korea, Republic of BIT (1997); Mauritius – Mozambique BIT (1997); Indonesia – Mauritius BIT (1997); Mauritius – Pakistan BIT (1997); Australia – Pakistan BIT (1998).

88 China – Italy BIT (1985) and China – Ghana BIT (1989), (both allowing the tribunal to choose between ICSID and SCC Rules).

89 ECE Projektmanagement & Kommanditgesellschaft Panta Achtundsechzigste Grundstücksgesellschaft MBH & CO v. The Czech Republic, UNCITRAL, PCA Case No 2010-5, Award, 19 September, 2013.

90 Ibid. para. 1.43.

91 Para. 4.

92 J Pohl, K Mashigo & A Nohen, p. 20.

state Sweden,[93] France regularly included ICC arbitration, especially in early treaty practice. Almost every other set of rules referred to in treaties have a connection to one of the state parties. In the treaty sample, there are in total one reference to arbitration under the rules provided by the Kuala Lumpur Regional Centre for Arbitration;[94] one reference to the Istanbul Center for Commercial Arbitration;[95] one reference to the Arbitration Court of Chamber of Economy of Bosnia and Herzegovina in Sarajevo;[96] two references to the Vienna International Arbitral Center[97] and 13 references to the Regional Cairo Center for International Commercial Arbitration.[98] Interestingly, the single references to the centres in Istanbul and Sarajevo are included in the respective Turkish and Bosnian BITs with Egypt, presumably as a *quid pro quo* for those treaties also allowing for arbitration at the Cairo centre. As of 2012, the centre in Cairo has been involved in three unpublished treaty cases.[99] There are no investment treaty cases reported at any of the other institutions.

Furthermore, the London Court of International Arbitration (LCIA) – one of the world's largest commercial arbitration institutions – is not referenced in a single investment treaty in this study. The LCIA has, however, administered a handful of investment disputes under the UNCITRAL Rules, as discussed below at 4.3.3.3.

While these other institutional rules are part of the general tendency studied in this text – that is, the tendency to arbitrate treaty disputes under rules that were traditionally used for contractual, commercial arbitration – their scarcity in treaty practice and lack of practical use mean that they are being left out of the rest of this study.

93 This has never been the Swedish government's policy, since it is considered to give a "biased" perception, email from former treaty negotiator at the Swedish Ministry for Foreign Affairs, Nils-Urban Allard, Friday November 6, 2015, on file with author.

94 Egypt – Sri Lanka BIT (1996).

95 Egypt – Turkey BIT (1996).

96 Bosnia and Herzegovina – Egypt BIT (1998).

97 Czech Republic – United Kingdom BIT (1990); Slovakia - United Kingdom BIT (1990).

98 Egypt – Spain BIT (1992); Egypt – Indonesia BIT (1994), stipulating that the arbitration at the Cairo centre must apply the UNCITRAL Rules; Egypt – Netherlands BIT (1996); Egypt – Sri Lanka BIT (1996); Egypt – Turkey BIT (1996); Belarus – Egypt BIT (1997); Egypt – Latvia BIT (1997); Croatia – Egypt BIT (1997); Bosnia and Herzegovina – Egypt BIT (1998); Cyprus – Egypt BIT (1998); BLEU (Belgium-Luxembourg Economic Union) – Egypt BIT (1999); Denmark – Egypt BIT (1999); Egypt – Georgia BIT (1999);

99 M A Raouf, *UNCITRAL Arbitration Rules and the settlement of investment disputes: The experience of CRCICA*. Available at http://www.crcica.org.eg/newsletters/nl201203/UNCITRAL_ARBITRATION_RULES_AND_THE_SETTLEMENT_OF_INVESTMENT_DISPUTES_%20THE%20EXPERIENCE_OF_CRCICA.pdf, visited 7 January 2019 and on file with author.

2.3.1.3 Summary

Alternatives to the ICSID Rules started appearing in the early 1980s but did not reach large numbers until the next decade. Towards the end of the century, the UNCITRAL Rules were a frequent alternative to ICSID arbitration, whereas references to the ICSID Additional Facility, ICC Rules and the SCC Rules were made on a regular basis, albeit less often. It is also common for treaties to set up "pure" *ad hoc* arbitration clauses, with or without references to existing arbitration rules and/or institutions. Finally, a handful of other commercial arbitration rules are also found in the treaty sample but not to any significant degree.

2.3.2 *Institutional Rules in Investment Treaties*

Whereas the UNCITRAL Rules are intended to be used as a flexible set of rules for non-administered as well as administered international arbitration, the ICC Rules and the SCC Rules have a closer connection to their respective institutions. The ICC Rules and the SCC Rules differ from the UNCITRAL Rules, as they are administered permanent secretariats, which form part of private, non-governmental, bodies.[100] The two following sub-sections aim at describing the development leading to their investment treaty arbitration work.

2.3.2.1 The SCC Rules

In section 2.2.1, it is explained how the many treaty references to ICSID were largely the result of active institutional promotion, with the ICSID Secretariat acting as an agent to promote the Center and its rules. The same cannot be said for the SCC. In fact, it appears many of the early SCC references were made without the Secretariat's knowledge.

By way of background, it should be emphasized that the SCC is an institution that traditionally administers commercial arbitrations, which to this day still make up the vast majority of the institution's caseload. It is, however, beyond doubt that in terms of administered cases, the SCC is second only to ICSID in terms of investment treaty arbitrations administered under its own rules.

For the present purposes, it should be noted that the SCC benefits from a historical reputation as a forum for disputes arising out of the East-West trade. The starting point for this development was the "Optional Arbitration Clause for Use in Contracts in USA-USSR Trade - 1977" (the "Optional Clause"), which was drafted by The American Arbitration Association and the USSR Chamber

100 This status is discussed further at 4.1.

of Commerce and Industry in 1977.[101] This clause, having been endorsed and promoted by leading trade institutions in both countries,[102] in essence served the purpose of a model arbitration clause to be inserted into commercial contracts between entities from the two states. The clause provided for the SCC to administer the disputes and for arbitrators to be chosen from a roster of six Swedish, six "Western" (non-American) arbitrators and six "Eastern" (non-Soviet) arbitrators.[103] Notably, the Optional Clause's governing arbitration rules is not the SCC Rules but rather the UNCITRAL Arbitration Rules.[104]

The SCC also cultivated early ties with Chinese entities. Following regular cooperation exchanges between the SCC and the China Council for the Promotion of International Trade in the 1970s and 1980s, SCC arbitration was for a long time the only politically acceptable alternative to arbitration in China for Chinese parties to international transactions.[105] Many of the largest and most complex Chinese foreign trade and investment disputes have been SCC disputes,[106] and a significant portion of SCC cases still involves Chinese parties.[107] Furthermore, China International Economic and Trade Arbitration Commission ("CIETAC") has regularly made reference to the SCC Rules in their revisions and scholars and judges in China pay close attention to developments in Swedish arbitration law.[108] The first Chinese BIT to be concluded, in 1982, was with Sweden.[109]

One person appears to be especially important in understanding how the SCC attained this prominent role in east-west arbitration. Ulf Franke worked at the institution between 1975 and 2010, during which time the institution grew from a small-scale domestic arbitration institution to a busy institution in a highly globalized field. During his tenure, most of it as Secretary-General but the last few years as Chairman of the SCC Board, the SCC also became

101 *Documents Exchanged January 12, 1977 between American Arbitration Association, USSR Chamber of Commerce and Industry and Stockholm Chamber of Commerce*, on file with author.

102 Ibid., para. 2.

103 Ibid., Enclosure 2.

104 Ibid., Enclosure 1, para. 2.

105 M Moser, "Ulf Franke, Stockholm Arbitration and the Bridge to China," in K Hobér, A Magnusson, M Öhrström (eds), *Between East and West: Essays in Honour of Ulf Franke*, Juris 2010, p. 348.

106 Ibid., p. 349.

107 A Håvedal-Ipp, "A Historical Perspective on the China-Sweden Arbitration Connection," China Business Law Journal, September 2015, p. 17.

108 M Moser, p. 349.

109 N Gallagher and W Shan, *Chinese Investment Treaties – Policies and Practice*, Oxford University Press, 2009, p. 300.

the second most frequently used institution for investment treaty arbitration under its own rules. Franke did not, however, have the institutional support available to Aron Broches at ICSID, but was rather for a long time the sole full-time employee of the institution. Even when SCC's caseload had taken off in the 1980s and 1990s, the SCC Secretariat consisted of Franke, one or two lawyers and a secretary.[110] To many, this made Ulf Franke synonymous with the SCC.[111] Franke was involved in initiating the Optional Clause, which ensured a steady stream of cases involving American and Soviet entities. In preparation for the agreement, Franke led a study of Sweden's legislative arbitration framework, which resulted in the first English-language publication about arbitration in Sweden and was important to the signing of the Optional Clause.[112] He also represented the SCC when the Soviet and American organizations met at the Swedish consulate in New York to review and reconfirm the Optional Clause in 1986.[113] Correspondence prior to that meeting, between the SCC and USSR Chamber of Commerce and Industry representative Professor Sergei Lebedev, indicates that Franke saw a large arbitration conference in New York as a good reason for the parties to meet and update the clause and the roster of arbitrators.[114] Franke wrote to the Soviet representatives with the proposal, which according to Franke was raised by Robert Coulson of the American Arbitration Association.[115] Franke noted the "brightening prospects in U.S-U.S.S.R trade" and that he had learned that "Soviet trade organizations have complained that they now and then meet American corporations which do not know about the agreement."[116] It is clear that the SCC Secretary-General acted as intermediary in a time and environment when Soviet and American organizations could not easily communicate directly. The 1986 meeting in New York led to a public

110 Franke Interview.

111 As demonstrated by the many texts submitted to his *liber amicorum* when he retired as Secretary-General in 2010, aptly named "Between East and West": K Hobér, A Magnusson and M Öhrström (eds), *Between East and West: Essays in Honour of Ulf Franke*, Juris, 2010.

112 K Hobér, A Magnusson, M Öhrström, p. xi. The publication is *Arbitration in Sweden*, published by the Stockholm Chamber of Commerce and Wetter & Wetter Advokatbyrå in 1977. It was the result of the work of a "panel," consisting of many leading Swedish procedural lawyers at the time.

113 Stockholm Chamber of Commerce, Press Release, *Soviet-US Arbitration Meeting on May 5, 1986 at the Swedish Consulate-General in New York*, on file with author.

114 Letter from Professor S. Lebedev to Ulf Franke, 14 March, 1986, on file with author.

115 Letter from Ulf Franke to Professor S. Lebedev (CC Professor Pozdniakov), on file with author.

116 Ibid.

reaffirmation of both sides' support of the Optional Clause, as communicated in an SCC press release.[117]

It was also Franke himself who, from his first days in office corresponded with Chinese representatives and on a dozen occasions travelled to China to cultivate relationships with public officials and businesses.[118] In an essay published when Franke retired, Hong Kong-based arbitrator Michael J Moser describes how the SCC's long-time Secretary-General "served as the main bridge between an emerging China and the international arbitration community."[119] Moser also reviewed extensive materials from the SCC archives reflecting the correspondence in which Franke replied to various Chinese inquiries into international arbitration law in general and Swedish practice in particular.[120]

These information activities were, however, never aimed at investment treaties specifically. On the contrary, for a long time the SCC secretariat was not aware of the SCC Rules being included in treaties and also treated its first treaty-based cases in the exact same way as those based on commercial contracts, without recognizing a distinction between the two.[121] Even after the first cases were brought in the mid-1990s, the SCC paid them only limited attention.[122]

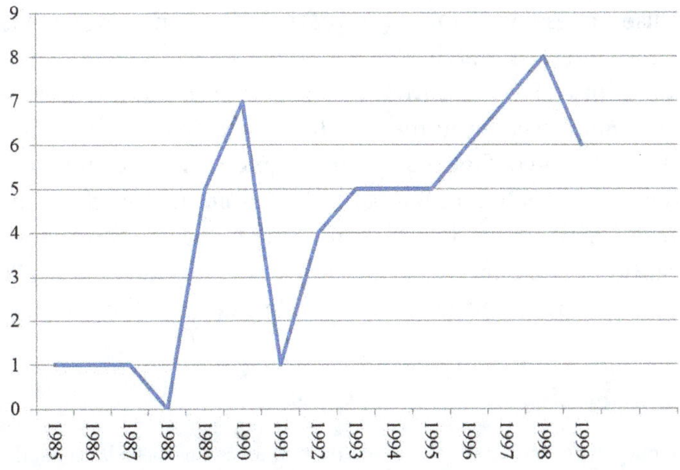

FIGURE 2.5 The SCC rules
SOURCE: THE AUTHOR

117 Stockholm Chamber of Commerce, Press Release, *Soviet-US Arbitration Meeting on May 5, 1986 at the Swedish Consulate-General in New York*, on file with author.

118 M Moser, pp. 346–348.

119 M Moser, p.344.

120 Ibid., pp. 344–346.

121 Franke Interview.

122 Ibid.

A good illustration of the Secretariat's view of the institution's role in investment treaties is the inclusion of the SCC Rules in the multilateral Energy Charter Treaty. As explained above, the ECT – which represents roughly a third of all treaty cases brought under the SCC Rules[123] – includes in its Article 26 consent to arbitration under either the ICSID, UNCITRAL or SCC Rules. Although this single treaty reference has provided a large part of the SCC's investment arbitration caseload, it appears the institution was unaware of the Rules' role in the negotiations. In an interview, Franke explains how he got a phone call from the Swedish government's representative in the ECT negotiations who asked, when the matter appeared to already be *fait accompli*, if the SCC would object to be included in the treaty's arbitration provision.[124] Ulf Franke did not object. A Swedish government official, who recalls the "Eastern European states" – particularly Russia – pressing for the SCC to be included alongside ICSID and UNCITRAL, confirms this account.[125] The Swedish government did not initiate the proposal but, naturally, supported such an inclusion when it was introduced by other states.[126] Given that one of the explicit ambitions behind the ECT was to bring the former East Bloc countries into a liberalized energy regime,[127] it likely made sense to accommodate a compromise in terms of the available dispute resolution fora, with ICSID arbitration being supplemented by both the UNCITRAL and the SCC Rules.

The apparent lack of active SCC advocacy aimed at investment treaties is confirmed by the general account in the 1996 book *Dealing in Virtue*, which devotes a chapter to the role of Stockholm's role in international commercial arbitration.[128] The authors note that the Stockholm arbitration world at the time "does not really compete for business" and "is not very entrepreneurial, not pushing to capture a larger market share."[129] Instead, they note that while the Stockholm market is reluctant to compete for business, it relies on large

123 As of 2017, 26 out of 74 treaty-based cases under the SCC Rules have been based on the ECT, see https://sccinstitute.com/statistics/investment-disputes-2017/, visited 6 January 2020.

124 Franke Interview.

125 Allard Interview.

126 Ibid.

127 Concluding Document of the Ministerial ("The Hague II") Conference on the International Energy Charter, available at http://www.energycharter.org/fileadmin/Documents-Media/Legal/ECTC-en.pdf, p. 14, visited 6 January, 2020.

128 Y Dezalay and B Garth, *Dealing in Virtue: International Commercial Arbitration and the Construction of a Transnational Legal Order*, Chicago Series in Law and Society, 1998.

129 Ibid., pp. 191–192.

international arbitrations coming there on their own accord, primarily thanks to the East-West connection.[130]

It is not particularly far-fetched to connect also the Eastern European insistence on SCC arbitration in the ECT to the long experience the Stockholm institution had with commercial disputes with an East-West aspect. This legacy would also explain the other, bilateral, treaty references to SCC arbitration; many of which predate the ECT. Of the 62 studied treaties referring to the Rules,[131] the vast majority includes at least one country that would have been on the "Eastern" side of the cold war, most notably China, Poland and Russia.[132] In this respect, the SCC seemed to have been able to "piggy-back" on its reputation as a reliable forum for commercial East-West disputes and carry this legacy on to investment treaties, despite the lack of active institutional promotion.

Furthermore, it is unusual that treaties refer exclusively to the SCC Rules.[133] Almost every reference is coupled with alternative options: ICSID,[134] UNCITRAL,[135] ICC,[136] or – most commonly – a combination of several rules.[137]

---

130 Ibid., pp. 190–193.

131 A study going further in time, covering every treaty until 2013, has shown that a total of 61 BITs refer to the SCC Rules, with an additional 64 naming the SCC as appointing authority in *ad hoc* arbitration, see K Hobér, *Selected Writings on Investment Treaty Arbitration*, Studentlitteratur, 2013, p. 543 et seq.

132 There are a few notable exceptions from this rule. For example, most treaties concluded by the Belgium-Luxembourg Economic Union provide for SCC arbitration, as do a few treaties concluded by Spain and Egypt with non-Eastern states.

133 The sole example from the 20th century being the Egypt – Kazakhstan BIT (1993).

134 China – Italy BIT (1985).

135 This is the case for most BITs concluded by the Russian Federation: Russian Federation – United Kingdom BIT (1989); Austria – Russian Federation BIT (1990); Russian Federation – Spain BIT (1990); Denmark – Russian Federation BIT (1993); Russian Federation - Vietnam BIT (1994); Russia - Albania BIT (1995); Hungary – Russian Federation BIT (1995); Egypt – Poland BIT (1995); Norway – Russian Federation BIT (1995); Russian Federation – Mongolia BIT (1995); Russian Federation - Croatia BIT (1996); Russian Federation - Laos BIT (1996); Russian Federation - Philippines BIT (1997); Lebanon - Russian Federation BIT (1997); Russian Federation - Moldova BIT (1997); Cyprus - Russian Federation BIT (1997); Russian Federation – Turkey BIT (1997); Russian Federation – Ukraine BIT (1998); Russian Federation - South African Republic BIT (1998); Russian Federation - Tajikistan BIT (1999).

136 Hungary – Spain BIT (1989),

137 This category includes most treaties concluded by Belgium/Luxembourg, as well as Cyprus – Hungary BIT (1989); Greece – Hungary BIT (1989); Czech Republic – United Kingdom BIT (1990); Czech Republic – Spain BIT (1990); Cyprus – Poland BIT (1992); Poland – Spain BIT (1992); Lithuania – Poland BIT (1992); Egypt – Spain BIT (1992); Latvia – Poland BIT (1993); The Energy Charter Treaty (1994); Slovakia – Poland (1994); Algeria – Spain BIT (1994); Egypt – Sri Lanka BIT (1996); Jordan – Poland BIT (1997); Mongolia – Turkey

2.3.2.2 The ICC Rules

There have been relatively few publicly known investment treaty arbitrations under the ICC Rules.[138] Still, the rules are frequently referred to in bilateral investment treaties: after the ICSID Rules, the UNCITRAL Rules and ICSID's Additional Facility Rules, they are in a safe fourth spot with a total of 127 references in the 20th century treaties studied.

As mentioned above, the first non-ICSID references were concluded in the late 1970s between France and other states, referencing both ICSID and ICC arbitration. After that, one ICC treaty was concluded in 1982,[139] two in 1983,[140] and one in 1984[141] and 1985[142] respectively. During the following years, the ICC references gained momentum and during most years in the 1990s, more than 10 treaties allowing for ICC arbitration were concluded annually. The ICC does not seem to have any documentation supporting that that these early references were the result of active ICC promotion. Rather, it is likely that the institution's dominance in international commercial arbitration at the time prompted (Western) states to insert ICC clauses in their investment treaties.

However, similar to the SCC Rules it is uncommon for treaties to allow exclusively for ICC arbitration; the ICC Rules are only referenced in conjunction with other options. This is consistent with the general increase in allowing the investor to choose between several arbitral *fora*, which can be detected as the number of treaties rises.

The UNCITRAL and the SCC Rules are included in significant multilateral investment treaties: both NAFTA and ECT in the case of the UNCITRAL Rules, and the ECT in the case of the SCC Rules. By contrast, the ICC Rules are not among the arbitration options under any of these treaties but were included in another, less well-known, multilateral instrument: the Lomé Convention.[143] The Convention, which is really four different treaties, was first signed in 1975 and thereafter updated on a regular basis. It is referred to by one commentator as one and the same "serial treaty,"[144] and is of interest in the general development of investment arbitration. Together the treaties set out the framework for investment cooperation between the European Union and a number of African, Caribbean and Pacific (ACP) countries. In addition to containing

---

BIT (1998); Cyprus – Egypt BIT (1998); Belarus – Cyprus BIT (1998); Lithuania – Russian Federation BIT (1999).

138 Although, as shown in Chapter 6, the number is bigger than often assumed.

139 Belize – United Kingdom BIT (1982).

140 Saint Lucia – United Kingdom BIT (1983); Haiti – United States of America BIT (1983).

141 France – Haiti BIT (1983).

142 Haiti – United Kingdom BIT (1985).

143 The Lomé Convention (1975).

144 J Paulsson, Arbitration Without Privity, p. 241.

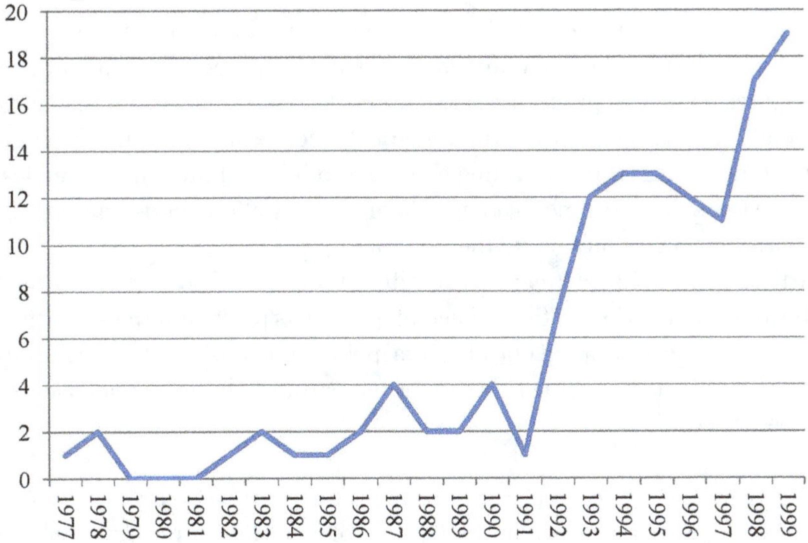

FIGURE 2.6 The ICC rules
SOURCE: THE AUTHOR

acknowledgments of the need for investment protection generally,[145] the treaties also provide for funding of investment projects by the European Development Fund (EDF), which has founded several infrastructure projects in the ACP. Disputes over such projects were regulated under the third Lomé Convention, signed in 1984, whose Article 238 sets out

> 1. Any dispute arising between the authorities of an ACP State and a contractor, supplier or provider of services, candidate or tenderer, on the occasion of the placing or performance of a contract financed by the Fund shall be settled by arbitration in accordance with procedural rules adopted by the Council of Ministers.
>
> 2. The procedural rules referred to in paragraph I shall be adopted by the decision of the Council of Ministers not later than its first meeting following the entry into force of this Convention, after consultation of the ACP-EEC Committee referred to in Article 193.
>
> 3. As a transitional measure pending the implementation of the decision provided for in paragraph 2, the final decision on all disputes shall be taken in accordance with the rules on conciliation and arbitration of the International Chamber of Commerce.

145 See R Dolzer & M Stevens, pp. 5–7.

No procedural rules were ever adopted by the Council of Ministers, leaving the door open for ICC arbitration under the treaty. The accounts of the number of disputes under this procedure varies from a few cases to a larger number.[146] It should be noted, that while the time of the conclusion of Lome III coincides with non-ICSID rules starting to appear in bilateral investment treaties, it seems to be the first time that a multilateral treaty allows non-state entities to arbitrate against states under the ICC Rules.

Article 238, and its reference to ICC arbitration, was subsequently replaced in the fourth Lome Convention, signed in 1990. In its place came a new Article 307, which made arbitration one of several possible avenues for dispute resolution. The particular sub-provision dealing with arbitration states that disputes may be settled

> [...] by arbitration in accordance with the procedural rules which will be adopted by decision of the Council of Ministers at the first meeting following the signing of this Convention upon the recommendation of the ACP-EEC Development Finance Cooperation Committee referred to in Article 325 of this Convention.

The procedural rules referred to were indeed adopted by the Council of Ministers. Rather than referring to an existing set of rules, an ad hoc system was set up.[147] The European states initially wished to model the rules on the UNCITRAL Rules but met with resistance from the ACP states, reportedly because of a general suspicion towards international arbitration.[148] The final form of the procedural rules instead included both arbitration and conciliation, in an effort to assuage the suspicions against arbitration as the exclusive mechanism. While the result of a compromise between two blocs with different views on arbitration,[149] the rules themselves are largely similar to established arbitration rules, primarily the 1976 UNCITRAL Rules.[150]

The dispute resolution clauses in Lomé III and IV demonstrate not only unilateral consent from the ACP states to private investors from foreign countries to arbitrate disputes but, more importantly for the purpose of this study, neither clause refers to the (at the time well-established) ICSID Convention – presumably because several of the Lomé states were not party to the Convention – but rather to the ICC and then to an *ad hoc* system closely modelled on the UNCITRAL Rules.

---

146 A Amissah, p. 168.
147 Described more in detail in A Amissah.
148 Ibid., pp. 169–170.
149 Ibid., p. 183.
150 J Paulsson, Arbitration Without Privity, p. 243. See also Amissah, p. 184.

As for bilateral investment treaties, many ICC references are contained in treaties concluded by at least one state that had not ratified the ICSID Convention at the time of the conclusion of the treaty. Common examples include Bulgaria,[151] China,[152] Cuba,[153] Poland,[154] and the Russian Federation.[155] However, a number of ICSID signatory states appear to have consistently opted for ICC arbitration in their investment treaties, even in cases where the other state party had also ratified the ICSID Convention at the time. These include the Belgium Luxembourg Economic Union,[156] Spain,[157] Turkey[158] and the

---

151 BLEU – Bulgaria BIT (1988); China – Bulgaria BIT (1989); Bulgaria – Ghana BIT (1989); China – United Arab Emirates BIT (1993); Bulgaria – Greece BIT (1993);

152 China – Kuwait BIT (1985); China – Malaysia BIT (1988); China – Bulgaria BIT (1989); China – United Arab Emirates BIT (1993).

153 Cuba – Spain BIT (1994); Cuba – United Kingdom BIT (1995); Barbados – Cuba BIT (1996); Cuba – Switzerland BIT (1996); Cuba – Greece BIT (1996); Brazil – Cuba BIT (1997); Cuba – Malaysia BIT (1997); Cuba – Indonesia BIT (1997); Cuba – Slovakia BIT (1997); Cuba – Turkey BIT (1997); BLEU – Cuba BIT (1998); Belize – Cuba BIT (1998); Cuba – Portugal BIT (1998); Cuba – Ghana BIT (1998); Cuba – Guatemala BIT (1999); Cuba – Hungary BIT (1999); Cuba – Mongolia BIT (1999); Cuba – Netherlands BIT (1999); Cuba – Panama BIT (1999); Cuba – Trinidad and Tobago BIT (1999).

154 BLEU – Poland BIT (1987); Greece – Poland BIT (1992); Albania – Poland BIT (1993); Iran, Islamic Republic of – Poland BIT (1998).

155 BLEU – Russian Federation BIT (1989); Russian Federation – United Kingdom BIT (1989); Austria – Russian Federation BIT (1990); Russian Federation – Spain BIT (1990); Denmark – Russian Federation BIT (1993); Russian Federation – Viet Nam BIT (1994); Albania – Russian Federation BIT (1995); Hungary – Russian Federation BIT (1995); Mongolia – Russian Federation BIT (1995); Norway – Russian Federation BIT (1995); Croatia – Russian Federation BIT (1996); Lao People's Democratic Republic – Russian Federation BIT (1996); Lebanon – Russian Federation BIT (1997); Philippines – Russian Federation BIT (1997); Argentina – Russian Federation BIT (1998); Russian Federation – Ukraine BIT (1998); Russian Federation – South Africa BIT (1998); Lithuania – Russian Federation BIT (1999); Russian Federation – Tajikistan BIT (1999).

156 BLEU – Malta BIT (1987); BLEU – Poland BIT (1987); BLEU – Bulgaria BIT (1988); BLEU – Czech Republic BIT (1989); BLEU – Russian Federation BIT (1989); BLEU – Slovakia BIT (1989); BLEU – Ukraine BIT (1996); BLEU – Moldova, Republic of BIT (1996); BLEU – Lithuania BIT (1997); BLEU – Cuba BIT (1998); BLEU – Mexico BIT (1998); BLEU – Uzbekistan BIT (1998); BLEU – South Africa BIT (1998); BLEU – Cote d'Ivoire BIT (1999); BLEU – Egypt BIT (1999); BLEU – Lebanon BIT (1999); BLEU – Macedonia, The former Yugoslav Republic of BIT (1999).

157 Armenia – Spain BIT (1990); Belarus – Spain BIT (1990); Czech Republic – Spain BIT (1990); Georgia – Spain BIT (1990); Kyrgyzstan – Spain BIT (1990); Russian Federation – Spain BIT (1990); Slovakia – Spain BIT (1990); Spain – Tajikistan BIT (1990); Spain – Turkmenistan BIT (1990); Cuba – Spain BIT (1994); Algeria – Spain BIT (1994); Honduras – Spain BIT (1994); Kazakhstan – Spain BIT (1994); Lithuania – Spain BIT (1994); Nicaragua – Spain BIT (1994); Pakistan – Spain BIT (1994); Latvia – Spain BIT (1995); Estonia – Spain BIT (1997).

158 Kazakhstan – Turkey BIT (1992); Kyrgyzstan – Turkey BIT (1992); Turkey – Turkmenistan BIT (1992); Turkey – Uzbekistan BIT (1992); Jordan – Turkey BIT (1993); Azerbaijan – Turkey BIT (1994); Lithuania – Turkey BIT (1994); Moldova, Republic of – Turkey BIT (1994);

United Kingdom.[159] Furthermore, ICC arbitration is included in a number of treaties concluded by Brazil,[160] which famously never ratified any of its early-generation investment treaties. It should also be noted that unlike Sweden, which has not concluded a single investment treaty which allows for SCC arbitration, there are a number of French investment treaties that allow for ICC arbitration.[161]

2.3.3 *The UNCITRAL Rules*

Of the arbitration rules studied in this project, the UNCITRAL Rules differ from the others. There are two primary reasons for this: (i) the UNCITRAL Rules are designed for *ad hoc* disputes and as such by default not administered by an institution (although such an institution is frequently appointed by the parties, as discussed below) and (ii) whereas the ICC and SCC Rules are drafted and maintained by their respective private institutions, the UNCITRAL Rules are subject to the work of UNCITRAL, a United Nations body made up of states. These distinctions are important to keep in mind as the UNCITRAL Rules are briefly introduced and their use in investment arbitration explained below.

Macedonia, The Former Yugoslav Republic of – Turkey BIT (1995); Egypt – Turkey BIT (1996); Croatia – Turkey BIT (1996); Iran, Islamic Republic of – Turkey BIT (1996); Nigeria – Turkey BIT (1996); Turkey – Ukraine BIT (1996); Estonia – Turkey BIT (1997); Latvia – Turkey BIT (1997); Bosnia and Herzegovina – Turkey BIT (1998); Mongolia – Turkey BIT (1998); Sudan – Turkey BIT (1999).

159 Belize – United Kingdom BIT (1982); Saint Lucia – United Kingdom BIT (1983); Haiti – United Kingdom BIT (1985); Malta – United Kingdom BIT (1986); Antigua and Barbuda – United Kingdom BIT (1987); Dominican Republic – United Kingdom BIT (1987); Bolivia – United Kingdom BIT (1988); Grenada – United Kingdom BIT (1988); Russian Federation – United Kingdom BIT (1989); Czech Republic – United Kingdom BIT (1990); Slovakia – United Kingdom BIT (1990); United Kingdom – Uruguay BIT (1990); Honduras – United Kingdom BIT (1993); Lithuania – United Kingdom BIT (1993); Trinidad Tobago – United Kingdom BIT (1993); Ukraine – United Kingdom BIT (1993); United Kingdom – Uzbekistan BIT (1993); Brazil – United Kingdom BIT (1994); Kyrgyzstan – United Kingdom BIT (1994); Pakistan – United Kingdom BIT (1994); South Africa – United Kingdom BIT (1994); Cuba – United Kingdom BIT (1995); Kazakhstan – United Kingdom BIT (1995); Swaziland – United Kingdom BIT (1995); Turkmenistan – United Kingdom BIT (1995); Slovenia – United Kingdom (1996); Croatia – United Kingdom BIT (1997); Tonga – United Kingdom BIT (1997); Lebanon – United Kingdom BIT (1999).

160 Brazil – Switzerland BIT (1994); Brazil – United Kingdom BIT (1994); Brazil – Portugal BIT (1994); Brazil – France BIT (1995); Brazil – Italy BIT (1995); Brazil – Korea, Republic of BIT (1995); Brazil – Cuba BIT (1997).

161 Bolivia – France BIT (1989); Czech Republic – France BIT (1990); Slovakia – France BIT (1990); France – Trinidad Tobago BIT (1993); France – Uruguay BIT (1993); Brazil – France BIT (1995); France – Qatar BIT (1996); France – Mexico BIT (1998).

2.3.3.1 UNCITRAL Background

The United Nations General Assembly created the United Nations Commission on International Trade Law in 1966. Today UNCITRAL works in six different Working Groups, each aimed at a specific legal area. Working Group II handles the work related to arbitration and conciliation and meets twice a year, in Vienna (where the UNCITRAL Secretariat is located) and New York respectively.[162] The membership at these meetings consists of 60 states who at the time are members of UNCITRAL, as well as many "observers" in the form of non-member states[163] and other non-state actors such as NGOs and arbitration institutions. In between the meetings, the Secretariat in Vienna works with preparation of agendas and documents relating to the meetings. At the meetings, the Working Group makes decision by "consensus," which is interpreted widely so that more than a few objections are needed to stop a proposal from moving forward.[164] This process arguably slows down the negotiations but also ensures that the resulting text has support from a wide range of states.[165]

UNCITRAL has for a long time been fostering international arbitration generally. Together with the New York Convention[166] and harmonization efforts aimed at domestic legislation,[167] the UNCITRAL Arbitration Rules constitute cornerstones of the international arbitration framework.[168] The first version of the Arbitration Rules, adopted by a General Assembly resolution on December 15, 1976, was intended to set up a global *ad hoc* system of international arbitration, partly as an alternative to the (private) institutions, such as the ICC, administering their own rules.[169]

The Rules, as well as the New York Convention and the Model Law, were drafted prior to the fast growth of investment treaties. Historically, therefore,

---

162 In July 2017, the UNCITRAL Commission tasked Working Group III with reform of investor-state reform, see UNCITRAL Doc A/72/17, Report of the United Nations Commission on International Trade Law Fiftieth session, para. 264.

163 States are UNCITRAL members for six-year terms, half of which expires every three years in order to ensure a regular rotation of member states.

164 See generally C R Kelly, "The Politics of Legitimacy in the UNCITRAL Working Methods," in T Brude, M L. Busch, A Porges (eds.), *The Politics of International Economic Law*, Cambridge University Press, 2011.

165 J Castello, "Unveiling the 2010 UNCITRAL Arbitration Rules," 65 Dispute Journal, Issue 2/3, p. 21.

166 The New York Convention, for which the UNCITRAL Secretariat acts as repository.

167 Most visibly by the issuance of the UNCITRAL Model Law on International Commercial Arbitration, adopted in 1985 and amended in 2006, which serves as the model for many domestic arbitration laws, as discussed further in Chapter 5.

168 Caron & Caplan, p. 2.

169 Caron & Caplan, p.4.

UNCITRAL's work was restricted to commercial arbitration. Nevertheless, the rise in investment treaties referring to UNCITRAL arbitration – and the accompanying cases brought under those treaties – meant that possible adaptions to treaty arbitration were discussed in Working Group II during the update of the Arbitration Rules, which finished in 2010.[170] In the end, despite suggestions to the contrary,[171] no specific language addressing this development was included in the 2010 Rules, which instead were largely an update of the existing language. This narrow approach is fully in line with the guiding principles adopted at the outset of the drafting, which stated that "the focus of the revision should be on updating the Rules to meet changes that had taken place over the last thirty years in arbitral practice, not on simply making them more complex."[172] A large part of the discussion circled around the need for a more transparent procedure for treaty-based arbitrations, but this matter was tabled and eventually led to the stand-alone 2014 UNCITRAL Rules on Transparency in Treaty-Based Investor-State Arbitration.[173]

Instead of specific language addressing treaty disputes, certain modifications were made to accommodate the Rules' use in non-contractual contexts more generally. Importantly, the Rules' scope of application was widened, since the 1976 UNCITRAL Rules never contemplated arbitrations based on treaties but instead were drafted for international commercial – meaning contractual – arbitration. Article 1(1) sets out the scope of application of the 1976 Rules:

> Where the *parties to a contract* have agreed in writing that disputes *in relation to that contract* shall be referred to arbitration under the UNCITRAL Rules, then such disputes shall be settled in accordance with these Rules

170 See for example UNCITRAL Report of the Working Group on Arbitration and Conciliation on the work of its forty-sixth session (A/CN.9/619); UNCITRAL Report of the Working Group on Arbitration and Conciliation on the work of its forty-eighth session (A/CN.9/646), esp. paras. 54–69. The revision process was initiated in 2006 following an article by the primary drafter of the 1976 UNCITRAL Rules, where the treaty arbitration development was not mentioned, see P Sanders, "Has the Moment Come to Revise the UNCITRAL Rules of Arbitration?," (2004) 20 Arb Intl 243.

171 See for example Center for International Environmental Law and International Institute for Sustainable Development, *Revising the UNCITAL Arbitration Rules to Address State Arbitrations*, available at http://www.iisd.org/pdf/2007/investment_revising_uncitral_arbitration.pdf., visited 6 January 2019.

172 Report of the Working Group on Arbitration and Conciliation on the work of its forty-fifth session (A/CN.9/614), para. 16.

173 UNCITRAL Rules on Transparency in Treaty-based Investor-State Arbitration, available at http://www.uncitral.org/uncitral/en/uncitral_texts/arbitration/2014Transparency.html.

> subject to such modification as the parties may agree in writing. (emphasis added)

The drafters of the 1976 Rules intentionally chose this narrow scope.[174] By contrast, the scope of application in the revised 2010 version of the Rules is expanded to "disputes [...] in respect of a defined legal relationship, whether contractual or not,"[175] a broader scope that also encompasses arbitration where one disputing party's consent is treaty-based.

Regardless of this revision made in the 2010 version of the Rules, the 1976 Rules will remain the most relied upon by investors for quite some time. This is so because of the relationship between the rules, as stipulated by Article 1(2) of the 2010 Rules:

> The parties to an arbitration agreement concluded after 15 August 2010 shall be presumed to have referred to the Rules in effect on the date of commencement of the arbitration, unless the parties have agreed to apply a particular version of the Rules. *That presumption does not apply where the arbitration agreement has been concluded by accepting after 15 August 2010 an offer made before that date.* (emphasis added)

The second sentence alters the presumption in cases of investment arbitrations where the treaty is older than 2010 and the request for arbitration is after 2010. Thus, for the 2010 Rules to apply automatically the treaty relied upon must be concluded after 15 August, 2010.

Furthermore, while, as discussed below, the Iran-US Claims Tribunal was empowered by the state parties to the Algiers Accords to modify the UNCITRAL Rules, very few bilateral investment treaties avail themselves of the Rules' inherent flexibility to tailor the Rules.[176] A notable exception is the trilateral NAFTA, which provides for detailed specification of various procedural aspects.[177] A few treaties also specify that the version of the Rules "as then in force" when the arbitration is initiated shall apply.[178]

The original, narrow scope of application is hardly surprising. Even though, by 1976, a small number of investment treaties referred to ICSID arbitration,

---

174 Report of UNCITRAL Committee of the Whole II, Annex II to Report on the Work of its 9th Session, UN Doc A/31/17, (1976), para 13.

175 UNCITRAL Rules 2010, Article 1(1).

176 J Paulsson & G Petrochilos, p. 3.

177 NAFTA Articles 1121 et seq.

178 This applies to most treaties concluded by the United Kingdom, following its early model BIT. See also Hong Kong SAR – Italy BIT (1995).

the first arbitration to be brought under an investment treaty was still over a decade away. Nevertheless, it did not take many years for the UNCITRAL Rules to find their way into treaties.

2.3.3.2 UNCITRAL and Investment Treaties

The UNCITRAL Rules entered the investment treaty scene in 1982 and grew slowly but steadily in prominence. By the 1990s, the UNCITRAL Rules were almost as likely as ICSID to be included in treaties. In fact, as mentioned above, the single most common type of clause towards the end of the century allows the investor to choose between either UNCITRAL or ICSID arbitration.

It appears the UNCITRAL Rules are included in early investment treaties in two scenarios: either (i) as a complement to ICSID arbitration, leaving the investor with the choice between the two (and sometimes also other rules), or (ii) as the primary option, mainly in treaties involving at least one state that is not an ICSID signatory.[179] In the latter, smaller category, several treaties allow only for UNCITRAL arbitration, thereby excluding the possibility of ICSID arbitration altogether.[180]

Significantly, the studied time period also includes two especially important multilateral investment treaties that both allow for UNCITRAL arbitration: the ECT and NAFTA.[181] A very large number of UNCITRAL cases have been filed

179 The fact that Poland had not "adhered" to the ICSID Convention was provided as the reason for including other arbitration rules in the US – Poland BIT, see Statement by Eugene J. McAllister in Hearing before the Committee on Foreign Relations of the United States Senate 18 September 1990, p. 8 (made available to the Qualitative Data Repository database by T St John). In the same statement, Poland's "acceptance of broader investor access to international arbitration" is hailed by McAllister.

180 For example Russia – Poland BIT (1992); Bulgaria – Russia BIT (1993); Russia – Cuba BIT (1993): Congo – Italy BIT (1994); Hong Kong, China SAR – Switzerland BIT (1994); Dominican Republic – Spain BIT (1995); Russian Federation – Sweden BIT (1995); Kyrgyzstan – Pakistan BIT (1995); Oman – United Kingdom BIT (1995): Hong Kong, China SAR – Italy BIT (1995); France – Hong Kong, SAR BIT (1995); Argentina – Cuba BIT (1995); Bulgaria – United Kingdom BIT (1995); Cuba – Lebanon BIT (1995): Armenia – Egypt BIT (1996); Eritrea – Italy BIT (1996); Italy – Russian Federation BIT (1996); Argentina – Viet Nam BIT (1996); Cuba – Romania BIT (1996); Bulgaria – Viet Nam BIT (1996); BLEU (Belgium-Luxembourg Economic Union) – Hong Kong, SAR BIT (1996); Cuba – France BIT (1997); Hong Kong, SAR – Japan BIT (1997); Hong Kong, China SAR – Korea, Republic of BIT (1997); Egypt – Russian Federation BIT (1997); Iran, Islamic Republic of – Switzerland BIT (1998); Argentina – Russian Federation BIT (1998); Hong Kong, SAR – United Kingdom BIT (1998).

181 Articles 26 and 1120 respectively.

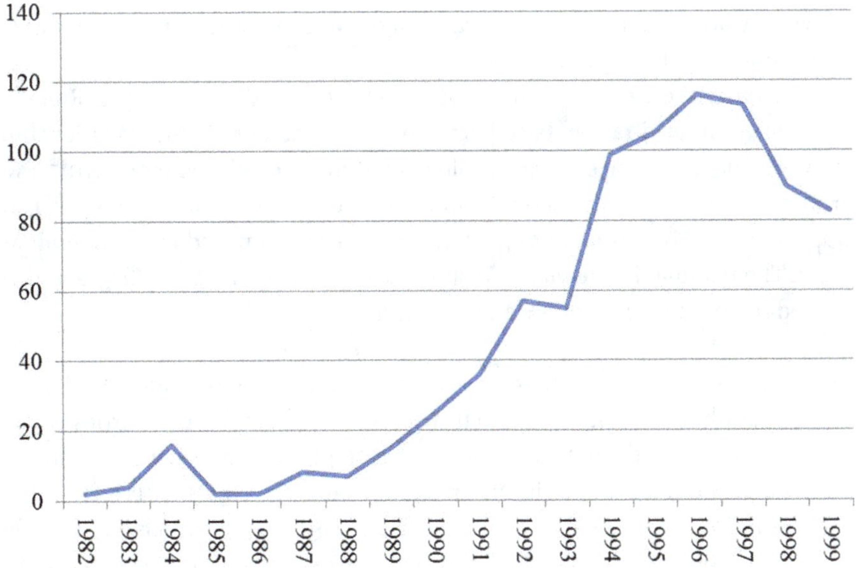

FIGURE 2.7 The UNCITRAL rules
SOURCE: THE AUTHOR

under these two treaties, which for a long time counted several non-ICSID states to its signatories.[182]

As discussed above, the combined consequence of the Rules' temporal applicability and states' historical lack to modifications to the Rules is that the 1976 version of the Rules, in their default shape, govern the vast majority of UNCITRAL treaty arbitrations. As of 2015, only four known treaty cases have been filed under the 2010 Rules, and in each case the disputing parties have agreed to applying the 2010 Rules even if the respective treaty otherwise does not provide for their application.[183] This number will most likely

182 For NAFTA, this is no longer the case: Canada (2013) and Mexico (2018) have now ratified the ICSID Convention, see https://icsid.worldbank.org/en/Pages/about/Database-of-Member-States.aspx, visited 7 January 2019.

183 *Enkev Beheer B.V. v. Republic of Poland*, PCA Case No. 2013-01, First Partial Award 29 April 2014; *Mytilineos Holdings SA v. Republic of Serbia*, UNCITRAL (not public but reported by IAReporter, *Serbia Disputes: Mytilineos Files a New Arbitration Claim in Long-running Fight, While Solar Park Investor Adds Treaty Claim to Threat of Contract Arbitration*, 10 December 2013, at http://www.iareporter.com/articles/serbia-disputes-mytilineos-files-a-new-bit-claim-in-long-running-fight-while-solar-park-investor-adds-treaty-claim-to-threat-of-contract-arbitration/); *ST-AD GmbH v. Republic of Bulgaria*, UNCITRAL, PCA Case No. 2011-06, Award on Jurisdiction, 18 July 2013; Windstream Energy LLC v. Government of Canada, UNCITRAL, PCA Case No. 2013-22, Award, 27 September, 2016.

grow over time but as of now, the vast majority of investment treaties in force were concluded before 2010.[184]

In theory, the restricted scope of Article 1(1) of the UNCITRAL Rules – providing for arbitration based only on a direct contractual relationship between the disputing parties – could constitute an obstacle for an UNCITRAL tribunal to assume jurisdiction based on a treaty. In practice, however, it appears that this particular objection has never been raised by a respondent state. The tribunal in the *ad hoc* dispute *Larsen v. The Hawaiian Kingdom* discussed the matter *sua sponte* and found that:

> [...] there appears no reason why the UNCITRAL Rules cannot be adapted to apply to a non-contractual dispute. For example, the parties could agree that a dispute as to tort, or occupier's or environmental liability might be determined in an arbitration applying the UNCITRAL Rules. Moreover they could so agree in relation to a dispute which had already arisen independently of any contractual relationship between them. In this manner the parties to an arbitration may specifically or by implication adopt or apply the UNCITRAL Rules to any dispute.[185]

Apparently, this explanation by the *Larsen* tribunal, based on the fact that the UNCITRAL Rules allow the parties to modify virtually every aspect of the Rules, is so well accepted by states that Article 1(1) has never been considered as a potential bar to arbitrating treaty disputes under the 1976 Rules. Thus, so the common assumption would seem to be, when a state consents to arbitration under the 1976 UNCITRAL Rules, and the investor subsequently accepts this offer, an agreement to arbitrate is formed, implicitly altering the language of Article 1(1).

2.3.3.3 Treaty Arbitration under the UNCITRAL Rules Administered by an Institution

Because of the *ad hoc* nature of the UNCITRAL Rules, it is common for parties to supplement their choice of the rules with the choice of an independent body to carry out various tasks that facilitate the arbitration. One of these is to act as appointing authority, which appoints and hears challenges to arbitrators. Under the UNCITRAL Rules, unless the parties agree to something else,

---

184 UNCTAD IIA Issues Note No. 1, February 2015, p. 2. Available at http://unctad.org/en/PublicationsLibrary/webdiaepcb2015d1_en.pdf

185 *Larsen v. Hawaiian Kingdom*, PCA Case 1999-01, Final Award 5 February, 2001, para. 10.7.

the Secretary-General of the PCA is tasked with designating the appointing authority.[186]

In addition to this designating role, the PCA appears to be the most-used appointing authority in UNCITRAL investment arbitrations.[187] Despite the fact that a number of treaties appear to directly designate the PCA,[188] in most such cases the PCA has provided its services because the disputing parties or the tribunal has requested them to do so.

The first investment treaty case administered by the PCA was an UNCITRAL case initiated in 2001 and concluded in 2006.[189] According to PCA Deputy Secretary-General Brooks Daly, the chairman in this case had previously worked with the institution in an interstate arbitration and preferred that the PCA act as registry in the case.[190] The tribunal put this suggestion to the parties, which agreed to it during the first organizational meeting in 2001.[191] Following this first case, the PCA has acted in 85 known investment treaty cases.[192] In none of these published cases did the PCA's involvement emanate directly from a designation in the underlying treaty, but rather by agreement of the parties. In addition to the PCA, it is clear that the Secretary-General of both the SCC[193] and ICC[194] is often designated as appointing authority in BITs.[195]

186 1976 UNCITRAL Rules Article 7; 2010 UNCITRAL Rules Article 6.

187 The UNCITRAL Secretariat does not issue information on these matters and the PCA web page does not contain such statistics but publicly known such cases are in the dozens.

188 The PCA lists 39 such treaties in force, http://www.pca-cpa.org/showpagee3a6.html?pag_id=1385, last visited May 1, 2016.

189 *Saluka Investments B.V. v. Czech Republic*, UNCITRAL, Partial Award, March 17, 2006.

190 B Daly, presentation to LLM students at Georgetown University Law Center, 28 October, 2015.

191 *Saluka Investments B.V. v. Czech Republic*, Decision on Jurisdiction, May 7, 2004, para. 7(ii).

192 Search in PCA Case Repository, 7 January, 2019.

193 For example China – Kuwait BIT (1985); Bulgaria – Italy BIT (1988); Finland – Russian Federation BIT (1989); BLEU (Belgium-Luxembourg Economic Union) – Czech Republic BIT (1989); Bolivia, Plurinational State of – France BIT (1989); Italy – Venezuela, Bolivarian Republic of BIT (1990); Algeria – France BIT (1993); Italy – United Arab Emirates BIT (1995). See also K Hobér, *Selected Writings on Investment Treaty Arbitration*, Studentlitteratur, 2013, for a complete overview.

194 For example Albania – Greece BIT (1991); Greece – Poland BIT (1992); Albania – Poland BIT (1993); Bulgaria – Greece BIT (1993); Albania – Croatia BIT (1993); Brazil – Korea, Republic of BIT (1995) (not in force); Germany – Qatar BIT (1996).

195 It is worth noting in this context that a surprisingly large number of treaties also refer to these institutions as appointing authorities in clauses envisioning "pure" *ad hoc* disputes, i.e. without any set of arbitration rules applying.

The LCIA has also acted in various capacities in a small number of publicly known treaty arbitrations under the UNCITRAL Rules.[196] The same is true for SIAC and CRCICA.[197] These institutions are not mentioned in any treaty covered by the study but have presumably, similar to the PCA, been appointed with the disputing parties' approval.

Finally, a few treaties that do not refer to ICSID arbitration still designate various ICSID entities to support the proceedings.[198] Many modern UNCITRAL arbitrations are administered by ICSID,[199] but the ICSID Secretary-General has also repeatedly been called upon to act as appointing authority, a practice that started already in the 1980s.[200] Yet again, it appears that most such cases have been made by virtue of the disputing parties, as opposed to the underlying treaty, designating ICSID to provide the services.

2.3.4 *The First Non-ICSID Treaty Cases*

There was a large gap in time between the first treaties allowing for ICSID arbitration and the first time an investor availed itself of such a treaty (in the ground-breaking *AAPL v. Sri Lanka* case, mentioned above at 2.2.1.1 and initiated in 1987). The corresponding gaps between treaty conclusion and early UNCITRAL and SCC cases are smaller, the first such cases having been brought relatively soon after the emergence of those rules in investment treaties.[201]

196 *Société Générale in respect of DR Energy Holdings Limited and Empresa Distribuidora de Electricidad del Este, S. A.v. The Dominican Republic*, UNCITRAL, LCIA Case No. UN 7927; *EnCana Corporation v. Republic of Ecuador*, UNCITRAL, LCIA Case No. UN3481; *Occidental Exploration and Production Company v. The Republic of Ecuador*, LCIA Case No. UN3467.

197 See above footnote 57.

198 See for example the ECOWAS Protocol on Community Enterprises (1984); Germany – India BIT (1995).

199 Particularly NAFTA arbitrations, for which it appears that ICSID administers most cases even if the ICSID Arbitration Rules have not been available historically.

200 A Parra, pp. 152–153 with further references.

201 The very first UNCITRAL cases were actually based on treaties providing for "pure" ad hoc proceedings but were heard under the UNCITRAL Rules after decisions of the respective tribunals. Depending on how the tribunal decides to apply the rules in the individual case, the lines between a "pure" ad hoc proceeding and an UNCITRAL proceeding becomes somewhat muddied in these cases. The first such award to be rendered, in the 1994 case between German investor Saar Papier and Poland, states that the UNCITRAL Rules apply "by the agreement of the parties," *Saar Papier Vertriebs GmbH v. Republic of Poland*, Interim Award of the Arbitral Tribunal, 17 August, 1994, para. 4. The same arguably applies for two early subsequent awards, still unpublished, under the Germany – Poland BIT (which does not refer to the UNCITRAL Rules), as both are reported as UNCITRAL awards Nordsucker v. Poland, see L E Peterson, *Poland Liable for Breach of Germany-Poland BIT; Arbitrators Grappling with Damages in UNCITRAL Proceeding*, 29 June, 2009, available at http://www.iareporter.com/articles/poland-liable-for-breach-of-germany-poland-bit

By contrast, the first use of an ICC arbitration clauses waited until the 21st century.[202]

2.4 Two Potential Explanations

The previous sections have shown that commercial arbitration rules were first included in investment treaties in the early 1980s, in a practice that gained momentum during that decade and the next. The investment treaties allowing for SCC arbitration were mostly concluded between one "Western" and one "Eastern" state, whereas the situation for both the UNCITRAL Rules and the ICC Rules is somewhat more fragmented. For all three rules, it is common, but not always the case, that at least one treaty state had not ratified the ICSID Convention at the time the treaty was concluded.

Below, two potential explanations are introduced that might help cast light on this development, through which ICSID lost its early monopoly on treaty references. First, it is argued that the Iran-United States Claims Tribunal's use of the UNCITRAL Rules might have broadened the understanding of the scope of traditionally commercial arbitration rules. The second potential explanation discussed is the discontent with the ICSID system that was voiced in the middle of the 1980s.

2.4.1 *A First Potential Explanation: The United States Claims Tribunal*

The first application of a set of commercial arbitration rules to non-contractual disputes is traced back to the Iran-United States Claims Tribunal (the Tribunal), constituted pursuant to the Algiers Accords in 1981. The Tribunal applied, and indeed still applies to the few outstanding cases, the 1976 UNCITRAL Rules, albeit in a slightly modified version. The Tribunal's unique history is well known and will not be restated in any great detail in this study. The argument

-arbitrators-grappling-with-damages-in-uncitral-proceeding/; Ingo Lutz v. Poland, see L E Peterson, *Cypriot Energy Trader Files Claim Against Poland Under Energy Charter Treaty; Poland has Faced At Least Eight Other Treaty Arbitrations*, 26 August, 2008, available at http://www.iareporter.com/articles/cypriot-energy-trader-files-claim-against-poland-under-energy-charter-treaty-poland-has-faced-at-least-eight-other-treaty-arbitrations/. While the SCC acted as appointing authority in the *Saar Papier* case, the first treaty case to be heard under the SCC Rules appears to be Biedermann v. Kazakhstan, L E Peterson, *Kazakhstan seeks to annul $125 Million ICSID Award in Telecoms dispute; we review earlier Kazakh arbitrations,* http://www.iareporter.com/articles/kazakhstan-seeks-to-annul-125-million-icsid-award-in-telecoms-dispute-we-review-earlier-kazakh-arbitrations/, Investment Arbitration Reporter, 12 November 2008.

202 See further Chapter 4.

put forward is, however, that the practice of the Tribunal likely influenced the choice of states to subsequently include references to UNCITRAL – and possibly other non-ICSID rules – in their investment treaties. In order to make this argument, it is necessary to first outline at least some basic background regarding the constitution of the Tribunal.

In early January 1981, 52 American hostages at the American embassy in Teheran were released after having spent 14 months in captivity. The hostage taking was the culmination of a dramatic deterioration in the relationship between Iran and the United States following the Iranian revolution in 1979. Prior to the revolution, the ruling Iranian Shah had entertained close relations with the West in general and the United States in particular.[203] As a consequence, at the time of the revolution many Americans lived in Iran and there were significant business ties between American and Iranian entities. This changed dramatically with the revolution, which sparked heavy anti-Western sentiments in Iran and eventually led to a complete breakdown in diplomatic and business relations between Iran and the United States, climaxing with the hostage taking at the embassy.[204]

The release of the hostages was part of a highly sensitive and complicated diplomatic exchange between United States and Iran, facilitated by the Algerian government as intermediary. The agreements forming the basis for the solution of the crisis are known as "The Algiers Accords." The Accords, which formally are pronouncements by the Algerian government to which Iran and the United States adhere,[205] consist of seven separate documents, of which the Claims Settlement Declaration is the most important for the purposes of this text.[206]

The background to the Accords – the severing of diplomatic and business relations between the two states – involved a freezing by the American president Carter of all Iranian assets held by American banks. Many of these Iranian assets were at the time of the Accords subject to litigation and interim

203 R Khan notes, with the benefit of historical hindsight, the irony in President Carter's statement on his new year's visit to Iran in 1977 that Iran is "an island of stability in one of the more troubled areas of the world," R Khan, *The Iran-United States Claims Tribunal – Controversies, Cases and Contribution*, Martinus Nijhoff Publishers, 1990. at p.7

204 Depicted in the 2013 Academy Award winning movie *Argo*.

205 G Wetter, "The Iran-United States Claims Tribunal," SvJT 1982 p. 194.

206 Declaration of the Government of the Democratic and Popular Republic of Algeria Concerning the Settlement of Claims by the Government of the United States of America and the Government of the Islamic Republic of Iran, 19 January 1981, reprinted in 1 Iran – U.S. Claims Tribunal Reports 1981–1982, at p.9. In addition to the Claims Settlement Declaration, the Accords consist of another declaration – usually referred to as the General Declaration – and five technical agreements.

measures in courts in America and elsewhere, usually with American claimants initiating the procedures. In the other declaration in the Algiers Accords, the General Declaration, the American government agreed to annul judgments and halt ongoing procedures against Iranian state entities and instead refer all claims relating to the Iranian assets to arbitration before a specially instituted body: the Tribunal.[207] As a lot of the assets were subject to attachment in ongoing proceedings, a simple lifting of the freeze would not have sufficed to secure the rights of American parties, who would still not be able to utilize the assets if they were simply unfrozen.[208]

The Algiers Accords consequently moved the assets to a fund, initially financed by $1 billion of the previously frozen assets, which the Iranian government is obliged to maintain at a level of at least $500 million and out of which all awards to American claimants are to be paid.[209] This fund in practice allows the Tribunal to conduct its work largely without having to consider enforcement issues: a fact that distinguishes the Tribunal from most other arbitral bodies. However, this only applies for awards in favour of American nationals,[210] but according to the wording of the Claims Settlement Declaration, any award rendered by the Tribunal is "enforceable in the courts of any nation in accordance with its laws."[211] In theory therefore, there is a possibility that an award that cannot be satisfied through the Security Account – such as a successful Iranian counterclaim – may be enforced through the New York Convention. This discussion will however be left outside of this text.

The Claims Settlement Declaration, in which the framework of the Tribunal is set up, is not an investment treaty but rather a response to the unique conflict between the Iranian and American governments. The declaration, arguably being a treaty under public international law,[212] however bears some

---

207 The constitutionality of this move was contested in the United States but finally settled by the US Supreme Court in Dames & Moore v. Regan, 453 U.S. 654 (1981).

208 DP Stewart & LB Sherman, "Developments at the Iran-United States Claims Tribunal: 1981–1983," in R Lillich (ed.), *The Iran-United States Claims Tribunal 1981–1983 (Seventh Sokol Colloquium)*, Virginia Legal Studies, 1984, p. 3.

209 Technical Agreement with N.V. Settlement Bank of the Netherlands, 17 August 1981, Art. 1(iv).

210 General Declaration, para. 7.

211 Art. IV(3).

212 The Vienna Convention on the Law of Treaties (VCLT) Art. 2(1)a states that a treaty is "an international agreement concluded between States in written form and governed by international law, whether embodied in a single instrument or in two or more related instruments and whatever its particular designation." See also the *Case A-1*, (1982), 1 Iran – U.S. Claims Tribunal Reports 1981–1982, at p.144; DL Jones, "The Iran-United States Claims Tribunal: Private Rights and State Responsibility," (1984) 24(2) Virg. J. Int'l L. 268.

relevance for the purposes of this study as it provides for, *inter alia,* "binding third party arbitration"[213] excluding the jurisdiction of any court.[214] While also providing for inter-state arbitration between the treaty parties in certain situations,[215] the vast majority of arbitrations conducted pursuant to the Declaration[216] – and the natural focus for the purposes of this study – are between nationals of one state directly against the other state. The cut-off period for lodging claims was set to October 19th 1981[217] and only certain types of claims were allowed.[218] Claims meeting these tests have been filed and processed in the thousands.[219] As of 2002, all claims by nationals were resolved[220] but a few interstate claims remain pending as of 2019.[221]

The Claims Settlement Declaration further stipulates that claims smaller than $250,000 must be presented by the claimant's government, whereas larger claims can be presented by the individual claimant directly.[222] This possibility for non-state entities to present claims directly against a state before an international tribunal, now common-place in the world of investment treaty arbitration, was very rare at the time.[223]

Article VI of the Claims Settlement Declaration specifies the Tribunal's seat to be in The Hague, where each government undertakes to designate an agent to receive notices or communications directed both to the states and their respective nationals. According to the terms of the Declaration, the Tribunal should consist of "nine members or such larger multiple of three" as the States may agree to.[224] In practice the number has never been extended and the day-to-day operations of the Tribunal are conducted before three separate chambers, each consisting of one Iranian, one American and one third-party arbitrator, although the Tribunal sometimes meets in full.

---

213 Claims Settlement Declaration, Art. II.
214 Ibid., Art. VII, para. 2.
215 Ibid., Art. II.
216 D Caron, The Nature of the Iran-United States Claims Tribunal, p. 120.
217 Claims Settlement Declaration, Art. III, para. 4.
218 Claims Settlement Declaration, Art. II.
219 A total of 3747 such claims involving a private party had been filed at the deadline on January 19th 1982, C Brower & J Drueschke, p.13. D Caron gives the number of "approximately 3,761," D Caron, The Nature of the Iran-United States Claims Tribunal, p. 130.
220 Caron & Caplan, p. 5.
221 http://www.iusct.net/Default.aspx, accessed 7 January, 2019.
222 Claims Settlement Declaration, Art. III(3).
223 DP Stewart & LB Sherman in Lillich (ed.), p. 6.
224 Claims Settlement Declaration, Art. III(1).

The Declaration also provides that the UNCITRAL Rules are to apply to the procedures of the Tribunal.[225] At the time of the initiation of the Tribunal the UNCITRAL Rules, having been enacted in 1976, were relatively untested.[226] The proceedings before the Tribunal therefore became an opportunity to "test the waters" in an environment when the awards and procedural orders would be published more widely than otherwise customary in international commercial arbitration.[227] The Tribunal did not adopt the UNCITRAL Rules wholesale but rather made some adjustments prompted by the peculiarities of the situation leading to the disputes. The Claims Settlement Declaration provides that the UNCITRAL Rules shall apply "to the extent modified by the Parties [the United States and Iran] or by the tribunal to ensure that this Agreement can be carried out."[228] No alteration was in fact done by the parties but the tribunal finally adopted its own modified version of the UNCITRAL Rules in May 1983.[229]

A lot has been written about the Tribunal's contribution to substantive international law, including whether or not its awards, given the Tribunal's unique circumstances, are in fact able to contribute to general international law at all.[230] It is clear that the Tribunal had to repeatedly rule on substantive matters of great relevance for both commercial law and public international law, especially on matters related to expropriation and compensation.[231]

In addition to the Tribunal's contribution to substantive law, there has also been a lot of scholarly discussion as to whether the Tribunal is "international," or "transnational" in nature, and whether or not it is best labelled as a purely international tribunal or something more akin to a conventional arbitral tribunal, presumably by virtue of being anchored in a domestic jurisdiction, with

---

225 "Oddly enough," according to one commentator, see S Toope, Mixed International Arbitration, p.202.

226 Brower & Drueschke, p. 17; S Abercrombie Baker & MD Davis, *The UNCITRAL Arbitration Rules in Practice – The Experience of the Iran-United States Claims Tribunal*, Kluwer Law and Taxation Publishers, 1992, pp. 2–3; K.H Ameli, "The Application of the Rules of the Iran-United States Claims Tribunal," in W.P. Heere (ed.), *International Law and The Hague's 750th Anniversary*, Asser Press, 1999, p. 279.

227 As discussed below, the Tribunal modified the UNCITRAL Rules so as to allow for a larger degree of transparency.

228 Claims Settlement Declaration, Art. III, para. 2.

229 Final Tribunal Rules of Procedure ("FTRP"), 2 Iran – U.S Claims Tribunal Reports at p. 405 et seq.

230 See for example C S. Gibson & C R. Drahozal, "Iran-United States Claims Tribunal Precedent in Investor-State Arbitration," Journal of International Arbitration 23(6): 521–546.

231 For an extensive discussion on these rulings, see Brower & Brueschke, pp. 359–613.

Dutch law being its *lex loci arbitri*.[232] For the purposes of the present study it is however sufficient to note that the Tribunal did not adjudicate contractual disputes, as the case would traditionally be in most commercial arbitrations, but rather rested its mandate on an inter-state treaty.[233] The vast majority of proceedings before the Tribunal therefore differed from any other previously conducted under non-ICSID rules, in that they were conducted between a state and a private party who, much like in modern investment treaty arbitrations, never directly agreed to arbitration between them.[234] Most disputing parties before the Tribunal instead relied on the consent expressed by the state parties in the Declaration. The consent between the disputing parties is thus formed, theoretically speaking, when the claimant accepts the respondent's standing offer to arbitrate and requests arbitration. This approach to consent is the one widely accepted in modern investment treaty arbitration[235] and the most reasonable one for understanding the Tribunal's jurisdiction,[236] since it would allow for the proceedings to be constituted without the respondent state participating actively. Another view is that both parties themselves are deemed to have agreed to arbitrate by filing their respective claims.[237]

This text has a procedural focus and intends to discuss the Tribunal's influence on the UNCITRAL Rules generally, and on the choice of those rules for disputes over foreign investment specifically: the latter, arguably, being a less studied matter.[238] It was claimed above that the Tribunal's application of the 1976 UNCITRAL Arbitration Rules was an important first test of the Rules. Much has been written about this application.[239] It has also been suggested elsewhere, but not investigated further, that the success of the Tribunal demonstrated that the UNCITRAL Rules are suitable for investment treaty

232 Brower & Brueschke, pp. 15–16 with further references; S Toope, Mixed International Arbitration, p. 268 et seq; H E Kjos, *Applicable Law in Investor-State Arbitration,* Oxford University Press, 2013. pp.48 et seq. See also generally D Caron, The Nature of the Iran-United States Claims Tribunal, arguing that maintaining the distinction between commercial arbitration and public international law disputes is futile when studying the Tribunal.

233 Article II, para. 1 of the Declaration states that the Tribunal is "an international arbitral tribunal."

234 Apart from the relatively few cases being arbitrated directly between the two state parties. See generally D Caron, The Nature of the Iran-United States Claims Tribunal, p. 130.

235 See most famously J Paulsson, Arbitration Without Privity.

236 D Caron, The Nature of the Iran-United States Claims Tribunal, p. 149.

237 J J van Hof, p.6 with further references.

238 For a general comment of the UNCITRAL Rules, including the Tribunal's influence, see Caron & Caplan.

239 See specifically about the application of the 1976 UNCITRAL Rules Baker & Davis; JJ van Hof; J Paulsson & G Petrochilos.

arbitration.[240] It is submitted that the Tribunal informed the potential users of the UNCITRAL Rules about their "usability" in hitherto unused contexts, thereby potentially influencing the development of the UNCITRAL Rules into a viable rule set for investment treaty arbitration. In order to further explain this thesis, the Tribunal's application of the UNCITRAL Rules will now be discussed more thoroughly.

2.4.1.1 Why the UNCITRAL Rules?

Before delving into the Tribunal's work with the UNCITRAL Rules, it might be worth asking a question that has eluded the academic discussion of the Tribunal: why did the state parties choose the UNCITRAL Rules as the procedural framework for the Tribunal? As emphasized above at 2.3.3.1, such an application was not envisioned during the drafting of the Rules, when only contractual disputes were contemplated.

The Algiers Accords were drafted in a unique fashion, with an Algerian delegation acting as intermediate between the Iranian and American governments, who at the time had no diplomatic relations. The communication at times suffered from considerable political pressure.[241] Under these circumstances it comes as no surprise that there are very little *travaux preparatoires* to the Algiers Accords; the sensitive situation surrounding the negotiation of the Accords probably rendered any thorough documentation of the underlying discussions impossible. The states have themselves been reluctant to disclose information; most of the documentation available at the American State Department remains classified, for example. Furthermore, as in most politically sensitive negotiations, the resulting language was not particularly detailed. On the contrary, the nature of the Tribunal was not clearly phrased at all.[242] It is reasonable to assume that the exact mandate for the dispute resolution was not carefully negotiated but rather left to specify at later stages; in that respect, the dispute resolution provision resembles those of most many commercial contract negotiations where such clauses are the last to be discussed, which famously have given arbitration clauses the nickname "midnight clauses." A commentator notes that the lack of precision in the Algiers Declaration is likely to be "either the product of legal ignorance and lacking foresight, or a result of flexible innovation required to face urgent and seemingly

240 N Horn, "Current Use of the UNCITRAL Arbitration Rules in the Context of Investment Arbitration, Arbitration International," Vol. 24, No. 4, p. 590; Caron & Caplan, p. 7.

241 For a detailed inside account of the intricate negotiations, see R B Owens "Final Negotiations and Release in Algiers," in W Christopher, *American Hostages in Iran: The Conduct of a Crisis,* Yale University Press, 1985.

242 S Toope, Mixed International Arbitration, p. 267.

insurmountable obstacles under time pressure."[243] One must keep in mind that, unlike most other international tribunals set up to handle specific disputes, the establishment of the Tribunal was not negotiated *after* but rather *during* a confrontational crisis.[244]

The Accords, including the Claims Settlement Declaration, were indeed "cobbled together in haste and confusion."[245] American witnesses from the negotiation give the impression of a rollercoaster process in which the American representatives drafted suggestions that were thereafter rejected and/or modified by their Iranian counterparts, sometimes for reasons that were not entirely clear to the American negotiators.[246] This confused process is also demonstrated by the fact that the initial American draft of the Claims Settlement Declaration was some 25 pages long, whereas the final result is just over three pages.[247]

The American international lawyer David Caron, who worked as legal assistant at the Tribunal, writes that several leading individuals within the American negotiation team were unfamiliar with the ramifications of choosing the UNCITRAL Rules and emphasizes that:

> one must remember that the UNCITRAL Rules were still quite new at the time the Accords were drafted and their UN origin might mistakenly lead one to conclude that they were designed for interstate arbitration rather than private international arbitration.[248]

Nothing suggests that the Iranian negotiating team had a more comprehensive understanding of the consequences of choosing the then relatively unknown UNCITRAL Rules. There is therefore some merit to the theory that the UNCITRAL Rules' express connection to the United Nations – after all, the organization is present in the official name of the Rules – made them an accessible option for both states. This is especially so when one contrasts the option with the most readily available alternatives, i.e. the ICC Rules (which to many states at the time had a distinct Western, commercial connection) and the ICSID Arbitration Rules (which would presuppose either that Iran signed the ICSID Convention or that the Additional Facility Rules, then still on their

243 G Wetter, "The Iran-United States Claims Tribunal," SvJT 1982 p. 193 (quote translated from Swedish by the present author).
244 Selby & Stewart, p. 216.
245 R Lillich (ed), preface, at vii.
246 R B Owens, pp. 313–322.
247 Ibid, p .312.
248 D Caron, The Nature of the Iran-United States Claims Tribunal, p. 140.

five-year review period as described above, were used).[249] Rightly or wrongly – and one could definitely argue that the connection between the United Nations and the average arbitration conducted under the UNCITRAL Rules is thin, to say the least – the perceived backing of the world organization made the Rules acceptable to both Iran and the United States.[250] This is emphasized by a statement by the lead US negotiator Warren Christopher, who writes that "the settlement itself was simplified because a reliable body of arbitration law already existed in the United Nations system and could be lifted by reference into the agreement."[251] In practice the United Nations, of course, has very little to do with *ad hoc* arbitrations: once the Rules have been accepted by the General Assembly each arbitration is a world of its own, existing without any relation to the world organization. It is thus entirely possible that the Tribunal's extensive use of the UNCITRAL Rules, which, as will be argued, probably turned out to be important for subsequent investment arbitrations, was in part a product of a limited understanding of international arbitration on behalf of the state parties to the Algier Accords.

2.4.1.2 The Tribunal's Relevant Modifications of the UNCITRAL Rules

Even though the state parties initially attempted to modify the UNCITRAL Rules,[252] they ultimately failed to reach an agreement and it instead fell upon the Tribunal itself to alter the Rules in order to make them more suitable for the very specific task at hand. Most alterations done by the Tribunal in the document known as the Final Tribunal Rules of Procedure (FTRP)[253] – such as the setting up of chambers to deal with the large number of disputes, the establishment of permanent government agents and a registry, as well as a system

249 D Caron, cites a second US negotiating response from Dec 3rd 1980, in which the American side indicates an agreement "that [...] arbitration may be conducted, at Iran's election by and under the rules of the International Chamber of Commerce or the World Bank's International Center for the Settlement of Investment Disputes," D Caron, The Nature of the Iran-United States Claims Tribunal, p.140. Mark B Feldman, who was involved in the negotiations, has suggested in an email to the present author, however, that the Americans assumed their Iranian counterparts would be sceptical towards rules developed by private institutions, Email from Mark B Feldman, 9 February 2015, on file with author.

250 This was also suggested in an email from US negotiator Arthur W. Rovine, 16 Dec 2014, on file with author; email from Mark B Feldman, previous footnote.

251 W Christopher (ed.), *American Hostages in Iran – The Conduct of a Crisis,* Yale University Press, 1985, pp. 10–11.

252 D Caron notes that United States especially desired to alter the provisions of the Rules providing for confidentiality, as well as making sure that the arbitrations were governed by the Dutch legal system, D Caron, The Nature of the Iran-United States Claims Tribunal, pp. 141–142.

253 FTRP, 3 May 1983, annexed in Brower & Brueschke, p. 726 et seq.

for cost-sharing by the governments – were made taking the sensitive and semi-permanent character of the Tribunal into consideration. The UNCITRAL Rules in their default outline are designed for one-off *ad hoc* disputes, which is different from the nature of the longstanding Tribunal because in the average *ad hoc* dispute, "everyone packs up and goes home" when the case is over.[254] The focus of commentary thus far has been largely on this aspect of the Tribunal's alteration of the Rules, emphasizing that the Tribunal is a long-standing body and as such had to alter the *ad hoc*-based UNCITRAL Rules.[255] In the present text, another aspect of the Tribunal's work with the 1976 UNCITRAL Rules will be treated as similarly relevant, *viz.* the fact that the Rules were drafted for contractual disputes but applied by the Tribunal to matters of substantive public international law, with sovereign states acting as respondents.

Some provisions of the UNCITRAL Rules were modified in a way that is interesting for the purposes of this study. The FRTP are essentially structured as a commentary to the 1976 UNCITRAL Rules, with large part of the latter being unchanged. Accompanying some provisions are either modifications of, or "Notes" to, the original language in the UNCITRAL Rules. For the purpose of succeeding investment treaty arbitration practice, a number of alterations or Notes are relevant.

For example, Article 1 of the 1976 UNCITRAL Rules provides the general scope of application of the Rules, leaving a large degree of autonomy to the parties to decide when and how the Rules are applicable. As such, it has been claimed that the Tribunal's use of this Article does not tell subsequent users a lot about the scope of the Rules, since the Algiers Accords constituted a party agreement that clearly rendered parts of Article 1 irrelevant.[256] It is easy to see why this theoretical and peripheral point would be of no interest to contemporary commentators.[257] Subsequent practice has shown, however, that the Tribunal's work has been instructive when it comes to the scope of application of the UNCITRAL Rules. This is because the 1976 UNCITRAL Arbitration Rules only contemplate arbitration based on contracts between the two disputing parties.[258] The FTRP added a third paragraph to this, stating that:

---

254 Brower & Brueschke, p. 660.

255 See for example Baker & Davis, p.2; G Aksen, "The Iran-U.S. Claims Tribunal and the UNCITRAL Arbitration Rules: An Early Comment," in Schultz & van den Berg (eds.), *The Art of Arbitration. Essays on International Arbitration. Liber Amoricum Sanders*, Springer, 1982.

256 Baker & Davis, p. 8.

257 JJ van Hof does not devote this matter any interest in her otherwise comprehensive 1991 doctoral dissertation on the Tribunal's application of the UNCITRAL Rules, see J J van Hof.

258 Article 1(1), see above at 2.3.3.1.

> The Claims Settlement Declaration constitutes an agreement in writing by Iran and the United States, on their own behalves and on behalf on their nationals submitting to arbitration within the framework of the Algiers Declarations and in accordance with the Tribunal Rules[259]

Thus, the Tribunal widened the potential scope of application of the UNCITRAL Rules in a way that was not contemplated in their default shape, but has come to be conventional in present-day investment arbitration.

Furthermore, one of the notes issued to the Article 15 of the 1976 Rules – one of the most important articles,[260] providing general provisions – allowed the tribunal to be assisted by non-disputing party submissions.[261] This was used several times.[262] This involvement of non-parties in arbitration was at the time a novel idea, shaped of course by the specific circumstances of the Tribunal.[263] However, subsequent to the Tribunal's practice, which found express support in Note 5, several other arbitration tribunals have found that the possibility to accept third party submissions generally falls within a tribunal's mandate to conduct the proceedings under UNCITRAL Rules Article 15. This possibility of allowing non-disputing parties to introduce material into the arbitration is not expressly provided for by Article 15, or any other specific provision in either version of the UNCITRAL Rules. In modern UNCITRAL arbitration practice, however, several tribunals have accepted that the general provision provides a tribunal with the power to allow such submissions under certain circumstances.[264] Also, in this respect, the Tribunal practice was a precursor.

---

259 FTRP, Article 1.

260 Caron & Caplan, p.30; JJ van Hof, p. 102; D Caron & M Pellonpää, *The UNCITRAL Arbitration Rules as Interpreted and Applied by the Iran-U.S. Claims Tribunal*, Finnish Lawyer's Publishing, 1995, p. 21.

261 Tribunal Rules of Procedure, Note 5 to UNCITRAL Article 15, as reprinted in Brower & Brueschke, p. 742.

262 Iran-United States Claims Tribunal, Award No. 264-264-1. 13 Iran-US CTR at 130; Iran-United States Claims Tribunal, E-Systems Inc. V. Islamic Republic of Iran, award No ITM 13-388-FT (4 February, 1983), 2 Iran-US CTR 51; Iran-United States Claims Tribunal, George W Drucker JR v. Foreign Transaction CO, Case No 121, Chamber Two, Order of 2 May, 1986, as reprinted in Caron & Caplan, p.70; Iran v United States, Case A/15 (Award No 63-Al15-FT), reprinted in 2 Iran-US C. T.R. 40, at p. 43.

263 JJ van Hof, p. 107.

264 *Methanex Corp v. United States of America*, Decisions on Petitions from Third Persons to Intervene as *Amici Curiae*, Jan 15th 2001, UNCITRAL, para. 24, relying on Iran-United States Claims Tribunal practice; United Parcel Service of America Inc. v. Government of Canada, Decision of the Tribunal on Petitions for Intervention and Participation as Amici Curiae, Oct 17th 2001, UNCITRAL; Grand River Enterprises Six Nations, Ltd., et al. v. United

In fact, the Tribunal's work can be characterized as more transparent than other contemporary international arbitrations, not only because of the express acceptance of non-party submissions but because the proceedings generally were more accessible than the average UNCITRAL arbitration at the time. Unlike the disputes between two commercial parties that the 1976 UNCITRAL Rules were initially intended for, the circumstances surrounding the Iran-US Claims Tribunal demanded a larger public interest in the proceedings.[265] The FTRP modify the UNCITRAL Rules and alter the presumption of confidentiality for the award once rendered. Article 32(5) is modified so that awards and decision shall be published unless the Tribunal approves a party request for keeping all or parts of the award confidential. JJ van Hof reports of 18 such requests being made, eight of which were denied by the Tribunal and nine were made confidential (in addition, one was made confidential temporarily and partially).[266] Similarly the provision in the UNCITRAL Rules prescribing *in camera* hearings is modified by the FTRP, albeit only slightly in the form of a Note allowing the Tribunal to permit counsel from similar cases to observe the proceedings when the parties so permit.[267]

Yet another aspect of the proceedings where the Tribunal altered the UNCITRAL Rules is the possibility to bring counterclaims. The 1976 UNCITRAL Rules only allow for counterclaims "arising out of the same contract."[268] As discussed above the Tribunal's jurisdiction was widened by the Claims Settlement Declaration, which for the purpose of the Rules constitutes the arbitration agreement, because the 1976 Rules only contemplate contractual arbitration. Correspondingly, the Tribunal's jurisdiction to hear counterclaims was widened to include counterclaims arising out of the "same contract, transaction or occurrence that constitutes the subject matter";[269] decidedly wider than the 1976 UNCITRAL Rules. The Tribunal regularly allowed counterclaims by

States of America; Glamis Gold, Ltd. v. The United States of America, UNCITRAL; US. Steel Global Holdings v. The Slovak Republic, PCA Case No. 2013-6.

265 In this respect, a similar argument has been made for a larger degree of procedural transparency in investment arbitration, as opposed to contractual disputes. See generally J Harrison, *Recent Developments to Promote Transparency and Public Participation in Investment Treaty Arbitration*, University of Edinburgh School of Law Working Paper No. 2011/01; JW Yackee and J Wong, "The 2006 Procedural and Transparency Related Amendments to the ICSID Arbitration Rules: Model Intentions, Moderate Proposals, and Modest Returns," in KP Sauvant (ed.), *The Yearbook on International Investment Law & Policy*, Oxford University Press, 2010, ch. 6.

266 JJ van Hof, p.224.

267 FTRP, Note 5 to Article 25.

268 1976 UNCITRAL Rules Article 19(3).

269 Claims Settlement Declaration Article II(1).

Iranian respondents,[270] also in cases where several different contracts were interpreted broadly as constituting part of the same "transaction" in the meaning of the Claims Settlement Declaration.[271] The possibility to raise counterclaims was subsequently extended in the 2010 UNCITRAL Rules, primarily to account for the increased use of the Rules in non-contractual arbitration.[272]

Finally, the Tribunals' approach to certain arbitrator-related issues likely proved instructive. For example, in modern UNCITRAL arbitrations argued before multi-member tribunals a resignation of one arbitrator generally has to be approved by the other arbitrators. This was not the case under the 1976 Rules but became the practice of the Tribunal. The possibility to proceed with two arbitrators was perceived to be consistent with a tribunal's general duty to conduct the proceedings; in fact, several Tribunal cases moved on successfully without a full tribunal.[273] The Tribunal practice in this respect has been quoted with approval by another UNCITRAL tribunal, where two arbitrators rendered an award against Indonesia despite the Indonesian-appointed arbitrator having been prevented by Indonesia to participate in hearings.[274] Furthermore, another mechanism proved crucial to the relatively uninterrupted work of the tribunal even amidst the lack of agreement between the treaty parties: the frequent use of an external body, the so-called appointing authority. For example, Article 13 of the UNCITRAL Rules states that "in the event of the death or resignation of an arbitrator during the course of the proceedings" an arbitrator shall be replaced in the same manner used to appoint him. During the redrafting of the 1976 Rules it was recognized, based on the Tribunal experience, that this provision could not deal effectively with cases of "mala fide or tactical resignation of arbitrators"[275] and the provision was substantially revised in the 2010 version.

The Tribunal Rules did not modify Article 13 in this respect, nor did they in any way change Articles 6–8, where the original appointment proceeding is stipulated. The Tribunal's work did however, given the frequent issues with

270 JJ van Hof, pp. 128 et seq; Caron & Caplan, pp. 436 et seq.

271 See eg. Iran-United Claims Tribunal, American Bell International Inc. v. Iran, Award No. ITL 41-48-3, 6 Iran-US CTR at 83.

272 Caron & Caplan, p.426.

273 J Paulsson & G Petrochilos, p. 59; Caron & Caplan, p. 283 et seq.

274 Himpurna California Energy Ltd. v. Republic of Indonesia, Final Award, October 16, 2009, paras 58–59. The Tribunal case relied upon is Uiterwyk Corp, et al v Islamic Republic of Iran, Final Award No. 501–381–1, 8 January 1991.

275 Report of the Working Group on Arbitration and Conciliation on the Work of its Forty-Fifth Session, UN Doc A/CN.9/614, at 15, para 67 (2007).

Iranian and third-country arbitrators,[276] become a test of the 1976 UNCITRAL Rules. Article 6(2) provides that if no appointing authority has been agreed upon the parties, either party may request the Secretary-General of the Permanent Court of Arbitration (PCA) to designate such an appointing authority. In the proceedings before the Tribunal, the Secretary-General has appointed current or former judges of the Dutch Supreme Court, Judge Moons and Judge Haak, to act as appointing authority.[277] The role of this person has however not primarily been to replace resigned arbitrators, but rather to hear challenges against arbitrators; between 1981 and 2006 there were eleven such challenges; nine were dismissed and in two cases the arbitrators withdrew.[278] Thus the appointing authority – nowadays an important staple of any UNCITRAL investment arbitration – was given an instrumental role in allowing the Tribunal to proceed its work.[279]

2.4.1.3 The Tribunal's Legacy and Demonstration Effect on the Use of the UNCITRAL Rules

There are plenty of reasons why the Tribunal should have failed. Indeed, the general sentiment in its early years seemed to be that it had a challenging future, to say the least.[280] Hostilities between both the treaty parties and within the Tribunal itself – the latter even manifested in physical violence among the arbitrators[281] – have indeed plagued the history of the Tribunal's work. Distrust and lack of collegiality at times characterized both the Tribunal's everyday

276 For an extensive recount of the various Tribunal cases involving arbitrators' failure to act, see Caron & Caplan, p. 290 et seq.

277 R Teitelbaum, "Challenges of Arbitrators at the Iran-United States Claims Tribunal Defining the Role of the Appointing Authority," Journal of International Arbitration 23(6): 547–562, 2006.

278 R Teitelbaum, 547. According to Caron & Caplan, "the Iran-US Tribual remains the most significant source of challenge practice [under the UNCITRAL Rules]," p.183. The same authors give an overview over some of the most instructive challenges heard by the appointing authority.

279 KH Böckstiegel, *A Special Arbitration Convention – The Algiers Declarations Creating the Iran-United States Claims Tribunal and Their Application, in Euro-Arab Arbitration Conference,* Port el Kantaoui, 1987; D Caron & M Pellonpää, pp. 271–279.

280 Most famously the United States Supreme Court in the 1981 Dames & Moore v. Regan case stated that "being overly sanguine about the chances of United States claimants before the Claims Tribunal would require a degree of ety which should not be demanded even of judges," Dames & Moore v. Regan, 453 U.S. 654 (1981) 28–29. See also R Khan pp. 3–38.

281 In what is perhaps the lowest point in the Tribunal's history, third-country arbitrator Nils Mangård was attacked by two Iranian arbitrators at the premises of the Peace Palace in The Hague. This assault, while illustrating the unique circumstances surrounding the

business and the surrounding political setting. In addition, the Tribunal faced a tremendous workload and limited resources. Despite this, the Tribunal managed to achieve unexpected success. As mentioned above, the Tribunal has issued thousands of awards; it has been noted that the Tribunal's greatest achievement has been its continuing existence.[282] Many studies have been published about the Tribunal and it is often held up as an inspiring example of peaceful settlement of international disputes.[283] In their treatise on the Tribunal's work Charles N. Brower and Jason D. Brueschke discuss the Tribunal's successful legacy. First and foremost, they emphasize that the Tribunal managed to navigate a fraught political landscape with a large degree of sensitivity, not upsetting the underlying tensions involved in any dispute involving sovereign states but of course unusually present given the Iran-US relations. Furthermore, the public nature of the Tribunal's work has led to many volumes of reported awards, decisions and orders together constituting the largest body of precedent, if one uses the word in the broadest possible sense, of public international and international commercial law produced by any international body.[284]

The flexible UNCITRAL Rules, slightly modified as discussed above, contributed to this achievement in a way that demonstrated the Rules' suitability not only for a more long-standing body, but also for other arbitrations based on treaties and involving state parties. Many of the characteristics of the Tribunal's work resemble those of present-day investment arbitration: not only the implied conflict between the treaty parties but also the wide discretion given to the Tribunal by vaguely drafted rules, in terms of both substance and procedure. The Tribunal's work further resembles that of investment treaty arbitration tribunals, in that both types of bodies are often faced with short and open-ended treaties, leaving tribunals with a mandate to interpret and fill gaps, leading to the development of a substantial jurisprudence.

Tribunal, is outside of the scope of this text. For more details, see Brower & Brueschke, p. 662 et seq.

282 S Toope, Mixed International Arbitration, p. 382. The remark is made in a slightly critical context, where the author points out that the Tribunal's general process, as opposed to its sometimes weak and compromised substantive awards, is a testament to its contribution to the rule of law.

283 K.M Ameli, "The Iran-United States Claims Tribunal," in P Hamilton (ed.), *The Permanent Court of Arbitration: International Arbitration and Dispute Resolution*, Kluwer, 1999, p. 246; see also generally KH Böckstiegel, *The Iran - United States Claims Tribunal - A Unique Example of Arbitrating for Peace*, in J Dahlquist, U Franke and A Magnusson (eds.), *Arbitrating for Peace,* Kluwer, 2017.

284 Brower, & Brueschker p. 669.

The Tribunal's role in interpreting and developing the UNCITRAL Arbitration rules generally is beyond doubt.[285] The 1976 Rules are, on their face, not very well suited for arbitrations based on anything other than contracts. Still, the Tribunal managed to solve thousands of sensitive disputes without the two states vacating the procedures. As discussed above, the Tribunal modified the 1976 UNCITRAL Rules in a way that allowed for, *inter alia,* third party participation, flexible administration of the submissions and hearings, and, crucially, for arbitration to proceed even when one party is trying to obstruct the proceedings. These and other modifications by the Tribunal were eventually included in one way or another in the 2010 version of the UNCITRAL Rules; a testament as good as any that the work of the Tribunal has been an important part of the successful story of the UNCITRAL Arbitration Rules.[286]

More generally, it is submitted that the Tribunal demonstrated a key feature of the Rules: their flexibility. The Rules were applied in a context for which they were not intended and they still worked well. Even if the parties to the dispute remained locked in durable disagreement, the Tribunal managed to utilize the Rules' inherent elasticity to safeguard a procedure acceptable, by and large, both to the involved states and to the individual disputants.

It is important to note, finally, a caveat. The direct influence of the Iran-United States Claims Tribunal on subsequent treaty arbitration is probably limited. The surrounding political circumstances, the extreme caseload and the semi-permanent institutional character together make the Tribunal a *sui generis* phenomenon in international dispute resolution.[287] Furthermore, as hinted above, the risk of the awards not being enforced has not been on the Tribunal's mind; this position is likely envied by many other arbitrators.

Keeping this caveat in mind, there still seems to be a connection in time between the Tribunal's work and references to the UNCITRAL Rules in investment treaties. As outlined above at 2.3.3.2, the spike of UNCITRAL references in investment treaties took place primarily in the late 1980s and early 1990s. During this time, or more precisely during the first 10 years of the Tribunal's work, 95% of all claims submitted to the Tribunal were disposed of and every award to American claimants paid in full, most often with interest.[288] To put it succinctly: the timing overlaps between the unlikely success of the Tribunal, or at least the impression of it, and the emergence of UNCITRAL references in

285 Caron & Caplan 2012, p. 6; Brower & Brueschke, pp. 19–20 with further references.

286 As mentioned above, however, due to the rules of temporal applicability, the 1976 Rules are still being used for most treaty arbitrations.

287 S Toope, Mixed International Arbitration, p. 383.

288 Brower, & Brueschker p. 658.

investment treaties. It seems likely that the Tribunal inspired later investment treaty negotiators, as an alternative to ICSID arbitration. This is also supported by the fact that both Iran[289] – which has never signed the ICSID Convention – as well as the United States[290] subsequently concluded several investment treaties allowing for arbitration with reference to the UNCITRAL Rules.

2.4.2 *A Second Potential Explanation: ICSID Backlash in the 1980s*

In the mid-1980s, the ICSID Convention had garnered close to 90 ratifications[291] and the first arbitrations had reached the award stage (although, it must be recalled, no case had yet been brought under a treaty). When *ad hoc* committees established under Article 52 of the ICSID Convention annulled two of those early awards,[292] it led to well-documented wave of criticism against not only the respective committees, but the ICSID system as a whole.

In the first of these two annulment cases, which was also the first ICSID annulment ever to be requested, the *Klöckner* committee unanimously annulled the award, which was rendered on 21 October, 1983.[293] Klöckner had requested annulment after the original tribunal had rejected the investor's claims, as well as the state's counterclaims. Before the annulment committee,

289 Belarus – Iran, Islamic Republic of BIT (1995); Georgia – Iran, Islamic Republic of BIT (1995); Iran, Islamic Republic of – Kazakhstan BIT (1996); Bosnia and Herzegovina – Iran, Islamic Republic of BIT (1996); Iran, Islamic Republic of – Turkey BIT (1996); Iran, Islamic Republic of – Lebanon BIT (1997); Iran, Islamic Republic of – Switzerland BIT (1998); Bangladesh – Iran, Islamic Republic of BIT (2001); Iran, Islamic Republic of – Malaysia BIT (2002); Greece – Iran, Islamic Republic of BIT (2002); Finland – Iran, Islamic Republic of BIT (2002); Ethiopia – Iran, Islamic Republic of BIT (2003). See generally about arbitration clauses in the Iranian BITs: A Atai, *Arbitration of Investment Disputes under Iranian Investment Treaties,* Journal of Money Laundering Control (JMLC), Vol. 14, No. 2, pp. 130–157, 2011.

290 See also for example Poland – United States of America BIT (1990); Argentina – United States of America BIT (1991); Kazakhstan – United States of America BIT (1992); Romania – United States of America BIT (1992); Russian Federation – United States of America BIT (1992); Bulgaria – United States of America BIT (1992): Armenia – United States of America BIT (1992); Kyrgyzstan – United States of America BIT (1993); Moldova, Republic of – United States of America BIT (1993); Ecuador – United States of America BIT (1993); Belarus – United States of America BIT (1994); Jamaica – United States of America BIT (1994); Ukraine – United States of America BIT (1994); Georgia – United States of America BIT (1994); Estonia – United States of America BIT (1994); Trinidad and Tobago – United States of America BIT (1994); Mongolia – United States of America BIT (1994).

291 A Parra, p. 122.

292 Klöckner I Annulment Decision; Amco I Annulment Decision.

293 *Klöckner Industrie-Anlagen GmbH and others v. United Republic of Cameroon and Société Camerounaise des Engrais,* ICSID Case No. ARB/81/2, Award 21 October, 1983.

Klöckner argued successfully that the tribunal manifestly exceeded its power by misapplying the applicable law.

The *Klöckner* tribunal had found that the investor withheld vital information from Cameroon, which ultimately led the tribunal to the reject the claims.[294] In doing so, the tribunal had assumed that French civil law embodied a "principle according to which a person who engages in close contractual relations, based on confidence, must deal with its partner in a frank, loyal and candid manner," which was also held to be a "universal requirement."[295] This application, according to the annulment committee, was an unacceptable way of applying Article 42(1) of the ICSID Convention, which in the committee's view "clearly does not allow the arbitrator to base his decision solely on the 'rules' or 'principles of international law'."[296] The committee also added that the tribunal had not demonstrated the content of French law, but rather just postulated the existence of a general principle, without making any references to legal sources.[297]

The second annulment committee, faced with an application to annul the *Amco v. Indonesia* award, also found that the tribunal had manifestly exceeded its power. The committee discussed Article 42(1) of the ICSID, emphasizing that the law of the contracting state is the primarily applicable law, only to be complemented by international law in the event of *lacunae* or a conflict between domestic law and international law.[298] Using this statement as a point of departure, the committee went on to find that the tribunal had failed to properly apply the law of the contracting state and thereby manifestly exceeded its mandate.[299] It seems the committee accepted that the tribunal had indeed applied Indonesian domestic law but not the relevant provisions of it.[300] This finding opened up the *Amco* committee to severe criticism for acting more like an appeals body than an annulment committee.[301]

---

294 Ibid., 61.

295 Ibid., 59.

296 Klöckner I Annulment Decision, para. 69.

297 Ibid. para. 79.

298 Amco I Annulment Decision, p. 515.

299 Ibid., pp. 534–535.

300 A Broches, *Observations on the Finality of ICSID Awards* (1991), reprinted in A Broches, *Selected Essays – World Bank, ICSID, and Other Subjects of Public and Private International Law,* Martinus Nijhoff (1995), p. 337.

301 M B Feldman, "The Annulment Proceedings and the Finality of ICSID Arbitral Awards," 2 ICSID Rev – FILJ 85, pp. 95–96; E Gaillard, *CIRDI:* "Chronique des sentences arbitrales," 114

In addition to the manifest excess of power found by both committees, they also both found that the respective tribunals had failed to state reasons for several of its conclusions. In one particular instance, the *Klöckner* committee even went so far, albeit *obiter* since the manifest excess of power had already been established, as to state that it found it "impossible to discern how and why the Tribunal could reach its decision."[302]

These two decisions provided a first test of the ICSID regime's internal annulment system, which is intended to insulate the arbitral awards from the jurisdiction of domestic courts, and instead subject them to a limited set of grounds for annulment under Article 52 of the ICSID Convention. They were both met with severe criticism from scholars and practitioners. Many contemporary commentators seemed to feel that the committees had overreached and not sufficiently respected the finality of ICSID awards, by venturing too far into scrutinizing the merits of the awards.[303]

The many critical voices questioning the functioning of the previously untested annulment mechanism prompted Aron Broches himself to publish an essay, where he in detail describes the drafters' intention behind the annulment system.[304] In the essay, Broches also recognized that the reaction in the arbitration community was not only focused on the specific cases but also

> [...] ranges well beyond that and includes comments as well on their effect on the future of ICSID, the proper place of annulment in the ICSID system and improvement of the annulment process by curing perceived shortcomings[305]

Broches still emphasized that in the years subsequent to the *Klöckner* and *Amco* annulments, several events had transpired that would justify a more nuanced view of the ICSID annulment, leading Broches to conclude that the process was "on track."[306]

Journal du Droit International 135 (1987). p. 189; A Redfern, "ICSID – Losing its Appeal?," 3 ARB. INT'L 98 (1987), pp. 116–117.

302 Klöckner Ad Hoc Committee Decision, p. 148.

303 See for example G R Delaume, "The Finality of Arbitration Involving States: Recent Developments," 5 ARB. INT'L 21 (1989); and the works cited in footnote 449.

304 A Broches, *Observations on the Finality of ICSID Awards* (1991), reprinted in A Broches, *Selected Essays – World Bank, ICSID, and Other Subjects of Public and Private International Law*, Martinus Nijhoff (1995).

305 Ibid., p. 333.

306 Ibid., p. 343.

The third annulment to be requested marked a departure from *Klöckner* and *Amco*. In the MINE *v. Guinea* annulment proceeding Broches himself, since then long retired from his position as Secretary-General, was on the committee.[307] The MINE committee emphasized the distinction between disregarding the applicable law, which would justify an annulment, and erroneously applying it, which would not.[308] It also pointed out that the function of an annulment committee is not to remedy an incorrect decision and the committee thus could "not in fact reverse an award on the merits under the guise of applying Article 52."[309]

While partially annulling the award on the ground of failure to state reasons, the MINE committee still also departed from the previous two decisions regarding the requirement in Article 52(1)(e) to provide reasons and stated that this requirement:

> [...] implies that it must enable the reader to follow the reasoning of the Tribunal on points of fact and law. It implies that, and only that. The adequacy of the reasoning is not an appropriate standard of review[310]

When it nevertheless annulled the damage part of the award, it did so because the tribunal did not address two matters which were argued by the parties, and which could have affected the damages outcomes.[311]

In the words of former Deputy Secretary-General Parra "[...] the fears for the ICSID system aroused by the *Klöckner* and *Amco* annulments were calmed by the ad hoc committee decision in MINE."[312] Furthermore, as emphasized by Broches in his 1991 essay, both annulled *Klöckner* and *Amco* cases were resubmitted and the two resulting awards were unsuccessfully challenged before new annulment committees.[313] Both the *Klöckner II* and *Amco II* annulment decisions have remained unpublished, but they have, together with the MINE

307 MINE Annulment Decision.
308 Ibid., para. 5.04.
309 Ibid., para. 4.04.
310 Mine Annulment Decision, para. 5.08.
311 Ibid., para. 6.701.
312 A Parra, p. 188.
313 A Broches, *Observations on the Finality of ICSID Awards* (1991), reprinted in A Broches, *Selected Essays – World Bank, ICSID, and Other Subjects of Public and Private International Law*, Martinus Nijhoff (1995), p. 343.

annulment, been described by a leading commentator as a "second generation" of decisions that alleviated the concerns raised by the two first decisions.[314]

It is unclear to what extent the arbitration community's doubts regarding ICSID's annulment mechanism affected contemporary treaty negotiators. It is possible that the controversy was a storm in a teacup and never seriously reached beyond the (at the time relatively small) community of international arbitration specialists. What is clear, however, is that the discussion coincided with the emergence of non-ICSID rules as serious contenders for states' advance consent to arbitration. In the time period between the *Klöckner* annulment and Broches' reassuring 1991 essay, eleven states that previously had only included ICSID arbitration in their treaties for the first time expanded their treaties with other ICSID states to include alternatives to ICSID.[315] During the same time period, a number of states concluded their first investment treaties with arbitration clauses and did so with reference to non-ICSID rules.[316] It is clear from the study of treaties that ICSID's monopoly on treaty references was challenged during the same time that the ICSID system was facing widespread criticism.

2.5 Interim Conclusion

This introductory chapter has provided a background to the emergence of non-ICSID arbitration rules in investment treaties and also provided a few attempted explanations for this development. In their early days, investment treaties referred exclusively to ICSID as the forum for disputes between investors and host states. To a large extent, this was the result of an active ICSID Secretariat, led by its first secretaries-general.

The clear number two in terms of treaty references, the UNCITRAL Rules, have primarily due to their *ad hoc* nature, never had a similarly active promoter. The UNCITRAL Secretariat is limited by its mandate to work with the Rules and do not engage in their active promotion, leaving the use of the Rules to the discretion of individual states. However, this text has argued that the visibility of the Iran-US Claims Tribunal might have indirectly promoted

314 C Schreuer, "Three Generations of ICSID Annulment Proceedings," in E Gaillard and Y Banifatemi (eds.), *Annulment of ICSID Awards,* IAI Series on International Arbitration, No. 1, Juris, 2004, p. 18. See also A Parra p. 190.

315 Belgium/Luxembourg, Egypt, Finland, Indonesia, Italy, Morocco Netherlands, Romania, Sweden, Tunisia and Turkey.

316 Albania, Argentina, Bolivia, Chile, Cyprus, Greece, Mongolia and Portugal.

the use of the UNCITRAL Rules. The Tribunal was tasked with modifying the UNCITRAL Rules at a time when they were largely untested and did so in a way that arguably exceeded expectations in terms of the type of disputes the Rules would be used for. While demonstrating the flexibility of the Rules more generally, the Tribunal also made several adjustments that have been of importance to subsequent investment treaty arbitration practice.

The presence of references to the ICC Rules and the SCC Rules is harder to explain. Here, more research is needed. While no clear pattern can be discerned in the treaties allowing for ICC arbitration, the SCC Rules appear to have benefited from their historically strong connection to disputes involving "Eastern" entities.

To a certain extent the discontent with ICISD in the late 1980s might also have inspired treaty parties to more generally include alternative references to ICSID in investment treaties. It cannot be ruled out that in this wave, the rules maintained by the two commercial institutions "piggy-backed" on the UNCITRAL Rules, which were the first to gain serious traction in state practice. This is confirmed by the fact that very few treaties allow only for SCC or ICC arbitration, but rather tend to combine them with consent also to UNCITRAL and/or ICSID. Conversely, while many treaties refer exclusively to the UNCITRAL Rules.

It deserves emphasizing that at the time when the commercial arbitration rules were introduced in investment treaties, it was a relatively small step compared to the big one taken when advance state consent, providing individual standing for investors against states, was first established by the ICSID Convention. Arguably, without the earlier work of ICSID, the idea of including traditionally commercial arbitration rules in investment treaties would have seem remote to many states.

Today, it can safely be concluded that the initial ICSID monopoly on treaty references is gone. This text has presented a clear answer to the question of *when* this happened. The *how* question, however, still hangs in the air. Compared to the emergence of ICSID arbitration, the appearance of commercial arbitration rules in investment treaties seems to have occurred in a relatively haphazard way. This finding would be consistent with other, more generally framed, accounts of the history of investment treaty arbitration, which reject notions of coordinated "grand bargains."[317]

Finally, it must be noted that this section has primarily addressed choices as expressed by states in their treaties. A related matter, only briefly touched

---

317 See for example J Pauwelyn, At the Edge of Chaos? and S Puig, Emergence & Dynamism.

upon so far, is the preferences of investors who requests arbitration based on these treaties. The next two chapters will discuss some consequences of an investor's choice to avail itself of advance state consent to commercial arbitration rules, focusing on how this choice has influenced the scope of arbitral tribunal jurisdiction.

CHAPTER 3

Domestic Courts and *Lex Loci Arbitri* in Treaty-Based Arbitration: Challenges of Awards

As calls for an increased role of domestic courts in the adjudication of investment disputes become more frequent,[1] little research exists on the *de facto* experience domestic courts already have of investment arbitration. In fact, while there is plenty of literature dealing with domestic courts and their interaction with international law generally,[2] little attention has been paid to the growing field of international investment law in this context.[3] Conversely, there is an abundance of writings on the application and interpretation of

1 See for example M Bronckers, 'Investor-State Dispute Settlement (ISDS) Superior to Litigation Before Domestic Courts? An EU View on Bilateral Trade Agreements', 18 Journal of International Economic Law 655–677 (2015); Open Letter, *220+ Law and Economics Professors Urge Congress to Reject the TPP and Other Prospective Deals that Include Investor-State Dispute Settlement (ISDS)*, available at https://www.citizen.org/sites/default/files/isds-law-economics-professors-letter-sept-2016.pdf, last accessed 1 September, 2018. For a description of Australia's and Indonesia's policies in this respect, see L E Trakman and K Sharma, "Jumping Back and Forth between Domestic Courts and ISDS: Mixed Signals from the Asia-Pacific Region," in S Hindelang and M Krajewski (eds.), *Shifting Paradigms in International Investment Law: More Balanced, Less Isolated, Increasingly Diversified,* Oxford University Press, 2016, pp. 320–328. Furthermore, some recent investment treaties exclude arbitration entirely in favor of domestic courts, see for example J Dahlquist, "Brazil and India Conclude Bilateral Investment Treaty," Investment Arbitration Reporter, 28 Nov, 2016, available at https://www.iareporter.com/articles/brazil-and-india-conclude-bilateral-investment-treaty/. See also generally S Gáspár-Szilágyi, "Let Us Not Forget about the Role of Domestic Courts in Settling Investor-State Disputes," The Law and Practice of International Courts and Tribunals 18 (2019) 389–415.

2 For a few notable examples, see Aust & Nolte (eds.); D Sloss, *The Role of Domestic Courts in Treaty Enforcement: A Comparative Study,* Cambridge University Press, 2009; O K Fauchald & A Nollkaemper (eds.); A Roberts, ICLQ; H P Aust, A Rodiles, and P Staubach, "Unity or Uniformity? Domestic Courts and Treaty Interpretation," Leiden Journal of International Law (2014), 27, pp. 75–112.

3 For example, the extensive Oxford Reports on International Law in Domestic Courts has only reported 6 instances of challenges in domestic courts as of September 2017. One of the very few texts dealing with domestic courts in investment arbitration is A Kulick and J Dahlquist, "International Investment Law and Arbitration Before Domestic Courts," in A Nollkaemper Y Shany and A Tzanakopoulos, *Engagement of Domestic Courts with International Law,* Oxford University Press, (forthcoming).

 | DOI:10.1163/9789004413689_004

international investment law, but few authors have considered the role of domestic courts in any systematic manner.[4]

Before it can be discussed how domestic courts should be involved in the future adjudication of investment disputes – which is not the primary focus here – it is submitted that it is helpful to address how courts already act in treaty-based investment disputes. This is the focus of this chapter, which focuses on one significant aspect, *viz.* the instances when treaty-based awards are challenged in domestic court. This chapter is based on a review of final court decisions as of January 1, 2020, and explores several issues raised by these court decisions.

Initially, domestic courts' general jurisdiction to hear challenges against treaty-based arbitral awards is discussed. The standard of review employed by courts is then analysed, as is the domestic court practice with respect to treaty interpretation, and a number of procedural particularities in different jurisdictions. In the final section 3.3, the consequences of the studied material, for both disputing parties and international investment law more broadly, are brought into context. Here, the proper function of treaty interpretation in domestic courts is discussed.

Each state has the sovereignty to determine the rules that will govern arbitrations within its jurisdiction. By choosing to locate the proceedings in such a jurisdiction, the parties to an arbitration not only create a territorial connection for the proceedings, but also submit to the laws of that state, as applied by its courts. Given this, surprisingly little attention has been paid to the issue of the seat of arbitration in the investment treaty context, by both treaty parties and the investment arbitration community. In commercial arbitration, disputing parties strive to ensure that any number of procedural issues connected to the legal seat are "known quantities and therefore controllable risks."[5] In the view of one prominent practitioner, besides the choice of applicable substantive

4 With respect to treaty interpretation, the practice of domestic courts in interpreting investment treaties is rarely mentioned by any of the major works, which instead focus solely on arbitral tribunals, see for example J R Weeramantry, *Treaty Interpretation in Investment Arbitration,* Oxford University Press, 2012 (which expressly excludes this practice from its scope, see p. 3); T Gazzini, *Interpretation of International Investment Treaties*, Hart, 2016; C Schreuer, "Diversity and Harmonization of Treaty Interpretation in Investment Arbitration," in M Fitzmaurice, O Elias, and P Merkouris (eds.), *Treaty Interpretation and the Vienna Convention on the Law of Treaties: 30 years on,* Martinus Nijhoff, 2010. Richard Gardiner's treatise does discuss this issue, but seemingly from the assumption that the treaty to be interpreted is binding on the court's home state, R Gardiner, *Treaty Interpretation,* 2nd. ed. (paperback), Oxford University Press, 2017, pp. 141–157. As will be discussed more extensively below, this is most often *not* the case when a treaty-based award is challenged in domestic court.

5 N Rubins, "The Arbitral Seat Is No Fiction," Mealey's Int Arb Rep, Vol. 16, Iss. 1, p. 26.

law, "the choice of arbitral seat is perhaps the most essential negotiating point of any international arbitration agreement."[6] The studied material suggests that the same has not been true in the investment arbitration sphere, but that the place of arbitration nevertheless matters a great deal also in this field, both for disputing parties in the individual case, and for the field more broadly in several ways.

Admittedly, the issues discussed in this text, which arise from set-aside proceedings, are only one part of courts' encounters with investment law, albeit the most common one; domestic courts may encounter jurisdictional issues also *during* treaty-based arbitration. For example, a court can be asked to order interim measures,[7] issue anti-arbitration injunctions, or to appoint[8] or decide challenge against arbitrators,[9] all of which potentially raise questions of tribunal jurisdiction. Such court interventions in pending arbitrations happen regularly in international commercial arbitration, but seem to be rare in investment treaty arbitration; only two challenges against arbitrators have been reported in such cases,[10] and no request for a court to appoint one seems to be known. There have also been a small number of attempts to halt pending treaty arbitrations by seeking an order to that effect from domestic courts.[11] In this chapter, however, the main focus is on the post-award stage,

6 Ibid, p. 27.

7 UNCITRAL Model Law, Article 17 J.

8 UNCITRAL Model Law Articles 11(4)-(5).

9 UNCITRAL Model Law, Article 13(3).

10 The first is the 2004 decision by the District Court of The Hague that an arbitrator in Telekom Malaysia v. Ghana was conflicted, see International Institute for Sustainable Development, *Investment Law and Policy Weekly News Bulletin, December 17, 2004*, available at http://www.iisd.org/pdf/2004/investment_investsd_dec17_2004.pdf, accessed 8 January 2019. The second is the rejection, by two different Brussels courts, of the challenge against an arbitrator in the first Eureko v. Poland case, see L E Peterson, *Backgrounder: Eureko v. Poland reaches anti-climax after notable liability award and battle over arbitrator challenge*, 14 October, 2009, https://www.iareporter.com/articles/backgrounder-eureko-v-poland-reaches-anti-climax-after-notable-liability-award-and-battle-over-arbitrator-challenge/, Investment Arbitration Reporter. Furthermore, it also seems that Argentina tried to overturn the decision by ICC to reject a challenge against an arbitrator in the *National Grid v. Argentina* challenge. Despite the case being legally seated in the United States, Argentina turned to a court in Buenos Aires, which ultimately ordered that the tribunal halt the arbitration while Argentina's challenge against the ICC decision be reviewed, see Federal Administrative Chamber of Appeals Buenos Aires, Causa 2.660/2006, 3 July, 2007.

11 See the Pakistani Supreme Court in *Societe Generale de Surveillance SA v Pakistan*, Secretary, Minister of Finance, Revenue Division and Islamabad, Appeal to Supreme Court, Civil Appeal No 459/2002, Civil Appeal No 460/2002, 2002 SCMR 1694, ILDC 82 (PK 2002), 3 July 2002. In addition, Belize unsuccessfully tried to halt two UNCITRAL arbitrations against the state in its own courts, see L Peterson, *In Lifting Injunctions against Two Investment Treaty*

where challenges against arbitral awards are often brought on jurisdictional grounds.

3.1 Challenges of Investment Treaty Arbitration Awards – The Legal Framework

All cases studied in this chapter were legally seated in 10 different jurisdictions: Belgium, Canada, Czech Republic, Denmark, England, France, Netherlands, Singapore, Sweden, Switzerland, and the United States.[12] The underlying arbitrations were governed by the UNCITRAL Rules, the SCC Rules, the ICC Rules or the ICSID Additional Facility Rules. While the last set of these rules occupies a special place on the investment arbitration map, as discussed above at 2.2.1.3, the three others were initially devised for contractual arbitration, on the premise that two (private) disputing parties agree directly to arbitration to the exclusion of other judicial proceedings. The rules allow for a large degree of autonomy for the parties to shape the arbitration's normative framework. This includes the choice of the arbitration's legal seat. Unlike the "self-contained" ICSID Convention, all four sets of non-ICSID rules – like all international commercial arbitration rules – are part of an intricate web of norms, involving both transnational and domestic law. Ultimately, however, the mandatory norms of the place of arbitration set the outer frame for the proceeding; commercial arbitration is a method of settling disputes outside of courts and as such is allowed only to the extent that the process complies with the parameters set out by the relevant state. Every international commercial arbitration must therefore have a place of arbitration, often referred to as its seat, which will determine

Arbitrations, Belize Court of Appeal Hews to Recent Caribbean Court of Justice Ruling, 4 Nov, 2013; https://www.iareporter.com/articles/in-lifting-injunctions-against-two-investment-treaty-arbitrations-belize-court-of-appeal-hews-to-recent-caribbean-court-of-justice-ruling/. Furthermore, after the time of writing this chapter, it was revealed that the Delhi High Court issued an injunction against a pending treaty arbitration against India, see A Ross, *Revealed: India's Three Attempts to Halt the Vodafone Case, Global Arbitration Review*, Global Arbitration Review, 26 August 2017, http://globalarbitrationreview.com/article/1146807/revealed-indias-three-attempts-to-halt-the-vodafone-case, accessed 30 August, 2017.

12 Subsequent to the finalization of this text, two different 2015 set-aside judgments from the Moscow Arbitrazh Court surfaced: *Stans Energy v. Kyrgyz Republic*, Moscow Arbitrazh Court Judgement 25 May, 2015; *Lee John Beck and Central Asian Development Corporation v. Kyrgyz Republic,* Moscow Arbitrazh Court Judgement 5 June 2015. These judgments, which have not been published in English or subject to much discussion in literature, are not dealt with further here.

the law governing the arbitration (the *lex loci arbitri*). The place of arbitration must be a domestic jurisdiction, whose legal system forms a key component of the legal framework governing the proceedings,[13] and which gives the arbitral award a "nationality" for purposes of enforcement.[14] Although the seat may be chosen by the parties, once chosen the law governing the arbitration restricts the parties' otherwise wide autonomy to structure the proceedings in any manner they see fit.[15]

The place of arbitration is important in several ways before, during and after the proceedings. Although the primary focus of this text is on a specific part of the latter aspect, i.e. set-aside proceedings, it should be noted that the *lex loci arbitri* most often governs various other matters such as arbitrability, the tribunal's powers, the form and validity of the award, and the availability of court assistance during the proceedings.[16]

As for the post-award stage, the *lex loci arbitri* has significant consequences for the status of the award, including the possibilities to correct, supplement, set aside, recognize and enforce it. The New York Convention, which deals with the recognition and enforcement of international arbitral awards, implicitly acknowledges that "annulment" of an international arbitration award may only be sought where the award was "made," in practice the place of arbitration.[17] This leaves the regulation of under what circumstances an award may be set aside to the respective jurisdiction and, ultimately, to the courts of that jurisdiction.

Although there have been challenges against the traditional assumption that every international arbitration is governed by a domestic legal system – primarily by proponents of the so-called delocalization theory[18] – the fact

13 JD M Lew, LA Mistelis, and S Kröll, *Comparative International Commercial Arbitration*, Kluwer 2003, p. 17.

14 New York Convention, Article I(1).

15 Lew, Mistelis and Kröll, pp. 27–29; Redfern & Hunter, pp. 176–177.

16 Redfern & Hunter, pp. 176–177.

17 New York Convention Articles V(1)(d)-(e). See further G Born, pp. 2992–3001.

18 This theory has attracted strongest support in France. In the words of the French Court de Cassation: "an international arbitral award – which is not anchored to any national legal order – is an international judicial decision," in PT Putrabali Adyamulia v. Est Epices, French Court de Cassation, Judgement 29 June, 2007. For a detailed discussion of other French cases, see E Gaillard, "L'exécution des sentences annulées dans pay d'origine," Journal du Droit international, 125e année (1998). For an early description of the theory, see J Paulsson, "Delocalisation of International Commercial Arbitration," 32 ICLQ 21 (1983), with further references. See also the exchanges of opinion in T Nakamura, "The Place of Arbitration in International Arbitration – Its Fictitious Nature and Lex Arbitri," Mealey's Int Arb Rep, Vol. 15, Iss. 10 and N Rubin's reply 'The Arbitral Seat Is No Fiction', Mealey's Int Arb Rep, Vol. 16, Iss. 1.

remains that for any international commercial arbitration, the place of arbitration is a central feature. Put simply, "non-ICSID" arbitration necessarily involves domestic courts, applying domestic law, and awards rendered under non-ICSID rules can only be challenged in the courts of the state where the proceedings took place.[19]

By contrast, in ICSID arbitration, there is no place of arbitration and no domestic court overseeing the arbitration. Presumably, the ICSID Convention itself is the *lex loci arbitri* in ICSID cases,[20] and ICSID awards are challenged in accordance with the ICSID Convention. This is one of the crucial differences between the "self-contained" ICSID system and the other arbitration rules available to investors under investment treaties.

Unlike the regulatory framework of most international commercial arbitrations, investment treaty arbitration is based on treaties, concluded between states. When such cases are arbitrated under rules that require domestic court supervision, there is always the potential that the domestic court will be required to interpret the treaty, in order to determine the scope of the state parties' agreement. This potential is the greatest when a domestic court is faced with a challenge against a treaty-based tribunal's jurisdiction, normally based on the argument that one or more of the jurisdictional criteria laid down in the treaty have not been respected. This fact raises a number of questions with respect to the role of domestic courts in interpreting international law, which are examined in the following text. They relate to (i) courts' general jurisdiction to hear such challenges; (ii) the standard of review when a tribunal's jurisdiction is challenged; (iii) treaty interpretation in these cases; and (iv) different procedural characteristics that are specific to a given domestic jurisdiction. First, however, the general legal framework will be introduced.

3.1.1 *Domestic Arbitration Legislation*

Courts in at least ten different jurisdictions have pronounced themselves in such cases. Consequently, ten different national legal systems have so far governed challenges against treaty-based cases. In theory, there is therefore a fragmented map of possible legal frameworks under which a non-ICSID challenge has been brought, contrasted with the single framework which by definition governs the attempt to annul an ICSID award.

In practice, most jurisdictions where international arbitrations tend to take place are similar in most important respects. The main reason for this is

---

19 G Born, 2nd ed., p. 2916.

20 C Schreuer, *The ICSID Convention – A Commentary*, Cambridge University Press, 2009, p. 1244; C Mclachlan, The Legal Framework, p. 123.

the 1985 UNCITRAL Model Law on International Commercial Arbitration (the Model Law), whose influence has been considerable, both by states adopting it directly, but also indirectly as a general inspiration in other states.[21] The ten studied jurisdictions are influenced by the Model Law to different degrees. According to the UNCITRAL Secretariat, Belgium, Canada, Denmark and Singapore all have legislation based on the Model Law.[22] Singapore has adopted the Model Law by way of a general reference clause incorporating it in its entirety subject to certain modifications,[23] while Belgium, Canada and Denmark have enacted domestic legislative acts based on the Model Law.[24] The six remaining states[25] are not listed as having legislation based on the Model Law, but have to various degrees incorporated its core elements. However, as will be shown in the text below, the frequently used jurisdictions, while inspired by the Model Law to different extents, are still separate and different in terms of arbitration legislation. Furthermore, many different types of more general rules might also be involved in a set-aside proceeding, including general principles of contract interpretation and other procedural norms not specific to arbitration. These will not be discussed separately here, but rather highlighted, when appropriate, in section 3.2 below.

With respect to the grounds for challenging an arbitral award, these are, broadly speaking, similar in the ten studied jurisdictions. Prior to the Model Law, there was a great variety in the grounds for setting aside an award in different states,[26] but it now seems that the general trend is to allow for only a limited set of grounds for challenges. Article 34(2) of the Model Law establishes six grounds for a challenge: (i) invalidity of the arbitration agreement, (ii) lack of notice or other inability for a party to present its case, (iii) the award deals

21 T Várady, JJ Barceló III, AT von Mehren, *International Commercial Arbitration – A Transnational Perspective*, Thomson West, 2006, p. 39; J Sekolec and N Eliasson, 'The UNCITRAL Model Law on Arbitration and the Swedish Arbitration Act: A Comparison', in L Heuman and S Jarvin, *The Swedish Arbitration Act of 1999, Five Years on: A Critical Review of Strengths and Weaknesses*, Juris, 2006.

22 http://www.uncitral.org/uncitral/en/uncitral_texts/arbitration/1985Model_arbitration_status.html, last visited 10 July, 2018.

23 Article 3(1), Singapore International Arbitration Act, 2002.

24 Chapter 6 of the Belgian Judicial Code, 2013 (see http://kluwerarbitrationblog.com/2013/07/04/belgium-adopts-a-new-law-on-arbitration/); Danish Act No. 553 of June 25, 2005 on Arbitration; International Commercial Arbitration Act (ICAA) on the federal level in Canada (each province has also adopted the Model Law).

25 Czech Republic, England, France, Netherlands, Sweden, Switzerland, United States (although several states within the country are listed as Model Law jurisdictions).

26 P Binder, *International Commercial Arbitration and Conciliation in UNCITRAL Model Law Jurisdictions*, Sweet & Maxwell, 2010, para. 7-005.

with matters beyond the scope of submission, (iv) irregularity in the composition of the tribunal or the procedure, (v) non-arbitrability, (vi) violation of domestic public policy.[27] As will be discussed above, it is the third ground, or versions of it, that has been the most frequently relied upon in the studied cases, and the one that is the most relevant for the purposes of this study.

In the drafting of the Model Law, there was "very wide support" for the view that an arbitral award should not be subject to court review on its merits.[28] This is the same in most of the jurisdictions where treaty-based awards have been challenged. There are two exceptions to this rule. First, Article 69 of the English Arbitration Act, allows for a limited court review of points of English law. Secondly, for arbitrations whose seat is in the United States, the extra-statutory ground of "manifest disregard of the law" applies.[29] However, few requests have been entertained under either of these grounds in challenges against treaty-based arbitral awards.[30]

It should also be noted that the Model Law, and similarly also most domestic arbitration statutes, is restricted to international arbitration that is "commercial" in nature.[31] This has two implications for the present study, one that is well established in arbitration doctrine and one that is less so. First, the question is whether a treaty-based arbitration between an investor and a state can be characterized as a dispute concerning a "commercial" relationship. The answer to that question seems to be yes; in the studied challenge proceedings, the applicability of domestic arbitration law has very rarely been questioned on this ground.[32] Furthermore, the UNCITRAL Working Group included a footnote to Article 1 of the Model Law, explaining that the term "commercial"

27 The first four grounds must be demonstrated by the party seeking the challenge, while the two latter grounds can also be established by the court *ex officio*.

28 UNCITRAL Doc. A/CN.9/216, para. 107. For more information on the drafting of the Model Law, see P Binder. Footnote 492, paras. 1-003-1-006 with further references.

29 N Rubins, 'Judicial Review of Investment Arbitration Awards', in T Weiler (ed.), *Investment Law and Arbitration: Past Issues, Current Practice, Future Prospects*, Brill, 2004, pp. 369–370.

30 See the discussion on *Thunderbird v. Mexico*, below at 3.2.2.6.

31 UNCITRAL Model Law, Article 1.

32 One exception is the challenge in *Metalclad v. Mexico*, discussed below at 3.2.1. There is also a recent case before the Delhi High Court concerning the (pending) arbitration between Vodafone and India, suggesting that investment arbitration is outside of the scope of the Indian Arbitration and Conciliation Act 1996, see P Ranjan and P Anand, "Vodafone Versus India – BIT by BIT, International Arbitration Becomes Clearer," https://thewire.in/business/vodafone-versus-india-bit-international-arbitration, 17 May 2018, accessed 18 May 2018.

> […] should be given a wide interpretation as to cover matters arising from all relationships of a commercial nature, irrespective of whether the parties are 'commercial persons' (merchants) under any given national law[33]

Secondly, "commercial" arbitration might imply "contractual" arbitration, meaning that the prospect of treaty-based arbitration has not been considered in the drafting of domestic arbitration statutes. This seems to generally be the case, in the sense that treaty-based arbitration has not been expressly taken into account in the drafting of either the Model Law or domestic statutes.[34] The implications of this fact are probably limited; although treaty-based arbitrations tend to require courts to engage in different types of exercises than those that are based on contracts – particularly with respect to challenges against a tribunal's jurisdiction – it is submitted that the general legislative framework is sufficiently flexible to accommodate the specificities associated with treaty-based awards. Instead, as will be discussed at length below, it is primarily matters *not* regulated in statutes that are of interest when studying domestic courts' role in investment treaty arbitration.

3.1.2 *Choosing the Place of Arbitration*

Given the potential ramifications of an arbitration's legal seat,[35] the choice of seat is important. In ICSID arbitration the choice is a non-issue, since the ICSID Convention establishes a "self-contained" arbitral system with no connection to any domestic jurisdiction.[36] In non-ICSID arbitration, by contrast, the choice of seat is effectively a choice of both law and forum for the review of the award.[37]

In international commercial arbitration – as opposed to treaty-based arbitration – the matter of choosing a seat is normally relatively straightforward: it is a matter of negotiations. In such cases, the disputing parties typically have a direct, contractual relationship and the legal framework for the arbitral

33 The language is (intentionally) similar to the "commercial reservation" available in Article I(3) of the New York Convention, see P Binder, *International Commercial Arbitration and Conciliation in UNCITRAL Model Law Jurisdictions*, 3rd. ed., Sweet & Maxwell, 2010, pp. 22–23.

34 In the directives to the commission tasked with revising the 1999 Swedish Arbitration Act, the frequent use of Sweden as forum for investment arbitrations was mentioned *en passant*, but does not seem to have justified any specific substantive considerations by the commission, SOU 2015:37, *Översyn av lagen om skiljeförfarande*, Bilaga 1, p. 206.

35 In this text "seat of arbitration" and "place of arbitration" are used interchangeably, for the sake of variation, to refer to an arbitration's legal seat.

36 Dolzer and Schreuer, p. 239.

37 W L Craig, 'Uses and Abuses of Appeal from Awards', 4:3 Arbitration International 174 (1988) p. 178.

proceeding is but one of several matters which the parties might negotiate as part of their general contractual bargaining.[38] Treaty-based proceedings, by contrast, are often characterized by the lack of a direct arbitration agreement between the disputing parties. Furthermore, very few treaties expressly provide for a seat of arbitration.[39] A notable exception is the NAFTA, which provides some guidance. Article 1130 states that the seat of arbitration shall be in a NAFTA state (which must also be a party to the New York Convention), to be chosen "in accordance" with the applicable arbitration rules. Every example of a challenge of a NAFTA award has been heard before a court located in one of the three treaty states (although never in Mexico). This fact highlights the contrast with challenges of BIT awards, which almost exclusively have been heard outside of the treaty states.[40]

The special status of NAFTA in this respect was highlighted in the *Apotex v. United* States dispute, which was heard under the ICSID AF Rules.[41] Although NAFTA Article 1130 gives some guidance, it does not specify the legal seat. Depending on the applicable arbitration rules, this leaves the choice to the disputing parties, the administrating institution or, ultimately, the tribunal. In *Apotex*, the disputing parties could not agree and the matter was left to the tribunal. Its decision in this respect represents a rare example of a tribunal giving extensive reasons for this choice.

The three arbitrators could not agree on the seat. Although the parties were in agreement that the geographical location of the hearings were to be at the World Bank in Washington DC, the Toronto-incorporated claimants had argued that Toronto should be designated as the legal place of arbitration, whereas the respondent state wished for Washington DC or, in the alternative, New York.

A majority of the tribunal designated New York, "by a whisker."[42] In an Appendix to the final award, the reasons for this decision are explained. The

38 See for example *2015 International Arbitration Survey: Improvements and Innovations in International Arbitration,* by Queen Mary University of London and White & Case Law firm, available at http://www.arbitration.qmul.ac.uk/docs/164761.pdf., pp. 11–24.

39 No reliable statistics seem to be available on this point, although the present author came across occasional references when reviewing 20th century BITs for Chapter 4. Furthermore, a compilation shows that 14 treaties expressly refer to Stockholm as the place of arbitration, see K Hobér, *Selected Writings on Investment Treaty Arbitration,* Studentlitteratur, 2013, p. 543. The practice of the SCC Board, as well as the ICC Court, in designating place of arbitration is discussed at 6.3.2.

40 The sole exception being the challenge against the unpublished *ad hoc* award in Binder v. Czech Republic, discussed below at 3.2.4.3.

41 Apotex Holdings Inc. and Apotex Inc. v. United States of America, ICSID Case No. ARB(AF)/12/1, Award 25 August 2014. This award does not appear to have been challenged.

42 Ibid., Appendix 1, Para. A. 39.

tribunal points out that it would have wished a "legal place of arbitration neutral for all parties" but that it was restricted by NAFTA, the arbitration rules and the parties' proposals.[43]

After consulting with the parties, the tribunal initially ruled out Washington, DC as a potential seat due to it being the respondent's capital. In the tribunal's view, it would not be appropriate for the investor to "play away in the Respondent's national home stadium."[44] In deciding between the two remaining choices, the tribunal stated that neutrality – which under other circumstances would be an important factor in its choice of seat – was an inapplicable criterion, since both Toronto and New York were located in the state of one of the parties.[45] Furthermore, the tribunal rejected the parties' respective submissions on the differing scope of court intervention in the two jurisdictions, noting that both seats have "acceptable laws for international arbitration, including the judicial review of investor-state arbitration awards."[46]

Similarly, the tribunal rejected the investor's worry over US courts' approach to international arbitration following the DC Court of Appeal's decision on the challenge in *BG Group v. Argentina*.[47] At the time of the award, that challenge had reached the US Supreme Court, which reversed the lower court's decision.

The tribunal devoted a large part of its reasons to addressing the investors' concern that US courts systematically favour the US government in interpreting treaties to which the US is a party. The concerns were based on several treaty interpretation cases (none of which concerned investment treaties) in US courts, from which the investors drew the conclusion that US courts are "required by established US law to defer to the US Government on issues of treaty interpretation."[48] Since treaty interpretation would likely be central to any post-award proceedings at the seat of arbitration, the investors argued that choosing an American seat under these circumstances would create an element of uncertainty, which the tribunal formulated in the following words:

> This Tribunal is not a US court. It cannot decide how US courts might resolve the tensions in this uncertain and disputed area of domestic US law. However, the possibility that a deference doctrine might be invoked and upheld in future litigation to set aside an award clearly creates an

43 Ibid., Para. A.3.
44 Ibid., para. A.34.
45 Ibid., para. A.35.
46 Ibid., para. A. 36.
47 Discussed below at 3.2.3.2.
48 Ibid., para. A.41.

> element of legal uncertainty. Is that theoretical uncertainty a bar to New York as a legal place for this arbitration?[49]

The majority of the tribunal, however, was hesitant to see this alleged uncertainty as a bar to choosing New York as the place of arbitration. Based on the reasoning that any US invocation of deference towards the state in a challenge proceeding would violate the NAFTA arbitration provision, it stated that it could not "assume that the Respondent, by its executive or judicial branches, would violate its obligation under international law."[50]

Ultimately, therefore, the majority of the tribunal favoured New York despite the investors' concerns, and gave three reasons that on balance made it more attractive than Toronto: (i) New York is an older and more established arbitral jurisdiction; (ii) the parties had already successfully arbitrated another dispute in New York, and (iii) Toronto was the principal place of business for the investors.[51]

The dissenting arbitrator argued that, on balance, Toronto was more suitable than New York. He emphasized the concerns raised about the risk of New York courts having to give "great weight" to the executive branch and was not convinced that this risk was absent from a potential challenge of the tribunal's jurisdiction in New York.[52]

3.1.2.1 What Do the Arbitration Rules Provide?

It seems that *Apotex* is a rare example of a tribunal giving extensive reasons for its decision on the seat of arbitration,[53] presumably because that decision was not made unanimously. In the absence of an agreement between the state

---

49 Ibid., para. A.46.

50 Ibid., para. A.47.

51 Ibid., para. A.39.

52 Ibid, para. A.51.

53 Other reported cases of tribunal's decision on seat include NAFTA cases with considerably shorter reasoning, see *Ethyl Corporation v. Canada*, UNCITRAL Decision on Venue of 28 November, 1997; *Methanex Corporation v. United States of America*, UNCITRAL, Decision On venue, 7 September 7, 2000; *Marvin Roy Feldman Karps v Mexico*, ICSID Case No. ARB(AF)99/1, Procedural Order No. 1 Concerning the Place of Arbitration, 3 April, 2000; *Vito G. Gallo v. Government of Canada*, UNCITRAL, PCA Case No. 55798, Procedural Order No. 1, 4 June, 2008; *Waste Management, Inc. v. United Mexican States*, ICSID Case No. ARB(AF)/00/3, Decision on the Venue of the Arbitration, 26 September 2001. In the latter case, similar to *Apotex*, the parties had argued for a seat in Canada and Washington, DC respectively. The tribunal stated that with respect to court review in the two states it could not: "[…] identify any particular issue on which there is likely to be a significant difference of approach by the courts of the two NAFTA states.", para. 19. The tribunal ultimately the tribunal designated Washington DC because an earlier case between the parties had been arbitrated there.

parties to the treaty, the choice has to be made by somebody else, either the disputing parties, the administering arbitral institution, or, as in the *Apotex* case, the tribunal. On whom the decision falls is normally regulated by the applicable arbitration rules. True to the principle of party autonomy, most sets of arbitration rules assume that the disputing parties decide the place of arbitration, while providing for fall-back options in the event that the parties cannot agree.

Given the *Apotex* discussion of *cities* rather than *states*, it might be useful initially to note that although it is sufficient under most domestic arbitration laws and arbitration rules for a state to be indicated as the place of arbitration, it is both advisable and common practice that a specific location within the state is specified. This is because the arbitration law might differ within different subsections of the country, such as provinces, cantons or states.[54] Furthermore, specifying a specific city or town as the place of arbitration also serves to clearly identify which court is competent to hear an eventual challenge.[55] In practice, therefore, the place of arbitration is generally a city.

With respect to the "non-ICSID" rules studied here, the two institutional rules allow their respective governing body to make the decision. Article 25 of the SCC Rules stipulates that unless the parties agree, the SCC board will determine the seat of arbitration.[56] Similarly, Article 18 of the ICC Rules provides that the ICC Court shall fix the seat, absent party agreement. The practice of these institutions with respect to deciding place of arbitration is discussed more in detail in Chapter 4.

The ICSID Additional Facility Rules constitute a special example of a "semi-institutional" framework. The mode of selecting the seat reflects this: Article 20 provides that "the place of arbitration shall be determined by the Arbitral Tribunal after consultation with the parties and the [ICSID] Secretariat."[57] In practice this consultation is usually made orally during the first procedural meeting.[58] According to an article written by officials from the ICSID secretariat, the secretariat's involvement is generally restricted to consulting on the suitability of hearing facilities at the seat.[59] Therefore, one would

---

Similarly, in *Lion Mexico Consolidated v. Mexico*, ICSID Case No. ARB(AF)/15/2, Procedural Order No. 2, the tribunal designated Washington DC over Toronto.

54 Fry, Greenberg & Mazza, para. 3-676.

55 Ibid.

56 This is longstanding SCC practice and was incorporated in earlier versions of the Rules.

57 It should be noted that this selection is "subject to Article 19," which provides that the seat must be in a state that is a party to the New York Convention.

58 F Nitschke & K Aït-El-Hadj, p. 246.

59 Ibid.

assume, the secretariat's involvement does not normally extend to the legal ramifications of the seat.

Unlike the other rules, the UNCITRAL rules are not by default tied to an administrative institution (although, in practice, one is often used) and therefore do not rely on one to determine the place of arbitration. Instead, therefore, the decision rests directly with the tribunal, provided that the parties have not agreed.[60] In this exercise, the tribunal has no institutional practice to rely on. However, the 2016 UNCITRAL Notes on Organizing Arbitral Proceedings (the "Notes") contain language on selecting place of arbitration. Generally, the Notes serve as "soft law" guidance for international arbitration proceedings, and were first adopted in 1996. The Notes are also understood to provide a useful point of departure when tribunals determine the place of arbitration in ICSID AF cases.[61] The 2016 version of the Notes contains extensive, but open-ended, guidance for determining the place of arbitration,[62] leaving wide discretion to tribunals to designate the seat of arbitration (albeit with an implied bias in favour of New York Convention states).

Moreover, the Notes emphasize that different considerations ought to guide the choice of the legal seat and the place of the hearings. The distinction between the two was introduced when the UNCITRAL Rules were updated in 2010.[63] In fact, only the more modern rules – i.e. the SCC Rules,[64] the ICC Rules[65] and the 2010 UNCITRAL Rules – expressly provide that the hearings may take place in different venues than at the place of arbitration. The ICSID AF Rules, as well as the 1976 version of the UNCITRAL Rules, take a different approach and do not expressly indicate that the two might be in separate jurisdictions. In practice, however, it is a well-recognized principle of international arbitration that hearings, meetings and deliberations can be conducted in places other than the place of arbitration.[66] It should therefore generally not be a problem to meet elsewhere, even if the arbitration rules do not expressly authorize it. In fact, ICSID AF practice shows that sometimes parties agree on the location of hearings, while leaving the choice of the legal seat to the tribunal.[67]

---

60 UNICTRAL Arbitration Rules, 2010, Article 18.

61 Nitschke & Aït-El-Hadj, p. 253

62 Paras. 29–31.

63 Article 18(2).

64 Article 25(2).

65 Article 18(2).

66 Redfern & Hunter, pp. 182–183. See also, for example, the UNCITRAL Model Law, Art. 20(2); the 2016 UNCITRAL Notes on Organizing Arbitral Proceedings ("The UNCITRAL Notes"), para. 31; ICSID Convention Article 63.

67 F Nitschke & K Aït-El-Hadj, p. 247, referencing *Mobil v. Canada* and *Apotex v. USA*.

3.1.2.2 Who Makes the Decision in Practice?

In no case studied for this chapter did the contracting states decide the place of arbitration. The court's jurisdiction in almost every challenge proceeding – to the extent it is possible to ascertain from documents in the public domain – has instead been a result of either a tribunal's decision, an agreement between the disputing parties (or a mix of the two), or and institutional designation.[68] It has been argued elsewhere that the fact that tribunals exercise such a large influence over the choice of place of arbitration in this context allows tribunals

> " [...] effectively to evade ex post-control by State courts of the interpretations they make of international investment law. States thereby are effectively prevented from intervening and correcting decisions of an investment treaty tribunal, for example because a tribunal gave an extensive reading to obligations contained in an investment treaty."[69]

This lack of direct state influence over the place of arbitration will be discussed below at 3.4.2 in the context of future treaty-making.

3.2 Specific Issues Arising from Challenges in Domestic Courts

Below, a number of issues arising from challenges of treaty-based awards in domestic courts are discussed.

3.2.1 *Court Jurisdiction to Hear Challenges of Treaty Awards*

No domestic court has declined jurisdiction to hear a challenge against an arbitral award because the award has been based on a treaty, as opposed to the contractually based arbitration that domestic arbitration statutes generally envision.[70] A number of parties, however, have tried to argue that domestic courts, as a general matter, lack jurisdiction to hear such cases.

---

68 It should be noted that the ICC encourages parties to choose seats on their own, which is reflected in a general decline in the amount of cases in which the ICC designates the seat, see Stone Sweet & Grisel, p.94 wth further references.

69 S. W. Schill, "System-Building in Investment Treaty Arbitration and Lawmaking," in A. von Bogdandy and I. Venzke (eds.), *International Judicial Lawmaking. On Public Authority and Democratic Legitimation in Global Governance,* Heidelberg, 2012, p. 148.

70 Challenges have been denied on other procedural grounds, and will not be discussed further here, see *Raymond L. Loewen v.* United States, United States District Court for the District of Columbia, Civil Action No. 04-2151 (RWR), 31 October 2005 (time-barred); *Tembec Inc. et al v. United States*, United States District Court for the District of Columbia, Civil Action

In the challenge brought by Russia against the award rendered in favour of Mr. Franz Sedelmayer,[71] the German investor argued that Swedish courts did not have jurisdiction over Russia's challenge because the 1929 Swedish Arbitration Act did not apply to the proceedings. The arbitration was instead, in Mr. Sedelmayer's view, governed by "international law":

> [...] Swedish courts should not have jurisdiction to annul an arbitral award rendered in arbitration proceedings, which is based on a provision of foreign law and which only involves legal subjects governed by foreign law, irrespective of where the arbitration proceedings took place.[72]

The Stockholm District Court did not accept this argument. It emphasized that the arbitrators had designated Stockholm as the legal seat of the proceedings, which "entails that the arbitral award shall be deemed Swedish and that applicable law to the proceedings shall, unless otherwise agreed, be the Swedish Arbitration Act."[73] In its conclusion in this respect, the court also emphasized that the fact that the arbitration was based on a treaty does not matter, "at least when the two parties are not two sovereign states, but one of them is a private individual."[74] In the Court of Appeal, Mr. Sedelmayer did not challenge this finding and it seems never to have been questioned in subsequent court cases in Sweden.

Similarly, in the first challenge of an award based on a treaty to be put before English courts, the American investor Occidental argued unsuccessfully that the question of a tribunal's jurisdiction under the US – Ecuador BIT was not "justiciable" in English courts, due to the dispute's public international law nature. Two instances rejected Occidental's contention and allowed Ecuador's challenge to proceed (although they both ultimately rejected the challenge on its merits).

The award was rendered in 2004 under the UNCITRAL Rules, by a tribunal legally seated in London. During both challenge proceedings, Ecuador argued that the tribunal had lacked substantive jurisdiction over the dispute, contrary to Section 67 of the English Arbitration Act. Occidental retorted that Ecuador's

---

No. 07-1905 (RMC), 14 August 2008 (*res judicata*, issue estoppel); *Argentina v. National Grid PLC*, United States District Court for the District of Columbia, Civil Action No. 09-248 (RBW), 28 November 2011 (time-barred).

71 *Russian Federation v. Franz J. Sedelmayer*, Stockholm District Court, T 6-583-98, Judgement, 18 December 2002.

72 Ibid., p. 8 (translated from Swedish by the present author).

73 Ibid., p. 16 (translated from Swedish by the present author).

74 Ibid (translated from Swedish by the present author).

challenge was not "justiciable" under English law, which prompted the High Court to hear this question as a preliminary matter.

Occidental's argument was based on the English law doctrine of "non-justiciability," and consisted of two parts: firstly, the court could not be required to interpret a treaty which had not been incorporated into English law and, secondly, hearing the case would be contrary to the principle of judicial restraint which prevents English courts from deciding on matters relating to transactions of other sovereign states.

In deciding this preliminary matter, both the High Court and the Court of Appeal rejected Occidental's claims, based on similar reasoning. The Court of Appeal concluded that the treaty clearly gave investors direct rights to pursue claims against a sovereign state.[75] The treaty could therefore be distinguished from other treaties, which operate only at the international level, because under the BIT, private subjects could enforce the treaty against a sovereign. The court therefore found that the doctrines of restraint and non-justiciability did not apply to the situation.[76] It also rejected Occidental's characterization of the arbitration as being concerned with "transactions between states." Instead the court emphasized that the BIT contemplated an arbitration agreement between the disputing parties – as opposed to the two state parties to the treaty – according to the UNCITRAL rules, which clearly envision a domestic court's jurisdiction to determine the scope of the arbitration agreement.[77]

The holding on justiciability in Occidental was subsequently referenced in an unrelated challenge proceeding in Singapore. The lower Singaporean court hearing the challenge against the *Sanum v. Laos* award, based on the BIT between China and Laos, was faced with a similar "non-justiciability" objection to that in Occidental.[78] The Singapore High Court expressly found the Occidental judgment to be applicable to the case before it, and cited it approvingly.[79] Similar to the English courts in Occidental, the court found that:

> [...] the present application does not raise questions of international law that are non-justiciable; it concerns the rights of parties seeking to invoke this court's jurisdiction under section 10 of the IAA to review the Tribunal's ruling on jurisdiction.[80]

75 *Ecuador v. Occidental*, Court of Appeal, para. 20.
76 Ibid., para. 37.
77 Ibid., paras. 37–41.
78 *Sanum v. Laos*, Singapore High Court.
79 Ibid., para. 30.
80 Ibid.

On appeal, Sanum did not contest the lower court's finding on this point.[81]

Finally, in the first the challenge of an award in Canada,[82] the Supreme Court of British Columbia faced an argument that it did not have jurisdiction under the International Commercial Arbitration Act (ICAA) – which, unlike the act governing challenges of domestic arbitration, is based on the UNCITRAL Model law and thus does not allow for a challenge based on alleged errors of law. The reason for this objection was the fact that the arbitration was supposedly not commercial in nature.[83] In deciding this matter, the court looked to the comment to the Model Law,[84] which states that "the term 'commercial' should be given a wide interpretation so as to cover matters arising from all relationships of a commercial nature."[85] Furthermore, the report emphasizes the wide and non-exhaustive list of examples of commercial relationships.[86] This list includes "investing." The court took this as an indication that the dispute, which was initiated under NAFTA's Chapter 11 under the heading "Investment," was covered by the scope of the ICAA:

> The arbitration did not arise under an agreement between Metalclad and the Municipality in connection with regulatory matters. Rather, the arbitration was between Metalclad and Mexico pursuant to an agreement dealing with the treatment of investors.[87]

Every Canada-seated challenge since Metalclad has been heard under the International Commercial Arbitration Act.

3.2.2 *Standard of Review for Jurisdictional Challenges*

While domestic courts' general jurisdiction to hear challenges against treaty-based awards seems largely undisputed – in fact, the matter seems not to have been much discussed in other cases than *Sedelmayer*, *Metalclad*, *Occidental* and *Sanum*[88] – the standard of review that courts are applying in such

81 *Laos v. Sanum*, Singapore Court of Appeal Decision, para. 15.

82 *Mexico v. Metalclad*, Supreme Court of British Columbia.

83 Ibid., paras. 39–40.

84 Section 6 of the Canadian International Commercial Arbitration Act expressly authorizes Canadian courts to do so when interpreting the act.

85 Comment to Article 1(1), Available at https://www.uncitral.org/pdf/english/texts/arbitration/ml-arb/07-86998_Ebook.pdf, last accessed November 12, 2017.

86 Ibid.

87 *Mexico v. Metalclad*, Supreme Court of British Columbia. para. 46.

88 However, in Ecuador's challenge against (another) *Chevron v. Ecuador* award before the Dutch Supreme Court in 2014 (discussed below at 3.2.2.5), the state had claimed its sovereignty was violated by the arbitration, since its constitution provides that the dispute

cases is more ambiguous. The question is primarily relevant when the tribunal's jurisdiction is challenged. Domestic courts have tended to make their own independent review of a tribunal's jurisdiction when it has been challenged in a set-aside proceeding. As a general rule, only matters of jurisdiction are reviewed anew. For issues that go the merits of the case, domestic courts will show considerable deference to the tribunal's determination, and decline to review it.[89] The distinction between jurisdiction and merits is therefore important.

As will be demonstrated below, domestic courts tend to allow for a wide scrutiny of jurisdictional matters, as opposed to substantive matters, where courts have tended to be very deferential towards arbitral tribunals. In practice, this has led to "jurisdictional" issues being treated as a distinct type of challenge ground, possibly creating incentives for challenging parties to frame their grievances as going to the jurisdiction of the tribunal. Jan Paulsson has deemed this the "tyranny of labels"; simply by calling something a jurisdictional question, it can be reviewed extensively by the court at the place of arbitration, unlike other questions.[90]

The extent to which a court may review a jurisdictional determination by a tribunal – as opposed to other determinations – is thus both of crucial importance and vaguely regulated. In practice, the type of review often seems to come down to the standard of review employed by the individual court.

3.2.2.1 The "*de novo*" Determination of Jurisdictional Issues at the Challenge Stage

Investment arbitration awards are governed either by non-ICSID rules (which allow for domestic courts to hear challenges against awards) or the ICSID Convention (which does not). Within the ICSID system, a challenge against an arbitral award must be brought according to the rules of the ICSID Convention,

---

should have been litigated in Ecuadorian courts. The Supreme Court swiftly rejected this objection, stating that "Ecuador has bound itself voluntary, unequivocally and without reservation to the BIT," including its arbitration clause, at para. 4.4.4.

89 See for example the challenges against *Ukraine v. Tatneft*; Paris Court of Appeal, Case No. 14/17964, Judgement, 29 November 2016; *Poland v. Saar Papier,* Swiss Federal Tribunal, Case No. 1P.113/2000/mks, Judgement, 1 March 2002; *Mexico v. Cargill*, Court of Appeal for Ontario, 2011 ONCA 622, Judgement 4 October 2011, all discussed further below.

90 J Paulsson, *The Idea of Arbitration,* p. 55. In Chapter 3 of this treatise, Paulsson argues in the context of jurisdictional determinations *during* the arbitration, that it is time to "reverse a jurisprudence of labels – which [...] leads to a dogmatic insistence that anything said to fall under one definition or another of 'jurisdictional' issues is subject to judicial review – and instead focus on what issues are encompassed by a sensible interpretation of the parties' intention.", p. 82.

primarily Article 52. The grounds for annulment in Article 52 of the ICSID Convention are close to a codification of existing international law in interstate cases at the time of the drafting of the Convention.[91] The grounds therefore have a different origin than those contained in domestic arbitration statutes, although they are very similar. Among the grounds enumerated is the "manifest excess of powers," under which most challenges against a tribunal's jurisdiction are framed. Excess of powers has long been accepted as a ground for nullity of arbitral awards in international law,[92] and it was included in Article 52 with the added requirement of "manifest" excess. The wording of the requirement makes no difference between jurisdictional errors and others.[93]

In the ICSID annulment system, the widely accepted position is that parties cannot re-litigate the merits of the case before ad hoc committees.[94] As put by the ad hoc committee in MTD v. Chile, ICSID annulment "is a form of review on specified and limited grounds which take as their premise the record before the Tribunal."[95] This is so because ICSID annulment is concerned with the process of the arbitral decision-making and not with the correctness of the decision.[96] In general, this assumption is the same in challenges brought before domestic courts. However, the question is arguably complicated by the fact that many courts, unlike ICSID annulment committees, approach jurisdictional questions differently from other questions.

The standard of review is not expressly regulated in Article 34 of the UNCITRAL Model Law. Similar to an ICSID annulment committee, however, it is well established that a domestic court does not act as an appeals court reviewing the decision of a lower court, but rather considers only whether one of a narrow list of grounds for annulment is present.[97] Generally speaking, the Model Law and most domestic arbitration statutes establish a framework intended to minimize the extent of judicial intervention; it is sometimes discussed in terms of a "presumptive validity" of arbitral awards.[98]

This presumption does not always exist when the challenge targets the tribunal's jurisdiction. In such cases, domestic courts tend to apply a standard

---

91 C McLachlan, The Legal Framework, p. 137.

92 H Lauterpacht, "The Legal Remedy in Case of Excess of Jurisdiction," British Yearbook of International Law 9 (1928), p. 117.

93 *Empresas Lucchetti, S.A. and Lucchetti Peru, S.A. v. Republic of Peru,* ICSID Case No. ARB/03/4, Decision on Annulment, 5 September, 2007, para. 101.

94 C Schreuer, ICSID Commentary, p. 902.

95 *MTD v. Chile,* ICSID Case No. ARB/01/7, Decision on Annulment, 21 March, 2007, para. 31.

96 C Schreuer, ICSID Commentary, p. 901.

97 Redfern & Hunter, p. 588; G Born, p. 3185.

98 G Born, pp. 3180–3185.

of judicial review that is often described as "*de novo*."[99] What is meant by this phrase is that the reviewing court engages in an independent jurisdictional determination, trying to ascertain whether the tribunal was right or wrong in asserting (or, as the case may be, refusing to assert) jurisdiction. If a tribunal accepts jurisdiction which it does not have, or on the contrary fails to exercise jurisdiction it does have, this would be contrary to the parties' agreement and, as such, should be set aside.[100]

A possible justification for why jurisdictional issues occupy a special status is that they go to the consent to arbitration. Therefore, for reasons of legal certainty, if an arbitral tribunal is legally seated in a particular state, the courts of that state must ultimately ensure that the tribunal has jurisdiction. This is because by agreeing to arbitration, parties opt out of what would otherwise be under court jurisdiction. In essence, courts' *de novo* review of tribunal jurisdiction can therefore be explained by the doctrine of *Kompetenz-kompetenz*: although the tribunal has the competence to determine the scope of its own competence,[101] ultimately, the court at the place of arbitration will have the final say. This applies equally before, during and after the arbitral proceedings.[102]

Thus, domestic courts commonly recognize that they have the authority to review freely the merits of a tribunal's jurisdictional determination. The following discusses the extent to which this general trend prevails in treaty-based cases. A number of judgments from various jurisdictions are discussed, in which the scope of the court's power has been an explicit issue discussed by the respective courts. In addition to these cases, there are also a large number of cases where the issue was not discussed but the court in question seems to have assumed its authority to review jurisdiction *de novo*. The latter category will not be analysed further, as the standard of review is not discussed, but seemingly assumed, by the respective courts.

3.2.2.2 Canada

The standard of review has been a repeat issue before Canadian courts, where courts have been somewhat reluctant to review jurisdictional decisions. A noteworthy exception is the early Supreme Court of British Columbia

99 See G Born, pp. 3206–3210, for a discussion of jurisprudence in both Model Law jurisdictions and others; G Verhoosel, To ICSID or Not to ICSID, pp. 131–132; A S Rau, 'Arbitral Jurisdiction and the Dimensions of Consent', Arbitration International, Vol. 24, No. 2, 2008, p. 219; K Bondar, p. 644.

100 G Verhoosel, p. 131.

101 UNCITRAL Model Law, Article 16.

102 Redfern & Hunter, p. 351.

judgment in the challenge against the Metalclad v. Mexico award.[103] While setting out, in theory, a restrictive standard of review based on the ICAA, [104] the court subsequently engaged with the merits of the arbitral tribunal's decision. Specifically, the court rejected the *Metalclad* tribunal's broad view that transparency formed a distinctive part of the fair and equitable treatment standard enshrined in Article 1105 of the NAFTA. In the view of the court, Article 1105 instead focused on the international minimum standard of treatment, whereas transparency formed matter of Chapter 18 of the NAFTA. Chapter 18 is not subject to investor-State dispute settlement under Article 1116 of the NAFTA.[105] Consequently, the court set aside those parts of the award where the tribunal had found Mexico liable for breaches of Article 1005, as these decisions were made on matters beyond the scope of the submission to arbitration.[106]

In the 2008 challenge against the *Bayview v. Mexico* award the Ontario Superior Court of Justice expressly declined to review the tribunal's jurisdictional determination *de novo*.[107] Among the investors' arguments in their application was that the tribunal should have accepted their factual contention that they owned water rights in Mexico. They made reference to the ICJ *Oil Platforms Case*,[108] as well as the *Methanex* and *UPS* arbitral awards,[109] arguing that for purposes of jurisdiction the tribunal should have assumed the facts as alleged by the investor.[110] Whether Bayview in fact owned water rights would have to be determined at a later merits stage. The fact that the tribunal made the determination at this early stage meant that it did not have access to a complete record and, by extension, that Bayview had not been able to fully present its case.

Mexico, by contrast, claimed that the state's position during the arbitration had not been that the investors owned the water rights as a matter of factual characterization, but rather that the rights did not constitute an investment in the meaning of NAFTA.[111]

---

103 *Mexico v. Metalclad*, Supreme Court of British Columbia.
104 Ibid., paras. 50–56.
105 Ibid., paras. 61–75.
106 Ibid., para. 134.
107 *Bayview Irrigation v. Mexico*, Ontario Superior Court.
108 *Case Concerning Oil Platforms* (Islamic Republic of Iran v. United States of America), ICJ Reports 1996, II, p.856.
109 *Methanex Corporation v. United States of America*, UNCITRAL, Final Award on Jurisdiction and Merits, 3 August, 2005; *United Parcel Service of America Inc. v. Government of Canada*, UNCITRAL, Award on Jurisdiction, 22 Nov 2002.
110 *Bayview Irrigation v. Mexico*, Ontario Superior Court, para. 42.
111 Ibid., para. 54.

The Court did not set aside the award. It made clear that its role was not to conduct a *de novo* review of the tribunal's jurisdictional determination.[112] Rather, it pointed out that:

> [...] while decisions by arbitral tribunals are not immune from challenge, any challenge is confronted with the 'powerful presumption' that the tribunal acted within its authority. An arbitral decision is not invalid because it wrongly decided a point of fact or law.[113]

In applying the standard – i.e. a "powerful presumption" that the tribunal acted within its jurisdiction – the court ultimately deferred to the tribunal's determination that the alleged water rights did not constitute an "investment" under the NAFTA definition.[114]

In its challenge against the 2009 ICSID Additional Facility award between *Cargill and Mexico*, the respondent state had initially argued that the court was authorized to determine whether the tribunal had been "correct" in its jurisdictional determination. This standard had been established without much discussion in the 2004 challenge in *SD Myers v. Canada*, where the Federal Court of Canada stated that jurisdictional questions were "pure questions of law" to be reviewed on their correctness, whereas mixed questions of law and facts were to be reviewed on a standard of "reasonableness."[115]

The essence of Mexico's challenge against the *Cargill* award was that the tribunal had gone beyond its jurisdiction, in violation of Article 34(2)(a)(iii) of the International Commercial Arbitration Act (ICAA), which is an enactment of the UNCITRAL Model Law. The state based its challenge on the fact that the tribunal had awarded the investor compensation, *inter alia*, for damages that occurred up-stream from its protected investment. In Mexico's view, Cargill's "investment," as defined by Article 1139 of NAFTA, was its wholly owned subsidiary in Mexico, which sold a low-cost substitute for cane sugar (HFSC). Furthermore, it was this subsidiary which by virtue of its Mexican incorporation was the covered "investor" under Article 1138 of the same treaty. The tribunal had, however, in addition to compensation for the "down-stream" losses sustained in Mexico also ordered compensation for the "up-stream" losses sustained in the United States. These losses stemmed from the cost of lost sales of products that the investor manufactured in the United States, which the tribunal found

112 Ibid., para. 60.
113 Ibid., para. 63.
114 Ibid., para. 75–77.
115 *Canada v. S.D. Myers*, Federal Court of Canada, paras. 58–60.

resulted from Mexico's breaches of NAFTA. Mexico had raised a jurisdictional objection during the arbitration and argued that the tribunal lacked jurisdiction over the up-stream losses because they were sustained in the United States.

The key question which the tribunal had addressed was whether the losses sustained in the territory of United States were sustained "by reason of, or arising out of" Mexico's treaty breaches, as required by Article 1116 of NAFTA. The tribunal had found that they were. Mexico ultimately moved to challenge the award, asking the courts to partially set aside the part of the award that was based on this finding.

The court of first instance, the Superior Court of Justice in Toronto, agreed with Mexico with respect to the standard of review and applied a test of "reasonableness" for legal issues. It applied this standard to find that the tribunal had not gone beyond its jurisdiction. Mexico appealed this finding to the Court of Appeal, which in 2011 found that a standard of reasonableness "inevitably leads to a review of the merits of the [tribunal's] decision."[116] According to the higher court, if domestic courts were allowed to enter into a reasonableness review, they would by definition have to consider the merits of the arbitral tribunal's decision and determine if it was acceptable.[117]

The Court of Appeal for Ontario further developed its view on the standard of review, opening the door for a further degree of review of the tribunal's determination, compared to *Bayview*. It first stated that under its domestic case law, as well as the *SD Myers* and *Metalclad* judgments, "the correctness standard would apply, implying possible considerations of, but no deference to, the decision of the tribunal under review."[118] In the present context, the court developed,

> [...] the role of the reviewing court is to identify and narrowly define any true question of jurisdiction. The onus is on the party that challenges the award. Where the court is satisfied that there is an identified true question of jurisdiction, the tribunal had to be correct in its assumption of jurisdiction to decide the particular question it accepted and it is up to the court to determine whether it was. In assessing whether the tribunal exceeded the scope of the terms of jurisdiction, the court is to avoid a review of the merits.[119]

116 *Mexico v. Cargill*, Court of Appeal for Ontario, para. 51.
117 Ibid.
118 Ibid., para. 35.
119 Ibid., para. 53.

When applying this standard, the tribunal found no reason to second-guess the tribunal's interpretation of Article 1116 of NAFTA. Mexico once again tried to appeal the refusal to set aside the award but the Canadian Supreme Court denied leave of appeal.

This reading of the court's role in *Cargill v. Mexico* was subsequently brought before the Supreme Court of Justice Ontario, in another case. At issue before the court in *Canada v. Murphy Oil/Murphy* al[120] was whether or not certain guidelines issued by the Canada-Newfoundland Offshore Petroleum Board (the Board) fell within the scope of a reservation made by Canada when it signed the NAFTA. The three NAFTA states agreed to exclude certain already existing domestic measures from the scope of NAFTA Chapter 11. These measures were specifically enumerated in a separate Annex. One of the questions before the tribunal was whether the guidelines enacted by the Board – imposing fixed rates of spending on research, development, education and training on offshore projects – fell within the scope of one such reservation made by Canada.

The tribunal majority held that the guidelines were not covered by Canada's reservation, and that it therefore had jurisdiction to hear the investors' claims based on the alleged breach committed by the guidelines. Ultimately, the tribunal found that the guidelines violated NAFTA Article 1106, which prohibits state parties from imposing "performance requirements" on foreign investors protected by the treaty.

In its set-aside attempt, Canada argued that the tribunal went beyond its jurisdiction because the disputed measures were indeed excluded from its mandate by virtue of the Annex and that the tribunal had applied the wrong criteria to find that they were not. Canada had expressly included the legislative act under which the guidelines were issued as part of its reservation to NAFTA. The key question before the tribunal was therefore whether or not the guidelines were covered by the reference to that legislative act. The majority of the tribunal found that the guidelines "significantly alter the legal obligations" and thereby went beyond Canada's reservation,[121] whereas the dissenting arbitrator found the guidelines to be consistent with the legislative act and therefore covered by the reservation.[122]

The Superior Court of Justice referred to the *Cargill* set-aside, which was brought before the Ontario Court of Appeal in the same jurisdiction, in order

120 *Canada v. Mobil/Murphy Oil*, Superior Court of Justice Ontario.

121 *Mobil Investments Canada Inc. and Murphy Oil Corporation v. Canada*, ICSID Case No. ARB(AF)/07/4, Decision on Liability and on Principles on Quantum, 22 May 2012, para. 411.

122 *Mobil Investments Canada Inc. and Murphy Oil Corporation v. Canada,* ICSID Case No. ARB(AF)/07/4, Declaration by Professor Sands Q.C, 22 May 2012.

to determine the standard of review and quoted that court's summary of its role when the jurisdiction of a NAFTA tribunal is challenged, finding that the court's role was to:

> ...identify and narrowly define any true question of jurisdiction. Specifically, under Article 34(2)(a)(iii), [ICAA] did the tribunal decide an issue that was not part of the submission to arbitration, or misinterpret its authority under the NAFTA? Another way to define the proper approach is to ask the following three questions:
>
> What was the issue that the tribunal decided?
>
> Was that issue within the submission to arbitration made under Chapter 11 of the NAFTA?
>
> Is there anything in the NAFTA, properly interpreted, that precluded the tribunal from making the award it made?[123]

In a relatively short reasoned decision, the Superior Court of Justice denied Canada's application to set aside the award. The court found that the question was not one of jurisdiction and stated that

> Canada has failed to establish that there was anything in the NAFTA that precluded the Tribunal from making the Award it made. To be a reserved subordinate measure, the Guidelines had to fall within the language of paragraph 2(f)(ii) [of the Annex]. However, this wording was subject to interpretation. Casting this interpretive exercise as a jurisdictional issue goes far beyond the narrow view of what constitutes a question of jurisdiction, as required by Cargill.[124]

In essence, the court found that the tribunal had made a determination on the merits of the case and not a jurisdictional determination. Under those circumstances, Article 34(2)(a)(iii) of the Canadian International Commercial Arbitration Act had not been violated and the award could not be set aside.

In summary, it seems Canadian courts have approached the standard of review in different ways. The earlier cases seemingly allowed for relatively extensive review similar to that conducted in contractual arbitration. Whether framed as a test of "reasonableness" (as in the earlier *Metalclad* and SD *Myers* cases, as well as the lower court in Cargill) or "correctness" (as in *SD Myers*, for

123 *Canada v. Mobil/Murphy Oil*, Superior Court of Justice Ontario, para. 39, citing *Mexico v. Cargill*, Court of Appeal for Ontario, para 52.

124 *Canada v. Mobil/Murphy Oil*, Superior Court of Justice Ontario, para. 50.

mixed questions of law and facts) of the tribunal's decision, they have in common that the tribunal's jurisdiction is reviewed anew, at least to some degree, by the court seized with the challenge.

By contrast, the *Bayview* judgment expressly reject the notion that Canadian courts can review tribunals' jurisdictional determinations *de novo,* and instead established a "powerful presumption" that the tribunal acted within its jurisdiction. Furthermore, the decision by the higher court in *Cargill*, subsequently endorsed also in *Murphy Oil*, would seem to suggest that the task of the court is to identify whether the issue in question is truly one of jurisdiction (which was ultimately not the case in either of the two challenges), and if so to review the issue with deference to the tribunal's decision; in the view of the *Cargill* decision: to avoid a review of the merits.[125] This later line of cases stands out from the situation in most other domestic jurisdictions, where it is generally accepted that the reviewing court may review also the "merits" of a jurisdictional decision, as part of a completely new jurisdictional determination. One such jurisdiction is England.

3.2.2.3 England

In addition to the justiciability question discussed above, the first challenge of an investment arbitration award to be brought in London – Ecuador's challenge against the award in favour of American investor Occidental – also raised the question of the standard of review. After rejecting Occidental's claim that the challenge was not justiciable, the High Court turned to Ecuador's arguments that the tribunal had (i) exceeded their jurisdiction in violation of Article 67 of the Arbitration Act 1996 and (ii) that the excess of mandate also constituted a serious procedural irregularity in violation of Article 68 of the same act.[126] Before reviewing these intertwined arguments, which the investor had characterized as a "thinly disguised attempt to challenge the award on the merits,"[127] the High Court stated the following with respect to the scope of its review:

---

125 *Mexico v. Cargill*, Court of Appeal for Ontario, para. 53.

126 Section 68 reads in selected parts:

1. A party to arbitral proceedings may (upon notice to the other parties and to the tribunal) apply to the court challenging an award in the proceedings on the ground of serious irregularity affecting the tribunal, the proceedings or the award. [...]
2. Serious irregularity means an irregularity of one or more of the following kinds which the court considers has caused or will cause substantial injustice to the applicant [...]

(b) the tribunal exceeding its powers (otherwise than by exceeding its substantive jurisdiction: see section 67).

127 *Ecuador v. Occidental*, High Court, para. 6.

> It is now well-established that a challenge to the jurisdiction of an arbitration panel under section 67 proceeds by way of a re-hearing of the matters before the arbitrators. The test for the court is: was the Tribunal correct in its decision on jurisdiction? The test is not: was the Tribunal entitled to reach the decision that it did?[128]

When Ecuador ultimately appealed, the High Court's decision to uphold the award the standard of review, as articulated by the High Court, was not discussed on appeal.[129] The Supreme Court did, however, make a full review of the tribunal's jurisdictional decisions, suggesting that it accepted the *de novo* standard as formulated by the High Court. Furthermore, this test was subsequently accepted by both parties in a separate English case. The High Court faced with the challenge against the *EMV v. Czech Republic* award stated that both disputing arties in that case had agreed with the *Occidental* standard,[130] and applied it to make its own interpretation of the scope of the arbitration clause in the underlying treaty.[131]

3.2.2.4 France

In France, the Paris Court of Appeal has repeatedly expressed that French courts reviewing arbitral jurisdiction should do so considering all elements of law and fact to assess the scope of the arbitration agreement.[132] The court has made clear that this scope of review is the same regardless of whether the arbitrators' mandate is based on a contract or a treaty.[133]

In *Venezuela v. Gold Reserve,* the Court of Appeal developed this scope of review. The court stated that it reviews (*contrôle*) the tribunal's jurisdictional decision, by researching all the elements of law or fact to assess the scope of the arbitration agreement.[134] This clear enunciation of a *de novo* review of the tribunal's jurisdiction was later echoed by the same court, with very similar wording, in *Venezeula v. Rusoro.*[135]

The line between a jurisdictional challenge – reviewed *de novo* – and a challenge that involves the merits/liability of a tribunal's reasoning is not always

128 Ibid., para. 7.

129 *Ecuador v. Occidental,* Court of Appeal.

130 *Czech Republic v. EMV*, High Court of Justice, para. 13.

131 Discussed further below at 3.2.3.2.

132 *Moldova v. Energoalians,* Paris Court of Appeal, p. 5; *Venezuela v. Garcia Armas and Gracia Gruber*, Paris Court of Appeal, p. 5; Schooner Capital et al v. Poland, p. 5.

133 Ibid.

134 *Venezuela v. Gold Reserve*, p. 3.

135 *Venezuela v. Rusoro*, p. 4

easy to distinguish. This was illustrated in the challenge against *Kaliningrad v. Lithuania*, which was arbitrated under the ICC Rules. The award has not been published. However, the underlying issues have been reported[136], and can to a certain degree be deduced by the challenge before the Paris Court of Appeal.

The property rights to a building owned by the Kaliningrad regional government in Vilnius had been frozen by Lithuanian courts in order to enforce an LCIA award against Kaliningrad. After failing to challenge the freeze in Lithuanian courts, Kaliningrad instead turned to investment treaty arbitration and argued that Lithuania had breached the Russia – Lithuania BIT by expropriating the building. The tribunal, however, found that it did not have jurisdiction to hear the claims.[137]

The arbitration involved several issues of relevance for general public international law. First, was the government of Kaliningrad, a Russian territory located between Lithuania and Poland, an investor in the meaning of the BIT? The tribunal found that it was, despite its semi-sovereign status. Secondly, can a national court decision made in accordance with the New York Convention, constitute an expropriation under the BIT? The tribunal found that it could not. Seemingly applying the VCLT to interpret whether Russia and Lithuania had intended for the BIT to modify the obligations both states have under the New York Convention, the tribunal held that it lacked jurisdiction to review rulings of domestic courts on questions of enforcement and recognition of foreign arbitral awards pursuant to the New York Convention.

Kaliningrad challenged the jurisdictional award at the seat of arbitration. The Paris Court of Appeals seemed to agree with the tribunal and stated that, with respect to the relationship between the BIT and the New York Convention:

> The BIT cannot be interpreted as including state responsibility when a state party simply complies with its obligations arising from the New York Convention, without that resulting, in the meaning of the Vienna Convention, in an incompatibility with the effective realization of the object and purpose of the New York Convention as a whole.[138]

Although short, one could argue that the French court's analysis did not concern the tribunal's *jurisdiction* – which it was asked to do – but rather the

---

136 IAReporter, *Lithuania Prevails in Investor-State BIT Claim over Enforcement of ICC Award in Case Brought by Russian Regional Govt*, http://www.iareporter.com/articles/lithuania-prevails-in-investor-state-bit-claim-over-enforcement-of-icc-award-in-case-brought-by-russian-regional-govt/, 17 March, 2009.

137 *Kaliningrad Region v. Lithuania*, Paris Court of Appeal, p. 6.

138 Ibid.

substantive claims brought by the investor. Under this view, the extent to which the respondent state's measures entail "state responsibility" is a matter for the merits of the case and, as such, not something for the court to review.[139]

Nevertheless, the award challenged by Kaliningrad was a jurisdictional award, which did not purport to determine any substantive aspects of Kaliningrad's claims. As such, the court was asked to review whether the tribunal's jurisdictional decision was in violation of French law; a task that by necessity involves at least a certain amount of analysis of the tribunal's reasoning.

3.2.2.5 The Netherlands

In the Netherlands, the standard of review has expressly been an issue in a number of separate court proceedings. The challenge against the still unpublished *Adria v. Croatia* award[140] was heard by the Hague District Court, which ultimately declined to set aside the award.[141] The investor, which lost the arbitration, did *not* argue before the court that the tribunal went beyond the scope of its mandate, but rather relied on an argument that the tribunal had failed to hear both parties, which would have been contrary to Dutch public policy according to Article 1065(1)(e) of Book Four of the Code on Civil Procedure (Burgerlijke Rechtsvordering - Boek vier, "RV"). The court initially stated that under Dutch law, the court should exercise restraint in reviewing arbitral awards, relying on domestic case law from challenges of commercial arbitrations.[142] The court further stated, however, that it will make a "full judicial review" when the challenge is based – as in this case – on an alleged breach of public policy.[143]

In *India v. CC Devas*, the state challenged an award on jurisdiction and merits,[144] arguing on three grounds that the tribunal had gone beyond its jurisdiction. In expressing its standard of review, the Hague District Court drew a distinction between the task before it and an appeal, stating that it should exercise restraint in assessing annulment requests, so as to ensure the effective functioning of arbitral proceedings.[145] However, the court also noted that the

139 Furthermore, it is not clear what the court meant with "state responsibility" (in the French original: *la responsabilite d 'un des Etats parties*).

140 *Adria Beteiligungs GmbH v. The Republic of Croatia*, UNCITRAL, Award, 21 June, 2010.

141 *Adria v. Croatia*, The Hague District Court.

142 Ibid., 4.2–4.4.

143 Ibid., 4.5.

144 The arbitration is still pending at the time of writing, with an award on quantum to be expected.

145 *India v. CC Devas*, 4.1.

final determination of existence of arbitration agreement lies with the court, not with the tribunal,[146] and moved on to review the tribunal's jurisdiction.

The narrow standard of review in Dutch courts was also expressed by the same District Court in the *Ecuador v. Chevron* challenge, which involved a question of the tribunal's jurisdiction.[147] The court, similar to the judgments in *Adria* and *CC Devas*, stated that as a general matter, the court "must exercise restraint" when reviewing arbitral awards.[148] The more precise type of review, however, "depends on the ground for setting aside that is being relied upon."[149] When the validity of the underlying arbitration agreement is being challenged, the court stated that it had to "fully review" the question, in order to protect the basic right to access to justice, as an arbitration agreement prevents parties from going to court.

Ecuador had argued that Chevron's investment ended almost five years before the entry into force of the US – Ecuador BIT, and that the company's only interests in Ecuador after that time were pending lawsuits.[150] In the state's view, therefore, there was no "activity associated with an investment" as required by Article I(1)(a)(iii) of the BIT and consequently no jurisdiction *ratione materiae* for the tribunal.

Chevron responded, *inter alia*, that the pending lawsuits constituted investments and that the company also had remaining activities in repairing environmental damages affected by their investments, as required by Ecuador.[151] In essence, Chevron claimed that the Article I definition should be interpreted to cover the whole "life cycle" of an investment, whereas Ecuador argued that only the operational phase of the investment should be protected.[152]

The District Court made an independent review of Ecuador's claim that the tribunal went beyond the agreement because there was no "investment" in the meaning of the BIT. It found that there was evidence of a valid arbitration agreement and declined to set aside the award on this ground.[153]

146 Ibid., 4.11.

147 *Ecuador v. Chevron*, Hague District Court. This is but one of many cases, in multiple fora, stemming from the same dispute between the parties.

148 Ibid., para. 4.4.

149 Ibid.

150 *Chevron Corporation and Texaco Petroleum Corporation v. The Republic of Ecuador*, UNCITRAL, PCA Case No. 34877, Partial Award on the Merits, 30 March 2010, paras. 15–16.

151 Ibid., paras. 34–57.

152 Ibid., paras. 18–19.

153 Ecuador v. Chevron, Hague District Court, para 4.13 (see 5.2.3.2 for further discussion).

The District Court decision was subsequently appealed to the Dutch Supreme Court.[154] At this stage Ecuador only argued a lack of arbitration agreement (i.e. that the tribunal did not have jurisdiction over the dispute). Furthermore, a new issue was introduced on appeal: which standard of review should the Supreme Court apply when reviewing the lower court's decision on the jurisdictional issue?

Initially, the Supreme Court reaffirmed that courts generally have the authority to fully review the jurisdiction of the tribunal; it made no distinction between arbitrations where the consent is located in a contract and those where the consent is located in a treaty, or between cases where the court is asked to determine a tribunal's jurisdiction during an ongoing arbitration and those where the question is brought to its attention as part of a challenge against the (final) award.[155]

Pursuant to Article 79(b) of the Dutch Judiciary Organisation Act (Wet op de Rechterlijke Organisatie, "RO"), however, the Dutch Supreme Court may not review matters involving "law of foreign states." Chevron had objected that the US – Ecuador BIT was covered by this provision, which would prevent the Supreme Court from examining the correctness of the lower court's decision. In ruling on this objection, the court stated that the legislative history accompanying this particular provision of the RO did not foresee this specific situation, when the alleged "law of foreign states" is a bilateral treaty concluded between two states, neither of which is the Netherlands.[156]

In ultimately finding that the BIT was indeed covered by the phrase – and thereby excluded from the Supreme Court's mandate – the court emphasized that the parliament had restricted the Supreme Court's ability to "decide with the same power on rules of foreign law as it does in relation to decisions on Dutch law."[157] Since the treaty constitutes public international law, and thus does not apply in the Dutch legal order, the Supreme Court denied to review, as a matter of law, the lower court's ruling on the BIT.[158]

After establishing this restriction, the Supreme Court still went on to review the aspects of the District Court's decision that involved the application of the VCLT, which apparently the Supreme Court did not consider to be "law of foreign states." Ecuador had in its appeal complained that the District Court's interpretation of the definition of investment was circular, a characterization

154 Ecuador v. Chevron, Supreme Court of the Netherlands.
155 Ibid., para. 4.2.
156 Ibid., 4.4.2.
157 Ibid., 4.4.2.
158 Ibid., 4.4.3.

which the Supreme Court did not agree with. Instead, the Supreme Court emphasized, the lower court had simply interpreted the treaty in accordance with the VCLT, as was its task.

When looking at the definition of investment, the Supreme Court recognized the problems in interpreting a term which is defined by using the same term: Article 1 of the BIT states that the term investment "Means every kind of investment in the territory of one Party (…); and includes (…) (iii) a claim (…) associated with an investment." The District Court had interpreted this definition with the aid of VCLT Article 31(4), taking into consideration the special meaning the parties gave to the term. The choice to define the term as 'every kind of investment', and to include a list of wide examples, suggested that the treaty parties, with respect to the second use of the term investment in the list of examples, "gave a broad meaning to the term, deviating from normal spoken language."[159]

The two uses of the term "investment," in the District Court's view, did not have identical meanings. In explaining this interpretation, the District Court had explained that giving the terms different meaning would render the definition meaningful whereas, by contrast, giving the terms the exact same meaning every time it appears in the treaty would render the definition circular and meaningless.

The Supreme Court expressly approved of the Court of Appeal's use of the VCLT. Quoting two ICJ decisions[160] the Court stated that "the interpretation of a treaty-definition on the basis of arts. 31 and 32 [VCLT] needs to be interpreted in principle as a definition that makes sense, and not in a manner that the definition is meaningless."[161]

Ecuador had also challenged the District Court's interpretation of Article XII, which states that the BIT applies to investments existing at the time of entry into force of the BIT, and to investments made or acquired thereafter. The Supreme Court once again pointed out that it was prevented from second-guessing the lower court's interpretation on appeal. It stated, however, that the District Court's judgment in this respect was consistent with its earlier reasoning on the circularity of the term "investment": the court had found that the parties had given "a broad and special interpretation to the term."[162] Part of this interpretation was the finding that the BIT had "instant effect," which

159 *Ecuador v. Chevron,* Hague District Court, para. 5.2.

160 *Georgia v. Russian Federation,* International Court of Justice, Preliminary Objections, Judgment, 1 April 2011, I.C.J. Reports 2011, p. 70; *Costa Rica v. Nicaragua,* International Court of Justice, Judgment, 13 July 2009 I.C.J. Reports 2009.

161 *Ecuador v. Chevron,* Supreme Court of the Netherlands, para. 5.5.2.

162 Ibid., para 5.7.4.

meant that Chevron's claims – which were pending at the time that the BIT entered into force – were covered by the definition. This interpretation would also be consistent with the text of the treaty's preamble, which states that the parties intend to stimulate "the flow of private capital and the economic development [of the parties]."

Ultimately, the Supreme Court did not find any reason to question the Court of Appeal's wide reading of the term "investment" and therefore did not allow the appeal to succeed.

3.2.2.6 Singapore

The award in *Sanum v. Laos*[163] was challenged by Laos at the seat of arbitration, in Singapore. It was initially set aside by the Singapore High Court, but that decision was ultimately reversed on appeal by Court of Appeals of Singapore.

In the proceedings, one of two key issues with respect to the tribunal's jurisdiction was the territorial scope of the China – Laos BIT. The tribunal had found that the treaty extended to Macao, where the investment was made. Subsequent to the award, however, the two state parties exchanged diplomatic letters stating that they did not intend for the treaty to encompass Macao, which similar to Hong Kong has the status of a special administrative region.

When the award was challenged by Laos, the lower court was faced with two jurisdictional questions: (i) did the BIT extend territorially to Macau (where the investment was made) and (ii) did the investor's expropriation claim fall within the BIT's arbitration clause, which required the claim to concern a "*dispute involving the amount of compensation for expropriation.*"

Before addressing these two questions, however, the Singapore High Court addressed two preliminary questions. In addition to its embrace of the *Occidental* judgment discussed above at 3.2.2.4, the court was also faced with the parties' disagreement over the applicable standard of review. It found that the *de novo* review generally recognized in Singaporean law – entailing a "fresh examination" of the award – was applicable also when the tribunal's jurisdiction is based on a treaty, finding that there was no basis for making a distinction between treaty-based cases and contractual cases in this respect.[164]

Unlike the arbitral tribunal, the Singapore High Court then answered the first jurisdictional question in the negative, with a line of reasoning that was made possible by the *de novo* standard. An important factor in this decision was that it relied on the diplomatic correspondence between the state parties

---

163 *Sanum Investments Limited v. Lao People's Democratic Republic,* UNCITRAL, PCA Case No. 2013-13, Award on Jurisdiction, 13 December 2013.

164 Sanum, Singapore High Court Decision, paras. 32–33.

(which had not been available to the tribunal). The court accepted the letters, even though the investor doubted their authenticity and also questioned the timing of the correspondence, arguing that Laos could have obtained the confirmation from its Chinese counterpart much earlier, during the arbitration.

The Singaporean International Arbitration ACT (IAA), based on the Model Law, does not expressly regulate the admittance of new evidence at the challenge stage. However, general procedural law allows the admittance of new evidence in the Court of Appeal if there are "special circumstances." The High Court distinguished such cases from the one before it, which was not an appeal but rather a challenge of an arbitral award under the IAA, but nevertheless applied a slightly modified version of the test for "special circumstances" under domestic procedural law by analogy. The test is based on three conditions:

– has the party seeking to admit the evidence demonstrated sufficiently strong reasons why the evidence was not adduced at the arbitration hearing;
– would the evidence, if admitted, probably have an important influence on the result of the case though it need not be decisive; and
– is the evidence apparently credible, though it need not be incontrovertible.

The modified condition (a) was applied by the court in a "slightly less stringent" manner,[165] but the two other criteria were applied unmodified. On this test, the court found the letters to be admissible in the challenge proceedings and moved on to find that, based on the state parties' demonstrated intention, the treaty did not extend to Macau.[166] Here it should be noted that by contrast, the Swiss Federal Tribunal hearing the challenge of the *Recife v. Vietnam* award found that, as a general rule, Swiss courts are bound by the facts as established before the arbitral tribunal.[167]

The lower court's decision was subsequently reversed on appeal by the Singapore Court of Appeal,[168] the court of final instance in challenges against international arbitration awards. With respect to the standard of review, however, the appeals court confirmed the High Court's finding and developed its view on what *"de novo* hearing" entails in this context. It cited a legal dictionary's definition of term, which included the phrase "giving no deference to a lower court's finding" and ultimately held that:

> In our judgment, the court should consider the matter afresh. In doing this, it will of course consider what the Tribunal has said because this

165 Ibid., para. 44.
166 Ibid., para. 111.
167 *RECOFI v. Vietnam*, Swiss Federal Tribunal, para. 3.1.2.
168 *Sanum*, Singapore Court of Appeal Decision.

> might well be persuasive. But beyond this, the court is not bound to accept or take into account the arbitral tribunal's findings on the matter.[169]

This express endorsement of a *de novo* review was later cited by the High Court of Singapore in the *Lesotho v. Swissbourgh et al* challenge. The court stated that it was "settled law and undisputed" that it must apply a *de novo* standard in assessing the state's jurisdictional objections against the award, citing the above paragraph from *Sanum,* where the Singapore Court of Appeal said that it was not bound to accept or take into account the tribunal's jurisdictional findings.[170]

3.2.2.7 Sweden

The Svea Court of Appeal in Stockholm has reaffirmed a strict standard of review in treaty-based challenges generally,[171] but when it comes to the jurisdiction of the tribunal, it is clear that Swedish courts try the matter anew, based also on new evidence and circumstances relied upon by the parties.[172] Generally, Swedish courts have seemingly assumed a *de novo* standard of review, and gone on to fully review jurisdictional issues, as will be discussed in the following sections.

3.2.2.8 Switzerland

Swiss courts have demonstrated a reluctance to inquire into arbitral tribunal's decisions, including their jurisdictional determinations. For example, in *Recife v. Vietnam* an UNCITRAL tribunal had rejected the investor's claims on jurisdictional grounds. As recounted by the court,[173] the tribunal, which following Vietnam's jurisdictional objections had bifurcated the proceedings, found that the sales contracts relied upon by Recife for the jurisdiction *ratione materiae* did not meet the treaty's definition of an investment. The tribunal therefore dismissed the case for lack of jurisdiction. The question – *viz.* the extent to which commercial sales contracts constitute investments – is familiar in arbitral jurisprudence.[174] The parties had therefore furnished evidence to support their respective interpretations of the definition in the particular BIT between France and Vietnam, including awards rendered by other investment

169 Ibid. para. 41.

170 *Lesotho v. Swissbourgh et al,* para. 87.

171 *Czech Republic v. CME*, Svea Court of Appeal, p. 85.

172 *Cem Uzan v. Turkey,* Svea Court of Appeal, p. 22.

173 *Recofi v. Vietnam*, Swiss Federal Tribunal. The award remains unpublished.

174 The Paris Court of Appeal has twice been faced with this very question, in *Moldova v. Energoalians* and *Czech Republic v. Pren Nreka,* see discussion below at 3.3.2.2

tribunals. Furthermore, the investor also submitted reports from the French parliament, stemming from the treaty's ratification process in France, which according to the investor showed that the parties had intended the definition of investment to be wide, for example by including "bonds, claims and rights to any performance having economic value" in its list of examples of what constitutes an investment. According to the French investor, therefore, Article 31(4) VCLT should have led the tribunal to find that the parties had intended for sales contracts to be covered by the definition of investment.

In determining whether the tribunal had violated Article 190(b) PILA when it denied jurisdiction, the court emphasized that it could not act as an appeals court although it could still "freely review the matter."[175] When looking at a tribunal's jurisdictional determination, however, it stated that it could "rectify or supplement the findings of the arbitrators," but that it has to act "on the basis of the facts found in the contested award."[176] It is unclear to what extent these statements also encompass the tribunal's findings on legal points, or if they are restricted to factual findings. This general approach was later echoed by the same court in the challenge against the *EDF v. Hungary* award.[177] Furthermore, the court stated that the three arbitrators were well-known experts appointed by the parties and that the court therefore would not "depart unnecessarily from the unanimous opinion issued by specialists on the question of the indefinite legal concept of investment."[178]

The Swiss Supreme Court's reluctance to review the *Recife* tribunal's jurisdictional decision is reflected also in the first challenge of an investment treaty award to be put before the court. In *Saar Papier v. Poland*, the investor had initiated an arbitration under the Germany – Poland BIT, and ultimately received an award of 2,3 million Deutsch Marks.[179] Saar Papier thereafter initiated a second arbitration in 1996, claiming that the 1995 award had only been a partial award and that the company was entitled to further damages. In 2000 the second tribunal, constituted under the same BIT and legally seated in Zürich, rendered an "interim award" finding that it had jurisdiction over the new claims. It also ruled on the merits of Saar Papier's second claim and found the state to be liable under the BIT's expropriation provision, but reserved the quantification of the damages to a later stage of the arbitration.

175 *Recofi v. Vietnam*, Swiss Federal Tribunal, para. 3.1.1.
176 Ibid., para. 3.1.2.
177 *Hungary v. EDF*, Swiss Federal Tribunal, para. 3.1.
178 Ibid., 3.4.1.
179 This appears to be the first known non-ICSID award based on an investment treaty.

Poland challenged the 2000 award before the Swiss Supreme Court and argued, among other things, that the interim decision covered matters that had already been settled in the 1995 award and, as a consequence, that the second tribunal went beyond its jurisdiction in violation of Article 190(2)(b) PILA.

The court did not agree with Poland's contention. Instead, it found that the question of whether or not the claims were covered by *res judicata* was one concerning the claims' admissibility and not the jurisdiction of the tribunal.[180] Therefore the court declined to review the tribunal's finding in this respect.[181]

Poland also challenged the tribunal majority's reading of the arbitration clause in the 1989 Germany – Poland BIT.[182] The treaty, similar to many others concluded by states in the Eastern bloc, restricts investors' access to arbitration. Article 11 allows for arbitration over disputes "under paragraph 2 of Article 4 or under Article 5" of the treaty. Saar Papier had alleged that Poland expropriated its investment contrary to Article 4, which mentions measures "tantamount to expropriation or nationalization in the territory of the other Contracting Party except for the public benefit and against compensation." Poland claimed no such measure existed and thus that there was no jurisdiction for the tribunal under Article 11. The state also argued that the court, within its power to review the tribunal's jurisdiction, had the mandate to examine the merits of the case, i.e. whether or not a measure tantamount to expropriation had taken place.[183]

The court, however, took a more restrictive view as to the scope of its jurisdictional review. It stated that although it could examine challenges to a tribunal's jurisdiction freely, including the correctness of the tribunal's determination, "this principle does not apply without limits."[184] The court stated that, under Art. 190 (2) (b) PILA, the court was not mandated to act as an appellate body, but that it is "generally bound by the findings of the arbitral tribunal and examines these findings only insofar as the objections concern the violation of procedural guarantees (…) or *ordre public.*"[185] The court therefore declined to review the findings of the tribunal with respect to the merits of the case.

Following the court's refusal to set aside the interim decision, a final award on quantum was rendered, holding that Saar Papier was not entitled to any

180 *Poland v. Saar Papier*, Swiss Federal Tribunal, 3(b).
181 Ibid., 3(b)
182 The third arbitrator, Poland's nominee, dissented.
183 *Poland v. Saar Papier*, Swiss Federal Tribunal, 4(a).
184 Ibid., 4(b).
185 Ibid.

damages. Saar Papier challenged the final award before the same court but this challenge did not raise the question of the court's standard of review.[186]

In more recent challenge practice, the Swiss Federal Tribunal had reason to discuss the scope of its review. In *Russia v. PJSC Ukrnafta* and *Russia v. Stabil LLC*,[187] two identical tribunals had found, in two separate awards resulting from a coordinated management of two cases, that they had jurisdiction over claims brought by two Ukrainian claimants against the Russian Federation. Russia challenged the separate awards before the Swiss Federal Tribunal, which rendered two identical judgments in dealing with the challenge.

The two claimants were owners of several Crimean petrol stations. They argued in the underlying UNCITRAL arbitrations that Russia's nationalisation of their network of petrol stations and other associated assets after the annexation of Crimea in 2014 violated the Ukraine – Russia BIT.

As an initial matter, the Swiss Federal Tribunal outlined the scope of its review of the awards under PILA. According to the court, an award on jurisdiction is a "preliminary award" in the sense of PILA article 190(1)(3),[188] and can therefore only be set aside under specific circumstances (in particular, when the arbitral tribunal wrongly accepted jurisdiction over the dispute).[189]

The court added that it could only consider arguments advanced by the challenging party, and that it could not review any factual determinations made by the arbitral tribunal. In particular, the court reasoned that it could not consider any factual arguments that had not previously been submitted to the arbitral tribunal.[190]

As a consequence, the Swiss court considered that two factual arguments submitted by the Russia which had *not* been raised in the arbitration proceedings were outside the scope of its analysis: (i) Russia's argument that Russia and Ukraine agreed that the BIT was not applicable to Crimea or to the city of Sevastopol and (ii) Russia's argument that Ukraine had no intention to offer protection under the BIT to Russian investors originating from Crimea.[191] By contrast, the court proceeded to review Russia's other arguments – relating to, *inter alia*, the territorial scope of the BIT, and the definitions of "investment" and "investor" in the BIT, ultimately rejecting the jurisdictional challenges.

---

186 *Saar Papier v. Poland*, Swiss Federal Tribunal.

187 *Russia v. PJSC Ukrnafta* and *Russia v. Stabil LLC*, Swiss Federal Tribunal 2018.

188 Article 190(1)(3) of PILA states that "Preliminary awards can be annulled on the grounds of the above paras. 2(a) and 2(b) only."

189 Article 190(1)(2)(b) of PILA states that an arbitral award may be annulled "if the arbitral tribunal wrongly accepted or declined jurisdiction."

190 *Russia v. PJSC Ukrnafta* and *Russia v. Stabil LLC*, Swiss Federal Tribunal, pp. 23–27.

191 Ibid., p. 29.

The notion that Swiss court only review jurisdiction on the same basis as the tribunal – i.e. without new facts being introduced at the challenge stage – was reaffirmed in *India v. Deutsche Telekom.* Here, the Swiss Federal Tribunal stated that it cannot "rectify or supplement ex officio the findings of the arbitrators, even if the facts have been established in a manifestly inaccurate manner or in violation of the law. [...] Furthermore, [the court's] mandate, in case of a civil matter appeal against an international arbitral award, does not consist of deciding with full power of review, like an appellate court, but only to examine whether the admissible complaints made against the said award are founded or not."[192]

3.2.2.9 United States

In the United States, in *Thunderbird v. Mexico*, a NAFTA tribunal seated in Washington DC dismissed the investor's case because it did not find that the investor had met its burden to demonstrate a *prima facie* case on the merits.[193] In reviewing Thunderbird's challenge to the award, the District Court for the District of Columbia initially stated that US courts "have long recognized that judicial review of an arbitration award is extremely limited,"[194] citing domestic court decisions to the effect that "a court may vacate an award only if there is a showing that one of the limited circumstances enumerated in the Federal Arbitration Act is present, or if the arbitrator acted in manifest disregard of the law."[195]

In its challenge, Thunderbird argued that the NAFTA tribunal had manifestly disregarded the law by stating a standard for burden of proof, which it then did not apply. The tribunal had expressed the view on the burden of proof in international law, that "the party alleging a violation of international law giving rise to international responsibility has the burden of proving its assertion. If said Party adduces evidence that prima facie supports its allegation, the burden of proof may be shifted to the other Party, if the circumstances so justify."[196]

In Thunderbird's view, it had met its burden to show a *prima facie* case and therefore, if the tribunal were to be true to what it stated, it should have

---

192 *India v. Deutsche Telekom,* p. 22.

193 *International Thunderbird Gaming Operations v. United Mexican States,* United States District Court for the District of Columbia, Civil Action 06-00748 (HHK), Judgement 14 February, 2007.

194 Ibid., p. 3.

195 Ibid.

196 *International Thunderbird Gaming Corporation v. The United Mexican States,* UNCITRAL, Arbitral Award, 26 January 2006, para 95.

required Mexico to rebut the presumption established by Thunderbird's *prima facie* case.

The court pointed out that this argument rested entirely on the assumption that Thunderbird had in fact showed a *prima facie* case, which it seemed that the tribunal did not consider that Thunderbird had done.[197] It stated that, for the court to set aside the award on the grounds claimed by the investor

> it would have to be plainly manifest that the tribunal both (1) determined that Thunderbird had met its prima facie burden and (2) refused to require Mexico to overcome the resulting presumption of a violation of international law. Otherwise, this court would be asked to improperly assess the factual question of whether that prima facie burden had been met in the first instance.[198]

Although this statement demonstrates considerable deference towards the tribunal's findings, it should be pointed out that the question was not one of jurisdiction, but rather one of alleged procedural error in determining the merits of the case. Similarly, the same court in a challenge brought by Argentina against an award rendered in favour of AWG,[199] found that the same strict standard applied to commercial arbitration awards should apply also in treaty-based cases. When applying this standard, the court found that Argentina "simply cannot overcome this high hurdle requiring deference to the Tribunal's determinations."[200] The court also stated that review of arbitral awards under the FAA must be "extremely limited,"[201] and added, aided by a quote from the Supreme Court judgment in *BG Group*, discussed below, that the fact that the document containing the arbitration agreement is a treaty and not a contract does not make a critical difference.[202]

Both *Thunderbird* and *AWG* concerned alleged tribunal errors when determining the merits of the case. In fact, it seems that the standard of review for jurisdictional challenges has not been expressly put before US courts in the investment treaty arbitration context. A related issue was discussed by the US

---

197 *International Thunderbird Gaming Operations v. United Mexican States*, United States District Court for the District of Columbia, Civil Action 06-00748 (HHK), Judgement 14 February, 2007, p. 5.

198 Ibid., p. 6.

199 *Argentina v. AWG Group Ltd.*, United States District Court for the District of Columbia, Civil Action No. 15-1057 (BAH), Judgement, 30 September, 2016.

200 Ibid., p. 32.

201 Ibid., p. 10.

202 Ibid., p. 11.

Supreme Court in the BG *Group* challenge, which is analysed more extensively below at 3.2.3.3. In that case, the majority of the court found that a local litigation requirement in the underlying BIT was a question of admissibility and not of jurisdiction. As such, the court stated,

> [...] the interpretation and application of the local litigation provision is primarily for the arbitrators. Reviewing courts cannot review their decision de novo. Rather, they must do so with considerable deference.[203]

Since none of the three cited US court cases expressly concerned the standard of review for jurisdictional challenges, it is not clear if the generally deferential standard employed by US courts under the FAA applies unmodified when the matters before the court concerns the jurisdiction of the tribunal. The cited paragraph from *BG Group* would seem to confirm, *e contrario*, that questions of jurisdiction are reviewable *de novo* under US law: since the local litigation requirement was found to be one of admissibility, the court could not review it. If the requirement instead had been found to be one of jurisdiction, the statement would seem to suggest, the court would have made such a *de novo* review of whether the local litigation requirement had in fact been complied with. Given the approach adopted by the *BG Group* majority – subsequently cited by the DC District Court in *AWG* – that treaty-based cases generally are not different from contract-based cases, this would seem a reasonable approach. It would similarly be the logic consequence of the dissenting opinion in *BG Group*, which argued that the nature of the local litigation requirement affected the tribunal's jurisdiction and as such could be reviewed by the court.[204]

3.2.2.10 Reviewing "Negative" Jurisdictional Decisions

Two court decisions stand out from the others, because they both concern an arbitral tribunal's decision not to accept jurisdiction. In these cases, the tribunal's determination was challenged by the party wishing for the arbitration to proceed, rather than by the party wishing to see the award set aside.

These decisions raise specific issues of standard of review: to what extent will a court review a tribunal's decision to *not* accept jurisdiction?

The first decision was rendered by Svea Court of Appeal in the challenge against the award in *Cem Uzan v. Turkey*.[205] The arbitral tribunal had found that Mr. Uzan was not a protected investor under the ECT, because he was

203 Ibid., p. 3.
204 Discussed further below at 3.2.3.3.
205 *Cem Uzan v. Turkey*, Svea Court of Appeal.

not an "Investor of another Contracting Party," as required by the arbitration clause in Article 26. Mr. Uzan then moved to challenge the tribunal's rejection of jurisdiction. Under Swedish arbitration law, a challenge against a tribunal's decision to reject jurisdiction is different from a challenge against the tribunal having gone beyond its jurisdiction. The latter scenario – which has been the ground relied upon in every other Swedish challenge proceeding discussed in this text – is governed by Section 34 of the SAA. By contrast, Section 36 of the SAA governs situations where "the arbitrators concluded the proceedings without ruling on the issues submitted to them for resolution [...]." In the case of an application under Section 36, the reviewing court will try the issue anew, which includes allowing new evidence to be introduced by the parties,[206] whereas the standard of review for Section 34, as discussed above, is not as unambiguously clear, although Swedish courts have generally reviewed the issue anew also under that provision.

In its review of Mr. Uzan's status as investor under the ECT, the court discussed both Article 1(7), which defines "investor," and Article 26, which contains the arbitration of the ECT, expressly with the aid of the Vienna Principles, which both parties had agreed would apply.[207] Mr. Uzan had argued that as soon as an investor meets the criteria for being an investor in one state, he is protected regardless of whether that investor is also a citizen of the respondent state. Turkey, on the other hand, claimed that a citizen of a contracting party can never be regarded as an investor from another state. In the court's view, the neutral wording of Article 1(7) encompassed both these competing interpretations.[208] When read together with Article 26, however, the court found that the contracting parties had not agreed to arbitration initiated by their own citizens who are permanently residing in another state.[209] In coming to this conclusion, the court looked at the systemic structure of the ECT, as well as the purpose behind the treaty (as supported by two legal expert opinions submitted to the court).

---

206 Ibid., p. 22 with further references. See also Swedish Supreme Court, NJA 2015, p. 991, Judgement, 21 December, 2015, in which the court stated that "the review under Section 36 SAA has sometimes been described as an appeal of a tribunal's decision to dismiss a case, and may involve a review of both the procedural main question and the tribunal's handling of that question. When acting under Section 36, the court may thus conduct a substantive review of the issue whether there is any procedural impediment to the arbitration," para. 12.

207 Ibid., p. 5.

208 Ibid., p 25.

209 Ibid., p. 27.

Therefore, although making an independent determination from that of the tribunal, the Svea Court of Appeal came to same conclusion as the arbitral tribunal and found that the ECT did not provide Mr. Uzan the right to initiate arbitration against Turkey. As put by the court, "the arbitral tribunal's conclusion that it lacked jurisdiction to determine such a dispute was correct."[210]

The other court to have been faced with a challenge against a tribunal's "negative" jurisdictional decision is the UK High Court of Justice. As mentioned in the introduction to this book, the tribunal in the SCC Case *Griffin v. Poland* had only accepted jurisdiction over one of the claims brought by investor, finding that the arbitration clause in the Poland – BLEU BIT did not cover the other claims.

In its submission under Section 67 of the English Arbitration Act, the investor claimed that the tribunal had erroneously rejected jurisdiction over some of its claims, a plea that resonated with the English court.

As for the standard of review, the court stated

> Suffice it to say at this point that I am satisfied that it is well established that the hearing is in the nature of a rehearing, and to the extent that Griffin advances any particular arguments not argued before the Tribunal, or adduces any new evidence, I am satisfied that Griffin may do so, and to the extent that permission is required to do so, I am satisfied that this is an appropriate case for permission to be granted, the Respondent not having adduced any evidence of prejudice in dealing with the same, and indeed having itself addressed such matters at length in its submission and evidence.[211]

After conducting such a "rehearing," the court ultimately interpreted the scope of Poland's consent to arbitration in a broader way than had the tribunal. The court therefore set aside the portions of the award in which the tribunal had rejected most of Griffin's claims, ordering instead that the tribunal's decision in this part be "substituted" with the court's declaration that the tribunal *has* jurisdiction also over claims based on indirect expropriation and breach of the fair and equitable treatment standard.[212] The court added a paragraph to the "substituted" text, to the effect that "The Tribunal will take the necessary steps for the continuation of the proceedings towards the liability phase dealing

210 Ibid., p. 29.

211 *Griffin v. Poland*, High Court, para. 7.

212 Ibid., para. 144.

with the measures identified [...]."[213] The consequence of the court's decision was therefore that the tribunal was ordered to assume jurisdiction over claims that the tribunal itself had found were not covered by its jurisdiction, as defined by the BIT.

These two court cases share similar traits. Most notably, they both contain express statements about the standard of review, making it clear that the courts review the tribunal's jurisdiction anew, including based on a different case file than that available to the respective tribunals, because of the way the parties pleaded their court cases.[214] Although both Sweden and England/Wales are generally jurisdictions where a significant degree of *de novo* review can be expected, these two cases contain clear language to that effect. In the case of Sweden, this is explained by the fact that a measure against a negative jurisdictional decision is governed by a different legislative provision than a measure against other alleged jurisdictional errors.

Presumably, the purpose of an action against a negative jurisdictional decision is to allow the arbitration to proceed and, in cases such as *Cem Uzan* where the tribunal has rejected the entire case due to lack of jurisdiction, to remove the *res judicata* effect of the tribunal's decision. As demonstrated by the *Griffin* case, if successful the case might be remanded back to the tribunal, even when the tribunal has already dismissed (part of) the investor's claim for lack of jurisdiction. In some regards, a challenge against a tribunal's rejection of jurisdiction might be less "interfering," in the sense that a tribunal decision not to accept a case does not rule out other remedies. For example, in the context of commercial arbitration, the Swedish Supreme Court has stated that parties may agree to exclude review of negative jurisdictional decisions under Swedish law, since the consequence of such a waiver is that there is still a competent court available to hear a case that has been rejected by a tribunal.[215] However, this is generally not the case in investment treaty arbitration, where domestic courts are typically not as easily available in the event that a treaty-based tribunal rejects jurisdiction. Thus, in treaty arbitration, the interest of having access to court review is as strong in cases where the tribunal has allegedly erroneously rejected jurisdiction, as it is in cases where the tribunal has assumed jurisdiction that it allegedly should not have exercised.

---

213 Ibid.

214 *Cem Uzan v. Turkey*, Svea Court of Appeal, p. 29; *Griffin v. Poland,* High Court, para. 7.

215 Swedish Supreme Court, 21 December 2015, NJA 2005, p. 991, paras. 17–19. The court also emphasized that under Swedish law, if the parties waive the right to use Section 36 of the SAA, Section 34, i.e. the more common set-aside procedure, is still available.

Furthermore, these two cases also demonstrate the consequence of this review when a domestic court assumes a *de novo*-type standard of review. In circumstances like in these cases, a party that believes the tribunal has misinterpreted a treaty in rejecting jurisdiction may turn to a domestic court in an attempt to have that determination tried again. In the *Cem Uzan* case, the Svea Court of Appeal found that there was no jurisdiction, but the High Court in *Griffin* "overruled" the tribunal. Regardless of the outcome, the *de novo* standard of review in practice allows a claimant a second bite at the jurisdictional apple, which would not be possible under the ICSID Convention.

3.2.3 *Treaty Interpretation*

International law and domestic law are formally separated.[216] This separation risks creating tension in challenge proceedings when the tribunal's jurisdiction is based on a treaty. When a domestic court is faced with the challenge against an arbitral award that is legally seated within that court's jurisdiction, it typically applies its home state's legislation in order to rule on the challenge. When the arbitral tribunal's jurisdiction is based on a treaty, the challenge might also involve matters of international law, primarily treaty interpretation. This sub-section discusses how courts have approached the task. In what situations have domestic courts been faced with interpreting investment treaty provisions? How have they approached this task?

3.2.3.1 The "Vienna Principles" in Domestic Courts Generally

Each jurisdiction has its own approach to the relationship between domestic law and international law. Most domestic courts try to interpret the former in conformity with the latter,[217] at least when it comes to the level of primary, substantive treaty norms, about which much has been written, including the effects of having various bodies deciding on the same international law norm.[218] Less focus has been put on the secondary, interpretative level,[219] which is arguably the most relevant in the case of arbitral set-aside proceedings, especially when the tribunal's jurisdiction is the object of the challenge.

---

216 Fauchald & Nollkaemper (eds.), p. 353.

217 V Lowe, *International Law*, Oxford University Press, 2007, p. 126.

218 The "substantive" aspects have been the primary focus of the extensive discussion on fragmentation in international law. See ILC Fragmentation Report. See also M Waibel, Uniformity versus Specialisation, p. 375 with further references.

219 See for example M Waibel, Uniformity versus Specialisation, p. 375 with further references; H. L. A. Hart, *The Concept of Law*, Oxford University Press, 1994, pp. 94–99.

With a few notable exceptions,[220] the studied cases involve a national court interpreting a bilateral treaty to which the court's home state is not a party. This is a special situation; most available literature and analysis on courts' treaty interpretation seems to presuppose that the treaty norm in question is binding on the court's home state.[221] When a BIT award is challenged in a third state, by contrast, the courts of that third state are by definition not bound by the treaty. To give a concrete example: when Singapore's Court of Appeal interprets the territorial scope of the China – Laos BIT in the *Sanum* case, the outcome has no direct consequences for Singapore, which is not a party to the BIT in question. In this typical scenario, the treaty is by definition not binding on the court's state. In fact, the court's home state was in all likelihood chosen to be the place of arbitration precisely because of its lack of connections to the parties.

Thus, the primary law (i.e. the treaty provision to be interpreted) is most usually not binding on the court's home state.[222] The interpretative principles of the Vienna Convention on the Law of Treaties[223] – as set out in Articles 31–33 (Vienna Principles) – by contrast, are most likely binding on the court in question. They constitute customary international law when interpreting treaties,[224] and have in the investment arbitration sphere found almost universal acceptance by tribunals.[225] The Vienna Principles are arguably equally applicable in domestic courts, which at least implicitly were considered by the ILC to be a "central audience" for the Vienna Principles.[226] As a basic premise, therefore, it is reasonable to assume that most domestic courts would utilize the Vienna Principles when faced with a treaty provision that needs to be construed. This is so despite the fact that not every state in which a treaty-based

220 The numerous occasions when awards based on the ECT or NAFTA have been challenged.

221 See for example the sources cited in footnote 469.

222 The significant exceptions from this, again, are NAFTA and ECT.

223 Vienna Convention on the Law of Treaties.

224 First pronounced by the ICJ in *Judgment on the Arbitral Award of July 31, 1989* (*Guinea-Bissau v. Senegal*), International Court of Justice, I.C.J. Reports 1991, para. 48. See also *Case Concerning Avena and Other Mexican Nationals* (*Mexico v. United States of America*), International Court of Justice, Judgment of March 31 2004, [2004] ICJ Rep. 12, a para. 83; *Case Concerning Sovereignty over Pulau Ligitan and Pulau Sipadan* (*Indonesia v. Malaysia*), International Court of Justice, Judgment, December 17, 2002, [2002] ICJ Rep. 625, para. 37, with further references; R Gardiner, Treaty Interpretation p. 13; J Weeramantry, Treaty Interpretation p. 6 with further references.

225 T Gazzini, Interpretation, p. 4; J Weeramantry, Treaty Interpretation pp. 26–30. Furthermore, an empirical study revealed, already in 2008, that about 40% of tribunals made express reference to the Vienna Principles, see O K Fauchald, 'The Legal Reasoning of ICSID Tribunals – An Empirical Analysis', 19 European Journal of International Law, at 314.

226 M. Waibel, 'Principles of Treaty Interpretation – Developed for and Applied by National Courts?', in Aust & Nolte (eds.), p. 13.

award has been challenged has ratified the VCLT. Most notably, neither the United States nor France is a VCLT state, but the executive branches of both states have expressed support for the Vienna Principles' status as customary international law.[227]

The Vienna Principles, which will not be described more extensively here, are by no means a magical set of interpretative guidelines that can be applied automatically and predictably.[228] Nevertheless, it should be pointed out that the principles constitute a "lowest common denominator among competing schools of interpretation."[229] The drafting history of the articles is well known and the result widely held to be a compromise between the competing interpretative schools advocated during the drafting of the VCLT,[230] although favouring textual and teleological schools over the role of the parties' intentions.[231]

Furthermore, there is no hierarchy among the interpretative elements set down in Article 31 of the VCLT. The International Law Commission stated that the elements should be included in a 'crucible'.[232] In fact, plenty of legal scholars have argued that the Vienna Principles only establish an outer framework, within which there is a wide flexibility to emphasize different aspects.[233] As will be shown below, the ways in which the Vienna Principles are evoked and applied differ considerably in the different court cases.

Finally, for the sake of completeness, it must be pointed out that some challenge proceedings do not raise issues of treaty interpretation or international law. These include instances when the challenging party based its application on an alleged failure to present its case before the tribunal,[234] or when the

---

227 US Department of State, https://www.state.gov/s/l/treaty/faqs/70139.htm, accessed 8 January 2019; Audit of Accounts Between the Netherlands and France in Application of the Protocol of 25 September 1991 Additional to the Convention for the Protection of the Rhine from Pollution by Chlorides of 3 December 1976 (Netherlands v France) 25 RIAA 267, para 57.

228 R Gardiner, Treaty Interpretation, p. 6.

229 M Waibel, Uniformity versus Specialisation, p. 380.

230 T Gazzini, Interpretation, p. 6 with further references.

231 Ibid., p. 7; J Weeramantry, Treaty Interpretation, p. 7. See also generally the criticism against the Vienna Principles by McDougal et al (known as the "New Haven School"), M S McDougal, H D Lasswell and J C Miller, *The Interpretation of Agreements and World Public Order: Principles of Content and Procedure,* Brill, 1994.

232 Doc A/CONF.39/11, Add 2., Yearbook of the ILC (1966), vol. II, para. 8. See also Gardiner, Treaty Interpretation, pp. 9–10.

233 See for example M Waibel, Uniformity versus Specialisation, pp. 377–379; C McLachlan, L Shore and M Weiniger, para. 3.71; T Gazzini, Interpretation, p. 4.

234 See for example *Mexico v. Marvin Roy Feldman Karpa*, Court of Appeal for Ontario, 11 January 2005; *Peter and Kristof de Sutter and others v. Madagascar,* Paris Court of Appeal, 14/19164, 15 March 2016.

award allegedly violates domestic public policy. Furthermore, a number of challenges have been dismissed on (domestic) procedural grounds, such as preclusion/time bar[235] and domestic *res judicata*/collateral estoppel.[236]

However, many challenge proceedings clearly involve elements of treaty interpretation, prompting the court in question to construe the terms of the underlying investment treaty. There are also examples of courts being faced with questions that do not fit squarely into either of these two clear-cut categories, but that rather raise questions of both domestic interpretative principles and treaty interpretation.

3.2.3.2 Express Applications of VCLT

A number of domestic courts have approached interpretative questions in challenge proceedings with express recognition that they should be solved by the principles enshrined in the Vienna Convention on the Law of Treaties.

Interpretation of Specific Treaty Language

For example, the Swiss Supreme Court was faced with construing the meaning of the phrase "the award shall be final and binding" in the arbitration clause in the Czech Republic – Netherlands BIT. When the Czech Republic moved to challenge an award rendered in favour of Dutch investor Saluka, the investor claimed that the phrase should be understood as an "exclusion agreement." Such agreements, which in advance prohibit the parties from challenging an award in court, are possible under certain circumstances in Switzerland and discussed further below at 3.2.4.1. The question for the court was whether the treaty language constituted such an agreement. The court found that it did not. According to the wording of the provision in Swiss law that allows for exclusion agreements in certain circumstances, the agreement has to be made explicitly. Although Swiss court practice had softened this provision so that it would suffice if the "unambiguous common will is visible," the court found that the treaty language did not constitute a waiver.[237] The court first analysed the alleged agreement by applying Swiss law and emphasized that given the far-reaching consequences of such an agreement, neither the phrase "final" nor the phrase "binding" could constitute an exclusion agreement. It then

---

235 *Raymond L. Loewen v. United States*, United States District Court for the District of Columbia, Civil Action No. 04-2151 (RWR), Judgement, 31 October 2005; *Argentina v. National Grid PLC*, United States District Court for the District of Columbia, Civil Action No. 09-248 (RBW), Judgement, 7 June 2010.

236 *Tembec Inc. et al v. United States*, United States District Court for the District of Columbia, Civil Action No. 07-1905 (RMC), Judgement, 14 August 2008.

237 *Czech Republic v. Saluka*, Swiss Federal Tribunal, para. 5.2.

moved on to interpret the wording in accordance with the VCLT. Interestingly, the court first noted that the Czech Republic only became a party to the VCLT after the entry into force of the BIT. Nevertheless, the court stated, the rules on interpretation enshrined in the VCLT "codify general principles of customary public international law and correspond to the practice of the federal court."[238] After establishing that Swiss courts generally approach the rules by focusing primarily on the wording of the treaty, it stated that:

> If the text is not obviously absurd after an interpretation of the common use of language as well as the object and purpose of the treaty an interpretation reaching – extensively or restrictively – beyond the wording is only possible if it can be clearly concluded from the context or the development history that the contracting states had a will different from the wording.[239]

The Court also stated – contrary to the investor's contention – that the contracting parties did not intend to exclude any involvement of domestic courts; only a limited number of states allow for exclusion agreements and the place of arbitration was not specified in the BIT. On the contrary, it was the disputing parties that chose the place of arbitration and they did so only after the arbitration was initiated.[240]

The court was similarly not convinced by the investor's argument that ICSID arbitration was not available at the time of the treaty's conclusion because the Czech Republic had not ratified the ICSID Convention at that stage. The investor seemed to have suggested that it would have preferred ICSID arbitration to UNCITRAL arbitration in order to avoid any intervention of domestic courts. However, the court pointed out that an ICSID award is not "final and binding" either, since it can be annulled under the mechanism provided in the Convention. In any event, if the states had indeed wanted to express any such preference, they could have agreed to future ICSID arbitration, provided that the Czech Republic ratified the Convention subsequent to the entering into force of the BIT; such agreements, the court pointed out, exist in other investment treaties.[241] In summary, neither domestic law nor international law would support the claim that the treaty language constituted a valid exclusion agreement.

---

238 Ibid., para. 5.4.1.
239 Ibid., para. 5.4.1.
240 Ibid., para. 5.2.1.
241 Ibid., para. 5.4.3.

In another case, as discussed above, the High Court of Justice of England and Wales determined that Ecuador's challenge against the award rendered in favour of Occidental was justiciable. This decision, which was confirmed by the Court of Appeal of England Wales, was decided as a preliminary matter.[242] In a subsequent stage of the challenge proceedings, the High Court faced the merits of Ecuador's challenge against the tribunal's jurisdiction. First, the court set out the standard of correctness in determining the jurisdiction *de novo*.[243]

Also before the High Court of England and Wales,[244] in *Czech Republic v. EMV*, the court confirmed the standard of review as summarized in *Ecuador v. Occidental*.[245] Furthermore, the court was also faced with a challenge against the tribunal's substantive jurisdiction under Section 67(1) of the English Arbitration Act. The Czech Republic argued that Article 8.6 of the Czech Republic – Belgium/Luxembourg BIT, which contains the treaty's arbitration clause, did not cover EMV's claims in the arbitration. The investor had alleged an indirect expropriation of its investment in a Czech television company and the tribunal found, in a partial award, that it had jurisdiction under the treaty. The particular clause is common in older BITs concluded by the Soviet Union, China and Eastern European states. Part of it reads as follows:

1. Disputes between one of the Contracting Parties and an Investor of the other Contracting Party *concerning compensation due by virtue of Art. 3 Paragraphs (1) and (3)* shall be the subject of a written notification, accompanied by a detailed memorandum, addressed by the investor to the concerned Contracting Party. To the extent possible, such disputes shall be settled amicably (emphasis added).
2. If the dispute is not resolved within six months from the date of the written notification specified in Paragraph (1), and in the absence of any other form of settlement agreed between the parties to the dispute, it shall be submitted to arbitration before an ad hoc tribunal.

The referenced Article 3 contains the treaty's prohibition on expropriation without compensation. In the view of the Czech Republic, the emphasized language in Article 8.6(1) restricted the tribunal's jurisdiction to quantifying damages in cases of expropriation; the underlying determination of whether an expropriation had occurred was to be decided in another forum. The tribunal, by contrast, had interpreted the clause as encompassing the question

242 Discussed at pp. 97–98. Ecuador v. Occidental Exploration and Production Company, Judgment of the Court of Appeal, (2007) EWCA Civ 656, July 4, 2007.

243 Discussed at pp. 97–98.

244 *Czech Republic v. EMV*, High Court.

245 Ibid., para. 13.

of whether an expropriation had occurred (but found it exclude any other non-expropriation claims).

In the English court, the argument between the parties largely revolved around the purpose and intention with the BIT, and both parties submitted interpretations based on the VCLT.[246] In making its own independent interpretation, the court initially stated that the BIT was governed by international law, including Articles 31 and 32 of the VCLT.[247] These interpretative principles, the court said, were accepted by the International Court of Justice as customary international law, and therefore part of English law. The court also laid down four preliminary points with respect to its treaty interpretation:

- Independent interpretation. This means that there can be only one true interpretation of a treaty, which does not take colour from the legal systems of any individual contracting state.[248]
- As a matter of wording, the jurisdiction is the same irrespective if the "concerned Contracting Party" is the Czech Republic or Belgium/Luxembourg.[249]
- The "ordinary meaning," as provided for by Article 31 VCLT, is the meaning given to the terms at the time the treaty is concluded (the principle of contemporaneity).[250]
- Finally, "as a normal principle of interpretation a Court or Tribunal should endeavour to give a meaning to each of the words being interpreted."[251]

The court looked at the language of the clause and found the phrase "concerning compensation" to give rise to the most difficulty.[252] While the term "compensation" established a jurisdictional restriction to one aspect of jurisdiction,[253] the court was unable to accept that the phrase meant, "relating to the amount of expropriation." In the court's view, the word "concerning" broadened the scope of the clause; the ordinary meaning of that term is to include every aspect of its subject, in this case meaning that it covers both "issues of entitlement as well as quantification."[254]

The court also looked at Article 3, which is referenced in Article 8. Article 3 contains a number of considerations, many of which may be relevant when

246 Ibid., para. 10.
247 Ibid., para. 14.
248 Ibid., para. 34.
249 Ibid., para. 35.
250 Ibid., para. 36.
251 Ibid, para. 37.
252 Ibid, para. 43.
253 Ibid, para. 44.
254 Ibid.

determining the level of compensation.[255] This cross-reference also supported the interpretation that a tribunal had jurisdiction to determine whether an expropriation had occurred. The effect of the opposite conclusion, as argued by the Czech Republic, would be to preclude the tribunal from making determinations relevant to the quantification of the amount of compensation.[256] The court therefore, similar to the arbitral tribunal, found that the tribunal had jurisdiction under the treaty to determine also whether compensation should be awarded.

Territorial scope – Laos v. Sanum

A similarly narrow arbitration clause was relied upon by the *Sanum v. Laos* tribunal. In the challenge proceedings in Singapore, Laos argued before two Singaporean courts that the tribunal exceeded the scope of the arbitration agreement in assuming jurisdiction under this clause, which reads as follows:

1. Any dispute between an investor of one Contracting State and the other Contracting State in connection with an investment in the territory of the other Contracting State shall, as far as possible, be settled amicably through negotiation between the parties to the dispute.
2. If the dispute cannot be settled through negotiation within six months, either party to the dispute shall be entitled to submit the dispute to the competent court of the Contracting State accepting the investment.
3. If a dispute involving the amount of compensation for expropriation cannot be settled through negotiation within six months as specified in paragraph 1 of this Article, it may be submitted at the request of either party to an ad hoc arbitral tribunal. The provisions of this paragraph shall not apply if the investor concerned has resorted to the procedure specified in the paragraph 2 of this Article.

In the High Court, Laos succeeded in challenging the award based on another ground, concerning the territorial scope of the treaty (discussed above at 3.2.2.6 in the context of the appropriate standard of review). Therefore, the proper interpretation of the arbitration clause in Article 8 was, technically speaking, moot. Nevertheless, the High Court analysed the provision in a *dictum*.[257] In the court's view, the tribunal did not have jurisdiction over Sanum's expropriation claim, because Article 8 only allowed for disputes over the amount of

255 Ibid., paras. 45–48.

256 Ibid., para. 49.

257 The court states expressly that the reasoning is "not necessary" but included since "counsel for both parties have made full submissions on this issue," Sanum v. Laos, Singapore High Court, para. 112.

compensation owed following an expropriation. The court emphasized the *context* leg of Article 31(1) VCLT, pointing out that Laos and China, as communist states at the time of the conclusion of the BIT, "possessed a certain degree of distrust regarding investment of private capital and were concerned about the decisions of international tribunals on matters over which they have no control."[258] It also disagreed with an ICSID tribunal's interpretation of a similar clause in a different Chinese BIT, stating that the tribunal placed "undue reliance" on the treaty's stated purpose to promote investment.[259] The court added:

> It is a truism to say that the purpose of any BIT is to promote investments. But it does not follow from this general proposition that every ambiguity found in such treaties should invariably be resolved in favour of the investor. Every BIT represents a negotiated bargain between two contracting states and the provisions therein reflect the extent to which the sovereignty of each contracting state has been curtailed. The bargains struck in BITs should therefore not be lightly displaced without due consideration of the context in which they were made.[260]

On appeal, the Court of Appeal of the Republic of Singapore reversed the High Court's decision and held that the tribunal had not gone beyond its mandate. It found both that the treaty extended to investors incorporated in Macao, and that the arbitration clause in the treaty encompassed Sanum's claims. With respect to the latter ground the appeals court, similar to the tribunal, interpreted the clause broadly. The court formulated is task in what seems to be a step-by-step analysis of three elements of Article 31(1) VCLT:

- the ordinary meaning to be accorded to the words used in Art 8(3) of the PRC – Laos BIT;
- the context of the PRC – Laos BIT; and
- the object and purpose of the PRC – Laos BIT.[261]

The court dealt with these three steps in turn. First, it stated that the ordinary meaning of the clause, and specifically the phrase "involving," could support both a broad and a narrow interpretation.[262] It therefore had to proceed to the context of the BIT. For example, the court stressed that the BIT also contained a so-called fork-in-the-road clause, as emphasized by the arbitral tribunal. The

258 Ibid., para. 123.
259 Para. 124.
260 Ibid.
261 Sanum v. Laos, Singapore Court of Appeal, para. 125.
262 Ibid., para. 126.

combined effect of Laos' proposed reading of Article 8(3) and the fork-in-the-road clause would lead to no investor-state arbitration at all: the broad language of the latter, the court said, prevents an investor from requesting arbitration if "any dispute" has already been submitted to court.[263] Therefore, the interpretation advanced by Laos, separating quantum from liability would violate the *effet utile* principle. The court also cited approvingly the same ICSID tribunal that was dismissed by the High Court.[264] However, the court also turned to "case authorities" relied upon by Laos, all of which seemingly supported a narrower reading of the clause. In total, five arbitral awards had been advanced; all were distinguished by the court and found to be less relevant due to factors of context, language or facts.[265]

After extensively reviewing the context of the treaty the court finally made reference to the treaty's object and purpose to confirm its broad interpretation of the clause. Having gone through the ordinary meaning of Article 8(3), as well as the context in which it was drafted, the court had at this stage in its interpretation established a broad understanding. It found that this understanding would also be "in line with" the treaty's objective of protecting investments.[266] By this exercise, the court felt it had done what was required of it by Article 31(1) VLCT, i.e. taking the different elements into account cumulatively.[267]

Furthermore, the Court of Appeal's analysis with respect to the treaty's territorial scope also involved significant elements of treaty law, not only the interpretative rules in Articles 31 and 32 VCLT. Specifically, the "moving frontier rule" was a decisive issue. The rule, which is expressed in Article 15 Vienna Convention on the Succession of Treaties ("VCST"), creates a presumption that a state's treaties are automatically extended to any new territory that becomes part of the state. Although not aimed expressly at treaty succession, the court stated that Article 29 VCLT implicitly codifies this principle.[268] There are exceptions to the presumptive rule, however, and one such exception, worded differently in VCLT and VCST but still found by the court to be "overlapping," was the focus of the Court of Appeal's analysis. The China – Laos BIT would apply automatically to Macao as of December 20, 1999 when Macao was restored to China from Portugal, unless:

263 Ibid., para. 128.
264 Ibid., para. 131.
265 Ibid., paras. 135–146.
266 Ibid., para. 150.
267 Ibid., para. 149.
268 Ibid., paras. 48–49.

> An intention appears from the [...] BIT, or is otherwise established, that the BIT does not apply in respect of the entire territory of [China].[269]

The BIT was silent on the issue, and nothing in its objects and purpose, or the circumstances of its conclusion pointed to any intention, which suggested to the court that the presumption would apply.[270] The court therefore turned to the evidence furnished by Laos to support its claim that the treaty did *not* extend to Macau.

First, the court determined that the standard of proof to establish a different intention under Article 29 VCLT should be "satisfaction on a balance of probabilities."[271] Furthermore, before turning to Laos' four different grounds supporting that the treaty parties had demonstrated a "different intention," the court clarified a principle of international law. The so-called critical date doctrine provides that evidence generated after the critical date cannot be relied upon by a party to improve its position. The court applied this principle when reviewing Laos' evidence, albeit in a flexible manner, stating that:

> In our judgment, the critical date doctrine remains relevant in this case when considering the various pieces of evidence that the Judge took into account. This does not mean that any evidence after the Critical Date is automatically inadmissible but special care would have to be taken in assessing the weight or relevance of such evidence.[272]

According to the court, the "critical date" was the date when the dispute had crystallized, i.e. in August 2012 when Sanum requested arbitration. By contrast, the lower court had not clearly stated what it viewed to be critical date, seemingly suggested that it could also have been the date of the conclusion of the BIT, or even the date of Macao's hand-over to China. Based on this, the lower court had found that the application of the critical date doctrine would be contrary to Article 31(3)(a) VCLT, because that no material generated after the hand-over could be relied upon.[273]

The Court of Appeal then reviewed the three pieces of evidence advanced by Laos that pre-dated the critical date: a 1987 China-Portugal Joint Declaration, a number of official statements with respect to Hong Kong and a 1999

269 Ibid., paras. 50, 53.
270 Ibid., para. 55.
271 Ibid., para. 62.
272 Ibid., para. 69.
273 Ibid., para. 68.

Chinese note to the UN Secretary General – but found that none of these was enough to displace the presumption of the moving frontier rule. The more intricate task was the 2014 notes between China and Laos, which *subsequent to the award* allegedly made clear that the treaty parties did not intend for the treaty to extend to Macao. The court stated that while it could rely on the 2014 notes, it would have to do so with special attention, allowing it greater weight only to the extent it confirmed a continuity and consistency with the pre-critical date evidence.[274] Since the notes rather contradicted the pre-critical date evidence, the court did not accord them any evidentiary weight.[275] In any event, the notes' stated justification was based on the internal laws of China and Macau, and thereby irrelevant considerations under Article 27 VCLT.[276]

Furthermore, the Court of Appeal also rejected Laos' argument that the 2014 notes were a subsequent agreement or subsequent practice under Article 31(1)(3)(a) or (b) VCLT. It found that giving the notes such an effect would constitute a retroactive amendment of the BIT, since there was nothing in the notes referring to a pre-existing agreement or understanding that pre-dated the critical date.[277] As part of this discussion, the court also distinguished a NAFTA award relied upon by Laos,[278] in which the tribunal had given effect to a subsequent interpretation by the three contracting states. The court stated that NAFTA is a special case, because Article 1131 NAFTA, unlike the China – Laos BIT, expressly permits contracting states to issue binding interpretative statements.[279]

Territorial Scope – Russia v. Stabil and Ukrnafta

The territorial scope was a key issue also when the Russian Federation challenged the two separate *Stabil* and *Ukrnafta* awards, concerning an investment in Crimea and Sevastopol.[280] In its challenge, Russia argued that the territorial scope of the Russia – Ukraine BIT only encompassed the territory of the two parties to the BIT at the time when the treaty was concluded (in 1998). Since Crimea and Sevastopol were part of Ukraine at that time, the territorial scope of the BIT did not extend to Crimea as a Russian territory, Russia argued.

The Swiss court rejected this argument. Instead, the court agreed with the arbitral tribunal's approach, interpreting the BIT in light of general rules of public international law. This had included Article 29 VCLT, which the tribunal

274 Ibid., para. 108.
275 Ibid., para. 112.
276 Ibid., para. 114.
277 Ibid., para. 116.
278 *ADF Group Inc v United States,* ICSID Case No ARB(AF)/00/1, Award, 9 January 2003.
279 *Sanum v. Laos*, Court of Appeal, para. 118.
280 *Russia v. Stabil and Ukrnafta,* discussed above at p. 120 et seq.

had applied in finding a "dynamic" approach to the territorial application of the BIT, ultimately concluding that the treaty applied to territories acquired by Russia after the conclusion of the treaty.

On review, the Swiss court found that this conclusion was "correct."[281] The Court also added that Russia failed to submit any convincing argument supporting its "static" interpretation of the territorial scope of the BIT.

Failure to apply law: Czech Republic v. CME

In another case involving the Czech Republic, which is well-known primarily for the fact that a parallel and very similar case was arbitrated in a different forum (and with a different outcome), the state argued before the Svea Court of Appeal that the tribunal had failed to apply Czech law and international law, despite an express instruction in the treaty to do so. The choice of law provision in the treaty reads as follows:

> The arbitral tribunal shall decide on the basis of the law, taking into account in particular though not exclusively:
>
> – the law in force of the Contracting Party concerned;
> – the provisions of this Agreement, and other relevant Agreements between the Contracting Parties;
> – the provisions of special agreements relating to the investment;
> – the general principles of international law[282]

The court analysed Article 8.6 of the BIT, relying on Article 31 of the VCLT. In its view, the initial part of the clause was clear, whereas the four exemplifying points left room for interpretation.[283] The wording "take into account in particular although not exclusively," however, suggested to the court that the tribunal was free to use also other sources of law. Furthermore, the fact that the sources of law were not numbered or in any other way structured to give the impression of a hierarchy "almost gives the impression that the contracting states have left to the arbitrators the determination, on a case by case basis, as to which source or sources of law shall be applied."[284] This finding, i.e. that the treaty provision allowed the arbitrators a certain discretion to apply the sources of law listed therein, was also "confirmed by" the agreed minutes from

281 Russia v. Stabil and Ukrnafta, para. 4.3.2.
282 Netherlands – Czech Republic BIT 1991, Article 8.6.
283 Czech Republic v. CME, Svea Court of Appeal, p. 92.
284 Ibid., p. 93.

a 2001 consultation between the treaty states, in which the interpretation and application of the BIT was discussed.[285]

Given this, the Court was not inclined to review each section of the award to see which law was applied but rather stated that "it is sufficient to clarify whether the arbitral tribunal applied any of the sources of law listed in the choice of law clause or whether the tribunal has not based its decision on any law at all but, rather, judged in accordance with general reasonableness."[286] Under those circumstances, the court found that the tribunal did not, as alleged by the Czech Republic, exceed its mandate by failing to apply the applicable law.

Tax Carve-Outs: Ecuador v. Occidental and Schooner Capital v. Poland

In the London-seated challenge against the *Occidental v. Ecuador* award,[287] the state argued that the arbitration had involved matters of taxation and thus was outside of the tribunal's jurisdiction subject to Article X of the US – Ecuador BIT, which excludes such matters from the protection of the treaty. Occidental countered that there were exceptions to the tax exemption: Article X(2)(c) provides that the treaty *shall* apply to matters of taxation with respect to "the observation and enforcement of terms of an investment agreement or authorization as referred."

Having set out the *de novo* standard of review, the High Court cited the Vienna Principles, without any comment as to their relevance or applicability.[288] In making its interpretation of the scope of Article X, the court found that the case involved a matter of taxation and as such could only be within the tribunal's jurisdiction in the event that any of the three exceptions in Article X applied.[289] The court therefore turned to the scope of these exceptions, ultimately finding that the dispute was covered by the exception in Article X(2)(c).[290] Although the court found the dispute to concern matters of taxation – which according to Article X would seemingly exclude it from the scope of the treaty – it also found the dispute to concern the performance and obligations of the underlying contract. The court gave three reasons for this finding, all having to do with the contract's connection to the potential VAT refund.[291] The *Occidental* judgment was subsequently cited by the High Court in *Griffin*,

285 Ibid., p. 6, p. 94.
286 Ibid., p. 94.
287 Discussed above at pp. 97–98.
288 *Ecuador v. Occidental*, para. 90.
289 Ibid., paras. 93–94.
290 Ibid., para. 110.
291 Ibid., paras. 107–108.

discussed above, as support for the assumption that the Vienna Principles guide the interpretation of investment treaties in set-aside proceedings seated in England.[292]

A similar tax exemption was discussed by the Paris Court of Appeal in the *Schooner Capital* case. In the arbitration, US investors owning shares in Polish companies was in a dispute with Polish tax authorities over deductible expenses for corporate income tax and VAT. After having filed for arbitration under the US – Poland BIT and the ICSID AF Rules, an award was issued in 2015 in favour of the state. One of the investors then brought an action for annulment to the Paris Court of Appeal based on several grounds. First of these was that, in the investor's view, the tribunal had wrongly assessed the BIT's exclusion of tax issues. The language of the clause in question related only to substantive tax provisions.

The court pointed out that pursuant to the VCLT there is no rule that would require a distinction to be made where the text does not make one. The BIT does not contain a definition of the expression "tax issue" and does not distinguish between substantive tax provisions and the procedures conducted in this area.[293]

To support this the court referred to the object and purpose of the treaty found in the preamble.[294] It further held that the comparison with the ECT, to which the US is not a party, is entirely unrelated to the BIT. And even if the terms did have a different meaning in the ECT, they are irrelevant for the interpretation of the BIT which must be made in the light of the common intention of the parties.[295]

Furthermore, the investor had, in its argument before the court, referred to a report on the BIT sent by the US State Department to the US Senate as means for interpretation. The court dismissed this as not relevant since the text of the BIT was clear. There was therefore no reason, the court found, to refer to the (alleged) preparatory work.[296] The Court further pointed out that an internal US document cannot represent the common intention of the parties.[297]

Ratione Temporis: Lesotho v. Swissbourgh et al

The *Lesotho v. Swissbourgh* challenge presented two courts in Singapore with interesting questions concerning, *inter alia*, the tribunal's *ratione temporis* jurisdiction.

292 Griffin v. Poland, High Court, para. 9.

293 *Schooner Capital v. Poland,* pp. 4–5.

294 Ibid., p. 6.

295 The French version of the Article 31(4) VCLT contains the wording *l'intention des parties.*

296 *Schooner Capital v. Poland,* p. 6.

297 *Ibid.,* p. 7.

The dispute arose out of mining investments made in the 1990s in Lesotho by nine investors, including South African entity Swissbourgh Diamond. The group of investors submitted expropriation claims to a tribunal pursuant to the Treaty of the Southern African Development Community (SADC) in 2016. However, Lesotho and the other SADC member states suspended the tribunal, which prevented the investors from seeking recourse. Instead, the investors brought a separate arbitration under the separate Finance and Investment Protocol ("*FIP*") of the SADC, administered by the PCA, and seated in Singapore. The PCA tribunal found, in a partial award by majority, that it had jurisdiction and that Lesotho had commited denial of justice. Lesotho applied for set-aside at the seat of arbitration and was successful in two instances.

In the set-aside proceedings, Lesotho's primary ground for its challenge was that the investors had been involved in one single dispute with Lesotho, which pre-dated the April 2010 entry into force of the FIP. This, the state argued, meant that the dispute fell outside of the protocol's express stipulation that it did not apply to disputes which "arose" before the treaty's entry into force.

In the first one, the Singapore High Court, the court interpreted the temporal scope of the FIP, in an express *de novo* review of the tribunal's jurisdiction.[298] The interpretation was preceded by a lengthy discussion of the Vienna Principles and their applicability, which relied on legal writings, international judicial practice, as well as the *Sanum* challenge in the same jurisdiction.[299] The court stated that the relevant terms in the FIP – "dispute" and "arose" – were not defined. Notably, the court also said that the stated objectives of the SADC Treaty (and the FIP) were "crafted too generally to be determinative of the question."[300]

The Court then turned to a long analysis of a number of investment arbitration awards cited by the parties, in its effort to interpret the scope of these terms.[301] As for the definition of "dispute," the court relied on the definition articulated by the *Maffezini v. Spain* tribunal in expressing a number of principles that the court found relevant to determine whether the arbitrated dispute was separate from an underlying dispute which the state alleged had arisen prior to the applicable treaty's entry into force.[302]

298 *Lesotho v. Swissbourgh et al*, Singapore High Court, para. 119.

299 Ibid., paras. 88–103.

300 Ibid., para. 120.

301 Ibid., paras. 121–161. These included *ATA v. Jordan, Lucchetti v. Peru, Chevron v. Ecuador, Mondev v. USA,* and *Jan de Nul v Egypt.*

302 Ibid., para. 170.

Ultimately, the court found that the dispute fell within the tribunal's jurisdiction *ratione temporis*. However, the award was set aside in its entirety on several other grounds, since the High Court found that the dispute was not contemplated by and not falling within the terms of the submission to arbitration, relying on Article 34(2)(a)(iii) of the UNCITRAL Model Law on International Commercial Arbitration (which, as discussed above, is implemented in Singapore by the Singapore International Arbitration Act). In an effort to revive the award, the investors appealed the decision to the Singapore Court of Appeal, where the *ratione temporis* question was reviewed again.

Similar to the lower court, the Court of Appeal initially set out the principles of treaty interpretation based on VCLT, relying on the same *Sanum* judgment which states that the Vienna Principles govern treaty interpretation in Singaporean courts.[303] The Court of Appeal further mentioned other principles, such as that investment treaties "should be interpreted neither liberally nor restrictively," "neither an unequivocally pro-investor nor pro-State approach should be adopted in interpreting the provisions of an investment treaty."

In the Court of Appeal judgment, the *ratione temporis* question was not as relevant. Instead, the Court of Appeal ultimately upheld the set-aside decision, finding that (i) the investors' alleged rights only existed on the international law plane, with no nexus in Lesotho, and (ii) there was no jurisdiction under the SADC in the first place, as disputes under that treaty were limited to application or interpretation of the treaty itself.[304]

"Investor" and "Investment"

The familiar objective jurisdictional thresholds of demonstrating an "investor" in possession of an "investment" are frequently relied upon in challenges before domestic courts. Although almost every investment treaty contains these threshold definitions, their proper interpretation must be ascertained based on the language of the specific treaty; the meaning of the definitions is similar, but not identical, in different treaties. In a number of cases, domestic courts have approached this task with the assistance of the VCLT.

The scope of both "investor" and "investment" was discussed when Canada challenged a NAFTA award in its own courts. In *S.D. Myers v. Canada*, the tribunal had held in a partial award that it had jurisdiction to hear S.D. Myers' claims. In Canada's view, the claims were beyond the scope of the arbitration agreement.

303 *Lesotho v. Swissbourgh et al*, Singapore Court of Appeal, para. 60.

304 Ibid., paras. 137–158.

Strictly speaking, there was no need for the court to rule on the merits of the jurisdictional objections raised by Canada, because the court found that the state had lost its right to claim that the tribunal lacked jurisdiction because it did not properly raise this jurisdictional objection during the proceedings.[305] However, the court still went on, in an *obiter dictum* in the alternative that it was wrong in finding that Canada had lost its right to raise the objection,[306] to review the tribunal's interpretations.

Although it was undisputed that the locally incorporated company in question constituted an investment under the NAFTA definition, Canada argued before the court that the company was not "controlled directly or indirectly" by the investor. The court therefore had to interpret the meaning of this phrase. Relying on the rules of interpretation enshrined in the VCLT – which the court had made clear at the outset of its judgment should be the governing rules when interpreting NAFTA[307] – it stated that the ordinary meaning of "control," as defined in the Canadian Oxford Dictionary means "the power of directing, command." This ordinary meaning, together with the purposive interpretation laid down both in the VCLT and NAFTA itself, led the court to find that the tribunal's legal interpretation was correct. It also found that the tribunal's analysis of the facts, which had shown that the president of the investor was clearly directing the operations of the locally incorporated company, was reasonable.

Canada had furthermore argued that whether the locally incorporated company was controlled by the investor was a question to be determined with reference to domestic Canadian law. This, in the court's view, would be a "narrow, legalistic, restrictive interpretation contrary to the objectives of NAFTA and contrary to the purposive interpretation which NAFTA Article 2.01 and Article 31 of the Vienna Convention stipulate."[308] Instead, the court reiterated that the ordinary meaning of the phrase "controlled" was the relevant basis for the determination.

The Swiss Federal Tribunal in *Recofi* pointed out that the ordinary meaning of the term investment, as examined for the purposes of jurisdiction in accordance with Article 31(1) of the VCLT, is "one of the most controversial to date in the litigation of international investment," as exemplified by the many tribunals attempting to define its contours.[309] In the challenge before it, the court found no reason to question the tribunal's determination, which was made

305 Canada v. S.D. Myers, Federal Court of Canada, para. 53.

306 Ibid., para. 57.

307 Ibid., para. 24.

308 Ibid., para. 69.

309 *Recofi v. Vietnam,* Swiss Federal Tribunal, 3.2.2.

relying on a reading of the treaty's Article 1 in its entirety, together with its preamble. The tribunal had found that this reading supported the conclusion that the treaty's definition of investment required a connection to the territory of the host state, which Recofi's contractual claims lacked.[310] The Swiss court was hesitant to second-guess this conclusion and stated that the tribunal was "correct" to focus on the text of the treaty and disregard the many other awards submitted by the investor, whose legal value was doubtful. Unlike the investor's contention, the court did not find that the tribunal had added criteria to the definition, but rather that it had properly made its own interpretation of the term in good faith, according to the ordinary meaning under the treaty in its context and in the light of its object and purpose.[311]

Recofi had also argued that certain parliamentary reports submitted during the French ratification of the treaty demonstrated the parties' intent to define the scope of investment broadly. The court pointed out that the reports could not be relied on to establish the intent of the parties, since it at most demonstrated the intention of only one of them.[312] The documents could also not be treated as "supplementary means of interpretation" in the meaning of Article 32 VCLT, because the tribunal – and now also the court – had found that the meaning of investment could be determined by employing Article 31, which would render Article 32 irrelevant.[313]

In *Hungary v. EDF*,[314] the state's primary ground for challenging the award was that the tribunal had gone beyond its jurisdiction in violation of Art. 190(2)(b) PILA.[315] The argument rested on a claim that the tribunal had adjudicated *contractual claims* – more specifically the consequences of the state cancellations of a number of power purchasing agreements – and not, as the tribunal had found, claims based on the fair and equitable standard contained in the Energy Charter Treaty.[316] The ECT contains a so-called umbrella clause, which under certain circumstances can bring contractual obligations of the host state in under the aegis of the treaty. However, when Hungary acceded to the treaty the state had undisputedly made a reservation under Article 26(3)(c), withdrawing claims from the umbrella clause from its consent to arbitration. The state had argued in the arbitration – and maintained in the challenge

310 Ibid.

311 Ibid., 3.4.2.

312 Ibid., 3.2.2.

313 Ibid.

314 Hungary v. EDF, Swiss Supreme Court.

315 Ibid., para. 3.

316 Ibid., para. 3.3.1. The underlying ECT award remains unpublished but is cited occasionally in the court judgment.

proceedings – that the tribunal *de facto* had based its award on the umbrella clause. The issue before the Swiss court was therefore if the tribunal had exceeded its jurisdiction when it adjudicated the alleged contractual claims although Hungary had excluded the umbrella clause from its consent to arbitration.

At the outset of this interpretation, the court referred to the VCLT, stating that

> [...] *like any other treaty,* the ECT must be interpreted in good faith according to the ordinary meaning of the words of the treaty, in their context, and in the light of the treaty's object and purpose[317]

The same basic approach, the court said, was relevant also in interpreting the reservation to the treaty, which "must be considered an integral part of the treaty."[318]

Although the court expressly cited the Vienna Principles – and also relied on various academic texts to support its statement on the general scope of Article 10 ECT, such as the umbrella clause's protection of investments even when there is no obligation towards the individual investor[319] – the VCLT rules of interpretation seem to not have been decisive.

Ultimately, the court found that the tribunal had been right to accept jurisdiction. The tribunal had analysed the claims as based on the fair and equitable treatment standard, in accordance with the investor's characterization. It had found that the state had failed to establish a reasonable system to compensate the investor for stranded costs in connection with the production of power. The court said that "one can only approve" of the finding that such a claim was within the framework of general duties imposed upon the host state to grant fair and equitable treatment, irrespective of the fact that cancelled contracts played part of the factual matrix.[320] Therefore, the state's reservation against the umbrella clause was not relevant; in fact, the court stated that Hungary sought to reshape the claim "as it sees fit in order to fit into the scope of the umbrella clause, the application of which would be prevented by the reservation it made."[321] The state's reading of the investor's claim would render Article 10(1) (except its umbrella clause) meaningless, since it would make

317 Ibid., para. 3.5.1. Emphasis added.

318 Ibid. The court here cited a judgment from the same court, 4A_736/2011 of 11 April, 2012, which concerned the application of the 1988 Lugano Convention.

319 Ibid.

320 Ibid., para. 3.5.4.2.

321 Ibid., para. 3.5.4.1.

treaty claims turn into contracts claims. This, according to the court, would be "contrary to the rule of interpretation of effectiveness of the law."[322]

This rejection of Hungary's interpretation of the relationship between the umbrella clause and the fair and equitable clause in Article 10(1) ECT was seemingly an independent interpretation of the treaty on behalf of the Swiss court. It does not, however, show traces of the principles described in Articles 31 and 32 of the VCLT, to which the court subscribed at the outset of its analysis. Instead, it seems largely based on principles of effectiveness and reasonableness. This is confirmed by the fact that the court, after announcing the result of its own interpretation, states that

> Finally, for the reasons already stated above, see [reference to the paragraph in which the court discussed the effectiveness and reasonableness of the state's interpretation], the general principles of interpretation of treaties and of the reservations therein are of no assistance to the Appellant.[323]

The status of contractual claims also featured in India's challenge against the award rendered in favour of CC Devas, by a tribunal seated in The Hague. In that dispute, the tribunal had found that India's cancellation of a satellite lease had constituted an unlawful expropriation, as well as breach of FET, in the India – Mauritius BIT. However, a tribunal majority also held that the state was partly protected from liability by the BIT's "essential security" clause. With the quantum phase still pending, the state challenged the partial award in the Hague District Court on, inter alia, the ground that CC Devas did not have a protected investment under the BIT, as the rights under the satellite contract did not meet the treaty's definition of investment, properly construed.

The state characterized the tribunal's analysis of the BIT as too "mechanical," with the result being manifestly absurd or unreasonable.[324] The court made its own analysis, coming to the same conclusion as the tribunal and thereby rejecting India's contention. When interpreting the scope of investment with the aid of the Vienna Principles, the court found that the textual interpretation of the definition of investment – which contained, in the court's view, a very broad definition – was sufficiently clear, there was no need to turn to the additional means of interpretation (proscribed by Article 32 of the VCLT).[325] The contract

322 Ibid., para. 3.5.3.1.

323 Ibid., para. 3.5.4.4.

324 *India v. CC Devas*, para. 4.12.

325 Ibid., paras. 4.13–4.15.

gave the investors exclusive rights to certain satellite capacity for twelve years, and the Indian Foreign Investment Promotion Board had approved the contract. Furthermore, it was undisputed that CC Devas had paid $13 million. Altogether, it was clear that the investment represented a "significant value" and as such must be regarded as a (protected) asset in the meaning of the treaty.[326]

Furthermore, addressing India's argument that the preamble to the treaty provides that its purpose is to "increase prosperity in the territories of both Contracting Parties," the court agreed that the object of the treaty must form part of its interpretation. However, it did not find that this fact altered its conclusion, since CC Devas had made its investment "with the intention to for a longer period, in this case a period of twelve years with the option of extension, contribute to the economic prosperity in India."[327]

Finally, the Paris Court of Appeal has several times been faced with the scope of "investor" and "investment" under investment treaties, and relied on the Vienna Principles in its judgments.

In the arbitration between Energoalians and Moldova, the state was ordered to pay Energoalians $49 million after the tribunal found that the state breached the fair and equitable treatment provision in the ECT. The award was rendered by majority; unusually, the two party-appointed arbitrators had found that the tribunal had jurisdiction under the ECT, while the chairman dissented and would have dismissed the case for lack of jurisdiction. The focus of the disagreement between the chairman and his co-arbitrators was the proper interpretation of the ECT's definition of investment, a question which was also at the centre of Moldova's challenge in the Paris Appeals Court.[328]

Energoalians' alleged investment,[329] as accepted by the tribunal majority, consisted of a right to recover debt from state-owned electricity company, Moldtranselectro, for electricity that was sold to, but never paid, by Moldtranselectro. The question whether contractual claims can constitute investments under international law is well-known in arbitration jurisprudence and the tribunal went through many cases in its analysis, including the *Salini* test relied

326 Ibid., para. 4.15.

327 Ibid., para. 4.16.

328 Moldova v. Energoalians, Paris Court of Appeal. Subsequent to the finalizing of this text, as mentioned in the introduction, the French Court of Cassation reversed the Court of Appeal's judgment, expressly coming to another conclusion with respect to the scope of "investment" in the ECT. See Energoalians SARL (Komstroy) v Moldova, Cour de cassation, Chambre civile 1, 16-16568, 28 March 2018.

329 By the time the case reached the Paris court, another entity, Komstroy, had obtained the rights to the award from Energoalians but for the sake of consistency, in this text the case is referred to by the name of the original investor.

on by Moldova.[330] When interpreting the relevant definition in the ECT, however, the tribunal had found it to be broader than in most other treaties, for example by expressly including "claim to money" in its list of examples. The tribunal also stressed the treaty's objectives of promoting economic development and protect investments.

When reviewing Moldova's challenge against the majority's jurisdictional finding the Paris court found that the majority had been wrong to declare itself competent. The court stated that the treaty's arbitration clause in Article 26(1) grants jurisdiction over disputes under Part III of the treaty, which concerns investment, but not under Part II, which concerns trade. This distinction between trade and investment, in the court's view, justified Moldova's contention that the ordinary meaning of the term, in the light of its purpose, would require some sort of contribution for an investment to have taken place.[331]

The court also pointed out that the definition of investment in Article 1(6) required a connection to an "economic activity in the energy sector," which the investor's claims to money did not fulfil. The underlying contract had as its "sole purpose" to sell electricity and did not constitute an investment in the meaning of the ECT. The award was therefore set aside for lack of jurisdiction. The wording of the Paris court has clear traces of the VCLT, which was presumably relied upon by Moldova in its challenge, and refers expressly to Article 31 and its status as international custom.[332] Furthermore, the court states, for example, that "the appellant relies rightly upon the condition of *contribution*, according to the ordinary meaning under the treaty in its context and in the light of its purpose."[333]

In *Tatneft v. Ukraine*,[334] the tribunal found that Ukraine was liable for violating the fair and equitable treatment standard in the Russia – Ukraine BIT and ordered the state to compensate Tatneft with $112 million plus interest. The two awards remain unpublished but it can be deduced from the Paris court decision that the investor successfully complained that several organs of the state acted to force Tatneft out of a joint venture, which owned an oil refinery.

Ukraine then moved to challenge the award on several grounds at the place of arbitration in Paris.[335] Among other things, the state claimed that the tribunal did not have jurisdiction *ratione personae*, because Tatneft was not a Russian investor but rather an official part of the Russian Federation. The

330 Moldova v. Energoalians, Paris Court of Appeal, p. 6.

331 Ibid.

332 Ibid., p. 4.

333 Ibid., p. 6. Emphasis added.

334 OAO *Tatneft v. Ukraine*, UNCITRAL, Award on the Merits, 29 July, 2014.

335 *Ukraine v. Tatneft*, Paris Court of Appeal.

BIT's arbitration clause allows for arbitration of disputes "between either Contracting Party and the investor of the other Contracting Party." According to Ukraine, a reading of this language must take into account the Vienna Principles, more specifically the ordinary meaning of the terms in their context and in the light of the object and purpose of the treaty. Under such a reading, taking into account that the treaty's purpose is to protect private investment and not to assist in the settlement of interstate disputes, the state argued, the tribunal did not have jurisdiction over Tatneft.[336]

Ukraine's case in this respect was built on the fact that Tatarstan, a semi-autonomous Russian republic, had a controlling interest in Tatneft and that the Prime Minister of Tatarstan chaired the company's executive board, which was also comprised by other minsters from Tatarstan. Ukraine also pointed out that Tatneft appears to have been specifically designed by the Republic of Tatarstan in order to participate in the joint venture, and that the Tatarstani government held a "golden share" in the company, which under Russian law entitled it to veto power over several major corporate decisions.

Furthermore, Ukraine argued that Tatneft met the tests laid down in Articles 8 and 9 of the International Law Commission's Articles on State Responsibility for attributing its conduct to Russia. This would also preclude Tatneft from bringing an arbitration under the BIT, Ukraine argued, since Tatneft in essence ought to be regarded as a state entity.

The Paris court did not accept these arguments. Like the state, the court referred to the Vienna Principles but stated that accepting Ukraine's contention would amount to adding a requirement which does not exist in the wording of treaty: that of the investor's "private" character.[337]

Furthermore, Ukraine's attribution argument was swiftly rejected without the court going into its merits: the court stated that the ILC rules regulate an "entirely different context" than the question of whether an entity is "assimilated" by a state for the purpose of a right to arbitration under a treaty.[338]

Instead, the court emphasized that Tatneft is a public limited company, publicly traded and listed on the Moscow Stock Exchange, and that although the government of Tatarstan held 36% of the shares, the remaining shares were spread over more than 50,000 shareholders.[339] Although the record showed that the Tatarstani government did hold a "golden share," the court stated that this did not mean that Tatneft could be characterized by an "absence of

336 Ibid., p. 4.
337 Ibid., p. 5.
338 Ibid., p. 6.
339 Ibid.

structural, organizational and decisional autonomy."[340] Rather, this type of arrangement, in the court's view, is not uncommon in the restructuring of certain markets in post-Soviet economies.

Another claim raised by Ukraine before the Paris court concerned Tatneft's alleged bad faith acquisition of two other shareholders in the joint venture, which was made after the dispute with Ukraine was foreseeable. This bad faith acquisition, according to the state, was an "artificial" attempt to become a protected investor under the BIT, which should have been rejected by the arbitral tribunal (which, one would assume, instead accepted jurisdiction over damages also relating to these two other shareholders).

This claim did not convince the court either. It stated that in order to be successful in its bad faith allegation, Ukraine would have to both demonstrate that the investment was made subsequent to the dispute had arisen, and that that it meant a 'significant advantage' to bring the shareholders under the Russia – Ukraine BIT, compared to the situation prior to the restructuring. With respect to the latter criterion, the court noted that the two shareholders each could have had access to investment treaties in the form of the ECT and the United States – Ukraine BIT, respectively. Compared to these treaties, Ukraine had "neither demonstrated nor even alleged" that the restructuring meant a significant advantage. Under these circumstances, an attempt to set aside the award based on bad faith on behalf of the investor could not succeed.[341]

The cases discussed above are not the only ones where the concepts of investor and investment have been discussed by domestic courts with the aid of the Vienna Principles. Other examples include whether dual nationals qualify as investors,[342] the jurisdictional consequences of corporate restructuring,[343] and whether investments are "invested" in a protected "territory."[344]

"Cooling off-periods"

In Kazakhstan's challenge against the ECT award rendered in favour of Ascom, Stati, and Terra Raf,[345] the state argued that the investors' failure to negotiate for three months prior to the request of arbitration meant that the arbitration

340 Ibid.

341 Ibid., p. 7.

342 *Venezuela v. Garcia Armas*, Paris Court of Appeal, succesfully appealed to the Cour de Cassation, which remanded the case to the Paris Court of Appeal (pending at the time of writing).

343 *Venezuela v. Gold Reserve.*

344 *Russia v. Stabil and Ukrnafta.*

345 *Anatolie Stati, Gabriel Stati, Ascom Group SA and Terra Raf Trans Traiding Ltd v. Kazakhstan, SCC* Case No. 116/2010, Award, 19 December 19.

agreement was never perfected. The investors did not contest that they had not complied with the cooling off period but argued that this fact did not deprive the tribunal of its jurisdiction.

This prompted the Svea Court of Appeal to interpret the cooling-off provision of the ECT, located in Article 26 of the treaty. Subparagraphs (1) and (2) of that article read as follows:

> 1. Disputes between a Contracting Party and an Investor of another Contracting Party relating to an Investment of the latter in the Area of the former, which concern an alleged breach of an obligation of the former under Part III shall, if possible, be settled amicably.
> 2. If such disputes can not be settled according to the provisions of paragraph (1) within a period of three months from the date on which either party to the dispute requested amicable settlement, the Investor party to the dispute may choose to submit it for resolution

The court recognized that a treaty should be interpreted according to the Vienna principles. In setting out its general approach to these principles, the court stated that the wording of the treaty provision is always the starting point: if the wording is clear, that should in principle be the end of the interpretation.[346] The object and purpose of a treaty cannot be an "independent" means of interpretation, but part of the general operation inscribed in Article 31. In this, the court made express reference to its own judgment in the *Renta 4* declaratory action, decided earlier the same year.[347]

The court stressed that nothing in the provision regulated which steps were to be taken during the three cooling-off months, nor what is the case if it is clear already before this time that any attempts at amicable solution would be futile. Already from this, the court said that the wording suggested that the provision did *not* contain formal conditions for a tribunal's jurisdiction.[348] Furthermore, the court compared the wording with that of Article 27 ECT, which regulates state-state disputes. It stated that the two articles are similarly structured but that Article 27 speaks of a "reasonable time"; the difficulty in determining what is reasonable further supported that such a requirement is not a condition for jurisdiction.[349]

From the wording and structure of the article the court therefore leaned towards finding that a failure to abide by the three-months negotiation

---

346 *Kazakhstan v. Ascom/Stati et al*, Svea Court of Appeal, p. 46.
347 Ibid. The *Renta 4* judgement is discussed further below at 3.2.4.2.
348 Ibid., p. 47.
349 Ibid., p. 47.

requirement did not deprive the tribunal of its jurisdiction. This conclusion was not "unambiguous," however, so the court proceeded to take further aspects into account.

These included the various arbitral awards and scholarly articles that had been brought to the court's attention by the parties. The court stated that the consequences of a failure to respect a cooling off period seems to be disputed in the academic literature. In fact, it was possible to find support for both parties' position. Although a few arbitral awards had been furnished to support Kazakhstan's position, the court pointed out that none of them had been based on the ECT; on the contrary, no ECT tribunal seemed ever to have rejected jurisdiction based on a failure to comply with Article 26(2).[350]

Still, the court did not find its reading of the requirement to be sufficiently supported. It therefore proceeded to discuss also the object and purpose of the treaty. The court stated that the main purpose behind Article 26 of the ECT appeared to be to "give investors an opportunity to use arbitration to solve ECT disputes with a contracting state."[351] Against this background, the court examined the consequences of reading the requirement as a bar to jurisdiction, finding that it would be both impractical and futile. Since the three months have normally elapsed when the tribunal is seized with the matter, a finding of no jurisdiction would simply be followed by an immediate new request for arbitration. It is also possible – and in fact common – that the underlying purpose of the requirement is fulfilled by the tribunal during the arbitral proceedings, for example by ordering the parties to negotiate. In the case before it, the court pointed out, the tribunal had in fact put the arbitration on hold in order for the parties to negotiate amicably.

Based on these considerations, delivered in a step-by-step manner which took into account various aspects of the Vienna principles, the court found that the three-month cooling off period was not a condition for jurisdiction and summed up its conclusion:

> The contracting states have given their unconditional consent to ECT arbitration in subparagraph (3). In the court's view, no further conditions for a valid arbitration agreement should be imposed unless they have express support in the wording of the provisions. No such support exists in the present case.[352]

---

350 Ibid., p. 48.
351 Ibid., p. 49.
352 Ibid., p. 51.

3.2.3.3 Interpretation without the VCLT

In contrast to the many examples of domestic courts expressly making use of, or at least recognizing the relevance of, the VCLT, there are also examples of national courts interpreting the underlying investment treaty without recognizing the VCLT or the interpretative rules inscribed therein. As discussed more extensively at 5.3.2.1, these cases are interesting when viewed from the perspective of the interplay between domestic law and international law, since it is not clear what type of interpretative exercise the courts perceive themselves to be engaged in.

At times, it is not clear if a domestic court is in fact interpreting a treaty or, rather, trying to subsume treaty provisions into their domestic order. By way of illustration, the Swiss Federal Tribunal – which in later cases has utilized the Vienna Principles frequently – was faced with such a crossover question in the early *Saar Papier* challenge.[353] As a preliminary question, the court had to address the rather fundamental question whether the BIT's arbitration clause could constitute an arbitration agreement in the meaning of the PILA, since Saar Papier was not a party to the treaty. In the court's view, the treaty was similar to a contract concluded in the interest of a third party (i.e. Saar Papier in this case), which constituted a standing offer to enter into an arbitration agreement.[354] The investor then accepted the offer by initiating arbitration.[355] This interesting conclusion – relatively novel at the time[356] – could possibly raise questions of international law.[357] It also bears resemblance to the theory of third party rights in international law.[358] Nevertheless, the Swiss Federal Tribunal proceeded to state that not only had Poland participated in the proceedings, but Zurich was the place of arbitration, and neither party had Swiss domicile or had excluded the application of the PILA.[359] Under these circumstances, the PILA was applicable, without any need to muse further on the exact nature of the nature of the treaty's dispute resolution clause.

353 *Poland v. Saar Papier*, Swiss Federal Tribunal.
354 Ibid., I, 1.c.
355 Ibid.
356 And subsequently confirmed by the same court in the *Saluka* challenge.
357 On the notion of host states' "public offer" to arbitrate, see above at 3.1, as well as A M Steingruber, pp. 61–62 with further reference.
358 See AM Steingruber, p. 63 with further reference.
359 *Poland v. Saar Papier*, Swiss Federal Tribunal, 1.d.

Interpreting "investment" without the VCLT principles

In the challenge against the *SwemBalt v. Latvia* award,[360] the key question put before the Maritime and Commercial Court of Copenhagen was whether SwemBalt owned an investment within the meaning of the Sweden – Latvia BIT. The Danish court interpreted the treaty's definition broadly – as argued by SwemBalt – and in doing so relied primarily on the fact that the provision contained a non-exhaustive list of examples.[361] It also pointed out that nowhere in the treaty was there support for Latvia's contention that the scope of "investment" should be construed narrowly. In reaching its conclusion, the Danish court seemingly relied on general principles of contract interpretation; it did not recognize that the fact that the provision is located in a treaty would justify treating the matter any differently than other interpretational tasks. Rather, the court's reasoning seems based on an implied intention by the parties to give the term investment a broad meaning by including a non-exhaustive list of examples.

Nevertheless, the ICSID award in *American Manufacturing & Trading, Inc. v. Zaire* was cited as support for the court's wide reading of the scope of investment, and one professor of international law, as well as employees from both states' foreign ministries, were heard as expert witnesses in order to determine the intention of the contracting states.

A similar approach was taken by the Paris Court of Appeal when the Czech Republic tried to set aside a partial UNCITRAL award in which the tribunal held the state liable for breaching the fair and equitable treatment standard in the Czech Republic – Croatia BIT.[362] The state advanced as its primary argument that the tribunal only had jurisdiction to hear disputes involving an investment protected by the BIT, which the Croatian investor, Mr. Pren Nreka, did not have. This prompted the Paris court to look into the treaty's definition of investment. Mr. Nreka had, through his Czech company, renovated parts of a commercial building owned by a state-owned entity. In exchange for the work, Mr. Nreka's company achieved a fifteen-year lease to operate a pizzeria in the building. A Czech ministry revoked the lease and repossessed the entire building, which prompted Mr. Nreka to request arbitration and ask for compensation.

360 *Latvia v. SwemBalt*, Maritime and Commercial Court of Copenhagen.

361 Ibid., pp. 21–22.

362 *Czech Republic v. Pren Nreka*, Paris Court of Appeal.

In the set-aside proceeding,[363] the state advanced that neither the work agreement for the renovation, nor the lease constituted an "investment." The state argued that Mr. Nreka's contract was a "mere commercial transaction" and relied on arbitration case law in general and ICSID case law in particular in this assertion, referring to the five criteria known as the "*Salini* criteria" as developed in ICSID jurisprudence.[364]

The Paris court rejected this challenge and found that Mr. Nreka had an investment covered by the BIT. In doing so, the court interpreted – without expressly applying the VCLT – the treaty's definition of investment and emphasized that it did not contain "any criteria identifying what is an investment, but rather give[s] a list, that is moreover non-exhaustive, of cases considered an investment."[365] This non-exhaustive list in Article 1 of the BIT includes "any right conferred under contract," which led the court to find that the right to a 15-year lease was indeed covered by the "very broad terms of the BIT."[366]

Similarly, the Svea Court of Appeal in *The Kyrgyz Republic v. Petrobart*,[367] interpreted several provisions of an investment treaty – including the definition of "investment" – without expressly discussing which interpretative standards it was using.

One jurisdictional question in the underlying arbitration had been the territorial applicability of the ECT, under which the claims were brought. Petrobart was incorporated in Gibraltar and the question before the tribunal was to what extent the United Kingdom's ratification of the treaty also covered Gibraltar. United Kingdom ratified the ECT provisionally on December 17, 1994 and then stated that the provisional application covered also Northern Ireland and Gibraltar. When the state finally ratified the treaty on December 13, 1996, it did so expressly covering Northern Ireland, The Bailiwick of Jersey and Isle of Man but without mentioning Gibraltar. Therefore, in Kyrgyzstan's view, the final ratification did not cover Gibraltar and the provisional application for that area seized when the ECT finally entered into force in 1998.

The tribunal, however, had found that it had jurisdiction over Petrobart.[368] It stated that the provisional application still applied to Gibraltar and that the United Kingdom would have to make the opposite clear when making its final ratification. When the award was challenged, Svea Court of Appeal stated

363 The English version of the decision available in MEALEY's International Arbitration Report, Vol. 24, #2, February 2009. The award remains unpublished.

364 MEALEY's International Arbitration Report, Vol. 24, #2, February 2009. p. 3.

365 Ibid., p.4.

366 Ibid., p.4

367 *Kyrgyzstan v. Petrobart*, Svea Court of Appeal.

368 *Petrobart v. Kyrgyzstan*, SCC Case No. 126/2003, Award, 20 March 2005, p.60 et seq.

that this particular situation – when the provisional application and the final application does not have the same territorial reach – was not regulated in the treaty. Therefore, the treaty had to be interpreted. Following this statement, the court agreed with the tribunal in its assessment that the United Kingdom "could not be assumed to have intended [to end the provisional application for Gibraltar], but rather that there likely were political reasons for not mentioning Gibraltar in the ratification document."[369] Thus the court found that Gibraltar was still covered by the treaty's provisional application and consequently that there existed a valid arbitration agreement between the parties in this respect.[370]

In addition, Kyrgyzstan's argued before the Svea Court that the tribunal had committed a procedural error in failing to properly analyse its own jurisdiction, given the state's claim that the United Kingdom's ratification of the ECT did not cover Gibraltar. The claimed damages were relatively modest and the parties had agreed that the arbitration would be conducted without any hearings. Instead, the parties agreed that the tribunal would pose questions to the parties and give each party the opportunity to comment on the other party's replies. Although the tribunal did not pose the issue of ECT's application to Gibraltar, Kyrgyzstan had asked it to request a comment from the ECT Secretariat, which the tribunal declined to do.

The court found that this decision did not violate any procedural principle: the tribunal had in fact extensively analysed the state's argument. Furthermore, the reason that the tribunal did not ask the ECT Secretariat for a view was based on the tribunal's assessment that the Secretariat would not have made such a comment if approached. This assessment was confirmed before the court, which heard Adnan Amkhan, Head of the Legal Affairs Department of the ECT Secretariat as a witness.

The state also argued that the gas contract in question did not constitute an investment under the ECT. The court rejected this argument in two short paragraphs, stating that the intention behind the ECT – confirmed by Mr. Amkhan's testimony – was to give the treaty's definition of investment a wide scope. The court could therefore not find that there was no valid arbitration agreement on this ground.

These three cases share similar traits. Seemingly, each court focused primarily on the respective parties' intentions when negotiating the treaties, which would be generally in line with civil law traditions of interpreting agreements. In interpreting the respective investment treaties' definition of investment,

369 *Kyrgyzstan v. Petrobart*, Svea Court of Appeal, p. 9, translation by the present author.

370 Ibid.

neither court made reference to the Vienna Principles. Instead, both the SwemBalt and Pren Nreka courts referred to the definitions' examples of investment as indications that the parties had wished for a broad understanding of the term. The Petrobart court came to a similar conclusion, relying instead on the testimony from an official involved in the treaty negotiations.

Furthermore, although neither court makes clear that the relevant "parties" are states, two of them nevertheless implicitly recognize the international character of the underlying instruments: both the Danish court and the French court relied on ICSID jurisprudence with respect to the definition of "investment" in international law, and the Danish court also heard testimony from the contracting states' government officials as part of determining the parties' intentions.

The judgments serve to illustrate the confluence of domestic and international law when the scope of a treaty-based tribunal's jurisdiction is challenged. While the Vienna Principles are no magic provisions fostering consistent interpretation – on the contrary – they say very little about the state parties' "intentions." By contrast, in many (civil law) jurisdictions' contract interpretation canon, finding out the parties' intentions, as expressed in the contract or as implied agreement, is the very purpose behind contract interpretation. By searching for the state parties' intentions when determining the scope of the term "investment," one could argue that all three courts essentially treated the investment treaty before them as if it were a contract between two private parties, governed by domestic law.

It is worth pointing out that these three cases, while not discussing standard of review, all illustrate clearly a *de novo* approach to jurisdictional review. The *SwemBalt* court's analysis of the definition of "investment" has even been criticized for venturing too far into the merits of the case, possibly in a manner not compatible with Danish arbitration law prohibiting such review of the merits.[371]

"Cooling off-periods"

If the three "non-VCLT cases" from Denmark, France and Sweden hint at an implicit tension between applying domestic interpretation principles on the one hand, and applying treaty interpretation principles on the other, that implicit tension was made explicit in the only treaty-based challenge to reach the United States Supreme Court so far. In *Argentina v. BG Group*, the state asked the court to set aside an award rendered in favour of British investor BG Group. Once the case reached the Supreme Court, the single legal question was how to interpret Article 8(2) of the BIT between the United Kingdom and

371 Christoph Liebscher, "The SwemBalt Case," 2 Stockholm Arb. Rep. 281 (2003).

Argentina. The provision, which contains the states' consent to arbitration, includes the following language:

> (2) The aforementioned disputes shall be submitted to international arbitration in the following cases:
> (a) if one of the Parties so requests, in any of the following circumstances:
> (i) where, after a period of eighteen months has elapsed from the moment when the dispute was submitted to the competent tribunal of the Contracting Party in whose territory the investment was made, the said tribunal has not given its final decision; [...]

Similar to the *Ascom/Stati* challenge in Stockholm, it was uncontested that BG Group had not complied with the 18-months local litigation requirement. The tribunal had found that under the particular circumstances of the case, this failure was not an impediment to the tribunal's jurisdiction and subsequently went on to render an award in favour of BG Group.

In the DC Court of Appeals, Argentina had successfully challenged the award on the ground that the tribunal had no jurisdiction, due to the 18-months requirement not having been respected. In the Supreme Court, the question, in essence, was this: who should determine the precise meaning of this language, the tribunal or the court at the place of arbitration?

The majority of the court held that this was a question for the tribunal, and not for the reviewing court. In arriving at this conclusion, the majority applied the same reasoning they would have if the arbitration had been based on a contract. In such cases, the court stated, the presumption is that the contracting parties intended for questions of "arbitrability" to be decided by courts.[372] However, the question of the precise meaning of the local litigation requirement was not such a question, but rather a "particular procedural precondition" which determines "*when* the contractual duty to arbitrate arises, not *whether* there is a contractual duty to arbitrate at all."[373] In such cases, the court held, the presumption is the opposite and the tribunal should answer the question.

---

372 *BG Group v. Argentina*, United States Supreme Court p. 7. It should be noted that the meaning of the phrase "arbitrability" is different in US arbitration law than in international commercial arbitration generally. In the former case, the phrase covers a variety of situations where the arbitration agreement is contested, whereas in the latter case the phrase has a more restricted meaning referring to the whether or not the particular dispute can be subjected to arbitration. For a summary of scholarly criticism of US courts on this point, see J Paulsson, The Idea of Arbitration, p. 72, under the heading "American struggles with 'arbitrability'."

373 *BG Group v. Argentina*, United States Supreme Court, p. 8.

After doing so, the majority also stated that the fact that this particular arbitration was *not* based on a contract – but rather on a treaty to which one of the disputing party was not, and could not be, a party – did not alter its conclusions. Relying on US court decisions, the court stated that "as a general matter, a treaty is a contract, though between nations. Its interpretation normally is, like a contract's interpretation, a matter of determining the parties' intent."[374] It supported this stance by referring to the language in the Article V(1)(e) of the New York Convention, which states that an award may be set aside by the competent authority at the seat of arbitration, as well as to arbitration treatises stating that in such circumstances, the domestic arbitration law controls the question of the validity.[375]

Having established a high degree of deference to the tribunal's finding, the court went on to apply this standard, holding that the tribunal stayed within its mandate.[376] Accordingly, the majority found that the tribunal's decision to uphold jurisdiction must be given deference and that its finding that the failure to observe the 18-month requirement did not impede access to arbitration, should be respected.

By contrast, the dissent, written by Chief Justice John Roberts and joined by Justice Anthony Kennedy, complains that the majority "starts down the wrong road and therefore ends up at the wrong place."[377] The dissenting opinion points out that a treaty is different from a contract when it comes to interpreting the arbitration agreement, due to the "important fact" that the investor is not party to the agreement, which is instead concluded between two sovereign nations.[378] Despite this initial statement, in substance the dissent seems to focus on the agreement between the investor and Argentina – of which there is none, at least not in the direct, traditional sense – and interprets that agreement in light of domestic contract law, finding that Argentina's intention was that the local litigation requirement be a precondition to jurisdiction. In substance, the dissent does not recognize that the agreement to be interpreted is between two states and should be interpreted accordingly, but instead focuses on the agreement between the respondent state and the investor. As discussed above, by ultimately siding with Argentina, the dissent found that the issue is one of jurisdiction and should therefore be reviewed *de novo* in accordance with US arbitration law, which was also the finding of the Court of Appeals.

---

374 Ibid., p. 10.
375 Ibid., p. 11.
376 Ibid., p. 18.
377 BG Group v. Argentina, United States Supreme Court, Dissenting Opinion, p. 1.
378 Ibid.

It is interesting to note that the US Solicitor General, in an *amicus* brief, had urged the court to interpret the nature of the treaty's local litigation clause with assistance of the VCLT.[379] The United States government recognizes the Vienna principles as customary international law but US courts have a well-known complicated relationship to the law of treaties generally.[380]

Ultimately, neither the majority decision nor the dissenting opinion mentions the VCLT or treaty interpretation more generally. Instead, both the majority decision and the dissent, while at least paying lip service to the relevance of international law, seem to proceed from the presumption that the question is one of domestic law, and should be interpreted accordingly. The majority described this approach succinctly when it stated that the fact that the consent was located in a treaty would not warrant "abandoning, or increasing the complexity of, our ordinary intent-determining framework."[381]

3.2.3.4 Non-Codified Principles of Treaty Interpretation

There are established principles of treaty interpretation that are not part of the Vienna Principles. These include various legal maxims such as *ejusdem generis* (of the same kind), *lex posterior derogate legi priori* (later law overrides earlier law) and *lex specialis derogat legi generali* (specific law overrides more general law).[382] Domestic courts have only very rarely utilized such non-codified principles of treaty interpretation in their practice. One exception is the principle of effectiveness, *effet utile*, which provides that a norm should be construed so as to have the greatest possible effect towards its aim. The principle of effectiveness has a long-standing role in treaty interpretation by international courts and tribunals,[383] and has often been invoked also by investment arbitration tribunals.[384] However, the principle is not part of the Vienna Principles, although it is sometimes held to be an implicit part of the "good faith" and

---

379 *BG Group v. Argentina*, United States Supreme Court, Case No. 12–138, *Brief for the United States as Amicus Curiae in Support of Vacatur and Remand*, pp. 16–17, available at https://www.italaw.com/sites/default/files/case-documents/italaw3020.pdf, visited 8 January, 2020.

380 See generally E Criddle, 'The Vienna Convention on the Law of Treaties in US Treaty Interpretation' (2005) 44 VJIL 431.

381 *BG Group v. Argentina*, United States Supreme Court, p. 12.

382 See J Weeramantry, Treaty Interpretation, paras 5.86–5.97.

383 A standard text on the matter still seems to be H Lauterpacht, "Restrictive Interpretation and the Principle of Effectiveness in the Interpretation of Treaties," 26 Brit. Y.B. Int'l L. 48, 85 (1949).

384 For an overview, see J Weeramantry, Treaty Interpretation, paras. 5.75–5.85.

"object and purpose" criteria in Article 31 VCLT.[385] In any event, a few courts have referred to this principle in their interpretative exercise, seemingly finding it to be relevant as an international principle, rather than a domestic one.

In the challenge against the *EDF v. Hungary* award, the Swiss Federal Tribunal set out its interpretative approach to the question of Hungary's reservation to the ECT, by pointing out that "the principle of good faith is intimately connected to the rule of interpretation of the effectiveness of the law, even if the latter does not expressly appear in Article 31 VCLT."[386] By recognizing this tension, the court was faced with several possible readings of Hungary's reservation to the treaty's umbrella clause. Hungary had argued before the court that the investor's (and the arbitral tribunal's) reading of the state's reservation rendered it ineffective: if the tribunal was allowed jurisdiction over any claim that is presented as either contractual or treaty-based, the state's reservation would be circumvented.[387] Essentially, the disputing parties argued before the court that the unclear scope of the reservation should be interpreted restrictively (in the case of EDF) or expansively (in the case of Hungary). The court ultimately found that the tribunal had been right in categorizing the relevant claims as treaty-based, leaving them outside the scope of Hungary's reservation.[388] Reading the reservation as suggested by Hungary would mean that any investment with a contractual element (such as the PPAs in the case before the tribunal) would be excluded from protection by Article 10(1) ECT, thereby depriving that article of any effectiveness.[389]

In *Sanum*, the Court of Appeal seemingly embraced the arbitral tribunal's reliance on the *effet utile* principle.[390] Although ultimately finding that the principle would not be violated by Laos' reading of the narrow arbitration clause, given the lack of a fork-in-the-road clause in the relevant BIT, the

385 R Gardiner, Treaty Interpretation, p. 66; M. Waibel, Uniformity versus Specialisation (Working Paper), p. 18; J. Weeramantry, Treaty Interpretation, para. 5.74. This contention has been criticized, see T Wälde, "Interpreting Investment Treaties: Experiences and Examples," in P Binder et al (eds.), *International Investment Law for the 21st Century: Essays in Honour of Christoph Schreuer*, Oxford University Press, 2009, pp. 738–740, in which Wälde calls this proposition "tenuous," stating that "ignoring a text element that the parties may have used in a duplicative way or without any particular meaning attached is not necessarily a breach of 'good faith'."

386 Hungary v. EDF, Swiss Federal Tribunal, para. 3.5.1.

387 Ibid., para 3.5.2.

388 Ibid., para. 3.5.3.1.

389 Ibid., para. 3.5.4.3.

390 Sanum v. Laos, Singapore Court of Appeal, para. 128, citing para. 333 of the award.

tribunal nevertheless assumed that the "principle of effective interpretation" was a relevant consideration.[391]

Finally, the Dutch Supreme Court embraced a lower court's use of effectiveness considerations as part of its interpretative exercise in the Occidental case. Citing two ICJ decisions, the Supreme Court stated that any use of Articles 31 and 32 VCLT involves interpreting a treaty term so that the result is not meaningless.[392]

3.2.4 *Procedural Particularities*

Unlike the one-stop shop of ICSID annulment, each domestic jurisdiction is different. There are countless specific varieties within the studied jurisdictions, which may or may not come into play during a challenge proceeding. Below, a number of specific domestic traits that *have* been brought to the surface by the material are discussed.

3.2.4.1 Availability of Court Review

Which court is competent to hear a challenge against an arbitral award? The UNCITRAL Model Law stipulates in Article 6 that a number of functions under the law shall be performed by a body, and states within square brackets that "Each State enacting this model law specifies the court, courts or, where referred to therein, other authority competent to perform these functions." Different jurisdictions have approached the task of court structure differently.

In Switzerland, for example, all challenges are heard directly by the Federal Supreme Court.[393] Other states, such as Sweden[394] and Singapore,[395] have also assigned specific courts for challenges against awards, leading to a certain level of specialization. By contrast, many other jurisdictions retain the same procedural hierarchy as in other private law matters. This means that a first challenge judgment may be appealed not only once but also twice, in states such as the Netherlands and the United States.

In addition to the relatively straightforward question of which and how many courts can hear a challenge against an award, there might also be various restrictions on how and what can be appealed to a higher court within

391 Ibid., paras. 128; 133; 146.

392 Discussed above at 3.2.2.5.

393 Art. 191(1) PILA.

394 In Sweden, the District Court is bypassed and a challenge has to be brought directly to the Court of Appeal at the place of arbitration. The decision of the Court of Appeal may only be appealed to the Supreme Court under certain circumstances, see Section 43 of the SAA.

395 In Singapore, the High Court is the first instance for any challenge, and its decisions may be appealed to the Court of Appeal.

a particular jurisdiction. A specific, but nevertheless clear, example of such a restriction is the limits on the Dutch Supreme Court's review that were brought to the surface in the *Chevron v. Ecuador* challenge.[396] Under Dutch procedural law, the Supreme Court may not review matters of "law of foreign states." No similar restriction exists for the District Court or the Court of Appeal. This provision, which restricts the Supreme Court from pronouncing itself on matters close to foreign powers' sovereignty, was introduced in 1963 and did as such not contemplate review of investment arbitration awards.[397]

Arguably, the reasoning of the Supreme Court in the *Chevron* challenge would suggest that every BIT to which the Netherlands is not a party is covered by the provision, and as such exempt from legal review at the final instance. A different question is whether treaties to which the state *is* a party are covered; a live question considering the several ECT tribunals seated in The Hague, including the largest investment arbitration award ever to be rendered, which at the time of writing is still pending appeal before the Hague Court of Appeal (and as such excluded from the scope of this text).[398] It would be sensible to presume, however, that the ECT is not "law of foreign states," as it is a treaty that the Netherlands has ratified;[399] The Netherlands is a monist state, although often described in doctrine as "moderately" monist, a view which has been endorsed by the Dutch government.[400] The qualifying phrase is explained by the fact that the Dutch constitution sets some limits to the application of international law (such as parliamentary approval and official publication) in the domestic order, and does not treat all sources of international law equally.[401] The ECT is however both approved by parliament and officially published,[402] and thus part of the Dutch legal order. Given the Supreme Court's emphasis in the *Chevron* case that a bilateral treaty "does not apply in the Dutch legal order"[403], the court's reasoning arguably does not extend to the ECT.

---

396 Ecuador v. Chevron, Supreme Court of the Netherlands, discussed above at 3.2.2.5.

397 Dutch Judiciary Organization Act, Article 79(1)(b).

398 Yukos Universal Limited (Isle of Man) v. The Russian Federation, UNCITRAL, PCA Case No. AA 227, Final Award, 18 July, 2014.

399 https://verdragenbank.overheid.nl/en/Verdrag/Details/005900, accessed 7 January, 2017. By way of comparison, the restriction on the Dutch Supreme Court does *not* comprise matters of EU law, which are not regarded to be law of foreign states.

400 E A. Alkema, 'Netherlands', in D Shelton (ed.), *International Law and Domestic Legal Systems: incorporation, transformation, and persuasion,* Oxford University Press, 2011, p. 408 with further references.

401 Ibid.

402 See footnote 832.

403 Ecuador v. Chevron, Supreme Court of the Netherlands, para. 4.4.2.

Therefore, the *Chevron* reasoning does not extend to ECT awards. In any event, it seems this approach to "law of foreign states" is not echoed in any other domestic jurisdiction frequently used for investment arbitration.[404]

A related question is the availability for the disputing parties to completely contract out of the possibility to bring a challenge of the award before the courts at the place of arbitration. Such agreements, commonly known as exclusion agreements, are allowed in a limited number of jurisdictions. Most notable for the present purposes is that France,[405] Sweden[406] and Switzerland[407] are among these jurisdictions. The domestic arbitration acts vary in the way they define how – and by whom – an exclusion agreement can be validly entered into. Since there is rarely any post-dispute, direct arbitration agreement between the disputing parties in the investment arbitration context, the question is to what extent the state parties to an investment treaty can waive any recourse against an award rendered between an investor and one of the states.

This question has been tried in Switzerland. In *Czech Republic v. Saluka*, the investor opposed the state's set-aside attempt by arguing that the following phrase in the BIT constituted an exclusion agreement: "the [tribunal] decision shall be final and binding upon the parties to the dispute."[408] The court was not satisfied that this wording constituted an exclusion agreement, as discussed at 3.2.3.2. However, there were seemingly no obstacles against the treaty states excluding review of the award in principle; the court stated that in order to have such a valid waiver in the treaty, it "would have required another sentence which clearly states that the parties waived the right for any form of review."[409]

Prior to the *Saluka* case, the Swiss Supreme Court had been faced with one treaty-based challenge in which the disputing parties *had* entered into a separate arbitration agreement. In *Lebanon v. France Telecom*,[410] the disputing parties agreed separately to submit a dispute to a tribunal constituted under the France – Lebanon BIT.[411] In the separate agreement, the parties had included the following clause:

---

404 The approach resembles the "justiciability" discussion in England and Singapore, as discussed above at 3.2.1.

405 French Code of Civil Procedure, Article 1522.

406 Swedish Arbitration Act, Section 51.

407 PILA 192(1).

408 Netherlands – Czech Republic BIT, Article 8(7).

409 *Czech Republic v. Saluka*, Swiss Federal Tribunal, para. 5.3.

410 *Lebanon v. France Telecom*, Swiss Federal Tribunal.

411 M Scherer, V Heiskanen and S Moss, "Domestic Review of Investment Treaty Arbitrations: The Swiss Experience," 27 ASA Bulletin 2/2009, p. 273. The award remains unpublished.

> The Parties undertake that they will not challenge the jurisdiction of the UNCITRAL Tribunal whether before the UNCITRAL Tribunal itself or before any national courts. For the avoidance of doubt, the [Parties] do not hereby waive their right to challenge any award in the UNCITRAL Arbitration in the place where the award is made or to resist enforcement thereof in the country or countries where enforcement is sought on the grounds contained in the applicable arbitration laws of those countries, save that the Parties will not do so on the ground that the UNCITRAL Tribunal lacked jurisdiction to consider one or more of the issues before it.

According to the court, this wording was sufficiently clear to constitute an exclusion agreement under Swiss law, albeit restricted to challenges against the tribunal's jurisdiction.[412]

Neither of these Switzerland-seated cases was an ICC case. As discussed in Chapter 4, most treaty-based ICC cases have been seated in either France or Switzerland, two jurisdictions which allow for exclusion agreements under certain circumstances. This fact raises the question of whether or not Article 34(6) of the ICC Rules could constitute an exclusion agreement. Under the headline "Binding Effect of the Award on the Parties," the article reads in its entirety:

> Every award shall be binding on the parties. By submitting the dispute to arbitration under the Rules, the parties undertake to carry out any award without delay and shall be deemed to have waived their right to any form of recourse insofar as such waiver can validly be made.

The second sentence could arguably be read as an exclusion agreement which, by virtue of an investment treaty's reference to the ICC Rules, would exclude domestic court jurisdiction to hear a challenge against an award (provided that this is allowed by the law at the place of arbitration, which might be the case in both Switzerland and France). In the Secretariat's comment to the ICC Rules, it is stated that although the extent of this waiver must be determined by the relevant domestic court according to the applicable procedural law, the provision is "unlikely to be deemed sufficient to constitute a waiver of the right to bring proceedings to set aside an award even in those jurisdictions where such a waiver is possible."[413] This statement is not supported by any reasoning and, although sensible as a matter of policy, does not sit comfortably with the

412 *Lebanon v. France Telecom*, Swiss Federal Tribunal, pp. 10–11.
413 Fry, Greenberg & Mazza, paras. 3-1252–3-1254.

wording of Article 34(6). If the parties waive *any* valid form of recourse against the award, surely that means also the recourse of a challenge, to the extent that is permitted by the law at the place of arbitration.

It is important to note that although exclusion agreements are only expressly allowed in a limited number of jurisdictions, this does not mean they are *prohibited* in other jurisdictions. The Model Law is silent on the question of waiver and the domestic court faced with a purported exclusion agreement would have to determine whether the relevant rules for set-aside proceedings are mandatory. In Canada, for example, the Ontario Court has held that Article 34 of the Model Law (which is replicated in the Canadian act incorporating the Model Law) is not mandatory, based on an earlier draft of the Model Law, as well as the absence of mandatory language.[414]

3.2.4.2 Parallel Declaratory Actions

In Article 16 of the UNCITRAL Model Law, the fundamental principle of *kompetenz-kompetenz* is enshrined. As discussed above at 3.1.1 the principle is generally incorporated in domestic arbitration laws, and provides (i) that an arbitral tribunal may rule on its own jurisdiction, and (ii) that notwithstanding this right, the tribunal's jurisdictional finding is subject to control by the court at the place of arbitration. While these basic features of the doctrine seem to have attracted universal acceptance, the exact shape and timing of the relationship between the tribunal and the court at the place of arbitration differs, however.

The Model Law presumes that the tribunal first rules on its own jurisdiction as a preliminary question.[415] In such a case, a party may ask the court at the place of arbitration, within 30 days of receiving notice of the tribunal's decision, to decide on the tribunal's jurisdiction.[416] While the matter is pending before the court, the tribunal may continue the arbitration, and even render an award.[417] If the tribunal does *not* rule on its own jurisdiction as a preliminary question, but rather incorporates such a ruling in a final award on the merits, only post-award remedies are available to the party wishing to challenge the tribunal's jurisdiction.

The 1999 Swedish Arbitration Act (SAA) deviated from the Model Law in this respect. This has now changed, following the 2019 revision of the SAA. Under

414 *Noble China Inc v Lei* (1998) 42 O.R. (3d) 69; 42 B.L.R. (2d) 262, as cited in B Leon and L Karimi, 'The Canadian Position: Can Parties to an Arbitration Agreement Vary the Statutory Scope of Judicial Review of the Award," ILSA Journal of International & Comparative Law, Vol. 14:2, pp. 7–8.

415 UNCITRAL Model Law, Article 16(3).

416 Ibid.

417 Ibid.

the old Section 2 of the SAA, however, a party could *at any time* during the arbitration ask the court at the place of arbitration to determine the scope and validity of the arbitration agreement. This approach was discussed in the drafting of the Model Law but rejected because it was found to open up for dilatory tactics, as well as not being fully compliant with the tribunal's right to rule on its own competence.[418]

Many jurisdictions have adopted the Model Law solution, which compared to the old Swedish approach limits the extent of potential court involvement, by only allowing parties to challenge in court a separate (positive) jurisdictional decision, and by imposing a relatively short time limit for this challenge. Furthermore, a number of states also subscribe to an approach that arguably favours the tribunal's determination, in the sense that once an arbitration has been initiated, the only way to ask a court to rule on the tribunal's jurisdiction is as part of a set-aside claim after the final award has been rendered; this is the situation in, for example, Belgium, France and Switzerland.[419]

The former "Swedish approach" invited parallel proceedings, which might be problematic. In fact, the commission tasked with proposing revisions of the SAA stated in 2015 that the solution showed traces of "system failure."[420] The commission therefore recommended to the Swedish legislator that the Model Law approach be adopted also in Sweden. Under the revised wording of Section 2, declaratory actions on the tribunal's jurisdiction can only be brought if the tribunal has found that it has jurisdiction, after which a party has 30 days to bring an action before Swedish courts.

This recent change notwithstanding, the Swedish court proceedings involving two different treaty-based cases serve to illustrate the potential for parallel proceedings under the old Section 2 of the SAA. Both cases were seated in Stockholm and saw the Russian Federation challenge BIT awards rendered against it.

In the first, brought by RosInvestCo under the UK – Russia BIT, the tribunal rendered a partial award finding it had jurisdiction in October 2007, and then, in September 2010, rendered its final award, in which it found Russia liable for expropriation.[421] Shortly after the tribunal's jurisdictional decision in 2007,[422]

418 Översyn av lagen om skiljeförfarande, SOU 2015:37, p. 112.

419 Belgian Judicial Code, Art. 1690 §4; French Code of Civil Procedure, Article 1465; Austrian Arbitration Act, Section 584(3).

420 Översyn av lagen om skiljeförfarande, SOU 2015:37, p. 115.

421 *RosInvestCo UK Ltd. v. The Russian Federation*, SCC Case No. V079/2005, Award, 12 September 2010.

422 There is no such thing as a partial award under Swedish arbitration law; under Section 27(3) SAA, what the tribunal deemed an "Award on Jurisdiction" is considered a decision,

Russia initiated an action under Section 2 SAA, asking the court to declare that the tribunal did not have jurisdiction over RosInvestCo's claims. The investor initially challenged the Swedish courts' mandate to hear Russia's declaratory action, arguing – among other things – that it was brought as a dilatory tactic, that there was no genuine need for a declaration, and that the Swedish court could not be asked to interpret the treaty when the treaty itself provided for international arbitration.[423] The Stockholm District Court,[424] the Svea Court of Appeal,[425] and ultimately the Swedish Supreme Court[426] all confirmed that Swedish courts could hear the Section 2 action brought by Russia.[427]

The merits of the action were therefore referred to the Stockholm District Court for review. At this stage, however, the investor no longer participated in the proceedings (presumably because the final award had now been rendered, awarding the relatively modest sum of $3,5 million, which did not justify further litigation). The Stockholm District Court therefore decided in a November 2011 default judgment[428] that the arbitration agreement "which was formed when RosInvestCo requested arbitration on October 28, 2005" did not – contrary to the tribunal's finding – cover the question of whether Russia had enacted expropriatory measures.[429] Thus, the tribunal – which by this stage had already rendered its award on the merits – did not have jurisdiction as a matter of Swedish law. Consequently, the challenge against the award, by now mostly a formality, succeeded and the award was set aside in September 2013 with reference to the 2011 default judgment.[430]

In *Renta 4 v. Russia*,[431] similar to RosInvestCo, the tribunal rendered a partial award, in March 2009, in which it found that it had jurisdiction over some of

---

which cannot be subject to set-aside proceedings.

423 Stockholm District Court, T 24891-07, 17 November 2008, p. 2.

424 Ibid.

425 Svea Court of Appeal, Ö 9773-08, 3 April, 2009.

426 Swedish Supreme Court, Ö 2301-09, 12 November 2010.

427 Unlike a challenge against the final award, which must be brought in the Svea Court of Appeal, an action under the old Section 2 follows general Swedish procedural law and must therefore be brought in the District Court. Following a revision in 2019, this was changed to the competent Court of Appeal.

428 The investors did not participate in the court proceedings and a default judgment in accordance with Russia's claims was rendered without the merits having been tried by the court. On default judgments, see below at 3.2.4.3.

429 Stockholm District Court, T 24891-07, 9 November 2011. Translated from Swedish by the author.

430 Svea Court of Appeal, T 10060-10, 5 September, 2013.

431 *Renta 4 S.V.S.A, Ahorro Corporación Emergentes F.I., Ahorro Corporación Eurofondo F.I., Rovime Inversiones SICAV S.A., Quasar de Valors SICAV S.A., Orgor de Valores SICAV S.A., GBI 9000 SICAV S.A. v. The Russian Federation,* SCC Case No. 24/2007, Award, 20 July 2012.

the investors' claims. Following this partial award, the Russian Federation then initiated a Section 2 motion in Stockholm District Court in September 2009. While the court case was pending, the tribunal proceeded with the arbitration and rendered a final award in July 2012, holding Russia liable for expropriation in violation of the BIT. In the court proceedings, a judgment was rendered in September 2014, over two years after the tribunal had already ruled on the merits of Renta 4's case. The District Court found that Article 10 (the arbitration clause) of the treaty covered the claims and that the tribunal thus had jurisdiction. This judgment was appealed by Russia, and in January 2016 reversed by the Svea Court of Appeal. The appeals court, finding that it had to "make its own interpretation,"[432] found that there was no jurisdiction for the tribunal under the treaty, either under Article 10 or by virtue of the MFN clause. Unlike the *RosInvestCo* case, the investors moved to have this judgment reviewed on appeal in the Swedish Supreme Court, but no leave was granted.[433] Thus, as a matter of Swedish law, the *Renta 4* tribunal was declared not to have jurisdiction under the treaty, although it had already rendered a final award 16 months earlier. The award was eventually set aside, with reference to the judgment in the declaratory action, on June 7, 2018.[434]

These two cases highlight the timing problems inherent in the Section 2 SAA, prior to the revision of this provision. Both court judgments were rendered after the respective arbitrations had been concluded. Thus, in each case an award was rendered following extensive arguments before an arbitral tribunal, after which Swedish courts declared that the tribunal in fact lacked jurisdiction.

3.2.4.3 Default Judgments

Default judgments against a non-participating respondent party are alien to international arbitration, including ICSID annulment. Procedural fairness, as expressed for example in the New York Convention Article V(1)(b), only requires that each party is given the *opportunity* to participate, not that each party in fact does participate.[435] This is the principle of non-frustration – i.e. that a party not showing up will not prevent the proceedings.[436] If the

432 Russia v. Renta 4, Svea Court of Appeal, T 9128-14, Judgement, 18 January 2016, p. 4.

433 Swedish Supreme Court, T 778-16, 14 December, 2016.

434 *Russian Federation v. ALOS 34 et al*, Svea Court of Appeal, Judgment, 7 June 2018, T 9294-12, p. 8.

435 J Butchers and P Kimbrough, "The Arbitral Tribunal's Role in Default Proceedings," Arbitration International, Volume 22 Number 2, p. 234 with further references.

436 C Schreuer calls this principle one of the guiding principles of the ICSID system, C Schreuer, ICSID Commentary, pp. 709–710.

respondent does not participate in an arbitration, or for that matter in an ICSID annulment proceeding, the arbitration will generally proceed and the tribunal or committee will not treat the failure to participate as an admission of the claimant's allegations.[437] Instead, with the removal of the otherwise adversarial character, the tribunal or committee must examine the participating party's submissions.[438]

This procedure is different from the default judgments used in many domestic court systems, whereby a judgment is rendered based on the submissions by the participating party, provided that the non-participating party has been served notice of the proceedings. In such cases, the merits of the claims are not tried by the court. Instead, the claims are made the basis for the default judgment.

If the winning party in an ICSID arbitration does not appear to "defend" the award before the annulment committee, the committee will "deal with the questions submitted to it."[439] When a challenge against a treaty-based award is brought *outside* of the system set up by the ICSID Convention – and thereby brought into a domestic legal sphere – the matter may be different. Depending on the law at the place of arbitration, a default judgment based on the challenging party's claims might be rendered, without the court actually making a determination of those claims.

Such default judgments have been rendered in two treaty-based challenges; in both cases the award was set aside when the "defending" party did not appear before the court. As already mentioned above, one of these was *RosInvestCo v. Russia*, when the challenge of the award took place while a declaratory action was pending simultaneously. After initially having contested, as a preliminary question, that Swedish courts could hear the declaratory action, the investors did not further participate in the Stockholm District Court when the declaratory action was heard.[440] This prompted the Russian Federation to ask for a default judgment in accordance with what it had claimed in its declaratory action, which the court issued without trying the merits of the action.[441] The court therefore declared that the tribunal in the underlying arbitration did not have jurisdiction over RosInvestCo's expropriation claim, while not giving

437 See for example UNCITRAL Model Law Article 25, UNCITRAL Arbitration Rules 2010 Article 30(1)(b), ICSID Convention Article 45 (applicable *mutatis mutandis* to annulment proceedings by virtue of Article 52(4)).

438 C Schreuer, ICSID Commentary, p. 712.

439 ICSID Convention Article 45(2).

440 Stockholm District Court, footnote X above, p. 4.

441 Ibid.

any independent reasons for this finding but rather referring to Russia's submission, which was attached to the judgment.

The other available example of a judgment rendered *in abstentia* – although probably not properly characterized as a default judgment – comes from the only challenge of an award in a treaty-based arbitration seated in the Czech Republic, Binder v. Czech Republic.[442] In June 2007, the UNCITRAL Tribunal issued a separate award, in which it rejected the respondent's state objections to its jurisdiction.[443] This partial award was challenged by the state. In June 2009, the District Court of Prague found – unlike the tribunal – that Mr. Binder's ties to the Czech Republic were too significant for him to be regarded as a German investor under the Germany – Czech Republic BIT (the treaty requires claimants to be "permanent residents" of their purported home state).[444] In fact, the court found Mr. Binder to be Czech for the purpose of the BIT.[445] Therefore, in the District Court's view, the tribunal did not have jurisdiction and the partial award was set aside.

The investor Mr. Binder did not appear in the District Court. According to the judgment, Mr. Binder had claimed that he would prefer any documents to be served in his native German language to his permanent residence in Germany.[446] Nevertheless, the court stated that Mr. Binder had also acquired Czech nationality and had demonstrated good knowledge in the Czech language. Therefore, the notice of the court hearing was written in Czech and served to Mr. Binder's place of business in Prague.[447] Mr. Binder never reacted on the notice, and the court proceeded without hearing him.

Strictly speaking, this decision was not a default judgment in the sense of RosInvestCo, because it was not rendered on the basis of the challenging state's submission. Nevertheless, the relatively short judgment was rendered without Mr. Binder having participate in the proceedings. The District Court's default judgment was appealed by Mr. Binder, arguing, *inter alia*, that the District Court did not have the mandate to set aside a partial award, and that the proper procedure had not been respected by the court, since he was not served and had

442 *Binder v. Czech Republic*, UNCITRAL, Award on Jurisdiction, 6 June 2007.

443 Ibid., para. 16.

444 *Czech Republic v. Rupert Joseph Binder*, District Court of Prague 1, 21 C 174/2007-78, 22 June, 2009, pp. 5–6.

445 Ibid. p. 5.

446 Ibid. pp .4–5.

447 Ibid.

only learned "accidentally" about the District Court judgment.[448] In July, 2010 the City Court of Prague overturned the lower court's decision, thereby ultimately confirming the tribunal's jurisdiction. It did so while noting, but not criticizing, the District Court's decision to proceed with a hearing *in abstentia*,[449] focusing instead on the fact that the arbitral award was not final and thus not (yet) subject to review by Czech courts.[450]

3.2.4.4 Stay of Enforcement

One question of practical relevance is the fate of the arbitral award during the time it is challenged. For the party who lost the arbitration and lodges a challenge against the award, it might be crucial to ensure that the award is not enforced while a *bona fide* challenge against its validity is pending. At the same time, such a stay risks affecting the balance of power between the disputing parties, as it might benefit the debtor: the stay allows the debtor to claim benefits on the money owed, as well as time to structure its assets, which might be especially problematic if the intention is to make enforcement more burdensome.[451]

Such a stay may be sought at the place of enforcement.[452] Although this is a common practice, it will be left out of this text because there is in principle little difference between ICSID and non-ICSID awards in this respect: both types of awards must ultimately be enforced before domestic courts, notwithstanding the self-enclosed nature of the ICSID Convention. It should be noted, however, that if an ICSID award is annulled, it could no longer be enforced. This is not necessarily the case with an award that is enforced under the New York Convention, which permits the court in the enforcing jurisdiction to recognize or enforce an award even if it has been annulled at the place of arbitration.[453]

A stay of enforcement can, however, also be sought at the forum hearing the challenge against the award. At this stage, there *is* a difference between ICSID and non-ICSID, in the sense that the latter is governed by the law at the place of arbitration, while the former is the governed by the ICSID Convention. The decision by one domestic court to stay enforcement of an award is

448 *Rupert Joseph Binder v. Czech Republic*, City Court of Prague, 2 July, 2010,18Co 164/2010 – 183, p. 3

449 Ibid., p. 2.

450 Ibid., p. 4.

451 Bjorklund & Vanhonnaeker, Stays of Enforcement, pp. 45–46.

452 This follows expressly from Article VI of the New York Convention.

453 Article V(1)(e) provides that "recognition and enforcement *may* be refused" in such circumstances (emphasis added). This has led a number of courts to allow enforcement of an award despite it having been set aside at the place of arbitration. See also Article VII.

arguably only valid in that court's home state. Therefore, despite a successful stay of enforcement at the place of arbitration, the award may still be enforced in other states, even if a challenge is still pending. In such cases, as mentioned above, it is up to the courts at the place(s) of enforcement to determine – in accordance with its own law – whether or not to stay enforcement pending the outcome of the challenge at the place of arbitration.

In the ICSID context the question of stay has been a frequent topic before *ad hoc* annulment committees, as the party seeking annulment normally requests a stay of enforcement; indeed, the seeking of an annulment has been deemed "irremediably intertwined" with the seeking of a stay of enforcement.[454] Despite the ostensible benefit of applying the same provision – Article 52(5) of the ICSID Convention – there has been considerable divergence in how different committees have approached the issue.[455]

In the non-ICSID setting, the matter is regulated by the law at the place of arbitration and subject to the jurisdiction of the domestic court hearing the challenge. Domestic courts rarely address the stay of enforcement in challenges of treaty-based awards; presumably this is because enforcement is not often sought at the place of arbitration, but rather in other jurisdictions. One exception is the *Sedelmayer v. Russia* case (which ultimately led to a much-publicized enforcement effort against Russian state assets at the place of arbitration in Stockholm). The challenge against the award was brought under the 1929 Swedish Arbitration Act, and therefore first argued before the Stockholm District Court.[456] In its petition, Russia argued that the investor, Mr. Sedelmayer, had assigned the rights under the award to a corporation in the British Virgin Islands for $580,000, although Mr. Sedelmayer himself had been declared bankrupt and therefore could not legally assign the rights under the award. Based on this information, in a short and unreasoned decision dated October 26, 1998, the court ordered a stay of enforcement of the award "until further notice."[457] The stay was subsequently lifted by the court once the set-aside was unsuccessful.[458]

454 J Fouret, "Stay(ing) on Track or Falling off the Edge: The Absence of Legal Security in the Ad Hoc Committees' Decision under Article 52(5) of the ICSID Convention," ICSID Review FILJ (2012) 27 (2): 303–334, p. 303.

455 For an overview, see B Kotick and J Dahlquist Cullborg, "A (Counter) Balancing Act: The Express Power to Order a Security on a Stay of Enforcement Pending Annulment," ICSID Review - Foreign Investment Law Journal, Volume 33, Issue 1, February 2018, pp. 260–279.

456 See above at 3.2.1.

457 The decision is in the form of a handwritten note on the petition, in Swedish and on file with author.

458 Russian Federation v. Franz J Sedelmayer, Stockholm District Court, T 6-583-98, 18 December 2002, Part 2 of the operative section, p. 1.

Domestic Law Approaches

Notwithstanding the general lack of stays of enforcement in the non-ICSID investment arbitration context, there is no regulatory difference between treaty-based arbitral awards and those based on contracts. Therefore, the general arbitration framework in each state is relevant in understanding how domestic courts might approach the matter in future challenges against treaty-based awards. Compared to the ICSID Convention, generally speaking, domestic courts' powers to order a stay of enforcement seem to be less frequently used. Partly, this as a result of a stay not being automatic in most states. Furthermore, domestic courts tend to review the merits of the set-aside application, and the likelihood of its success, as part of their balancing act when determining whether to allow the stay.[459] By contrast, this consideration is largely absent from the reasoning of ICSID annulment committees.[460]

The UNCITRAL Model Law is silent on the question of stayed enforcement at the place of arbitration. Most arbitration statutes are similarly silent on the matter, which means that one has to look at surrounding legislation and domestic court practice in order to determine the scope and conditions of courts' powers in this respect.

The only frequently used jurisdiction in which enforcement, at least historically, was automatically stayed pending a set-aside proceeding was France.[461] This was changed in 2011,[462] so that instead the court hearing the challenge may halt the enforcement if it risks seriously prejudicing the rights of one of the parties.[463] The change – although it arguably creates a relatively high standard – brought France more in line with other jurisdiction in which challenges against treaty-based awards have been lodged.

For example, an international arbitration award rendered in Switzerland is enforceable as of the notification to the parties. Therefore, in order for the enforcement to be stayed, the Federal Tribunal has to order this as an exceptional measure.[464] A party has to request a stay, and the request is only admissible once a set aside application has been filed.[465] The Federal Tribunal has a

459 Bjorklund & Vanhonnaeker, Stays of Enforcement, p. 61.

460 Ibid., p.62.

461 G Verhoosel, To ICSID or Not to ICSID, p. 144.

462 Decree 2011-48. See also E Kleiman and J Spinelli, *'La réforme du droit de l'arbitrage, sous le double signe de la lisibilité et de l'efficacité'*, Gazette du Palais 2011, No 26- 27, p 9.

463 French Code of Civil Procedure, Article 1526.

464 E Geisinger and A Mazuranic, "Challenge and Revision of the Award" in Elliott Geisinger and Nathalie Voser (eds), *International Arbitration in Switzerland: A Handbook for Practitioners*, 2nd ed., Kluwer Law International 2013, p. 234.

465 Ibid.

wide discretion to decide on the request. The conditions to be considered by the court are the following:

- The party requesting the stay has demonstrated that the immediate enforcement of the award exposes it to serious and irreparable harm in its 'legitimate legal interests';
- The interests of the party requesting the stay prevail those of the party objecting to such stay; and
- The challenge itself very strong *prima facie* chances of success.[466]

Under these conditions, stays of enforcement are rarely granted: in practice, the award creditor must be either on the verge of bankruptcy or located in a country where it would be impossible to recover amounts that have already been paid if the award is then set aside.[467]

Most other jurisdictions where challenges against treaty awards have been brought are characterized by a similar approach to that of Switzerland, in the sense that the filing of a challenge against the award does not automatically halt enforcement, but rather involves a separate analysis of the merits of the challenge.

In Sweden, a stay can only be ordered by the court hearing the set-aside, which has to balance the parties' respective interests, taking into account the objective of a final and binding award.[468] In practice, the test under Swedish law often turns on the likelihood of the award being set aside.[469] The situation in the Netherlands seems to be similar: a stay is not automatic and only granted if the court finds "important reasons" justify it.[470]

Another example of a jurisdiction where the merits of the set-aside is examined when determining whether to stay enforcement is Canada. In the words of the Ontario Court of Justice, courts must judge "whether there is a serious issue to be tried" in the challenge against the award.[471]

In 2015, the English Commercial Court clarified the situation under English law.[472] In the case, one party had successfully asked an English court to

---

466 Ibid.

467 Ibid., with further references.

468 L Heuman, *Arbitration Law of Sweden: Practice and Procedure*, Juris, 2003, p. 656.

469 Ibid.

470 2014 Dutch Arbitration Act, Article 1060(8), translation provided by the Netherlands Arbitration Institute, http://www.nai-nl.org/downloads/Text%20Dutch%20Code%20Civil%20Procedure.pdf, last visited April 25, 2017. Another translation, provided by Linklaters law firm in Amsterdam, uses the phrase "serious reasons," http://www.linklaters.com/Insights/Pages/New-Dutch-Arbitration-Law.aspx, last visited April 25, 2017.

471 *Europcar Italia SpA v. Alba Tours International Inc* [1997] OJ 133, at para 22, as cited by A Bjorklund and L Vanhonnaeker, Stays of Enforcement, p. 61.

472 *Y and S*, English Commercial Court, [2015] EWHC 612, 13 March 2015.

pre-emptively stay the enforcement of the arbitral award pending a challenge of the award, even though no enforcement had yet been sought. The original stay was modified by the Commercial Court, which made clear that it applied only to enforcement effort in England and Wales and not, as the language of the original order implied, globally.[473] Subsequently, the other party applied to have the stay discharged in its entirety, arguing that it should not have been ordered in the first place.

In ruling on the application, the Commercial Court was "prepared to assume" that it had jurisdiction to order a stay of enforcement,[474] but found it inappropriate to exercise that mandate in this particular case.[475] The court pointed out that the stay order, as modified in its second version, did not apply globally, and that there was no intention to seek enforcement in England or Wales (where the debtor did not seem to have any assets).[476] Furthermore, if the award creditor *did* subsequently seek enforcement in England or Wales, the civil procedure rules would allow the debtor to request a stay at that stage, pending the outcome of the set-aside proceeding.[477] The stay was therefore lifted.

Security as a Condition for Stay of Enforcement

With respect to the posting of security as a condition for allowing a stayed enforcement, both the UNCITRAL Model Law and the New York Convention expressly allows for this at the enforcement stage,[478] whereas the ICSID Convention is silent on the matter.[479] However, the extent to which domestic jurisdictions grant their courts this power also during set-aside proceedings within their own jurisdiction seems to be less studied – and less frequently a live issue.

However, the English Commercial Court addressed also this question in its 2015 judgment. Referring to previous English case law, the court stated that it accepted, as a matter of principle, that it may "in an appropriate case, make

473 Ibid., paras. 16–19.

474 Ibid.

475 Ibid., para. 20.

476 Ibid.

477 Ibid.

478 Articles 36(2) and VI, respectively. For an overview of domestic court practice in this context, see N C Port, J R. Simonoff, et al., "Article VI," in H Kronke, P Nacimiento et al. (eds.), *Recognition and Enforcement of Foreign Arbitral Awards: A Global Commentary on the New York Convention,* Kluwer, 2010, pp. 433 et seq.

479 Schreuer has noted that the preliminary draft of the ICSID Convention authorized an annulment committee to order unspecified measures to protect the rights of the parties during the annulment, but that this was rejected by the states and excluded from later drafts, see C Schreuer ICSID Commentary, p. 1076.

any order restricting enforcement of an award conditional upon the respondent putting up security."[480] On the facts before it, however, the court found no reason to make an order restricting enforcement conditional on the provision of security.[481]

Investors have twice asked the United States District Court for the District of Columbia, to order Argentina – the challenging party – to post a bond, not in order to obtain a stay of enforcement during the challenge, but rather in order to have the challenge considered by the court. The request was rejected in both cases, since Argentina's challenges failed before the court had to consider the ordering of such a bond.[482]

In summary, while conditions for a stay of enforcement pending annulment has received significant attention in the ICSID context, it has barely registered on the non-ICSID radar. Presumably this is because the practical relevance of such a stay at the place of arbitration is relatively limited; the resulting order of the court would *prima facie* only be valid at the place of arbitration, where enforcement is rarely sought.

Nevertheless, there are several important differences between the ICSID regime and most domestic jurisdictions. Contrary to what some have argued is the position under the ICSID Convention, no frequently used jurisdiction automatically stays enforcement when a challenge is brought, meaning that the issue has to be initiated by a party. Furthermore, domestic courts hearing the stay petition generally consider the potential of a successful challenge as a factor when deciding whether to stay enforcement, thereby reviewing the merits of the pending challenge. It is also worth pointing out that most jurisdictions allow for the enforcement – and consequently the possible stay of such enforcement – of "partial" awards, i.e. decisions issued by a tribunal prior to the final award.[483] Partial awards often deal with the jurisdiction of the tribunal. Under the ICSID system, there are no such partial awards.[484]

---

480 *Y and S*, English Commercial Court, [2015] EWHC 612, 13 March 2015, para. 31.

481 Ibid., para. 34.

482 *Argentina v. BG Group*, United States District Court for the District of Columbia, 17 January, 2012, p. 5; Argentina v. AWG Group Ltd., United States District Court for the District of Columbia, Civil Action No. 15-1057 (BAH), 30 September 2016, p. 3, footnote 4 (citing the earlier ruling in BG Group).

483 See for example UNCITRAL Model Law, Article 16(3); English Arbitration Act 1996, Section 67(2.)

484 ICSID Convention, Article 48(3).

3.2.4.5 Language

A minor question concerns the language in which a challenge proceeding may be conducted. Within the ICSID regime, the three official languages are English, French and Spanish.[485] In practice the vast majority of proceedings are conducted in either of these languages, although the parties may agree to another language if that choice is approved by the ICSID Secretary-General.[486] The language used before the tribunal is likely to be used also in the committee when annulment is sought.[487]

In domestic courts the point of departure is the language(s) of that particular jurisdiction. However, many non-English speaking jurisdictions seem to allow for parties to submit original documents such as arbitral awards in English, without having to translate them into the court's language.[488] Furthermore, the possibility for international parties to conduct their set-aside proceedings in English has been discussed in a two non-English speaking jurisdictions. In both states, there are currently pending proposals to allow for English to be allowed to a larger extent than what is currently possible.

In Sweden, the Committee tasked with updating the Swedish Arbitration Act has proposed that the Court of Appeal should be mandated to allow that a challenge proceeding is conducted in English, if the parties so agree.[489] Decisions and judgments by the court shall however always be drafted in Swedish, albeit that the parties can request to obtain them simultaneously in English.[490]

In Switzerland, a draft bill for a revision of Chapter 12 of PILA, governing international arbitrations seated in the country, was issued in 2017.[491] It includes a codification of current court practice, which allows parties to file written submissions in English. Similar to the Swedish proposal, the Supreme Court's correspondence and decisions would still be in one of the four official Swiss languages.[492]

---

485 ICSID Administrative and Financial Regulations, Regulation 34.

486 ICSID Rules of Procedure for Arbitration Proceedings, Rule 22.

487 ICSID, *Updated Background Paper on Annulment for the Administrative Council of ICSID*, 5 May, 2016, para. 40.

488 SOU 2015:37, *Översyn av lagen om skiljeförfarande*, p. 138.

489 Ibid., p. 143.

490 Ibid., pp. 143–144.

491 Available in German or French via the Swiss Arbitration Association: https://www.arbitration-ch.org/en/asa/asa-news/details/995.asa-comments-on-revision-of-swiss-international-arbitration-law.html, last visited July 31, 2017.

492 S Nessi, *Introducing English as a possible language in setting-aside proceedings before the Swiss Supreme Court: a good idea?*, Thomson Reuters Practical Law Arbitration Blog, 20 February 2017, http://arbitrationblog.practicallaw.com/introducing-english-as-a-pos-

With the (proposed) exceptions in Switzerland and Sweden, a challenge proceeding must still be conducted in the official language of the relevant court. In Switzerland, where the most challenge proceedings have been challenged, there are four official languages. As pointed out by the Federal Tribunal in its decision on the *EDF* challenge, in non-arbitration settings the court normally uses the language of the decision under appeal. When that language is an unofficial one (such as English, in the *EDF* example), the court instead uses the official language agreed to by the parties. In the *EDF* challenge, the initial brief to the court was in French. Thus, the Federal Tribunal issued its own judgment in French.[493]

In frequently used jurisdictions such as (most of) Canada, England, Singapore, and the United States the official language is of course English, the *lingua franca* of international arbitration and the language in which almost all of the challenged awards were conducted.[494] In other commonly used jurisdictions, the procedural language could potentially be Dutch, French, or German. Even with good knowledge of the *lex arbitri* in the relevant jurisdiction, parties may therefore still need to retain local counsel fluent in the language of the challenge proceeding, and risk delays and expanded costs in the adjudication of the challenge.

3.2.4.6 Precedents

Without venturing into the intricacies of different domestic doctrines of precedent, it is fair to say that, unlike international courts and tribunals generally – and those within the ICSID system specifically – domestic courts are, to various degrees, bound by previous decisions by other courts within their own jurisdiction. Although the "*de facto*" practice of reference to earlier ICSID tribunals is well established,[495] one *ad hoc* annulment committee is not formally bound by how another committee has interpreted the grounds for annulment in the ICSID Convention; it follows from the very name that the committees

sible-language-in-setting-aside-proceedings-before-the-swiss-supreme-court-a-good-idea/, accessed 9 January 2019.

493 *Hungary v. EDF*, Swiss Federal Tribunal, para. 1.

494 The exceptions are the Paris-seated *Energoalians v. Moldova* (Russian), and *De Sutter and others v. Madagascar* (French). The procedural language in the unpublished *RECOFI v. Vietnam* award is not known.

495 See generally J Paulsson, "The Role of Precedent in Investment Arbitration" in K Yannaca-Small (ed), *Arbitration Under International Investment Agreements: A Guide to Key Issues*, Oxford University Press, 2010; C Schreuer and M Weininger, "A Doctrine of Precedent?" in P Muchlinski, F Ortino and C Schreuer (eds), *The Oxford Handbook on International Investment Law*, Oxford University Press, 2008.

are established "*ad hoc*." The situation is different in domestic courts, which are part of a domestic legal system.

Court decisions are normally publicly available. Disputing parties can therefore consult court decisions on issues similar to those expected to arise in an eventual challenge proceeding. This practice is well-established in the sphere of commercial arbitration, and the considerations in that context are to a large degree relevant also for treaty-based arbitrations. However, as more treaty awards are challenged before domestic courts – and because most of the jurisdictions where such challenges are heard are "repeat players" – it is only a matter of time before a number of those jurisdictions have heard enough cases for an investment arbitration-specific jurisprudence to develop. Still, it seems that this point has not yet been fully reached. It seems very rare that investment treaty-specific jurisprudence from the relevant jurisdiction has been at issue in the studied challenge proceedings.[496]

3.3 Consequences of Challenging Treaty-Based Awards in Domestic Courts

It is submitted that the foregoing text has shown that the place of arbitration matters; in fact, it has potentially wide ramifications that, with the exception of the trilateral NAFTA, do not seem to have been expressly considered by treaty parties at all. The following section discusses in which ways the choice matters, both by contrasting non-ICSID arbitration (which requires a national place of arbitration) with ICSID arbitration (which does not), and by scrutinizing the experience of different legal seats in non-ICSID arbitration.

In this discussion, an analytical distinction must be made between how having domestic courts adjudicate the validity of treaty-based awards affects the disputing parties – one of which, by definition, is not a subject of international law – and which consequences the practice has for international investment law more widely. In the former case the consequences are primarily practical, affecting several aspects of how the individual case is adjudicated. Viewed through the latter, more macro-focused lens, there are a number of

---

496 One exception is The United States District Court for the District of Columbia's rejection of Argentina's request for the posting of a security, in which it referenced the same court's rejection of Argentina's request in BG Group, see *Argentina v. AWG* Group Ltd., United States District Court for the District of Columbia, Civil Action No. 15-1057 (BAH), Judgement, 30 September, 2016, discussed above.

implications for international investment law more widely, as domestic courts are increasingly engaged in the adjudication of investment disputes.

3.3.1 *Consequences for Disputing Parties*

Given the degree of convergence in frequently used states' domestic arbitration legislation, it is sometimes assumed that the difference between the leading alternatives is relatively small, mostly thanks to the widespread acceptance of the New York Convention and the UNCITRAL Model Law.[497] There is certainly some merit to the proposition that the procedural framework for international arbitration is converging, especially compared to the historical situation. Nevertheless, the foregoing text has shown that there are differences, big and small. It does not suffice to assume that "most states are similar."

Seasoned counsel in commercial cases regularly advise their clients on the relative virtues of different domestic *fora,* including the potential for judicial review.[498] There is very limited data on this practice that is specific to investment treaty arbitration, although a reasonable assumption would be that the experience from contractual arbitration spills over. The question is therefore this: does the experience of challenges against non-ICSID awards justify any specific consideration when choosing place of arbitration?

3.3.1.1 Challenges in Domestic Courts as Opposed to ICSID Annulment

The most obvious difference between ICSID annulment and challenges before domestic courts is that in most cases parties can expect to retry the tribunal's jurisdictional determination in the latter scenario. Despite repeated reaffirmation by many courts that the task of reviewing an arbitral award must be done with considerable deference, in most instances when the challenging party has argued either that the tribunal lacked a mandate, or that it went beyond it, most courts have reviewed the question independently, in most cases after hearing new arguments from the parties (the two exceptions to this are Swiss and Canadian courts, discussed further below at 3.3.2.1). This fact is significant, because given investment treaty arbitration's characteristics – such as the

497 K Bondar, p. 629; B W. Daly & F C Smith, 'Comment on the Differing Legal Frameworks of Investment Treaty Arbitration and Commercial Arbitration as Seen Through Precedent, Annulment, and Procedural Rules' in Albert Jan van den Berg (ed), *50 Years of the New York Convention: ICCA International Arbitration Conference*, ICCA Congress Series, Volume 14, Kluwer Law International 2009 ("2009 ICCA Congress Series"), pp. 162–163; C McLachlan, The Legal Framework, p.128.

498 A prominent review of this practice is the regular International Arbitration Survey published by the School of International Arbitration at Queen Mary University London and the law firm White & Case.

asymmetric consent and the objective jurisdictional requirements contained in investment treaties – most arbitrations involve extensive jurisdictional debate, which often spills over into set-aside proceedings. Frankly put, most challenges against treaty-based awards can be framed as a challenge against the tribunal's jurisdiction, at least partially, meaning that a second attempt to test the tribunal's determination is usually available at the place of arbitration. Parties must therefore be prepared to argue these issues a second time, not always with the same result as in the original arbitration; as demonstrated by several cases, it is not a given that a domestic court shares a tribunal's understanding of, for example, a treaty's definition of investment,[499] investor,[500] the scope of the arbitration clause,[501] territorial scope[502] or cooling-off period.[503]

In ICSID annulment, such issues are not re-litigated before an *ad hoc* committee. ICSID annulment is concerned with "the integrity of the process"[504] and, as such, does not involve any assessment of the substantive outcome. Jurisdictional questions are no different from other grounds of annulment in this respect. A *de novo* review of arbitral jurisdiction has been expressly rejected several times.[505] In fact, several annulment committees have expressed discontent with the tribunal's jurisdictional findings but still upheld the award, stressing the limited mandate of committees under the ICSID Convention.[506] In this respect, it must be recalled that Article 52 requires an excess of power to be "manifest" – language that is absent from domestic arbitration statutes and arguably restricts the scope of an annulment committee's review considerably.

Given this, it would be reasonable to expect that a party challenging an award outside of the ICSID sphere would have a higher likelihood of success than a party who brings the case before an ICSID annulment committee.

499 *Moldova v. Energoalians*, Paris Court of Appeal; *Hungary v. EDF*, Swiss Federal Tribunal; *RECOFI v. Vietnam*, Swiss Federal Tribunal.

500 *Ukraine v. Tatneft*, Paris Court of Appeal; *Cem Uzan v. Turkey*, Svea Court of Appeal; *SD Myers v. Canada*, Federal Court of Canada.

501 *Griffin v. Poland*, High Court; *Czech Republic v. EMV*, High Court; *Russia v. Renta 4*, Svea Court of Appeal, T 9128-14, Judgement, 18 January 2016.

502 *Laos v. Sanum*, Singapore High Court.

503 *BG Group v. Argentina*, United States Supreme Court; *Kazakhstan v. Ascom/Stati et al*, Svea Court of Appeal.

504 C Schreuer, ICSID Commentary, p. 914 with references to ICSID Annulment decisions.

505 *Total SA v. Argentina*, ICSID Case No. ARB/04/01, Decision on Annulment, 1 February, 2016, paras. 175–176; para. 250; *Impreglio SpA v. Argentina*, ICSID Case No. ARB/07/17, Decision on Annulment, 24 January 2014, paras. 134–141; *Standard Chartered Bank (Hong Kong) v. TANESCO*, ICSID Case No. ARB/10/20, Decision on the Application for Annulment, 22 August 2018, para. 63.

506 *Duke Energy International Peru Investments No. 1 Ltd. V. Republic of Peru*, ICSID Case No. ARB/03/28, Decision on Annulment, 1 March 2011, para. 99.

However, one study found that by the end of 2007, 40% of ICSID annulment applications had been successful (partially or wholly), while the corresponding number for non-ICSID challenges was 6%.[507] Furthermore, following a wave of successful, and controversial, ICSID annulment cases in 2010, Christoph Schreuer stated that "it has become considerably easier to overturn an ICSID award in annulment proceedings than to have a non-ICSID award set aside by a domestic court."[508]

A mere comparison between the rates of successful reviews in the two systems would not sufficiently address whether this contention rings true. Such a quantitative exercise says little by way of comparison between the two types of review; each case is too specific for there to be reasonable to draw any conclusions from such a small amount of aggregated cases. With this in mind, of the 37 concluded non-ICSID challenges, only four were set aside, partially[509] or in their entirety.[510]

With the exception of the early partial set-aside in *Metalclad* – which long stood as the sole example of a (partially) successful challenge of a non-ICSID award – all other successful set aside decisions are from 2013 and later. It has therefore been suggested that perhaps national courts have "become increasingly emboldened in reviewing at least certain aspects of awards."[511] Yet again, such a conclusion seems somewhat premature given the limited amount of data.

3.3.1.2 Differences across Different Legal Seats

With respect to the differences among national jurisdictions, while there are plenty of state-specific aspects that may be relevant to a set-aside proceeding, there are simply too few cases (yet) to distinguish different potential *fora* from each other with any kind of refinement. Viewed from the perspective of state parties or disputing parties considering a potential place of arbitration, few general lessons can be learned from the experience of the concluded challenges so far.

507 G Verhoosel, To ICSID or Not to ICSID, p. 287.

508 C Schreuer, "From ICSID Annulment to Appeal: Half Way Down the Slippery Slope," (2011) 10(2) L & Practice of Intl Courts & Tribunals, at p. 222.

509 *Mexico v. Metalclad*, Supreme Court of British Columbia.

510 *de Sutter et al v. Madagascar*, Paris Court of Appeal; *Moldova v. Energoalians*, Paris Court of Appeal (subsequently re-instated by the Court of Cassation); *RosInvest*.

511 K B Reisenfeld and J M Robbins, "Finality under the Washington and New York Conventions: Another Swing of the Pendulum?," ICSID Review – Foreign Investment Law Journal, Volume 32, Issue 2, May 1, 2017, pp. 371–384, p. 383.

However, one general point is that, all other things being equal, the jurisdictions where courts have had the most exposure to treaty-based challenges seem to have developed a more sophisticated practice. At the time of writing, states such as Canada, Sweden, Switzerland, and the United States have had the largest quantity of such cases. Partly, the increasing sophistication is a function of time more generally; the field is maturing and so are parties involved in the cases. Much like the early arbitral awards from the turn of the previous century feel crudely written to the modern-day investment lawyer, a lot has happened in the corresponding sphere of challenges against awards.

Furthermore, the institutional experience within individual courts cannot be discounted. Courts such as the Court of Appeal for Ontario, the Paris Court of Appeal, the Svea Court of Appeal, the Swiss Federal Tribunal, and the United States District Court for the District of Columbia have all faced a handful of treaty-based challenges. This means that although the individual judges may change over time, there is a bourgeoning body of legal precedent, as well as a reasonable expectation of a certain degree of institutional knowledge as to how to approach cases in which the underlying award is based on a treaty. Parties wishing to seat a non-ICSID arbitration in any of these jurisdictions will be certain that, in the event that the award is challenged, it will be argued before a court that is relatively familiar with the subject matter.

Irrespective of the explanation, therefore, a challenge that is lodged in any of these jurisdictions can now go straight to the core of the disputed issues. In this respect, the difference between early challenges such as, for example, *Saar Papier* in Switzerland or *Sedelmayer* in Sweden, and the more recent cases concluded in those jurisdictions, are significant. While the earlier judgments demonstrate an unfamiliarity with investment law more generally, later practice from these courts are characterized by extensive engagement with sources and practice from the field. Nowadays, little effort in judgments is made to establish the preliminary issues such as the applicability of the domestic arbitration law and the standard of review to be applied. It is also the case that courts in the last couple of years almost universally apply the Vienna Principles when called upon to interpret the scope of the underlying investment treaty, as discussed below.

3.3.2 *Consequences for International Investment Law*

If, when viewed from a party perspective, the implications of having domestic courts hearing challenges mainly affect the actors involved in the individual dispute, the potential implications for international investment law generally are more fruitful soil to explore.

Investment treaties grant investors rights under international law, which like most rights under international law rely on domestic courts for their ultimate effectiveness.[512] When deciding whether to *enforce* a non-ICSID award, a domestic court seized with the matter is interpreting and applying the New York Convention, or its domestic incorporation, to which its home state is presumably a party. In practice, the losing party resists many such enforcement efforts on the ground of public policy, a concept which is intrinsically linked to the internal interest of the court in the enforcing jurisdiction.[513] Furthermore, the other grounds available in New York Convention Article V are to be judged according to the enforcing court's law, or, conversely, are dependent on the status of the award under the applicable domestic law.[514] In this respect, the enforcement of a treaty-based award before a domestic court usually involves the application of domestic norms and seldom raises issues of international law. Challenge proceedings, on the other hand, often concern both primary and secondary norms of international law.

3.3.2.1 Domestic Law and International Law – The Proper Role of the Vienna Principles

When domestic courts are asked to review the validity of an arbitral award based on an investment treaty, this practice is *prima facie* governed by domestic law, to which the parties have submitted by reference in their arbitration agreement. Such review often also involves matters of international law, because the arbitration agreement is based on a treaty and must be construed accordingly.[515] Consequently, most challenge proceedings involve matters of both domestic law and international law. It would be too simplistic to reduce this operation to a binary one: domestic courts are neither pure enforcers of international norms, nor solely agents of the domestic system within which they primarily operate.[516] However, when the question put before the domestic court is whether or not the arbitral tribunal went beyond the mandate as defined by the treaty, the matter is somewhat different; the *de novo* review of jurisdictional questions means that courts, with a few exceptions, have tended to make their own independent decisions, as if they were the primary

512 A Nollkaemper, National Courts and the International Rule of Law, p. 6.

513 New York Convention, Article V(2)b.

514 In the words of Paulsson, Article V(2) "leaves it to any of a multitude of enforcement fora to evaluate the conformity of an award with their particular conceptions of arbitrability and public policy," Jan Paulsson, The Idea of Arbitration, p. 39.

515 C McLachlan, The Legal Framework, p. 141; R Gardiner, Treaty Interpretation, p. 141.

516 A Nollkaemper, National Courts and the International Rule of Law, p. 10.

decision-makers. In this operation, the role of domestic law has often been more limited than in other instances.

An appropriate preliminary question is the extent to which courts are aware of the international framework of treaty-based awards and, by extension, of the rules for treaty interpretation in the VCLT. It could be argued, rather technically, that domestic courts are agents of the state and as such addressees of an obligation to interpret treaties in accordance with the Vienna Principles, either by virtue of their home state being a VCLT party or by virtue of the Principles' status as customary international law.[517] Yet, it has also been argued that whether domestic courts are bound to apply the Vienna Principles is ultimately a matter of domestic law.[518]

The interesting question for the present purposes is the extent to which domestic courts recognize any obligation of this nature. Outside of the sphere of investment arbitration, different studies have dealt with domestic courts' treaty interpretation. One comparative study of other spheres of treaty law has suggested that there are, by and large, similarities in how domestic courts use the Vienna Principles.[519] A later article, however, casts doubts on this proposition, arguing instead that there is a certain degree of adaption to domestic environments.[520] In the investment arbitration context, it seems that most domestic courts at least recognize that a treaty-based award is different from one based on a contractual relationship, although the extent and manner in which the Vienna Principles are employed differs considerably. The number of judgments that approach interpretative questions without acknowledging – expressly or implicitly – the need to resort to treaty interpretation is small.

Two of those cases are from the early days of challenge practice. As discussed at 3.2.3.1, neither the Commercial Court of Copenhagen in the 2001 *SwemBalt* challenge, nor the Svea Court of Appeal in the 2005 *Petrobart* challenge clarified which interpretative standards they were using. Both courts seemingly sought to construe the intention of the parties, in a way similar to how they would approach the matter under their respective domestic canons of contract interpretation. This could have many explanations. First and foremost, the role of the parties must be emphasized; in neither of the cases did the parties advance arguments based on the VCLT, opting instead to frame their arguments in more generic language focusing on the reasonable

517 H P. Aust, "Between Universal Aspiration and Local Application – Concluding Observations," in Aust and Nolte, p. 340.

518 M Waibel in Aust & Nolte (eds.), p. 21.

519 M P. van Alstine, "The Role of Domestic Courts in Treaty Enforcement: Summary and Conclusion," in D. Sloss (ed.), pp. 588–9.

520 Aust, Rodiles, Staubach, Unity or Uniformity.

intention of the parties.[521] Furthermore, it is a well-known maxim that domestic courts are more comfortable with applying domestic norms than are other treaty interpreters.[522] Especially this early in challenge practice, it seems likely that the two courts turned to basic domestic principles of contract interpretation, rather than the Vienna Principles, whose relative formality is probably unfamiliar to Scandinavian courts. This would also be in alignment with international lawyers' traditional scepticism towards domestic courts' use of the Vienna Principles, on the assumption that they are prone to a certain "interpretive home bias."[523]

In addition, there is another factor, which might shed some light on these early judgments' reliance on contractual analogies in their search for the parties' "intentions." Among the several ways of categorizing different types of treaties, a distinction is commonly drawn between "law-making" (*traits-lois*) and "contract-like" (*traité-contrats*) treaties.[524] The latter are characterized by a reciprocal undertaking of obligations, and as such resemble private law contracts, which would suggest that contract interpretation analogies are appropriate.[525] This arguably applies even more convincingly in the typically bilateral, contract-like relationship that forms the basis for most investment treaties (although not for the multilateral ECT). It is therefore attractive for domestic courts, in the view of the US Supreme Court in BG *Group*, to approach a bilateral investment treaty "as if it were an ordinary contract between private parties."[526]

The Vienna principles are however, different from most contract interpretation canons, in the sense that they contain no reference to the parties' "intent," but rather has a relatively objective, textualist focus, which might sit uncomfortably with some domestic courts.[527] Nevertheless, as discussed more extensively below, the lack of hierarchy in the holistic Vienna Principles leaves them open to various methods of interpretation.

---

521 In neither court case did any party made express reference to the VCLT in their written submissions (on file with author).

522 M Waibel in Aust and Nolte (eds.), p. 28.

523 M Waibel in Aust & Nolte (eds.), p. 26.

524 H Lauterpacht, *Private Law Sources and Analogies in International Law*, Longman, 1927, p. 70; M Waibel in Aust & Nolte (eds.), p. 14. This categorization finds no support in the VCLT itself, see C Schreuer, "The Interpretation of Treaties by Domestic Courts," 45 British Year Book of International Law 255-301 (1971), p. 256; E Bjorge, "'Contractual' and 'Statutory' Treaty Interpretation in Domestic Courts? Convergence around the Vienna Rules," in H P. Aust and G Nolte (eds.), p. 51.

525 M. Waibel in Aust & Nolte (eds.), p. 14.

526 BG Group v. Argentina, United States Supreme Court, p. 6.

527 Aust, Rodiles, Staubach, Unity or Uniformity, pp. 80–81 with further references.

There are two further cases when domestic courts did not apply the Vienna Principles, although arguably presented with the opportunity. The cases were argued in France and the United States respectively, two jurisdictions that are not party to the VCLT and have a well-documented complicated relationship to the Vienna Principles.

In *Pren Nreka*, the first treaty-based challenge to reach the Paris Court of Appeal, the court found that a commercial contract was covered by a bilateral treaty's definition of "investment." Similar to the *Petrobart* and *SwemBalt* cases above, the court arrived at that conclusion without any reference to the secondary norms guiding its interpretation, although its emphasis on the broad, non-exhaustive terms of the treaty's definition rings of contractual interpretation. Interestingly, as discussed below, the same court came to a different conclusion in the later *Energoalians* case, which was based on the ECT and in which the court *did* rely on the Vienna Principles.

As already alluded to in this text, perhaps the most significant example of a domestic court's non-reliance on the Vienna Principles, is the *BG Group* challenge before the US Supreme Court, in which the court engaged extensively with the UK-Argentina bilateral investment treaty without recognizing any need to resort to any interpretative exercise different from that under domestic law.[528] This decision stands out from the other "non-VCLT" cases, because at the time of its rendering, a number of treaty-based cases had already been heard in the court's jurisdiction.

In addressing the key question – whether the reviewing court should defer to the tribunal's reading of the treaty's cooling off-clause – the majority focused on the state parties' intent, stating expressly that it treated the treaty "as if it were an ordinary contract between private parties,"[529] also stating that "a treaty is a contract, though between nations."[530] The court found that its task was to determine the parties' intention as to who should determine the nature of the cooling-off clause: the arbitral tribunal or the reviewing court. US law provides that contracting parties are entitled to agree whether certain issues should be decided by the tribunal or by a reviewing court, but absent such agreement there is a presumption that the tribunal decides disputes about procedural preconditions.[531] The treaty – as well as the arbitration rules incorporated therein – is silent on the matter, and since the court's majority found that the cooling-off

528 See discussion above at "Cooling off-periods."
529 *BG Group v. Argentina*, United States Supreme Court, p. 6.
530 *BG Group v. Argentina*, United States Supreme Court, p. 10.
531 A Roberts, *BG Group v. Argentina.*

period was a procedural precondition (as opposed to a jurisdictional requirement), it deferred to the tribunal's findings on this point.

This approach has been criticized by several authors,[532] although the criticism generally relates more to the method of reaching the conclusion, than to the conclusion itself. For the purposes of this text, the absence of reference to the Vienna Principles is manifest, even more so because it was left out also of the dissenting opinion, which otherwise criticized the majority's equation of a treaty with a private contract.[533] Furthermore, in an *amicus* brief, the court had been encouraged by the Solicitor-General to apply the Vienna Principles.[534] Nevertheless, the reluctance to refer to rules of treaty interpretation has a long-standing tradition in the United States,[535] and the *BG Group* case confirms this in the investment arbitration context.

With the few exceptions discussed above, most courts *have* engaged with the Vienna Principles when faced with jurisdictional challenges. Generally speaking, domestic law has played a less significant role in this exercise than in challenges decided on other grounds,[536] and instead courts have at least recognized the need to avail themselves of the Vienna Principles. It would be reasonable to assume that part of the explanation for this is *de novo* review conducted by most courts. Put in other words, when reviewing challenges against investment tribunal's jurisdiction, the *de novo* standard has led domestic courts to answer the question "did the tribunal have jurisdiction?," rather than the question "is the tribunal's determination compatible with our domestic law?." The resulting interpretation is arguably an independent pronouncement on the content of an international treaty (rather than a test against norms of domestic arbitration law), inviting treaty interpretation.

A good illustration of this approach is the *EMV* challenge before the High Court of Justice in London, in which both parties accepted the *de novo* standard previously established in the *Occidental* challenge,[537] and proceeded accordingly by presenting arguments as to the scope of the treaty's arbitration clause. A further example is the *Ascom/Stati* challenge, in which the question whether the ECT's cooling-off period constituted a jurisdictional requirement

532 See for example J Wong, A Supreme Misunderstanding; A Roberts, BG Group v. Argentina, A Bjorklund, BG Group.

533 See above at 3.2.2.10.

534 See above at 3.2.2.10.

535 A Roberts, BG Group v. Argentina, pp. 4–5 with further references.

536 Although most challenges involved, at least partially, a jurisdictional question, a number of cases were dismissed on reasons related to domestic procedural law, see above at footnote 70.

537 Czech Republic v. EMV, High Court, para. 13.

was argued anew by the parties. Both the investors and the state submitted legal opinions – by Gary Born and Thomas Grant respectively[538] – in which the experts relied on extensive international arbitral practice, scholarly writings and the Vienna Principles to support their opposing views on the cooling-off period. The way the submissions on this point were structured in the challenge proceedings before the Svea Court of Appeal, the parties might as well have been arguing before the *Ascom/Stati* tribunal (whose findings on this point were barely referred to in the submissions or in the oral hearing before the court). The *Petrobart* and *Renta 4* challenges before the same court also involved similar *de novo* arguments, with a full review of the tribunal's jurisdiction, focusing on the legal question itself rather than the tribunal's determination on this point.

If one were to place the different approaches to standard of review on a spectrum, these Swedish cases would be accompanied at one end of the spectrum by the English decisions in *Occidental* and *EMV*, and by judgments rendered in the Netherlands[539] and Singapore.[540] Together, these cases demonstrate, in different language, a clear articulation of full review of the tribunal's jurisdiction.[541] The *BG Group* decision from the US Supreme Court, as discussed above, could arguably be read *a contrario* as an embrace of this approach as well: if the court had found that the cooling-off period concerned the tribunal's jurisdiction, the court would have had to review the tribunal's finding *de novo*.

On the opposing end is the practice of some Canadian courts, which have been hesitant to review jurisdictional determinations by tribunals. Both the *SD Myers*[542] and *Bayview Irrigation*[543] judgments contain statements to the effect that courts must exercise restraint in conducting such reviews. Arguably, the later *Cargill*[544] and *Murphy Oil/Mobile* judgments[545] opened for a larger degree of review, while not expressly mentioning the *de novo* standard. Instead, both these decisions focus on whether or not the challenge in question brought genuine jurisdictional issues, as opposed to questions going to the merits.

Similarly, somewhere on this end of the spectrum is the Swiss Federal tribunal. While recognizing its power to freely review questions of jurisdictional determinations, this court has been hesitant to exercise this power, preferring

538 Both expert opinions are on file with the present author.
539 Adria v. Croatia, The Hague District Court; Ecuador v. Chevron, The Hague District Court.
540 Laos v. Sanum, Singapore High Court.
541 Discussed above at 3.2.2.
542 Canada v. S.D. Myers, Federal Court of Canada.
543 Bayview v. Mexico, Ontario Superior Court.
544 Mexico v. Cargill, Court of Appeal for Ontario.
545 Canada v. Mobil/Murphy Oil, Superior Court of Justice Ontario.

instead to defer to the tribunal's decision unless particular reasons suggest otherwise.[546]

Most other literature dealing with domestic courts' interpretation of international law focuses on the extent and manner to which the relevant norm of international law has been incorporated in the domestic order.[547] In this respect, there is a spectrum of examples. At one end are cases where the treaty to be interpreted has been fully integrated into the domestic order – such as many multilateral treaties that have been translated and made into domestic law in dualist countries – to the extent that the international origin of the instrument is remote. In those cases, it is appealing for the domestic court to rely primarily on its internal, domestic rules of interpretation. At the other end of the spectrum are many of the court challenges discussed in this text: with the exception of NAFTA and ECT awards, they have all been based on a treaty to which the court state has no connection other than that the arbitration clause therein requires a domestic court to be competent to hear challenges. The court in question is only very rarely specified in the treaty, but rather designated at a later stage. In these situations, the norms of the treaty clearly retain an international character and should arguably be interpreted accordingly, i.e. with the assistance of the Vienna Principles. The treaty norm to be interpreted – typically a jurisdictional requirement – is in these cases located in an instrument with limited association with the court's domestic order.

3.3.2.2 Influence of Sovereign Interests

Unlike ICSID annulment committees, domestic courts are organs of a state. This raises the question of whether courts are more inclined than international tribunals to show deference to sovereign interests, either of other states, or of its own government, when they hear challenges of investment treaty awards. It might be suspected that such deference is exercised in many instances – from the overarching standard of review of awards, to occasions when the court is considering whether or not to stay enforcement of an award rendered against another state. However, the reviewed challenge proceedings do not support this suspicion. Any potential deference shown to sovereign interest is outside of the text of the judgments. One exception is the deference that has been incorporated in Dutch legislation, by virtue of RO Article 79, discussed at 3.2.4.1. This provision prevents the Dutch Supreme Court from reviewing "law of foreign states," which the Supreme Court held included BITs to which the

---

546 See Poland v. Saar Papier, Swiss Federal Tribunal, RECOFI v. Vietnam, Swiss Federal Tribunal, Hungary v. EDF, Swiss Federal Tribunal. All discussed above at 3.2.2.2.

547 See for example the contributions in Aust & Nolte (eds) and in Section II of D Sloss (ed.).

Netherlands is not a party. Treaties to which the Netherlands *is* a party – such as the ECT, for example – is presumably a different matter.

Furthermore, several jurisdictions historically required their domestic courts to consult the executive branch, i.e. the foreign ministry, before ruling on a question of treaty interpretation.[548] This tendency is widely perceived to have been abandoned,[549] and has not been formally exercised in any of the studied proceedings.

Normally, the court seized with the challenge is not located in a state that is party to the investment treaty in question, meaning that the interest of the court state's government is limited. The legal seat for the proceedings is determined by either the tribunal, the disputing parties or the administering arbitration institution, and not by the treaty parties.[550] In established practice, the seat tends to be chosen for its lack of connection to the disputing parties and therefore, to be located in a state other than those parties to the treaty. The resulting arbitral award, which can only be challenged before the domestic court at the place of arbitration, is in such cases therefore based on a treaty which, by design, has not been incorporated in the relevant jurisdiction, in the case of bilateral investment treaties. In the case of the multilateral treaties, however, the court seized with the challenge has always been located in a treaty state, meaning that there is a larger potential for the executive branch of the legal seat to have an interest in the case.

In some NAFTA challenges, the executive branch of the court's home state has in fact been arguing the treaty case before its "own" court. Sometimes this has been in conjunction with other treaty states. VCLT Article 31(3)(a) provides that "any subsequent agreement between the parties regarding the interpretation of the treaty or the application of its provisions" shall be taken into account when interpreting a treaty. In investment treaty arbitration, this creates a tension for contracting states: they are treaty parties, but also potential respondents in disputes under the treaty.[551] In theory, therefore, contracting states have a tool not available to the private investors with which they are in dispute, in the sense that they may directly influence the interpretation of

---

548 C Schreuer, "The Interpretation of Treaties by Domestic Courts," 45 British Year Book of International Law 255-301 (1971), pp. 261–263. See also generally J Arato, "Deference to the Executive – The US Debate in Global Perspective," in Aust & Nolte (eds.), pp. 204–207. See also generally E Benvenisti, "Judicial Misgivings Regarding the Application of International Law: an Analysis of the Attitudes of National Courts" (1993) 4 European J Intl L 159.

549 Aust, Rodiles, Staubach, Unity or Uniformity?, p. 76.

550 See above at 3.1.2.2.

551 A Roberts, Power and Persuasion, p. 180.

the underlying treaty (provided, of course, that the other state(s) share this interpretation). In particular, this is available through a so-called *amicus curiae* submission as a non-disputing state party.[552] This question has indeed been raised in several arbitrations,[553] and also attracted extensive interest in the literature.[554]

Arguably, the same dynamic could be present also when the forum is a domestic court, which is seized with a challenge against a treaty-based award. This is a less discussed matter, although several domestic jurisdictions allow for *amicus* submissions. One example is Canada, where non-disputing state parties have twice been allowed to intervene with written submissions on the interpretation of the underlying investment treaty. In the *SD Myers* challenge, an award rendered in favour of an American investor against Canada was challenged on jurisdictional grounds by the state in its own courts. In cases like this, the state as the challenging party is by definition advancing an interpretation of the treaty, in its capacity as disputing party. Canada is the only state that has done this before its own courts.

What is interesting with the *SD Myers* challenge, however, is that Mexico, another NAFTA contracting state, intervened as *amicus curiae* in support of Canada's position that the tribunal had gone beyond its jurisdiction. While Canada focused its challenge primarily on the definitions of investor and investment, as discussed at 3.2.2.3, the state also argued that SD Myers' business activities in Canada were best characterized as cross-border trade in services, which is governed by NAFTA Chapter 12 and not, by Chapter 11 (which contains the arbitration clause). In this view, Canada was supported by Mexico's amicus submission. However, the two states failed to convince the court, which instead

552 Such submissions are expressly allowed under Article 5 UNCITRAL Transparency Rules but have also been accepted by tribunals under other arbitration rules.

553 Such a submission has been admitted in two cases: *Everest Estate LLC et al. v. The Russian Federation*, PCA Case No. 2015-36, PCA Press Release on Issues of Jurisdiction and Admissibility and Non-Disputing Party Submission, 13 January 2017; *Eureko v. Slovak Republic*, PCA Case No. 2008-13, Award on Jurisdiction, Arbitrability and Suspension, 26 October 2010. It has also been rejected in one: *SGS v. Pakistan*, ICSID Case No. ARB/01/13, Decision of the Tribunal on Objections to Jurisdiction, 6 August 2003.

554 See for example A Roberts, *Power and Persuasion*; T Gazzini, Interpretation, pp. 341–345; M Paparinskis and J Howley, "Submission by Non-disputing Party to the Treaty," in D Euler, M Gehring and M Schrer (eds.), *Transparency in International Investment Arbitration*, Cambridge University Press, 2015; E de Brabandere, Investment Treaty Arbitration as Public International Law, pp. 160–174; V Živković, *Rethinking Interested Parties in ISDS: The Case of 3rd States*, Kluwer Arbitration Blog, 3 December, 2015, available at http://kluwerarbitrationblog.com/2015/12/03/rethinking-interested-parties-in-isds-the-case-of-3rd-states/, visited 9 January 2019.

found that NAFTA's chapter overlapped and that SD Myers was entitled to the cumulative protection of both.[555]

This is not the only time another state party to the underlying treaty has intervened in Canadian court. In Mexico's challenge of the *Cargill* award,[556] both the United States and Canada submitted *amici* briefs on several points. The tribunal had, *inter alia*, awarded the investor damages for up-stream damages. Mexico asked the court to set aside this part of the award, arguing that the tribunal did not have jurisdiction to award damages for losses incurred outside of Mexico. In their respective submissions, Canada and the United States supported Mexico's argument that the states had established a "subsequent practice" for the purpose of Article 31(3)b of the Vienna Convention to the effect that damages could only be awarded for losses sustained within the host state. Although NAFTA expressly allows for binding interpretations of the treaty, this specific mechanism was not exercised in this case.

The Court of Appeal did not follow the interpretation suggested by the treaty parties. It stated that there was no "clear, well-understood and agreed common position," as required by VCLT Article 31(3)(b) between the state parties as to the availability of damages sustained in the investor's home state.[557] Despite the alleged subsequent interpretative statement to the contrary, the court found that the *Cargill* tribunal's finding that there was an investment made by an investor was in line with the treaty parties' "common position" and that damages awarded on this basis did not constitute a jurisdictional error.[558] This deviation from the three treaty states' submissions is notable. The court recognized that, as a matter of principle, subsequent practice could be binding on the tribunal (and, implicitly one would assume, also on the court) but did not find it established that the three parties had indeed come to such an agreement on the specific question at hand. As already discussed, Canadian courts are generally among the most restrictive in reviewing jurisdictional issues. It is possible that the fact that the alleged subsequent agreement postdated the award influenced the court's decision, although that fact is not mentioned in the judgment. By contrast, in the *Sanum* challenge in Singapore, the lower court first faced with the matter allowed for such a subsequent agreement – reached outside of court, through the exchange of diplomatic notes – to inform its decision on the territorial scope of the China – Laos BIT. This was later reversed by the Singapore Court of Appeal, which found that if states

555 Canada v. S.D. Myers, Federal Court of Canada, para. 71.

556 Mexico v. Cargill, Court of Appeal for Ontario.

557 Ibid., para. 84.

558 Ibid.

could issue interpretative notes during a challenge proceeding, it would allow retroactive amendments of the BIT in question.[559]

Not every jurisdiction allows for *amicus curiae* submissions. Does this mean that non-disputing contracting states are prevented from influencing the court's interpretation? Probably, at least in the unilateral sense: in jurisdictions where no third-party interventions are allowed in court, the proceedings are generally closed to a non-disputing state. However, if the treaty states are in agreement, it is possible for the non-disputing state to get its view before the court, by being included the disputing state's submissions.

Finally, when discussing domestic courts' relationship to sovereign interests, it must be pointed out that a *de novo* review of an arbitral tribunal's jurisdictional decisions might be questioned on the ground that it cannot reasonably have been the intention of treaty parties to have a court in a third state conduct such a review. This has been argued in the context of the *BG Group* challenge in the US Supreme Court: why would Argentina and the UK ever wish for this court – which is not mentioned in their BIT – to apply its own domestic law to review the tribunal's decision on the treaty's cooling-off period's nature?[560] In the view of Jarrod Wong:

> [...] to permit the *lex arbitri* exclusively to determine the standard of review of any investment treaty arbitral award would lead to the unsettling result that an award issued under any single investment treaty is potentially subject to as many different standards of review as there are jurisdictions – depending solely on which seat of arbitration the investor and host state happen to agree upon. Equally troublesome, then, is the corollary consequence that the various awards issued under any single investment treaty (between different investors and the relevant host state) could be subject to varying standards of review. Surely the state parties must have intended any and all awards issued under the same investment treaty to be reviewable or binding to the same degree?[561]

As a general proposition, this argument is unconvincing. Admittedly, if one were to construe such an "intent," it seems unlikely that two treaty states wished for the Supreme Court of a third, unrelated state to review an otherwise final and binding international arbitral award. However, the proposition's reliance

559 See discussion above at 3.2.3.2.
560 J Wong, "A Supreme Misunderstanding," pp. 545–546.
561 Ibid., p. 546.

on a notion of treaty parties' "intent" is misguided.[562] As discussed above, such considerations are absent from the Vienna Principles. Instead, one would have to rely on the good faith interpretation of the arbitration clause, in light of its object and purpose. By agreeing expressly to, for example, UNCITRAL arbitration in a treaty, states consent to a type of proceeding which necessarily involves domestic courts applying domestic law (at least to a certain extent) in the event of a challenge of the award. In order to read an implied intention to modify courts' role in this context, one would have to deviate from the ordinary meaning of the arbitration clause: UNCITRAL arbitration unavoidably entails a reviewing domestic court, relying at least partly on domestic law in its review.

That being said, Wong's general point seems to be that domestic courts authorized in this manner should refrain from relying solely on their domestic practice to the exclusion of international law,[563] an undesirable approach of which the *BG Group* decision is "Exhibit A." This is a reasonable idea, which further emphasizes the argument that application of the Vienna Principles might work to reduce the potentially fragmenting consequences of domestic courts' review of treaty-based awards, which will be discussed further at 3.3.2.1.

562 See generally A Bjorklund, "BG Group."

563 J Wong, "A Supreme Misunderstanding," p. 547.

CHAPTER 4

Investment Treaty Disputes at Commercial Arbitration Institutions

In Chapter 2, the lack of involvement on behalf of the ICC and the SCC in the early practice of investment treaty arbitration was discussed. Over time, however, this has clearly changed. Today the two institutions are very much involved in the administration of investment arbitrations, and both have extensive experience of such disputes. Based on a review of documents from the respective institutions' case-loads, the following chapter discusses this experience, and whether it has influenced arbitral tribunal jurisdiction.

Arbitral institutions perform work that is not related to case management, such as promotional and educational activities.[1] The focus in this text, however, is on case-related work, as supported by the arbitration rules to which the disputing parties have agreed.[2] In a monograph dedicated to the subject, Remy Gerbay has explained that arbitral institutions' work is often represented on a spectrum, ranging from "administrative" to "jurisdictional" functions.[3] Although Gerbay critically examines this spectrum, and the dichotomy upon which it is based,[4] it is a helpful tool to keep in mind for the presentation of the material studied in this text, which only deals with "jurisdictional functions," leaving aside purely administrative tasks such as cost decisions, service of notice, and the setting and extending of deadlines.

After first introducing the organizational framework of the two institutions, this chapter addresses issues that arguably relate to matters of both tribunal and institutional jurisdiction. These include (i) institutions' *prima facie* jurisdiction decisions, (ii) institutional designations of the place of arbitration and (iii) ICC Court scrutiny of draft awards, including jurisdictional awards. Then, the institutional experience of emergency arbitration is discussed, focusing on the general availability of this mechanism, where the two institutions have opted for different paths.

---

1 For an overview of both types of activities, see R Gerbay, Chapter 3.

2 For an argument that arbitral institutions also act in manners that go beyond those designed to safeguard the parties' interests, to the extent that institutions possess certain "regulatory power," see B A Warwas, in particular pp. 80–93.

3 R Gerbay, p. 112.

4 Ibid., pp. 147–173.

 | DOI:10.1163/9789004413689_005

The primary aim of this Chapter is not to discuss issues relating to legitimacy or the desirability of commercial arbitration institutions' administration of investment treaty cases, but rather to attempt to explain and analyse actual practice. This notwithstanding, the text is concluded by a discussion putting the studied material in context.

4.1 Organization

Before the experience of the ICC and the SCC in administering investment disputes is discussed, the organization of the two institutions is briefly explained below.

4.1.1 *The ICC*

The International Chamber of Commerce is also known as the World Business Organization. It is headquartered in Paris and incorporated as a private non-profit association under French law.[5] The Court of Arbitration is only a minor part of the activities of the Chamber of Commerce, which has more than six million members from the private sector.[6] The members belong to different National Committees, and the National Committees are represented at the ICC World Council,[7] which is the "supreme authority" of the Chamber of Commerce.[8]

Generally speaking, the National Committees consist of business members; no public officials are represented.[9] Each National Committee has one to three votes in the World Council's decision-making process, depending on the size of contribution to the Chamber of Commerce's budget.[10] The World Council – and thereby the National Committees – appoint the members of the ICC Court, the decision-making body of the arbitration institution. Each National Committee proposes one member, who is then approved by the World Council. The President and Vice Presidents are also elected by the World Council.

Under the ICC Rules, the ICC Court is independent from the wider organization[11] and members of the Court are independent from the National

5 Y Derains and E A. Schwartz, *A Guide to the ICC Rules of Arbitration*, Kluwer, 2005, p. 1.

6 International Chamber of Commerce, https://iccwbo.org/about-us/global-network/, visited 11 January 2019.

7 Article 3.5a ICC Constitution of June 2017.

8 Article 5.1 ICC Constitution.

9 OECD Appointing Authority Paper, p. 31.

10 Article 5.4, ICC Constitution.

11 ICC Rules, Article. 1, Appendix. I.

Committees by which they were nominated.[12] As of 1 July 2018, The Court consists of 17 Vice-Presidents, and 176 Members and alternate members,[13] which meet every month in Paris with the President of the Court. In practice, however, attendance is low; reportedly, 25–40 members are normally present.[14] The required quorum is six members.

In the practical case management, the decision-making Court is assisted by the ICC Secretariat, lead by its Secretary General. According to the ICC Rules, the ICC Court is the only body authorized to administer cases,[15] but some of the more practical aspects of day-to-day case management may be delegated to the Secretariat.[16]

Under Article 33 of the ICC Rules, an arbitral tribunal must submit the award to the ICC Court for approval. In this process, the Court "may lay down modifications as to the form of the award and, without affecting the arbitral tribunal's liberty of decision, may also draw its attention to points of substance."[17] This feature, which has the purpose to guarantee the quality and enforceability of the award, is generally held to be one that distinguishes the ICC Rules from other arbitration rules.[18] The scrutiny practice of the ICC Court is discussed in some detail further down in this text.

The ICC also has a separate rule-making body, the Commission on Arbitration and ADR ("the Commission"). This body drafts and revises the arbitration rules, as well as researches new policies.[19] The Commission consists of ICC officials, arbitrators, counsel and academics and typically work in special committees focusing on narrower aspects of reform work, which is then presented to the plenary Commission, which meets twice per year.[20]

---

12 ICC Rules, Article 3.1, Appendix. II.

13 International Chamber of Commerce, https://iccwbo.org/dispute-resolution-services/icc-international-court-arbitration/court-members/#1478195489936-1a1acd15-7f6d, visited 11 January, 2019.

14 OECD Appointing Authority Paper, p. 32 with further references.

15 ICC Rules, Article 1(2).

16 ICC Rules, Article 5, Appendix II.

17 ICC Rules, Article 33.

18 Fry, Greenberg & Mazza, para. 3-1181. See however Gerbay, pp. 99–103, who points out that a large number of other institutions also perform this function.

19 International Chamber of Commerce, https://iccwbo.org/dispute-resolution-services/commission-on-arbitration-and-adr/, visited 11 January 2019.

20 Stone Sweet and Grisel, p. 84.

4.1.2 *The SCC*

Similar to the ICC Court, the Arbitration Institution of the Stockholm Chamber of Commerce is an independent part of a business organization. The Chamber of Commerce has 2,000 member companies,[21] and is managed by a Board of Directors consisting of 12 representatives from Swedish companies.[22]

The arbitration institution operates independently of the Chamber of Commerce.[23] It is governed by its own Board, consisting of arbitration practitioners from both Sweden and abroad, as well as a Secretariat, lead by a Secretary-General. Similar to the relationship between the ICC Court and its Secretariat, the SCC Board makes decisions in ongoing disputes, when called upon to do so by the SCC Rules, while the Secretariat manages the day-to-day operations of disputes. The Board may also delegate certain decision-making functions to the Secretariat. For example, decisions on advance on costs are typically delegated this way.[24]

Thus, there are similarities in how both institutions are structured. A body composed primarily of external experts makes the more significant decisions connected to the administration of an arbitration, while a secretariat employed at the institution conducts the daily administration of cases, and make certain decisions in the course of this work. Examples of types of decisions made by the former include determining whether the institution has jurisdiction,[25] appointing and deciding on challenges against arbitrators,[26] and deciding the place of arbitration.[27] The ICC Court also scrutinizes draft versions of all awards. Once the case is referred to a tribunal, the two Secretariats typically only make minor decisions, including decisions regarding the payment of advance on cost and extending certain deadlines.[28] However, as will be discussed below, both secretariats play an informal but important part in the decision-making, as they make suggestions and present material for the consideration of the formal decision-makers.

---

21 Stockholm Chamber of Commerce, *A Global Stockholm – A Strategy to Internationalize Sweden's Capital Region, Executive Summary,* Introduction.

22 Stockholm Chamber of Commerce, https://english.chamber.se/board-of-directors.htm, visited 11 January 2019.

23 SCC Rules, Appendix 1, Article 1, 2017.

24 C Salinas Quero, *Investor-state disputes at the SCC,* available at https://sccinstitute.com/media/178174/investor-state-disputes-at-scc-13022017-003.pdf, p. 1.

25 SCC Rules, Article 12(i)

26 SCC Rules, Article 17 and 19 respectively.

27 SCC Rules, Article 25(i).

28 Furthermore, both secretariats engage in research, events and publications. Since these tasks fall outside of the management of cases, they also fall outside of the scope of this text.

4.2 The Arbitration Rules

As mentioned in the introductory chapter, at both institutions, commercial case work constitutes the vast majority of the business. For a long time, this was reflected in the respective arbitration rules, which did not distinguish treaty-based cases from those based on contracts. More recently, both sets of Rules have shed this distinction. In the work leading up to the 2012 revision of the ICC Rules, a Commission Task Force on Arbitration Involving States and State Entities produced a report (ICC Task Force Report).[29] In addition to discussing past ICC experience of cases with states and state entities – which goes beyond treaty-based cases, and also includes cases when such entities are involved in contractual disputes – the Task Force Report led to a number of provisions being added, or modified in, the 2012 ICC Rules, in order to take this experience into account. For example, Article 1 of the ICC Rules now refers to "disputes," rather than the earlier "business disputes," thereby covering also investment treaty disputes.[30] Other changes will be discussed further below in this text, including changes to the institutional decision of *prima facie* jurisdiction, and emergency arbitration.

At the SCC, the Rules have been expressly adapted to treaty-based cases to a lesser degree than the ICC Rules. A separate Appendix III was added to the 2017 version of the SCC Rules. In this Appendix, three provisions specific to treaty-based cases were introduced, jointly constituting the first time the SCC Rules regulate such disputes separately. These new provisions stipulate that the default number of arbitrators is three,[31] and that a tribunal under certain circumstances may allow for submissions from third persons[32] and non-disputing states[33] respectively.

These changes notwithstanding, the procedure at both the ICC and the SCC is very similar for commercial cases and treaty cases, at least as far as the respective Rules are concerned. Before proceeding to the practice at both institutions, however, it must be pointed out that it is not always clear which set of rules are to apply in a given treaty-based dispute.

Investment treaties that refer to ICC or SCC arbitration tend to do so without much specificity. When an investor requests arbitration with reference to a treaty clause – typically mentioning "an arbitral tribunal of the International

29 ICC Task Force Report.
30 Ibid., para. 28.
31 SCC Rules, Appendix III, Article 2.
32 SCC Rules, Appendix III, Article 3.
33 SCC Rules, Appendix III, Article 4.

Chamber of Commerce in Paris"[34] or arbitration "at the Institute of Arbitration of the Chamber of Commerce of Stockholm;"[35], two questions might arise with respect to the various potential applicable versions of the rules: (i) as the rules are regularly updated, which temporal version should apply?, and (ii) as there are several different *types* of arbitration rules maintained by each institution, could a special rule set, rather than the "standard" version, be applicable? The answers to these questions could have important implications.[36] In the investment treaty context, this has primarily manifested itself in the context of emergency arbitration, which is discussed at length below at 6.4, but the questions are potentially of more general relevance.

4.2.1 *Which Rules Apply?*

As with many things arbitration, the parties may agree to which version of the relevant arbitration rules they wish should apply to their dispute. In the context of international commercial arbitration, it is not uncommon that the arbitration clause stipulates, for example, that "the rules for expedited arbitration shall apply"[37] or "the version of the arbitral rules in force at the time of the conclusion of this contract shall apply." Although there are a few investment treaties that regulate these matters in similar detail,[38] it appears that no such treaty has been relied upon at the ICC or the SCC. Naturally, if the "pre-dispute" arbitration agreement – be it located in a contract or in the form of a unilateral offer in a treaty – is silent, the disputing parties can also agree directly after the dispute has arisen. This seems to have been similarly rare in the practice at the ICC and the SCC. Instead, when the parties do not agree, these matters are regulated by the arbitration rules themselves, which contain default solutions for the situation.

4.2.1.1 Temporal Application

The arbitration rules at both institutions are regularly updated, taking into account the experience of the institution as well as feedback from users. According to the institutions' web sites, the ICC Rules exist in versions from 1975, 1988, 1998 and 2012 and 2017, whereas the SCC Rules are available in versions dated in 1999, 2007, 2010 and 2017.[39] A preliminary question is therefore

34 See for example the 1997 Croatia – Slovenia BIT, Article 8(2).
35 See for example the 1989 Russian Federation – United Kingdom BIT, Article 8(3).
36 R Gerbay, p. 62 with further references.
37 Both the ICC and the SCC provide "model clauses" to this effect.
38 See Caron & Caplan, p. 22 for a discussion in the UNCITRAL context.
39 Both sites last visited 11 January 2019. There are older versions of both rules: for the ICC, see M Schinazi, *Between Renewal and Anxiety: The Three Ages of International Commercial*

which of these applies to any given dispute, especially given the fact that, as discussed in Chapter 2, many investment treaties containing references to the ICC and the SCC entered into force in the 20th century. Both Rules contain presumptions to the effect that the Rules in force on "the date of the commencement of the arbitration" shall be applied.[40] The consequence of these provisions is that when the parties have not agreed otherwise, the most recent version of the arbitration rules always applies, regardless of when the arbitration agreement is deemed to have been formed.

4.2.1.2 Different Types of Rules

Even once the applicable temporal version of the arbitration rules has been determined, both institutions in practice maintain several sets of rules. Traditionally, this was not the case: ICC arbitration, for example, for a long time meant arbitration under the only ICC Rules available. Presently, however, in addition to the "standard" arbitration rules, both the ICC and the SCC maintain (i) expedited arbitration rules, (ii) rules for administering cases under the UNCITRAL Rules and (iii) mediation rules. The latter category typically does not raise any issues of applicability in the treaty-based context: application of the mediation rules, rather than the arbitration rules, requires a clear reference to mediation.

As for the respective rules for expedited arbitration, these seem to never have been applied in treaty-based cases at either institution, although a few times, their potential application has been discussed. Generally speaking, under the SCC Rules the expedited arbitration rules apply only if the disputing parties so agree. By contrast, the ICC Rules provide for a presumption that the expedited arbitration procedure applies in certain circumstances. According to Article 30 of the 2017 version ICC Rules, read together with Appendix VI of the Rules, the expedited procedure shall apply if the amount in dispute is below $2 million, *unless* either (i) the arbitration agreement pre-dates 1 March 2017, (ii) the parties have opted out of expedited procedure, or (iii) the ICC court decides such an application is inappropriate given the circumstances of the case. Since this was introduced only in 2017, it has never been an issue in any of the arbitrations forming the material for this study, but it should be pointed out that very few treaty-based cases concern less than the $2 million that would trigger the presumption for application of expedited arbitration at the ICC.

Arbitration, (PhD thesis, Sciences Po Law School, forthcoming), Sweet Stone and Grisel, p. 87. For the SCC, the present author has rules from 1976 on file.

40 ICC Rules Article 6(1); SCC Rules Preamble.

Finally, the availability of so-called emergency arbitration, which is included in separate appendices in both Rules, is regulated differently by the two Rules. This issue is discussed separately below at 6.4.4.1.

4.3 "Jurisdictional" Considerations by Institutions

Generally speaking, issues that affect an arbitral tribunal's jurisdiction are to be taken by the tribunal itself. According to the doctrine of *kompetenz-kompetenz,* a tribunal has the mandate to rule on its own jurisdiction, subject to the competent domestic court's final decision on the matter.[41] However, in administered arbitration – as opposed to "pure" *ad hoc* proceedings[42] – the administering institution might perform decision-making functions that arguably have consequences for the tribunal's jurisdiction. These functions are discussed in the following.

First, the text explores the ICC and SCC experience in making *prima facie* determinations on whether the institution in question is competent to administer the cases. Neither the ICC, nor the SCC has had any extensive experience grappling with the *prima facie* determination in treaty-based cases. Although the matter has been raised repeatedly, it has seldom led to the decision-making bodies having to engage extensively with the matter. Generally, there is instead a preference for having the arbitral tribunal determining the scope of jurisdiction, and the bar for early institutional rejection of a case is thus set very high. At least once, however, the ICC has rejected a treaty-based case before a tribunal was put in place.

The second focus is the designation of the place of arbitration. As discussed more thoroughly in Chapter 5, the legal seat of the dispute could have several different consequences, both during and after the arbitration. In a relatively large number of cases, treaty-based arbitrations have been seated in jurisdictions that have been determined by the ICC Court and the SCC Board respectively.

Finally, the ICC Court's scrutiny of jurisdictional issues is discussed. This scrutiny is exercised for all types of awards, but in the treaty-based context issues of jurisdiction have been common occurrences in the Court's scrutiny process.

---

41 On the doctrine of *kompetenz-kompetenz,* see 5.1.

42 A Carlevaris in C Giorgetti (ed.), p. 175.

4.3.1 Prima Facie *Jurisdiction of the Arbitral Institutions*

At both institutions, there are mechanisms in place to allow for early review of whether the institution in question has jurisdiction to administer the arbitration. This early review is structured somewhat differently in the respective arbitration rules, but it serves the same purpose: to ensure that cases in which there is clearly no institutional jurisdiction do not proceed.[43] Strictly speaking, the determination made at this stage is often understood to not be a jurisdictional decision, but rather an administrative one, determining whether a case should proceed to an arbitral tribunal.

A review of treaty-based cases shows that deference to the (future) tribunal's determination is considerable. This is in line with the general assumption in international arbitration that jurisdictional decisions are generally reserved for the tribunal,[44] and so are all decisions with respect to the merits of the case; even manifestly unfounded *substantive* claims must also be dismissed by an arbitral tribunal.[45]

The institutional *prima facie* determination of jurisdiction has sometimes been referred to as "gatekeeping."[46] A similar procedure exists under Article 36(6) ICSID Convention and Article 6(1)(b) ICSID Rules, which is commonly referred to as a "screening procedure."[47] This phrase is sometimes used also to describe the corresponding mechanisms in the commercial rules.[48]

Under Article 12 of the SCC Rules, the SCC Board "shall dismiss a case, in whole or in part, if [...] the SCC manifestly lacks jurisdiction over the dispute." The review by the Board is typically made upon request from a party – in practice the respondent – unless the respondent has not been in contact with the

43 Fry, Greenberg & Mazza, para. 3-209; R Raljovic, "Screening Powers in Investment Arbitration – Questions of Legal Change and Legitimacy" in F Baetens (ed.), *Legitimacy of Unseen Actors in International Adjudication*, Cambridge, 2019.

44 ICC Rules Article 6(5); K Hobér, *International Commercial Arbitration in Sweden*, Oxford University Press, 2011, p. 195; Fry, Greenberg & Mazza, para. 3-209.

45 A Carlevaris in C Giorgetti, p. 175 with further references.

46 Fry, Greenberg & Mazza, para. 3-210; K Claussen in F Baetens (ed.), Legitimacy of Unseen Actors; S.D. Sutton, "*Emilio Augustin Maffezini* v. *Kingdom of Spain* and the ICSID Secretary-General's Screening Power," Arbitration International 21 (2005), p. 126.; A Carlevaris in C Giorgetti (ed.), p. 175.

47 A R Parra, "The Screening Power of the ICSID Secretary-General," *News from ICSID* 2(2), 1985, Obadia & Nitschke in C Giorgetti (ed.); S Puig and C Brown, "The Secretary-General's Power to Refuse to Register a Request for Arbitration under the ICSID Convention," (2012) 27 ICSID Review FILJ.

48 See for example R Radovic, "Screening Powers in Investment Arbitration: Questions of Legal Change and Legitimacy," in F Baetens (ed.), Legitimacy of Unseen Actors; A Carlevaris and J Dahlquist Cullborg, p. 26.

SCC, or the issue in question appears to be non-arbitrable;[49] in these latter cases, presumably, the SCC Board examines the institution's jurisdiction *sua sponte*. The Board's review is not designed to analyse complicated jurisdictional issues – which, again, are rather left to the tribunal – and consequently the procedure is based only on a review of documents, with no oral hearing.[50] The Board makes its determination based on a recommendation made by the Secretariat, which has the benefit of institutional knowledge from previous cases.[51]

The ICC Rules are formulated differently, in the sense that the ICC Court "has to be *prima facie* satisfied that an arbitral tribunal under the Rules may exist."[52] Unlike the negatively formulated standard of the SCC Rules – and, for that matter, of the ICSID Convention[53] – this requires the ICC Court to make an active determination whether the institution's administration of the dispute is in fact covered by the (alleged) arbitration agreement.

In the most recent version of the ICC Rules, it is up to the Secretary-General of the Secretariat to refer decisions to the Court; previously *any* jurisdictional objection automatically triggered the Court's preliminary screening.[54] Article 6(4) now reads:

> If any party against which a claim has been made does not submit an Answer, or raises one or more pleas concerning the existence, validity or scope of the arbitration agreement or concerning whether all of the claims made in the arbitration may be determined together in a single arbitration, the arbitration shall proceed and any question of jurisdiction or of whether the claims may be determined together in that arbitration shall be decided directly by the arbitral tribunal, unless the Secretary General refers the matter to the Court for its decision pursuant to Article 6(4).

In practice, the screening competence at the ICC is now therefore shared between the Secretary-General and the Court. It should be pointed out, however, that Articles 6(3)-(4) are only triggered if the respondent party does not submit an answer, or does so and raises a jurisdictional objection. In this respect, the ICC Rules are similar to the SCC Rules in that neither set of Rules

49 K Hobér, *International Commercial Arbitration*, p. 196.
50 Ibid., p. 195.
51 F Mutis Tellez, *Prima Facie* Decisions, p. 2.
52 ICC Rules, Article 6(4).
53 ICSID Convention Article 36(6) and ICSID Rules Article 6(1)(b).
54 A Carlevaris and J Dahlquist Cullborg, p. 27.

require the institution to make a *prima facie* determination if the respondent is participating in the arbitration without raising jurisdictional objections.

Only if the ICC Secretary-General finds it appropriate to refer the question to the Court will the latter make a determination; otherwise the determination is made by the tribunal.

4.3.1.1 ICC Practice

In the studied cases, it seems that on only three occasions have treaty-based cases actually been referred by the Secretary-General to the Court under Article 6(3). In one case, the Court decided to stop a case from proceeding to a tribunal, and in the two other the Court ultimately decided that the determination should instead be made by the tribunal.[55] In all these cases, the Secretariat also provided the Court with an analysis of the issues in question.

The sole investment treaty case to have been rejected at this *prima facie* stage is a case in which the claimant requested arbitration based on a BIT. The alleged respondent was not, however, the claimant's host state, but rather another private company. The alleged investment in question was a set of contracts, which contained a choice-of-court provision referring all disputes to a specific court in the respondent's home state. The claimant argued that the respondent had a "serious dominance" in its home state, to the extent that the bilateral investment treaty's arbitration clause – which allows for ICC arbitration – should prevail over the choice-of-court clause in the contracts, "in order for the impartiality of the courts and judiciary not to be overshadowed."

The respondent raised several jurisdictional objections, the primary one being that it was a private company and as such could not have consented in a treaty to be the respondent in arbitration. Furthermore, the respondent's ultimate owners were established outside of the state that was a party to the bilateral investment treaty in question.

The Secretary-General referred the matter to the Court under Article 6(3). In then deciding that the case should not proceed, the Court emphasized that a private entity could not be a signatory to the treaty and as such could not have consented to ICC arbitration in the way argued by the claimant. Consequently, the case was dismissed due to lack of ICC jurisdiction.

---

55 The former Secretary-General of the ICC has commented generally that arbitral institutions only reject jurisdiction in "extreme cases," with reference to the principle of kompetenz-kompetenz, A Carlevaris, "Preliminary Matters: Objections, Bi-furcation, Request for Provisional Measures," in C Giorgetti (ed.), *Litigating International Investment Disputes: A Practitioner's Guide*, Brill, 2014, p. 176.

In the two other cases to have been referred to the Court, it found that there was *prima facie* jurisdiction, while leaving the finer legal points to the tribunal's determination. One of these cases presented an unusual jurisdictional question. The respondent state had objected that the treaty clause relied upon by the claimant had been misrepresented. Specifically, the respondent claimed that an incorrect version of the treaty in question – a bilateral investment treaty – had been submitted by the claimant. In the respondent's view, there was a sentence missing as compared to the authentic version of the treaty. Crucially, this missing sentence supposedly required both disputing parties to agree expressly to ICC arbitration. To support its contention, the respondent submitted diplomatic notes between the two treaty states, allegedly confirming the existence of the missing sentence. It also made jurisdictional objections to the effect that were no "investor" or "investment" under the treaty. The investor in turn argued that its version of the treaty was available at both the web page of its home state and in the UNCTAD database. In any event, it claimed, the host state had consented to ICC jurisdiction by initially participating in the arbitration.

After receiving the issue from the Secretary-General, the ICC Court ultimately decided to refer this matter to the tribunal. This was motivated by the fact that a determination of which version of the treaty was the authentic one would require both factual and legal analyses better conducted by a tribunal.

4.3.1.2 SCC Practice

Despite being faced with jurisdictional objections against SCC jurisdiction several times, the SCC Board seems never to entirely have rejected a treaty-based case at the early stage, instead leaving such determinations to the arbitral tribunal. This is in line with general SCC practice for commercial cases: a 2012 study of such *prima facie* decisions during the two preceding years found that two out of 14 objections were sustained by the Board, and the cases thereby dismissed.[56] In one case the arbitration agreement made reference to another arbitration institution,[57] and in the other it clearly provided for *ad hoc* arbitration.[58]

One relatively early case *could* have raised the question of *prima facie* jurisdiction, but the Board decided to refer the question to the tribunal. In SCC Case No. 97/1996, the request for arbitration referred to a bilateral investment treaty that does *not* make reference to the SCC Rules, while also making reference to a joint venture contract. The request was sent to the SCC Secretariat, which

56 F Mutis Tellez, Prima Facie Decisions.

57 SCC Case No. 086/2010.

58 SCC Case No. 067/2012.

responded to the claimant that it had interpreted the request as a request for application of the SCC Rules, but asked for the claimant's confirmation of this interpretation.[59] The Secretariat also added that it would invite the respondent state's confirmation regarding the application of the SCC Rules. Furthermore, in addition to the arbitration initiated against the respondent state, a separate arbitration against another (corporate) respondent had also been requested.

In its reply to the SCC,[60] the claimant stated that the joint venture contract referred to the SCC Rules. Claimant wished to rely both on this contract and the treaty, since the arbitration clause of the latter made reference to *"previously agreed dispute-settlement procedures"* as well as *"other arbitration rules, as may be mutually agreed between the parties to the dispute."* In the claimant's view, the joint venture contract's arbitration clause constituted such an agreement, and would therefore provide for jurisdiction also under the BIT. The respondent state replied to the SCC that it contested the institute's jurisdiction, as well as the merits of the claims.[61] The respondent also objected to consolidating the case with the one pending against the corporate respondent, which had been requested by the claimant.[62]

The SCC made two decisions: first, it found that it was "not obvious" that SCC lacked competence to administer the case.[63] Thus the jurisdictional issues connected to the two instruments relied upon would have to be dealt with by the tribunal. Secondly, the SCC also noted that it had no competence to consolidate the two cases without the consent of all parties. The two cases therefore proceeded separately. Following subsequent exchanges between the parties, the respondent state ultimately agreed to the jurisdiction of the tribunal based on the joint venture contract, but not on the investment treaty. The question of jurisdiction under the treaty was thereafter subject to the tribunal's determination. Ultimately, the tribunal decided to procced under both instruments, relying on declarations made by the respondent at a later stage of the proceedings.

The sole case in which the SCC Board partly rejected jurisdiction is *Amto v. Ukraine*. According to the final award, the respondent state requested in its

---

59 SCC Case No. 97/1996, Letter from SCC Secretariat, 17 April 1997.

60 SCC Case No. 97/1996, Letter from Claimant, 23 April 1997.

61 SCC Case No. 97/1996, Reply from Respondent, 29 April 1997

62 Ibid.

63 SCC Case No. 97/1996, SCC Board Decision, 25 June, 1997. The exact formulation of the *prima facie* test has varied over the years. The 1999 version of the Rules provided that the Board shall reject the case if it is "clear" that the institute lacked jurisdiction. In this case, presumably, the 1988 version of the Rules was applicable. Article 10 of this version provides that the claimant's request be dismissed if it is "obvious" that the institute lacks jurisdiction.

reply that the SCC dismiss the case for manifest lack of jurisdiction.[64] After receiving Amto's comments, the SCC Board found that it manifestly lacked jurisdiction over one of the two claimants, EYUM-10. Consequently, only the claims raised by Amto were allowed to proceed to the tribunal.[65] While the award does not recount the nature of the respondent's objection, presumably it related to the nationality of the investor: EYUM-10 was a Ukrainian corporate entity, the same nationality as the respondent state.[66]

The Board's decision to reject jurisdiction over one of the two original claimants in *Amto* raises question as to the scope of the Board's review. In at least one other arbitration, there was arguably a similar case to be made that the SCC manifestly lacked jurisdiction. However, unlike in *Amto*, the Respondent in question did not raise such an objection. The case was the first treaty case to be heard by a sole arbitrator.[67] It is not made clear in the award whether the SCC examined its own jurisdiction, but the sole arbitrator ultimately rejected jurisdiction over two out of three claimants. The sole arbitrator found that the two (corporate) claimants lacked the nationality of the home state under the BIT they sought to initiate the arbitration under, finding instead that for the purposes of the BIT they held the nationality of the host state.

Even if the SCC Board had made a decision in this case, it is likely that it still would have opted for a positive *prima facie* determination, since the determination of the claimants' status as investors would require interpretation of the applicable BIT, a task typically reserved for the tribunal. Furthermore, the documentation in the case does not clarify whether the lack of home state nationality was evident already from the request of arbitration, or whether it became clear once further material had been provided to the sole arbitrator. By contrast, in the *Amto* case the Board rejected jurisdiction over an alleged investor who clearly had the nationality of the host state. Interestingly, the administration of these two cases was relatively close in time: the sole arbitrator's award was rendered in September 2005, while the Board's decision in *Amto* was rendered in March 2006.

4.3.1.3 Discussion

Procedurally, neither institution conducts an adversarial process in deciding on its *prima facie* jurisdiction.[68] That being said, under both Rules the

64 *Amto v. Ukraine*, para. 3.
65 Ibid., para. 4.
66 Ibid., paras. 17–18.
67 SCC Case No. 093/2004.
68 Cf. A Carlevaris in C Giorgetti (ed.), p. 178.

screening power seems to only be activated if the respondent makes a jurisdictional objection, or does not participate at all. If no such objection is made, both institutions assume that the respondent is consenting to proceeding with the arbitration.

In cases where the respondent does not participate, the institutions seemingly differ in their approach. Under Article 6(3) of the ICC Rules, the screening process is not triggered by a non-participating party, unless the Secretary-General refers the matter to the Court. The SCC Rules do not regulate this, but it is institutional practice in cases where the respondent does not participate – and thus does not make an objection to the alleged jurisdiction – that the Secretariat determines whether the jurisdiction of the institute should be put before the Board.[69] This is the case, for example, in most emergency arbitrations,[70] where the respondent typically has not contested jurisdiction.

Thus, in practice the procedure is similar at both institutions in cases of non-participating respondents: the issue does not automatically go to a formal decision, but is subject to the discretion of a "pre-screening" by other entities than the Court and the Board. The difference between the institutions lies in who makes this pre-screening determination, i.e. deciding whether the issue should be put before the decision-making body within each respective institution. At the ICC, the Secretary-General exercises this function, whereas at the SCC the Secretariat makes the determination. Neither set of rules gives express guidance as to the standard applied in order to determine whether to put the issue before the decision-making bodies: once the issue is before the ICC Court or the SCC Board, there are standards ("is *prima facie* satisfied" and "does not manifestly lack jurisdiction," respectively) but what about the prior stage? A review of the treaty-based cases at the institutions gives no guidance in this respect, since Secretariat practice is not recounted in the awards, and only limited internal institutional documentation has been available. This raises the question of the Secretariats' ability to potentially influence decision-making in a matter not expressly regulated by the arbitration rules, an issue which is discussed further at 4.5.3.

Furthermore, neither the ICC nor the SCC provide the parties with reasons for their *prima facie* decisions, irrespective of whether the decision is "positive" or "negative."[71] By contrast, ICSID provides the parties with reasons in cases when the case is refused at the preliminary stage.[72] Given how rarely

69 F Mitus Tellez, Prima Facie Decisions, p. 2.
70 Discussed at 4.4.
71 A Carlevaris in C Giorgetti (ed.), p. 180; E Obadia and F Nitschke, in C. Giorgetti (ed.), p. 83.
72 ICSID Arbitration Rule 6(1)(b).

the screening power is used, the lack of reasons has likely not been a big issue among arbitration users. It must be noted, however, that under Article 6(6) ICC Rules, a party that is not content with a negative decision under Article 6(4) retains the right to ask a domestic court whether there is a binding arbitration agreement. Presumably, this right is retained also in SCC arbitrations, although it is not specified in the Rules; if the institution finds there is no SCC jurisdiction, the parties cannot be restricted by the SCC Rules from actions that are otherwise available to them. However, there seems to be no reported cases – commercial or treaty-based – where such a court action has been brought in relation to an SCC arbitration.

Are the institutions making jurisdictional determinations in deciding whether to allow the case to proceed? Formally, the answer is clearly no;[73] only arbitrators are authorized to make such decisions, and there is by definition no tribunal in place at the early stage where the institutions exercise their "screening power." Nevertheless, one could argue that an institutional decision to prevent a case from proceeding directly precludes a party from accessing arbitration.[74] Conversely, a "positive" decision is a condition for getting access to arbitration. Jan Paulsson has argued that "the stakes involved are often even more significant than those of a challenge action (because, unlike the latter, they put in doubt the very availability of the arbitral mechanism)"[75]. In essence, a negative *prima facie* decision removes the issue of arbitral jurisdiction from the tribunal,[76] in practice preventing a party from accessing arbitration. Admittedly, the bar for accessing arbitration under both Rules is very low, and consequently a decision to reject the case is only made in cases where there clearly is no agreement to arbitrate under the Rules.

A party that is not content with the institutional decision might want to challenge it. In theory, such a negative decision could be reviewed. ICC Rules Article 6(6) presupposes that there is a "court having jurisdiction" to hear such an action. The same arguably applies in cases where a party wants to bring

73 A Carlevaris in C Giorgetti, p. 176. In the ICSID context, see M. Polasek, "The Threshold for Registration of a Request for Arbitration under the ICSID Convention" (2011) 5 Dispute Resolution International, pp. 177–179.

74 Cf. in the ICSID context, A R Parra, "Provisions on the Settlement of Investment Disputes in Modern Investment Laws, Bilateral Investment Treaties and Multilateral Instruments on Investment," ICSID Review, F.I.L.J. 12 (1997), p. 12, arguing that in cases of rejection, "the screening authority will in effect assume a role normally reserved to the tribunals." See also generally R Radovic in F Baetens (ed.), Legitimacy of Unseen Actors, nuancing the contention that institutional screening power is purely administrative in nature.

75 J Paulsson, Vicarious Hypochondria, p. 243.

76 Ibid., p. 245. See also R Gerbay p. 71 with further references.

an action related to a rejection under the SCC Rules, although this is not expressly contemplated by the SCC Rules. Which court has jurisdiction over such an action? Presumably, this would be a task for the same court that would be competent to hear a challenge against a tribunal's negative jurisdictional decision, i.e. the competent court at the place of arbitration. However, in treaty-based arbitrations it is unlikely that there will be a place of arbitration at this stage of the dispute; unlike in commercial cases, there is typically no place of arbitration in the arbitration "agreement," given the fact that the agreement is not negotiated directly by the disputing parties. As discussed in Chapter 3, the place of arbitration is typically designated by either the institution (which by definition cannot be the case if the institution has rejected the case), or the tribunal (which by definition has not been appointed if the institution has rejected the case). Instead, presumably, the party dissatisfied with the institution's decision would have to choose the domestic court in which to bring the action. According to *The Secretariat's Guide to ICC Arbitration,* "determining the competent court in this respect is a matter for the parties, but it will usually be a court at what would be the place of arbitration."[77] The fact that there is generally no competent court specified for these actions serves to illustrate a general point made repeatedly in the present study: the place of arbitration matters. An institutional rejection of an arbitration at the *prima facie* stage effectively transfers the competence to decide on the validity of the arbitration agreement from a tribunal to a competent domestic court.[78] Which court is competent is not always clear.

In the ICSID context, by comparison, there is no place of arbitration and thus no court competent to review a negative screening decision. During the drafting of the ICSID Convention, the risk of interfering with the tribunal's kompetenz-kompetenz power prompted suggestions to subject the screening power to some form of review,[79] but no review mechanism was ultimately included in the ICSID Convention. It should be noted that the ICSID Convention, unlike the commercial arbitration rules studied here, contains jurisdictional requirement that the parties cannot derogate from.[80]

The SCC test is clearly developed for contractual cases, and formed in a context in which commercial institutions seek to give effects to arbitration

---

77 Fry, Greenberg & Mazza, para. 3-271.

78 See further I Houtot, "Les Pouvoirs de la Cour d'Arbitrage de la C.C.I de Décider ou Non d'Organiser l'Arbitrage," ASA Bulletin 1990, p. 26.

79 *History of the ICSID Convention,* 4 vols., ICSID, 1968, pp. 770–772, as cited by R Radovic.

80 Article 25, ICSID Convention. See also R Radovic; S Puig and C Brown, "The Secretary-General's Power to Refuse to Register a Request for Arbitration under the ICSID Convention," (2012) 27 ICSID Review FILJ, pp. 181–187.

agreements.[81] Although one could argue that the ICC Rules leave room for a more extensive *prima facie* review, in that the ICC Court must positively find that the dispute is covered by an arbitration agreement, the same notions of commercial arbitration arguably influenced also the ICC test. Treaty-based arbitrations often involve more intricate jurisdictional issues than do contract-based cases. Furthermore, treaty cases are part of a public international law web, with potentially larger systemic implications than contractual cases. The primary concern with institutional screening power is therefore arguably its potential to unduly adjudicate issues that are better reserved for the tribunal.

The present survey of ICC and SCC *prima facie* jurisdictional decisions does not seem to support this fear. For the reasons provided above, it seems to be a reasonable approach to maintain a high bar for institutional dismissal on jurisdictional grounds, instead leaving ambiguous cases to the tribunal.

4.3.2 *Designating the Place of Arbitration*

As discussed in Chapter 3, the place of arbitration is a distinctive feature of non-ICSID arbitration, as compared to the "self-contained" ICSID Convention. In that Chapter, a number of issues related to the post-award stage were discussed. The place of arbitration is relevant also *during* a non-ICSID proceedings, because the arbitration law – *lex loci arbitri* – of the seat typically applies to the proceedings, thereby giving the case its outer procedural framework.

Yet, the designation of the legal seat is rarely made by the disputing parties, and virtually never by the state parties to the treaty. Occasionally, investment treaties clearly stipulate a seat of arbitration,[82] but this is not typically the case. In fact, only a few cases appear to have been arbitrated when the seat was agreed by the disputing parties, while no case has been found at either the ICC or the SCC where the place of arbitration was designated directly by way of the underlying investment treaty. Instead, the decisions have presumably been

81 In his review of SCC practice, F Mutis Tellez concludes that the SCC "has maintained and is consolidating a 'pro-arbitration' approach, p. 20.

82 For Stockholm, see for example Italy – Venezuela BIT; Kuwait – China BIT; Ukraine – United Arab Emirates BIT. See K Hobér, *Selected Writings on Investment Treaty Arbitration*, Studentlitteratur, 2013, p. 543pp for an overview of treaties referring to SCC and/or Stockholm. For Paris, no similar study has been published of the (more numerous) treaties referring to ICC arbitration, but in the survey conducted for Chapter 2, the present author came across two examples in the Azerbaijan – Italy BIT (1997) and the Congo – Italy BIT (2006). A number of Italian BITs authorize UNCITRAL arbitration while stipulating that the place of arbitration shall be "Stockholm or Paris," see for example Dominican Republic – Italy BIT (2006) and Guatemala – Italy BIT (2003).

made by the institution in question; the matter is often not mentioned in the awards or other procedural documents made available to the present author but, as discussed below, both Rules provide for this particular decision to be made by the institutions.[83] The following subsection discusses this practice at the ICC and the SCC with respect to deciding the place of arbitration in treaty-based cases.

4.3.2.1 What Do the Rules Provide?

Both institutions provide in their Rules that their respective governing body shall decide the place of arbitration, unless the parties agree to one.[84] In the case of investment treaty arbitration, the "parties" could refer to both the treaty states and to the disputing parties. As to the former, there seems to be no case heard at either institution in which the place of arbitration was designated in the treaty. In the latter case, the disputing parties have agreed in a limited number of cases. This was the case, for example, in an ICC case where the disputing parties agreed to the Respondent's capital (located in an EU state) as the legal seat.[85] At the SCC, the disputing parties have once designated Madrid, and, on two different occasions, London.[86] In all other cases, the decision-making bodies of the two institutions have designated the place of arbitration.

Neither set of Rules provides any guidance as to how the decision is to be made. On the contrary, the ICC Court and the SCC Board both have wide discretion in designating the place of arbitration as they see fit. This contrasts with some other institutional rules, which provide a presumptive seat in case the parties do not agree to one.[87] Given the lack of regulation, there is room for institutional practice to develop.

Without full access to internal documents it is hard to ascertain the extent to which this question is discussed internally at the respective institutions, and what type of research is done by the Secretariats prior to the matter being

83 By contrast, pursuant to the UNCITRAL Rules and the ICSID AF Rules, in such a scenario it would be for the tribunal to designate the place of arbitration.

84 ICC Rules, Article 18; SCC Rules, Article 25.

85 ICC Case. No. 20662.

86 This information is not available from the studied awards, but provided directly from the SCC Secretariat. The Madrid-seated case is *Charanne and Construction Investments v. Spain*, SCC Case No. V 062/2012, Award, 21 January 2016, wheras the London-seated cases are unidentified, one under the ECT and one under a BIT, email from the SCC dated 19 December 2017, on file with author.

87 See for example LCIA Rules, Article 16(2) and of the VIAC Rules, Article 2(1) providing for London and Vienna respectively as the default seat. Article 7 of the CIETA Rules provides that the default place of arbitration shall be the domicile of CIETAC or its sub-commission administering the case.

put before the decision-makers. However, despite there being no presumption under either Rules, it is clear that both institutions tend to designate their respective "home town," thereby turning what is in theory a very wide discretion into a *de facto* presumption. The ICC Court has twice designated Geneva as the place of arbitration, but have otherwise tended to choose Paris. Similarly, the SCC Board seems to have been consistent in designating Stockholm, with a few exceptions. It is important to note that this does not mean that treaty-based arbitrations under these rules are always seated in Paris or Stockholm: sometimes, the disputing parties agree to a seat directly, as mentioned above.

Furthermore, it is expressly stated in both the ICC Rules and the SCC Rules that hearings may take place elsewhere than the legal seat of arbitration.[88] As far as can be deduced from the studied material, parties and tribunals exercise this opportunity relatively often in SCC cases,[89] while most Paris-seated ICC cases are physically heard in Paris.[90]

4.3.2.2 ICC Practice

As already mentioned, the ICC Court has a wide discretion under Article 18 of the ICC Rules. In practice, the Court makes an independent determination of the suitability of the seat, and may also designate a seat that was not proposed by either party.[91] Factors considered in this determination include the neutrality and geographical location in relation to the parties, as well as the seat's reliability as an "arbitration friendly" place.[92]

Given that the ICC Court is located in Paris, it is not uncommon that investment treaties refer to the ICC Rules while also mentioning the city of Paris, without stipulating clearly that the latter reference is a designation of the place of arbitration. In such cases, it is general Court practice to invite the disputing parties' view on whether the reference was intended to designate Paris as the place of arbitration.[93] In this scenario, if the parties do not agree on another seat, the Court will designate Paris. This was done in two treaty-based cases, where the respective treaties contained a reference to Paris. In Case No.

---

88 ICC Rules Article 18(2); SCC Rules Article 25(2).

89 SCC Case No. 010/2000 (case settled but hearing was scheduled in Washington DC); SCC Case No. 096/2008 (hearings in Brussel); SCC Case No. 094/2013 (hearings in London); SCC Case No. 023/2014 (hearing in Paris).

90 The sole exception where it is clearly stated that a hearing was heard elsewhere seems to be ICC Case No. 2020-1, where the jurisdictional hearing was held in the capital city of the claimant's home state (an EU state).

91 A Carlevaris and J Dahlquist Cullborg, p. 26.

92 Ibid.

93 Ibid.

2020-1,[94] which is discussed more extensively below, the claimant suggested Paris and the Respondent did not reply. The Court then designated Paris.

In Case No. 2020-2 the treaty in question referred to arbitration at the ICC "of Paris" (as opposed to "in Paris"). Similarly, in another case the BIT clause provided for arbitration at the "court of arbitration *of* the Paris International Chamber of Commerce (emphasis added)." Ultimately, the Court designated Paris. This decision was later cited by the Court in another case, Case No. 2020-3 where the investor had initially proposed the capital of its home state as the place of arbitration. Once again, the respondent state did not participate in the proceedings. The Court designated Paris as the place of arbitration.

4.3.2.3 SCC Practice

Unlike most other aspects of SCC decision-making, the institution has not published any material on the practice of determining legal seats. Furthermore, the material forming the basis for this study has not contained any information on the seat designation, other than the few times it is recounted in awards. However, although not codified clearly in the Rules, it seems that Stockholm is the default place of arbitration in SCC cases where the Board designates the seat. The only case seated elsewhere by virtue of a Board decision is an unidentified ECT case in which the Board designated The Hague.[95] In every other case where the Board made the designation, the arbitration has been seated in Stockholm.

4.3.2.4 Discussion

In order to explain both institutions' "home town preference," an argument could be made that in most cases the parties have indicated at least a preliminary intention to submit to French or Swedish arbitration law, respectively, by submitting their case to the ICC in Paris or to the SCC in Stockholm. This is supported by the fact that many treaty clauses referencing the two institutions tend to mention the two cities, albeit without expressly designating them as the place of arbitration.

This argument is more convincing in the SCC context. Stockholm is a relatively small and niched arbitration market, and SCC historically has had a less international outlook than the ICC. By agreeing to SCC arbitration, it is reasonable that as a default rule – when the parties do not indicate otherwise – the arbitration is governed by Swedish arbitration law. By contrast, the ICC Rules

---

94 As a matter of updated policy, the ICC no longer publishes case numbers. Hence, each referenced case has been given a generic number, used only for the purposes of this book.

95 Email from the SCC Secretariat, see above footnote 86.

do not have a similarly strong connection to Paris. Quite the contrary: to many in the arbitration community, the ICC is the only "truly international" arbitration institution, often chosen by commercial parties for precisely that reason. While most other arbitral institutions are more or less tied to the local community,[96] the *International* Chamber of Commerce is just that: international. Taking this into account, it would seem a stretch to assume that parties agreeing to ICC arbitration do so under the assumption that French arbitration law will govern the proceedings. In fact, the ICC Secretariat's guide to the ICC Rules states that having a default place of arbitration "would not be appropriate in ICC arbitration, which has a global caseload."[97] This notwithstanding, it seems that in treaty-based cases Paris is the *de facto* default place of arbitration. This is different from the commercial case-load: although Paris is the most frequently selected seat also in this context, it is only selected in 18% of the cases, with both London, Geneva and Zurich being frequent alternatives.[98] The much more differentiated map in the context of commercial arbitration is probably explained by the fact that disputing parties agree to a seat much more often. In investment treaty arbitration, as discussed above, there is rarely such an agreement, which means that the institution typically designates the seat. At the ICC and the SCC alike, this has led to a less diverse result than when disputing parties agree themselves.

Given the seat's legal ramifications, an argument could be made that this decision is better made by the tribunal. This is the default situation under the two other non-ICSID rules frequently used in treaty-based cases, the UNCITRAL Rules[99] and the ICSID AF Rules.[100] Although sensible as a general proposition, this approach necessarily means that the place of arbitration is designated at a later stage of the proceedings, once a tribunal has been put in place. In fact, it has been argued that this late designation of the seat should be reconsidered, for example by amending the UNCITRAL Rules and the Model Law to allow for an appointing authority to (at least preliminarily) designate the seat prior to the tribunal's constitution, or in the ICSID AF Case to involve the ICSID Secretariat at the outset of the case.[101] With an institutional arbitration, such as those conducted by the ICC and the SCC, such an authority is already in place to designate the seat. It should be pointed out, however, that if the disputing

96 As mentioned above, many such institutions even contain an express presumption that the city in which the institution is located is the default place of arbitration.

97 Fry, Greenberg & Mazza, para. 3-671.

98 Based on statistics from 2007-2011, Fry, Greenberg & Mazza, Tables 25-27.

99 Article 18(1).

100 Article 20(1).

101 A Sabater, pp. 454–455.

parties so wish, both the ICC Rules and the SCC Rules allow for the parties to agree that the seat be decided by the tribunal instead.[102]

Similar to most decisions made by the ICC Court and the SCC Board, no reasons are given to the parties under either institutional practice. It is therefore unclear which criteria go into the decision, although the ICC Secretariat has provided generic information about what considerations generally play a part, as discussed above. It has been argued that institutions should always establish the seat of arbitration having allowed the parties to express their views, and if needed submit evidence, on the matter.[103] Both institutions have wide discretion and nothing prevents them from choosing either a seat suggest by one party or one that has not been suggested by either party. In the latter case, it is reasonable that the disputing parties are given the chance to comment on this potential seat.[104]

Based on a review of the treaty-based awards at both institutions, as well as some sporadic internal documentation, it seems evident that among the many issues regularly dealt with within the course of an institutional arbitration, the place of arbitration is treated with relatively limited attention. Little information on institutional practice has been published by either institution, and in the vast majority of cases the disputing parties have, at least tacitly, accepted that ICC arbitrations are seated in Paris and SCC arbitrations are seated in Stockholm.

4.3.3 *ICC Court Scrutiny*

As mentioned at the beginning of this Chapter, ICC tribunals are required to submit draft awards to the ICC Court for scrutiny. The scrutiny procedure is a distinguishing feature of the ICC Rules and has been part of the rules since the 1927 version.[105] In the 2012 version of the Rules, Article 33 provides that:

> Before signing any award, the arbitral tribunal *shall* submit it in draft form to the Court. The Court may lay down modifications as to the form of the award and, without affecting the arbitral tribunal's liberty of decision, may also draw its attention to points of substance. No award shall be

102 This is longstanding ICC practice in commercial cases, see H Verbist, "The Practice of the ICC International Court of Arbitration with Regard to the Fixing of the Place of Arbitration," 12 ARB. INT'L, 1996, p. 349.

103 A Sabater, p. 458.

104 A Sabater, p. 462.

105 G Flecke-Giamarco, p. 47. It should be pointed out, however, that scrutiny of draft awards is not as specific to ICC arbitration as often assumed: R Gerbay lists 10 other institutions with a similar feature, p. 100.

rendered by the arbitral tribunal until it has been approved by the Court as to its form (emphasis added)

The scrutiny is mandatory and the parties cannot derogate from it.[106] The Court scrutinizes points of form as well as substance. However, the Court can require changes in the form of the award, but may only suggest changes as to substance.[107] In 2010, the ICC Secretariat released a checklist for arbitrators, which is submitted to all ICC tribunals.[108] The checklist sets out a number of formal points that tribunals must consider before submitting a draft award for scrutiny.

The result of Court scrutiny is one out of three scenarios: (i) either the draft award is approved as is, (ii) the draft award is approved "subject to" certain comments, or (iii) the draft award is not approved.[109] The vast majority of scrutinized draft awards belong to the second category, and are approved subject to comments, which are provided for the tribunal's consideration.[110] Much smaller portions of the scrutinized awards are either approved directly, with no comments from the Court, or sent back to the tribunal for revision.[111] These figures – taken from the general ICC caseload – correspond well with the specific situation for treaty-based awards reviewed as part of the present study.

Before the award is put before the Court, the responsible managing counsel at the Secretariat will prepare a report on the background of the case and also include the Secretariat's suggested comments.[112] Most such reports are then submitted to one of the weekly committee sessions at the Court (which is more frequent but attended by fewer Court members than the plenary sessions). However, in cases – such as investment treaty arbitrations – when one party is a state, standard practice is to submit the award to a plenary session.[113] In these cases, a member of the Court serves as a *rapporteur* (or "Court reporter"), preparing an extensive written report on the draft award.[114]

---

106 G Flecke-Giammarco, pp. 56–57.

107 Ibid., p. 61.

108 Fry, Greenberg & Mazza, paras. 3-1195-6.

109 Ibid., para. 3-1205.

110 In a 2014 article written by an ICC Counsel, it is stated that 91,19% of all draft awards submitted to the Court in 2013 were approved subject to comments by the Court, while 7.83% were not approved, G Flecke-Giammarco, p. 2.

111 Ibid.

112 Fry, Greenberg & Mazza, para. 3-1201.

113 Fry, Greenberg & Mazza, para. 3-1202.

114 G Flecke-Giammarco, p. 60.

Scrutiny is equally applicable to all draft awards under the ICC Rules, including partial awards. Consequently, awards in which jurisdictional questions are treated before the merits – which is common in treaty-based arbitration – are also subjected to Court scrutiny. In fact, the Court "strongly encourages arbitral tribunals to treat their decisions on their jurisdiction as awards,"[115] thereby making them susceptible to Court scrutiny. Typically, jurisdictional issues in treaty-based arbitration concerns more complicated legal issues than in contractual arbitration.[116] Consequently, the ICC Court has several times been asked to exercise its scrutiny power with respect to draft jurisdictional awards.

In the first treaty-based case to reach the merit stage at the ICC, the tribunal submitted such a partial award on jurisdiction.[117] The Court invited the tribunal to develop its analysis with respect to the nationality of the claimants and their right to invoke the bilateral investment treaty in question. The tribunal eventually did so in the final award.

In another case, the state's jurisdictional objections were referred to the arbitral tribunal under Article 6(3). When scrutinising the draft partial award on jurisdiction, rendered by a majority, the Court invited the majority to expand upon its finding that a loan agreement constituted a protected investment under the relevant investment treaty. Specifically, the tribunal's attention was drawn to the lack of reasoning on whether or not a loan agreement could result in a 'contribution' to the host state economy, and whether the claimant could be considered as an investor within the meaning of the treaty. The Court also invited the arbitral tribunal to examine certain aspects of its own jurisdiction that had not been raised by the parties, including the six-month waiting period provided by the treaty and whether or not the claimant had established a *prima facie* case sufficient for the tribunal to uphold its own jurisdiction.

In yet another case, the claimant relied on several instruments in support of the tribunal's jurisdiction. It referred firstly to the contract and then, as alternatives, to a bilateral investment treaty and a domestic investment statute. The ICC Court invited the tribunal to expand on its reasoning as to whether the alternatives were excluded from the analysis of the tribunal's jurisdiction, as both investment protection instruments provided that they could be used only 'in the absence of an agreed procedure' and the contract provided for ICC arbitration.

---

115 Fry, Greenberg & Mazza, para. 3-1188.

116 K Hobér & N Eliasson, para. 28.162.

117 The discussion below draws upon Carlevaris & Dahlquist Cullborg, pp. 27–28.

4.4 Emergency Arbitration

In the world of commercial arbitration, many institutional rules have seen the introduction of so-called "emergency arbitration" in the last few years. This type of procedural mechanism allows a claimant, under certain circumstances, to request provisional or conservative measures prior to the constitution of a full tribunal. It also possible to obtain such measure by a full tribunal pending an arbitration,[118] but in some cases, it might already be too late at that stage. Emergency arbitration is intended to bridge this gap, and allow claimants to obtain provisional measures without having to wait for a full tribunal to be constituted.

Although emergency arbitration has been a popular mechanism in international commercial arbitration – introduced, in addition to the rules discussed here, for example, in the SIAC Rules,[119] the HKIAC Rules,[120] the LCIA Rules,[121] and the ICDR Rules[122] – its application in investment treaty arbitration is a somewhat different issue. Neither of the two most frequently used arbitration rules[123] for investment arbitration contains provisions on emergency arbitration. The same is true for the ICSID AF Rules. The two other sets of arbitration rules, which are the focus of this chapter, reflect different approaches to the matter: the ICC Rules seemingly exclude it for treaty-based cases, while the SCC Rules allow for it. Consequently, the experience of such cases is limited at the ICC, and more extensive at the SCC.

4.4.1 *Emergency Arbitration at the ICC*

Emergency arbitration was introduced in the 2012 version of the ICC Rules. While the mechanism has been used frequently in commercial cases, there have been no treaty-based emergency arbitrations at the ICC. Article 29(5) of the Rules states that

> Articles 29(1)–29(4) and the Emergency Arbitrator Rules set forth in Appendix V (collectively the "Emergency Arbitrator Provisions") shall apply only to parties that are either *signatories* of the arbitration

---

118 See generally G Born, p. 2428 et seq.

119 SIAC Rules, Article 26.2.

120 HKIAC Arbitration Rules, Schedule 4.

121 LCIA Rules, Article 9B.

122 Article 6.

123 UNCITRAL Arbitration Rules and the ICSID Convention with its associated arbitration rules.

> agreement under the Rules that is relied upon for the application or successors to such signatories. [emphasis added]

It has been argued, in legal doctrine[124] as well as in the 2012 Commission Task Force Report,[125] that this provision excludes investment arbitration from the scope of the emergency arbitrator rules' application. The reason for this exclusion – which according to the 2012 ICC Report was the very purpose behind introducing Article 29(5)[126] – is that an investor and a host state involved in an investment treaty arbitration cannot be considered to be "signatories" to an arbitration agreement. However, this conclusion is not evident from the wording of the provision. Who is a "signatory" to the arbitration agreement when the arbitration is based on a state's offer in an investment treaty? The assumption of the drafters seems to be that this description does not cover an investor availing itself of such an offer. Supposedly, the underlying reasoning is that an investor does not "sign" an arbitration agreement by accepting an offer. If that is indeed the intended interpretation, that is a rather technical view of the consent mechanism in investment arbitration, as it is conventionally understood. One could argue that a broader reading of the term "signatories" covers also investors accepting a host state's offer to arbitrate.[127] Albeit technically not a signed contract in the traditional sense, there is little doubt that an arbitration agreement is formed when the investor requests arbitration.[128]

Furthermore, Article 29(6) concerns the timing of the parties' consent. According to this provision, emergency arbitration is not available if "the arbitration agreement under the Rules was concluded before 1 January 2012." Similar to the lack of clarity under Article 29(5), Article 29(6) raises another question with respect to the parties' consent to arbitration, *viz.* the question of timing. When is an arbitration agreement formed in treaty-based arbitration? This is a live issue, since the majority of investment treaties referring to ICC arbitration were concluded before January 2012.[129] Yet again, the conventional

---

124 P Mayer and E Silva Romero, "Le nouveau Règlement d'arbitrage de la Chambre de Commerce Internationale (CCI)," Revue de l'arbitrage 2011, p. 919; N Voser & C Boog, "ICC Emergency Arbitrator Proceedings: An Overview," in *Interim, Conservatory and Emergency Measures in ICC Arbitration*, ICC International Court of Arbitration Bulletin, 2011 Special Supplement, at 83–84; N Voser, *Overview of the Most Important Changes in the Revised ICC Arbitration Rules*, 29 ASA Bull. 83, (2011), p. 817.

125 ICC Task Force Report, paras. 51–52.

126 Ibid.

127 A Carlevaris and J Dahlquist Cullborg, p. 29.

128 See discussion at 2.1

129 A Carlevaris and J Dahlquist Cullborg, p. 29. See also Chapter 2.

understanding of consent to treaty-based arbitration would suggest that the agreement is formed at the time of the investor's acceptance of the host state's offer, in this particular instance in the form of applying for emergency arbitration. Under this reading, only emergency arbitration procedures initiated prior to 2012 would be excluded from the scope of the ICC Rules: an absurd conclusion, given that emergency arbitration was introduced in 2012. Therefore, the only plausible reading of Article 29(6) is that the "arbitration agreement" referred to is in fact the investment treaty, and not the agreement formed when the investor avails itself of the treaty. This reading could be justified by the policy consideration that states entering into a treaty prior to 2012 did not have the opportunity to consider that future disputes would also include emergency arbitration.

As discussed further below, the ICC approach to temporal application of the arbitration rules differs from that of the SCC, which in practice clearly gives retroactive effect to the introduction of emergency arbitration by providing expressly that the date of the request of arbitration is determinative for which version of the Rules is applicable.

Articles 29(5)-(6) have been tested on at least one occasion, by an investor asking for emergency relief in a treaty-based case, where the President of the ICC Court decided that the emergency arbitration provisions were not applicable.[130] The request was filed in 2014, relying on a BIT which was signed in 2001 and entered into force in 2003, several years before emergency arbitration was introduced in the ICC Rules in 2012.

It is worth pointing out that in this particular case, the ICC instead sped up the general process: following the unsuccessful application for emergency arbitration, a draft award on the claimants' application for provisional measures was scrutinized and approved by the ICC Court at the first available committee meeting, as opposed to the more infrequent plenary sessions, as is ICC practice in arbitrations with state parties.[131]

In summary, despite this decision by the President of the ICC Court, it is not clear from the wording of Articles 29(5)-(6) that investment arbitration is exempt from the application of emergency arbitration.[132] Under the conventional understanding, an arbitration agreement in investment treaty arbitration is formed by a combined offer by the host state and an acceptance of that offer by the investor. Although not "signatories" to the same agreement in the technical sense, an arbitration agreement is formed by the parties. Similar

130 Carlevaris & Dahlquist Cullborg, p. 29.

131 This practice is discussed at 4.3.3.

132 See also A Carlevaris in C Giorgetti (ed.), p. 204.

considerations would apply in instances when the state's offer is located in other unilateral acts, such as investment legislation. In any event, this case appears to have been the only time a request for emergency arbitration was filed in a treaty-based case. Without access to the reasons, if any, given by the President of the Court, it is hard to tell whether the door to such measures is closed at the ICC, or whether that door remains at least possible to open in the future.[133]

4.4.2 *Emergency Arbitration at the SCC*

Emergency arbitration was introduced in the 2010 version of the SCC Rules. In contrast to the ICC Rules, the SCC Rules allow for emergency arbitration also in treaty-based cases. In fact, no distinction is made between treaty-based arbitration and arbitration based on contracts in the SCC Rules.[134] Therefore, the same preliminary issues that apply to every case also apply to the question of whether emergency arbitration is applicable to any given investment disputes. These include the institution's *prima facie* jurisdiction,[135] and the temporal applicability of the rules, i.e. which version of the SCC Rules are applicable. In this respect, the SCC adopted a different solution from that by the ICC. In its 2010 version, unchanged in the updated 2017 version, the Preamble to the SCC Rules provides the following:

> Under any arbitration agreement referring to the Arbitration Rules of the Arbitration Institute of the Stockholm Chamber of Commerce (the "Arbitration Rules") the parties shall be deemed to have agreed that the following rules, or such amended rules, in force on the date of the commencement of the arbitration, or the filing of an application for the appointment of an Emergency Arbitrator, shall be applied unless otherwise agreed by the parties.

133 In addition to the Carlevaris text cited above, Philippe Pinsolle has gone even further in arguing that emergency arbitration should be available to investors in treaty-based cases under the current Rules, see P Pinsolle, "A Call to Open the ICC Emergency Arbitrator Procedure to Investment Treaty Cases," in A Carlevaris, L Lévy, A Mourre and E Schwartz (eds.), *International Arbitration Under Review: Essays in Honour of John Beechey*, ICC, 2015.

134 The sole exception is Appendix III to the 2017 version of the Rules, which regulates the number of arbitrators and submissions by non-disputing parties in treaty-based cases.

135 Discussed above at 4.3.1. This issue does not seem to ever have been considered by an SCC Board decision, presumably because no respondent state has raised an objection against the institution's *prima facie* jurisdiction.

Thus, it is made clear that it is the date of the application for emergency arbitration that is determinative. If an investor applies for emergency arbitration after 1 January 2010 (when emergency arbitration was introduced), emergency arbitration is available, provided that there is an arbitration agreement referring to the SCC Rules. There have been a number of such cases, most of which are discussed below,[136] with a focus on issues relating to the administration and jurisdiction of such cases. The merits of the cases, as ruled upon by the emergency arbitrators, are discussed to a more limited extent. As will be elaborated upon, most decisions have been issued within five days of the registration of the application, as provided by the Rules. Naturally, this short time frame means that the reasoning of the emergency arbitrators typically is limited. The following accounts attempt at gathering the various issues facing the emergency arbitrators, as well as putting those issues into context.

Three out of seven known treaty-based emergency cases have been heard under the Russia – Moldova BIT, and involved similar fact patterns. These will be discussed in sequence, since they cross-reference each other and concern similar issues. The remaining four cases will then be discussed in chronological sequence.[137]

4.4.2.1 TSIKInvest v. Moldova

The very first application for emergency arbitration in a treaty-based based dispute is the case *TSIKInvest* LLC *v. Moldova*, which was brought under the 1998 Russia – Moldova BIT.[138] In this case, the application was registered at the SCC on 23 April 2014, and the emergency arbitrator (EA) appointed the following day. The decision was rendered by the EA on 29 April 2014. In the application, the claimant sought an order to protect its alleged investment in Moldova from the consequences of a decision issued by the National Bank of Moldova (the NBM Decision). According to the claimant, the NBM Decision had suspended the claimant's voting rights in a Moldovan bank, and ordered it to divest its shares in the bank by 5 May 2014, based on an allegation that the claimant had unlawfully acted in concert with other foreign investors to acquire a too substantial a share of a Moldovan bank. The NBM decision was

136 At the time of writing, there were seven such cases. Since then, a further two have been reported.

137 At the time of writing, a small number of further treaty-based emergency arbitrations have been reported, namely in the cases *Komaksavia v. Moldova* (two separate emergency arbitrations), *Zaza Okuashvili v. Georgia,* and *Vnesheconombank* (*VEB*) *v. Ukraine* (all reported by Investment Arbitration Reporter but not publicly available).

138 *TSIKInvest v. Moldova,* Emergency Decision. Commented more extensively in J Dahlquist, *The First Known Investment Treaty Emergency Arbitration,* JWIT 17(2016) 261–271.

claimed to violate several provisions of the BIT, and the claimant sought an order for its immediate suspension.

As to the jurisdiction of the EA, the claimant professed to be an investor holding an investment in the meaning of BIT. In its application, it also addressed the so-called "cooling off" clause in the BIT's Article 10. Pursuant to that clause, an investor cannot initiate arbitration before six months has elapsed from the date it first notifies the state of a dispute. The claimant had notified Moldova of the dispute on 31 March 2014. Since the application for emergency arbitration was registered on 23 April 2014, six months had not elapsed. In the claimant's view, however, the six-month period did not apply to emergency arbitration: applying the cooling-off requirement to this particular type of dispute would be "inequitable and procedurally unfair."[139] Furthermore, the claimant stated that Moldova had not engaged in any amicable settlement efforts, despite claimant's efforts to that end. In the alternative, the claimant also argued that the BIT's MFN clause would allow it to "import" an unspecified treaty provision which does not contain a cooling-off clause.

Moldova did not participate in the proceedings, and thus did not present any objection to the EA's jurisdiction (or, for that matter, any arguments on the merits of the claimant's case). On the same day that the EA was appointed by the SCC Board, the EA issued an order calling for a response from the state by 25 April 2014. According to an SCC report of the case, Moldova confirmed receipt of the EA application on April 25.[140] This is not reflected in the account in the decision, which rather states that the EA was informed on April 28 that "Receipts of service of process with respect to the aforementioned couriers [the application and its exhibits, sent by the SCC via courier to two different Moldovan ministries] were submitted to the Emergency Arbitrator on 28 April 2014."[141] Furthermore, the EA stated that:

> Respondent has not submitted such a response [to the application], nor has it made any other contacts with the Emergency Arbitrator or the SCC Institute in these emergency proceedings.[142]

The EA accepted jurisdiction over the claims. On a "*prima facie* basis," the EA accepted, without discussion, that the claimant had established both an

---

139 *TSIKInvest v. Moldova*, Emergency Decision, para. 59.

140 L Knapp, SCC Practice: Emergency Arbitrator Decisions Rendered 2014, http://www.sccinstitute.com/media/62020/scc-practice-emergency-arbitrators-2014_final.pdf, last visited 12 January 2019, Section 3.

141 *TSIKInvest v. Moldova*, Emergency Decision, para. 8.

142 Ibid., para. 9.

"investor" and an "investment" under the treaty.[143] With respect to the "cooling off" clause, the EA held that it did not prevent the claimant from making the application.[144] The EA stated that:

> […] it would be procedurally unfair to Claimant and contrary to the purpose of the Emergency Arbitrator procedure to apply the Cooling-Off Period to the appointment of an Emergency Arbitrator or to an emergency decision on interim measures to be made by the Emergency Arbitrator, not least since Claimant seems to be facing a serious risk of suffering irreparable harm before the expiry of the Cooling-Off Period if interim measures are not granted.[145]

Having found that the cooling-off did not prevent the claimant, the EA did not have to address arguments as to Moldova's alleged failure to respond to amicable settlement attempts, nor the application of the treaty's MFN clause.

Ruling on the application for provisional measures, the EA granted the claimant's request to order a stay of the NBM Decision. In a few short paragraphs, the EA set down three criteria for granting the request, drawing from Swedish law, as the law of the seat of arbitration and thus, in the claimants' view, the applicable law.[146] All criteria are, however, generally accepted in arbitral jurisprudence. They are (i) a *prima facie* case on the merits, and (ii) the harm to be prevented by the ordered measure is of an urgent or imminent nature, and (iii) irreparable harm if the measure is not granted.[147] As for the first criterion, the EA based the decision on the facts as presented by the claimant, and was convinced that there was a reasonable possibility that a tribunal would find that the NBM Decision breached either the FET clause or the expropriation clause of the BIT.[148] With respect to the urgent or imminent harm, the EA stated that complying with the NBM Decision would result in the claimant being permanently and irrevocably deprived of its shareholders rights, whereas Moldova would suffer limited harm if the measure were ordered.[149] In this balancing act, the EA found it proportional to allow the requested measure.[150]

143 Ibid., para. 61.
144 Ibid., para. 66.
145 Ibid.
146 Ibid., para. 53.
147 Ibid., paras. 62–63.
148 Ibid., para. 62.
149 Ibid., paras. 64–65.
150 Ibid., para. 65.

4.4.2.2 Evrobalt v. Moldova

Following the *TSIKInvest* case, there have been two subsequent EA proceedings under the Russia – Moldova BIT. They both arose out of similar fact patterns as the *TSIKInvest* case, involving measures taken by the Moldovan authorities in the state's banking sector. In *Evrobalt LLC v. Moldova*,[151] the claimant was successful in obtaining emergency relief, while in *Kompozit v. Moldova*,[152] it was not.

Evrobalt applied for emergency arbitration on 24 May 2016. On 25 May an EA was appointed by the SCC Board, which also designated Stockholm as the seat of arbitration, since the parties had not agreed in advance.[153] On 26 May 2016, the SCC obtained proof of delivery of the EA application to two different Moldovan ministries, and on the same day Moldova responded briefly to the allegations put forward by Evrobalt. The state never participated further in the proceedings, however, despite the EA's attempts to "strongly invite" it via email to the two ministries.[154]

Similar to *TSIKInvest*, Evrobalt's claims centered on the actions of the National Bank of Moldova (NBM). Evrobalt asked the EA to suspend one decision and one decree, which in Evrobalt's view violated several provisions of the BIT.

Prior to the EA application on 24 May 2016, Evrobalt had notified the state of a dispute under the BIT, on 16 May the same year. Thus, similar to the *TSIKInvest* case, the six-month cooling-off period in Article 10 of the Russia – Moldova BIT had not been observed by Evrobalt, prompting the EA to discuss the consequences of this fact.

The claimant submitted that the cooling off did not prevent it from accessing emergency arbitration,[155] and the EA agreed with this reading.[156] In particular, the EA pointed that out that irrespective of one's reading of cooling-off clauses (*viz.* whether or not they constitute a procedural precondition or a question of admissibility), the key question was whether the insistence of observing the six-month period would be futile.[157] For the EA, the futility exception was met in the case, given that the Moldova intended to implement the decisions within three months, and had confirmed that it had no intention to suspend

151 *Evrobalt v. Moldova*, Emergency Decision.
152 *Kompozit v. Moldova*, Emergency Decision.
153 *Evrobalt v. Moldova*, Emergency Decision, para. 3.
154 Ibid., para. 5.
155 Ibid., para. 21.
156 Ibid., para. 22.
157 Ibid.

them, as confirmed by the letter issued when Moldova had been served notice by the SCC.[158]

The EA also stated that he was *prima facie* satisfied that Evrobalt was an "investor" in possession of an "investment" in the meaning of the treaty.[159] In doing so, the EA emphasized that Moldova had not disputed these assertions in its letter responding to the initial notice of dispute on 16 May 2016.

As a final jurisdictional consideration – and here it should be re-emphasized that Moldova did not raise any objections to the jurisdiction of the EA – the temporal application of the SCC Rules was discussed. In a relatively long analysis, the EA discussed "how the terms of Article 10 of the treaty may be said to encompass the 2010 version of the SCC Rules, and the emergency interim measures [available therein]."[160] As is discussed further below, this is a live issue since the 1998 BIT contains a generic reference to the SCC Rules, which were updated to include emergency arbitration in 2010. Evrobalt had argued that the SCC Rules themselves contained the answer to the question, by virtue of the Preamble to the Rules.[161] The claimant also relied upon a Svea Court of Appeal decision embracing the interpretation that whenever parties refer generically to a set of arbitration rules, this is to be understood as referring to the rules in effect at the time of commencement of the arbitration.[162] This latter argument, one would presume, was made because the place of arbitration was Stockholm. The EA did not rely on the Svea Court decision, but rather stated that the meaning of Article 10 should be interpreted by reference to international law, more specifically the Vienna Principles.[163] In this exercise, the EA framed the question in the following way: "[…] whether it may be said, on a *prima facie* basis, that the 2010 SCC Rules were within the reasonable contemplation of the Contracting Parties to the Treaty."[164]

By the time that the BIT entered into force in 2001, the applicable SCC Rules were those that entered into force in 1999. They contain the same preamble as the 2010 version.[165] For the EA, this was decisive, as it indicated that the two states had reasonably contemplated future arbitrations under the treaty to be governed by the version of the SCC Rules applicable at the time of the

158 Ibid., para. 23.
159 Ibid., para. 19.
160 Ibid., para. 24.
161 Ibid., para. 26.
162 Ibid. The case referred to is the *Auto Connect Sweden AB v. Consafe IT AB*, Svea Court of Appeal, T 754-09, 18 May 2009.
163 *Evrobalt v. Moldova*, Emergency Decision, para. 25; para. 27.
164 Ibid., para. 28.
165 Which was also retained in the 2017 version, as discussed below.

commencement of the arbitration.[166] This convinced the EA that, at least on a *prima facie* basis, the 2010 version of the rules applied to the proceedings.[167] Furthermore, the EA also stated another, independent basis for this conclusion. In his view, the fact that the BIT was intended to be in force for a long time demonstrated that the states could easily have opted to "freeze" the applicable version of the SCC Rules, especially since at the time when the BIT was signed, the SCC Rules had already been issued in updated version several times.[168] This fact also supported a "dynamic" interpretation, in the EA's view.

As for the standard for ordering the provisional measures requested, the EA in *Evrobalt* reasoned along similar lines as the EA in the *TSIKInvest* case. Relying partly on Swedish law as *lex loci arbitri,* and partly on Article 26 of the (non-applicable) 2010 UNCITRAL Rules as codification of established practice, the EA set out four "substantially uncontroversial" elements: (i) a risk of non-compensable harm or unenforceability of award,[169] (ii) a *prima facie* case on the merits,[170] (iii) urgency,[171] and (iv) proportionality.[172] In the view of the EA, it was sufficient in this case to discuss the two former criteria, which he found not to have been satisfied on the facts: the potential harm could be adequately repaired by an award of damages, as Evrobalt's potential loss was purely economic in nature.[173] The EA therefore dismissed the application already on this ground. Consequently, the three other elements, *viz.* a *prima facie* case on the merits, urgency and proportionality elements were not discussed by the EA.[174] This notwithstanding, the EA added a few words on the *prima facie* aspect, given that Evrobalt had relied on the decision in *TSIKInvest,* which had found that such a case on the merits existed in that dispute. The Evrobalt EA distinguished the *TSIKInvest* case from the Evrobalt case, because the NBM decision in the *TSIKInvest* case had not been motivated.[175] In Evrobalt's case, the decision targeted in the application had in fact been accompanied by reasons, and it also seemed that judicial review of the decision in question was still available in Moldovan courts.

---

166 *Evrobalt v. Moldova*, Emergency Decision, para. 29.
167 Ibid.
168 Ibid., para. 30.
169 Ibid., paras. 40–58.
170 Ibid., paras. 59–62.
171 Ibid., para. 63.
172 Ibid.
173 Ibid., paras. 51–52.
174 Ibid., paras. 59–62.
175 Ibid., para. 60.

4.4.2.3 Kompozit v. Moldova

In yet another emergency arbitration application targeting a decision by the National Bank of Moldova and brought under the Russia – Moldova BIT, the claimant Kompozit LLC was ultimately successful in its application.[176] Kompozit had notified Moldova of a dispute, thereby triggering the six-month cooling-off period, on 2 June 2016. On 9 June 2016, the claimant applied for emergency arbitration. The day after, on June 10, the SCC Board decided that it did not manifestly lack jurisdiction, appointed the EA and designated Stockholm as the seat of arbitration.[177] On the same day, the EA invited the respondent state to respond to the application, including informing whether it would be represented by outside counsel.[178] On June 11, when the EA had received no response from the state, he sent another email asking whether the state wished to submit any comments. Moldova responded the same day that it had no comments. This was seemingly the only time the state participated in the proceedings.

The case raised similar jurisdictional discussion as the two previous EA cases against Moldova, focusing on (i) whether the claimant was an "investor" in possession of an "investment," (ii) the BIT's cooling-off clause and (iii) the temporal application of the SCC Rules. The first issue was swiftly dealt with by the EA, who accepted Kompozit's allegations as the basis for a *prima facie* finding that it was an "investor" in possession of an "investment."[179] Kompozit had also, similar to the claimants in *TSIKInvest* and *Evrobalt*, claimed that the non-observance of the cooling-off period did not bar it from accessing emergency arbitration. The EA focused his analysis on the futility of observing the cooling-off. The Moldovan Ministry of Justice had indicated on June 3 that it was not authorized to negotiate, nor could it take any actions with respect to the bank's decisions.[180] Based on this, the EA stated that

> since the dispute was not resolved within the Cooling-Off Period due the Respondent's attitude, the Claimant became entitled to refer the dispute to arbitration, as provided for in Article 10(2) of the Treaty, without having to wait until the expiration of the six-month period[181]

176 *Kompozit v. Moldova*, Emergency Decision.
177 Ibid., paras. 7–8.
178 Ibid., para. 10.
179 Ibid., paras. 48–50.
180 Ibid., para. 54(e)ii.
181 Ibid., para. 56.

As for the applicability of the 2010 SCC Rules, the *Kompozit* decision is similar to the *Evrobalt* decision. The EA was satisfied, on a *prima facie* basis, that the 2010 Rules would apply, and thereby that emergency arbitration was available. The EA stated that it was "fair to assume that when the contracting parties to the Treaty included a reference to the SCC Arbitration Rules, they anticipated that [the Rules] could be amended in the future."[182]

In discussing the standards to be met, the EA in the *Kompozit* case reasoned along similar lines as both the *TSIKInvest* and *Evrobalt* EAs. In addition to the SCC Rules (which are silent in this respect), the EA relied on the UNCITRAL Model Law, as well as Swedish Arbitration Act, by virtue of its status as *lex loci arbitri*. The EA based his reasoning on similar requirements as those set down in the two earlier cases, but came to a different conclusion than the *Evrobalt* EA.

4.4.2.4 SCC Case No. 183/2014

Moving to the other four EA cases at the SCC, the second-ever treaty-based emergency case to be registered at the SCC was brought by an investor incorporated in the EU against another EU state.[183] The investor had already notified the state of a dispute under the BIT between the two EU states. That notification was filed in October 2013, and in 2014 the claimants also requested arbitration at the SCC.[184] Eventually, after the registration of the request for arbitration but prior to the constitution of the tribunal in the arbitration, the claimants also applied for emergency arbitration on December 31, 2014. In its application, the claimants asked the EA to enjoin the effects of a local court judgment in the respondent state.

This case stands out from the others discussed in this section, in several significant ways. First, the application for emergency arbitration was registered after the investor had also initiated a full arbitration.[185] Second, the six-month cooling-off period had been observed prior to both the request for arbitration and the request for arbitration. Thus, two issues which could otherwise have been problematic for the purposes of EA jurisdiction[186] were not on the table in this case.

---

182 Ibid., para. 39.

183 SCC Case No. 183/2014, Emergency Decision.

184 SCC Case No. 168/2014.

185 As indicated by the respective SCC case numbers, which are chronological based on the registration of a case. The fact that an arbitration agreement had been perfected, through the request for arbitration prior to the filing of emergency measures, was also pointed out by the EA at para. 32.

186 Discussed further below at 6.4.4.

Furthermore, the state seemingly participated actively in the proceedings. The application for emergency arbitration was registered on December 31 2004. On the same day, the EA was appointed and the state was served notice of the application (a fact that, according to the decision, the state did not dispute). The disputing parties could not agree on a seat of arbitration. In accordance with the SCC Rules, the SCC Board therefore designated Stockholm as the place of arbitration. Both disputing parties attended the initial case management telephone conference, and two more were conducted during the five-day span. As recounted by the EA, both disputing parties also agreed that proper procedure had been followed, and that they had been able in the circumstances to present their respective case.[187]

As for the EA's jurisdiction, there was a discrepancy in the different language versions of the investment treaty, it was not addressed by the EA, because the disputing parties agreed that the determination of which version of the treaty was authentic was outside of the mandate of the EA.[188] In any event, the EA stated, the discrepancy was not relevant for the emergency proceedings, but rather for the subsequent arbitral tribunal to determine.[189]

In determining its own jurisdiction, the EA reiterated what was common ground between the parties that the determination in this respect could only be made on a *prima facie* basis.[190] The EA further stated:

> By definition, an emergency arbitrator, who steps in where a tribunal is yet to be constituted and has very tight time-frames for a decision, can only make a prima facie finding; hence his or her decision does not bind the tribunal [footnote omitted]. [...] [S]atisfaction of prima facie jurisdiction does not equate with any presumption in favour of jurisdiction. Arbitration being a forum available by consent and election of the parties, he must be satisfied – albeit on a preliminary basis – that there is a good prospect for a finding (by the Tribunal) that the parties have agreed upon the procedure set out in Appendix II to the 2010 SCC Rules[191]

Having set out this general framework, the EA proceeded to briefly recount further specific objections that the state intended to make before the full tribunal, stating that the state "accepts that in respect of neither of them can it make a

187 SCC Case No. 183/2014, Emergency Decision, para. 12.
188 Ibid., para. 19 with footnote.
189 Ibid, paras. 19, 26–27.
190 Ibid., para. 24.
191 Ibid., paras. 24–25.

showing of manifest absence of jurisdiction, as would be necessary within the constraints of the present emergency proceedings. Consequently, these objections cannot be determined in the present proceedings, and will have to be submitted to the Tribunal in due course and determined by it."[192] There is no reference in the EA decision to the requirement that the state show that the EA "manifestly" lacks jurisdiction. Under this standard, most of the state's jurisdictional objections would instead have to be developed before the full tribunal.

The sole jurisdictional objection dealt with by the EA was that the respondent had not consented to arbitration under the 2010 SCC Rules, or at any rate to the Appendix II of these rules, (which provide for emergency arbitration).[193] The state argued that the investment treaty, which predates the 2010 Rules, only contains consent to arbitrate under the SCC Rules in force at the time of the treaty, i.e. the 1976 version of the SCC Rules.[194] In the alternative, even if the state's consent were found to encompass the 2010 Rules, it did not encompass emergency arbitration, which was a "qualitative change," rather than a change in degree. The state argued that it could not have given advance consent to a procedure that was unknown at the time of the conclusion of the treaty.[195]

The EA approached this objection by interpreting the treaty's arbitration clause with the aid of Article 31 of the VCLT. The clause in question provides for a number of potential arbitration avenues, including the "SCC Arbitration Institute," albeit without reference to the SCC Rules as such.[196] The EA pointed out that other treaties by the same state referenced specific arbitration rules, which might imply that the present treaty's reference to institutions was a deliberate choice not to freeze in time the version of the relevant institution's rules. Furthermore, the EA discussed the utility of an "evolutionary" or "dynamic" interpretation, citing the ICJ's *Dispute regarding Navigational and Related* Rights judgment as support for this approach in cases where treaty terms are susceptible of evolving over time.[197]

However, in the view of the EA, the state's objection could be dealt with in a more "straightforward" manner. The 1976 SCC Rules in effect at the time of the treaty's conclusion contains a temporal provision which states that "if a party invokes an arbitration agreement concluded prior to [the entry into force of the 1976 Rules] which refers to arbitral proceedings under the auspices of the Institute, the former Statutes shall apply unless the parties have otherwise

192 Ibid, para. 27.
193 Ibid., para. 22.
194 Ibid., para. 28.
195 Ibid.
196 Ibid., para. 34.
197 Ibid., para. 35.

agreed."[198] The 1988 SCC Rules, which were in force once the treaty entered into force, contains a similar temporal provision.[199] In short, the EA found:

> both at the time of the signature of the Treaty and at the time of its entry into force, the critical time for selection of the applicable version of the SCC Rules was the time of the conclusion of the parties' arbitration agreement. This was the only inter-temporal rule that could have been within the contracting states' reasonable contemplation [at the conclusion and entry into force of the treaty].[200]

Based on this reasoning, the EA concluded that the states gave advance consent to the version of the SCC Rules in effect at the time an eligible investor would accept the standing offer to arbitrate. As for the state's other argument, that emergency arbitration could not have been within the states' reasonable contemplation when entering into the treaty, as the jurisdiction of a body other than the tribunal to issue binding interim measures was a "sea change" that occurred in 2010,[201] the EA pointed out two things. First, the state's argument is "inferential," whereas the reading of the 1976 and 1988 versions of the SCC Rules is specific. Secondly, the state's inference would be difficult to apply in principle, because there have been several qualitative changes of importance since the 1976 Rules. Granting adjudicative functions to a body other than the Tribunal was not as extraordinary as the state would suggest: for example, already in the 1976 Rules the SCC Board was authorized to dismiss claims for manifest lack of jurisdiction. Here, the EA stated that "while it is true that the Board has been a fixture of SCC arbitration for several decades, it is also true that an emergency arbitrator is appointed by decision of the Board."[202]

Although accepting jurisdiction, ultimately, the EA rejected the application for interim relief.[203] At the time of writing, the full arbitration is still pending.

4.4.2.5 SCC Case No. 002/2015

On 7 January 2015 the claimants filed an application for the appointment of an emergency arbitrator in Case No. 002/2015. Prior to this application, the claimants had sent a letter to the state on 13 November 2014 seeking amicable

198 1976 SCC Rules, Rule 20.
199 1988 SCC Rules, Article 34.
200 Para. 38.
201 Para. 41.
202 Para. 41.
203 Para. 65.

settlement of a dispute under the ECT, as well as under two BITS. All treaties contain cooling off-periods of three months.

The SCC Board appointed an EA on the same day as the application, and notified the Respondent by email and courier the same day.[204] The Board also designated Stockholm as the place of arbitration.[205] The state never confirmed receipt of notification, nor did it participate in the proceedings.[206] As a consequence, the EA stated that it had "the power to draw inferences from Respondent's default," and proceeded to render its decision based on the facts submitted by the claimants.[207]

The decision is short on jurisdictional analysis. The EA states that the claimants accepted the state's standing offer to arbitrate under the ECT by sending its 13 November letter.[208] The EA went on to state that "no thorough review of [the EA's jurisdiction] can be undertaken."[209] However, the Claimants "appear to satisfy the jurisdictional requirement under the rules of the ECT." More specifically, Claimant appeared to be investors with an investment, and to have accepted the state's offer to arbitrate. The EA also concluded that the Claimant's factual allegations which may support a claim if verified in the main arbitral proceedings. One potential jurisdictional hurdle was identified by the EA, however: the so-called "tax carve-out" in Article 21 of the ECT. However, the EA stated that this question could not be decided in an emergency proceeding, but was rather better dealt with by the subsequent tribunal.[210]

Based on this analysis, the EA proceeded to discuss the merits of the sought interim measures, ultimately ordering the state to refrain from imposing certain royalties on the production of gas.

4.4.2.6 SCC Case No. 092/2017

In SCC Case No. 092/2017, the application for emergency arbitration was registered on June 2, 2017. An emergency arbitrator was appointed by the SCC the next day. On June 4, the EA issued Procedural Order No. 1, directing the Respondent to submit a reply no later than June 6 at 22.00 CEST.[211] The order was sent to various email addresses, collected from the official Facebook page of the Presidency of the host state, and to the official email address of the state's

204 SCC Case No. 002/2015, Emergency Decision, para. 11.
205 Ibid., para. 19.
206 Ibid.
207 Ibid., para. 16.
208 Ibid., para. 18.
209 Ibid., para. 52.
210 Ibid., para. 57.
211 Ibid., para. 3.

ministry of foreign affairs. On June 6, the claimant also provided the EA with further email addresses, and the procedural order was sent to these the same day. No communication was registered from the Respondent before the deadline set by the EA. This notwithstanding, the EA found that the application and the procedural order had been properly communicated to the respondent state. The EA found it "important to underline that no one of the email addresses used to liaise with the Respondent (or the Applicant for that matter) in respect of any email message has generated an irregularity report."[212]

In the relatively short analysis on jurisdiction, the EA stated that the treaty relied upon by the claimant provides for arbitration under the SCC Rules, and that the claimant relied on this offer in making its request.[213] The EA further dispensed with the treaty's cooling off-clause, in the following way:

> Even if [the cooling off-provision] were to be regarded as a condition precedent for arbitration – which the Emergency Arbitrator does not need to take a position on – this would still not bar a request for emergency relief at this time. Emergency measures do not seek to resolve a dispute or result in the final disposition of a dispute; they seek to preserve the status quo or to provide other temporary relief in the anticipation of or in the course of contentious proceedings. Due to their very nature of provisional and temporary relief in support of contentious proceedings follows that any reference to arbitration rules – such as the SCC Rules – encompassing emergency relief grounds jurisdiction irrespective of whether a cooling-off period carries with it jurisdictional implications for the tribunal proper.[214]

Based on these reasons, the EA was satisfied that there was jurisdiction to render interim measures. It also pointed out that the finding in favour of jurisdiction is "without any prejudice to a future tribunal's inquiry and conclusion on this threshold issue."[215]

Regarding the merits of the claimant's case, the EA stated that, although granted a "wide sphere of discretion" by the SCC Rules, the EA's exercise of this discretion should be guided by criteria which are generally recognized in adjudicatory practice and which are, on the whole, "not at all controversial."[216]

212 Ibid., para. 9.
213 Ibid., paras. 14–15.
214 Ibid., para. 17.
215 Ibid., para. 20.
216 Ibid., para. 36.

These included, in the EA's view, a risk for irreparable harm, that the risked damage is "imminent" and "urgent," and that there is a *prima facie* case on the merits.[217] The EA found that all of these tests had been met by the investor and thus granted the requests for emergency relief, ordering the state to restrain its judiciary and other state organs from aggravating the dispute in the arbitration.

4.4.2.7 Munshi v. Mongolia

The most recent treaty-based emergency arbitration, *Munshi v. Mongolia*[218] involves a slightly different set of facts than the earlier cases. The application was filed under the ECT by an alleged investor who is a physical person with dual nationality. Both of the investor's home states are ECT states, and the respondent is a third state, also party to the ECT. The application was registered on 19 January 2018 and was served on the state on 31 January 2018, when the EA was appointed by the SCC Board.219 It is not clear why there is a time gap between the application and the formal initiation of the case, but presumably the applicant did not pay the SCC fees at the time when the application was sent, thereby rendering the application incomplete. In accordance with the Rules, the SCC serves the application on the respondent only once an application is complete. In any event, on the same day that the SCC Board appointed the EA, the Board also designated Stockholm as the place of arbitration.[220] The EA issued a first procedural order on the same day. On 2 February, the EA wrote to the respondent state to confirm that it had received the first procedural order, also asking whether it intended to make submissions.[221] Two days later, on 4 February, the investor made further submissions.[222] The state never participated in the proceedings.[223]

The investor claimed to have been subject to severe legal difficulties in the respondent state. The alleged investment in question was a coal exploration company, which the investor chaired but claims to have been forced out of. Furthermore, the investor claims to have been kept from leaving the country lest an unspecified sum of money was paid to a powerful individual in the host

217 Ibid., paras. 38–60.

218 This decision is in the public domain, *Munshi v. Mongolia*, Emergency Decision. See also L E Peterson, *Emergency arbitrator Bernardo Cremades orders Mongolian state to ensure businessman has "reasonable access" to counsel, but declines to order state to free him from prison*, Investment Arbitration Reporter, 3 April 2018.

219 *Munshi v. Mongolia*, Emergency Decision, paras. 1–2.

220 Ibid., para. 5.

221 Ibid., para. 9.

222 Ibid., para. 10.

223 Ibid., para. 11.

state, who at the time of the EA application controlled the coal exploration business.

In 2015 the investor was arrested and kept in prison until July 2017, when he was convicted to 11 years for a type of fraud that was only criminalized after the alleged acts leading up to the 2015 arrest and the 2017 conviction. In the EA application, the investor claims to be working on a request for arbitration which would outline how the state has violated the FET (more specifically the denial of justice element of that standard) and expropriation clauses of the ECT.[224] More relevant to the application for interim relief is that the investor at the time of application was still imprisoned in the state, allegedly with danger to his life. The investor claims to have been targeted by the powerful individual and that the terms of the imprisonment were a consequence of his refusal to pay this person. In prison, the investor has very limited access to legal counsel – the emergency application had been prepared by international counsel who had to rely indirectly on local counsel, who in turn had very limited access to the investor – and medical personnel. In the latter case, this was supposedly life-threatening to the investor, who had developed several serious medical conditions but been refused access to treatment. The notification of a looming ECT arbitration allegedly made the situation worse.

The EA did not grapple extensively with jurisdictional issues; once again, it bears repeating that the respondent state did not participate and thus did not raise any jurisdictional objections. The two passports submitted by the applicant were seemingly deemed sufficient to establish the investor's nationality, and thus his status as protected investor under the ECT.[225] Without much discussion, including on jurisdiction *ratione materiae*, the EA thus found that its jurisdiction was *prima facie* satisfied.[226] In coming to this conclusion, the EA also cited the fact that the SCC Board had decided that it did not manifestly lack jurisdiction.[227]

Instead, most of the decision was concerned with the merits of the application, in which the investor requested the EA to order that the investor be released from detention, allowed to leave the state, or in the alternative only released from detention. The investor also asked to be allowed to travel to a specified third country for medical care, and to have access to national and international legal counsel. The EA recognized its broad powers to order "any interim measure it deems appropriate," and discussed four elements that by

224 Ibid., para. 20.
225 Ibid., para. 29.
226 Ibid., para. 33.
227 Ibid., para. 33.

now are familiar to the reader of this text. Two of them were relatively unproblematic: irreparable harm (which the EA found to have been met, given the fear for the investor's life),[228] and urgency (where the EA relied on Art 7 of Appendix II, which provides that the arbitration shall be conducted "taking into account the urgency inherent in such proceedings," to find that there was no indication that the conditions of the detainment would change) were both found to have been met.[229] However, the EA was less convinced by the investor's arguments on the points of necessity and proportionality, respectively.

On necessity, the EA was not convinced that the investor's right to develop his international arbitration case justified an order allowing him to leave the country. Instead, the EA stated that he was "not satisfied that Claimant's fundamental rights in the procedural running of the arbitration extend so far as to interfere with the justice system of a sovereign state."[230] Allowing the investor to leave the state would go beyond what was strictly necessary for him to file his request for arbitration. Furthermore, the EA distinguished the case before him from the ICSID case *Nova Group v. Romania*, because unlike that case the investor in *Munshi* was already convicted and the EA was not in a position to suggest that he was in fact innocent.[231]

As to the proportionality of the requested measures, the EA, while convinced that a *prima facie* case had been established, found that allowing the measures would place a burden on the host state. Interfering with sovereign actions, in this case a criminal proceeding, would place a burden on the state that would not be proportional. Furthermore, the EA did not find that there was a legal basis to order a person released from prison in order to commence an international arbitration.[232]

Ultimately, given the lack of necessity and proportionality, on 5 February 2018 the EA rejected the investor's request for an order to be released from detention, but instead ordered that the state give the investor access to (local and international) legal counsel.[233]

Interestingly, the investor's request, as recounted by the EA decision, was to be released from prison or, in the alternative, to be allowed to leave the country. Thus, the EA's order that the state give the investor access to legal counsel had not, strictly speaking, been requested by the investor. In his discussion on the necessity aspect of the claims, however, the EA emphasized that he

228 Ibid., paras. 42–44.
229 Ibid., paras. 50–52.
230 Ibid, para. 47.
231 Ibid., para. 48.
232 Ibid., para. 53–57.
233 Ibid., para. 58.

was "endowed with inherent powers to preserve the integrity of the arbitral process," which led him to find it "necessary for Claimant to have reasonable access to both Mongolian and international counsel in order to advance his ECT claims."[234] Presumably, this led the EA to order such access, even if it was not requested by the investor. This reasoning is arguably complicated by the fact that at the time of the rendering of the EA decision, there was no arbitration yet, in the strict sense of the word; the investor had not yet requested arbitration. The SCC Rules do not require that an arbitration has been initiated prior to the request for emergency measures, which is discussed further below at 4.4.4.2.

4.4.3 *The Place of Arbitration in Emergency Arbitration Cases*

Given this text's repeated insistence on the importance of the place of arbitration, it deserves pointing out that every known treaty-based emergency arbitration has been legally seated in Stockholm. The SCC Board made the decision in each case.[235] Once, in Case No. 183/2014, did the disputing parties directly discuss the issue but could not come to an agreement, leading the Board to designate the seat in that case as well.[236]

The SCC Board, which according to the Rules should consist of one chair, three vice-chairs and additionally 12 people at the most,[237] may make a decision if at least two members are present.[238] Decisions may also be delegated to the Secretariat.[239] The exact constitution of the Board is not specified in any of the EA awards. In practice, however, given the very short time-frame, it is unlikely that such designations have been made at one of the regular board meetings, which occur on a monthly basis. Instead, a limited number of Board members are likely to have designated the place of arbitration in each case

234 Ibid., para. 46.

235 *TSIKInvest v. Moldova*, Emergency Decision, para. 4; *Kompozit v. Moldova*, Emergency Decision, para. 8; *Evrobalt v. Moldova*, Emergency Decision, para. 4; *Munshi v. Mongolia*, Emergency Decision, para. 5. The same holds true for two of the three remaining cases which are not in the public domain: SCC Case No. 183/2014 (para. 4); SCC Case No. 002/2015 (para. 4). In SCC Case No. 092/2017, the designation of the place of arbitration is not described in the decision, but the decision is signed "in Stockholm," p. 15. Given that the respondent did not participate, it is unlikely that there was a party agreement on the seat, which would have prompted the SCC Board to designate it.

236 SCC Case No. 183/2014, para. 6.

237 SCC Arbitration Rules, Appendix I, Article 3. At the time of writing, the Board consists of the maximum amount of members.

238 SCC Arbitration Rules, Appendix I, Article 7.

239 Ibid.

(and, as discussed below, to simultaneously have decided on the *prima facie* jurisdiction of the institution).[240]

The place of arbitration may be particularly significant in emergency arbitration, because the SCC Rules are relatively open-ended in terms of which standards to apply for determining the core question in each case, i.e. whether to order the requested provisional measures. For example, the *TSIKInvest* EA, the *Evrobalt* EA and the *Kompozit* EA all referenced Swedish arbitration law, as argued by the claimant, in determining the test for provisional measures to be accepted. As is evident from these decisions, Swedish arbitration law, in the form of Section 25 of the Swedish Arbitration Act, does not provide much by way of further guidance, which may explain the slightly different elements emphasized by different EAs in their discussion. This being said, the choice to designate Stockholm as the place of arbitration is also necessarily a choice not to designate other jurisdictions; there are plenty of other alternative *leges arbitri* that are more specific on the points of interim measures.[241]

What is more, the place of arbitration could play a role with respect to challenges of an emergency decision. Swedish arbitration law does not allow the challenge of non-final awards, such as EA decisions. Although the SCC Rules provide that an EA's decision can take the form of either an "order" or an "award,"[242] this is subject to the law at the place of arbitration. Swedish arbitration law does not recognize this distinction, regardless of the brand put on the decision by the arbitrator(s). Under Section 27 of the Swedish Arbitration Act:

> The issues which have been referred to the arbitrators shall be decided in an award. Where the arbitrators terminate the arbitral proceedings without deciding such issues, such shall also take place through an award. [...] Other determinations, which are not embodied in an award, are designated as decisions.

Only "awards" may be challenged in Swedish court, and not "decisions."[243] Thus, when Swedish arbitration law is *lex loci arbitri,* a party cannot go to court to apply for the set aside of an emergency arbitration decision. In *Kompozit,* the EA asked the parties whether they wished the decision to be framed as an

---

240 K Hobér states that "emergencies occur from time to time" which have to be handled in between monthly Board meetings, usually by "the chairman of the Board together with another member of the Board," K Hobér, *International Commercial Arbitration,* p. 10.

241 See for example Articles 17-17 J of the 2006 UNCITRAL Model Law; Sections 35–38 of the 2011 Hong Kong Arbitration Ordinance.

242 SCC Rules, Article 32(3).

243 Sections 34 and 36 of the Swedish Arbitration Act speak only of "awards."

"order" or an "award." As per the answer from the claimant, the EA opted for "award."[244] Furthermore, although not discussed expressly in any decision, all the other (Stockholm-seated) EAs have also styled their decision as "awards," with the sole exception of the *TSIKInvest* case.[245] This notwithstanding, for the purposes of Swedish law, these are properly characterized as "decisions,"[246] and as such not open to challenge. Rather, a disgruntled party would have to wait for an "ordinary" tribunal to determine the matters and render a final award. This is not the same in all jurisdictions; some jurisdictions allow for the recognition and enforcement of "non-final" decisions.[247] Presumably, if an emergency arbitration were seated in such a jurisdiction, it would be theoretically possible to challenge it in court.[248] Ultimately, however, the need to challenge an emergency order is likely to be of limited relevance, given that such orders are by definition temporary and their applicability restricted in time.

A related – and arguably more pertinent – issue is that the place of arbitration may also influence the recognition and/or enforcement of an EA's decision. For the purposes of the New York Convention, the award has the "nationality" of the place of arbitration.[249] Without discussing the enforcement issue further, as such issues are excluded from the scope of this text, it is not entirely clear whether an order from an emergency arbitrator is "final and binding" for the purposes of the New York Convention.[250] This being said, the Convention only establishes a bottom-line, allowing the enforcing court to always recognize or enforce an award if it so sees fit.[251]

---

244 *Kompozit v. Moldova*, Emergency Decisio, para. 12. Note that this para states that "the Respondent informed the Emergency Arbitrator, with copy to the Respondent [that the decision should take the form of an award]." This is likely a typographical error, and the former "Respondent" is better understood as referring to "Claimant."

245 The *TSIK* decision is consistently framed as a "Decision," and was rendered by Kaj Hobér, a Swedish arbitrator and former Chairman of the SCC Board.

246 The SCC Rules speak of emergency "decisions," see Appendix II, Articles 8–9.

247 For an overview of practice, see G Born, pp. 2429–2439.

248 Given the limitations of an EA order, the practical use of such a challenge is likely to be very limited.

249 The New York Convention consistently refers to the place where the award was "made."

250 For an overview of literature and jurisprudence dealing with the enforcement of provisional measures generally, see G Born, pp. 2510–2521.

251 Article V(1) provides that the enforcing court "may" refuse recognition or enforcement based on the enumerated grounds provided in the article; nothing in the Convention prevents the court to allow enforcement. Furthermore, some jurisdictions expressly allow for the enforcement of orders of interim measures, see for example Article 183(2) of the Swiss International Arbitration Law.

4.4.4 *Discussion: The Function of Emergency Arbitration in Treaty-Based Disputes*

In many ways, emergency arbitration is at the apex of the questions asked in this dissertation, as it is an instrument that has been developed in a commercial arbitration framework but is sometimes also applied in the treaty-based sphere. Depending on the perspective, emergency arbitration can be viewed either as an efficient way of protecting the rights of consenting disputing parties, or a disproportionate infringement upon sovereign rights, which could not have been foreseen by treaty states. In any event, the use of emergency arbitration in investment cases has not been discussed frequently in literature, probably because the decisions presented above have all been rendered in the last couple of years.[252]

Below, a number of questions raised by these cases are discussed in a wider context. These include the different approaches by the ICC and the SCC, as well as more general questions relating to the jurisdiction of emergency arbitrators, and the nature of the requested measures.

4.4.4.1 The Different Approaches – Opt In or Opt Out?

Although not executed in the clearest of terms, it seems that the intention behind Article 29 of the 2010 ICC Rules was to exclude emergency arbitration from investment treaty disputes. The SCC, on the other hand, undoubtedly introduced emergency arbitration in 2010 and maintained it in the 2017 update of the Rules. In practice, therefore, it seems that parties wishing to allow for ICC emergency arbitration in an investment treaty arbitration would have to make that expressly clear, whereas the inverse is true for the SCC Rules. The two institutions have thus established different default frameworks for emergency arbitration, meaning that when the parties do not to take active action, emergency arbitration is available under one set of rules, but not under the other.

During the drafting of the 2017 SCC Rules, a specific working group was designated to deal with issues relating to investor-state arbitration. It is unclear if emergency arbitration was discussed in this context, but during the public

252 For an early identification of potential issues – prior to any treaty-based case having been filed - see however C Brower, A Meyerstein and S W Schill, "The Power and Effectiveness of Pre-Arbitral Provisional Relief: The SCC Emergency Arbitrator in Investor-State Disputes" in K Hobér, A Magnusson, M Öhrström (eds.), *Between East and West: Essays in Honour of Ulf Franke,* Juris, 2010. For more recent texts, see K S Yen, "The Use of Emergency Arbitrators in Investment Treaty Arbitration," ICSID Review, Vol. 31, No. 3 (2016), pp. 534–548; J Dahlquist, "The First Known Investment Treaty Emergency Arbitration," (2016) 17 JWIT 261.

consultation period, the present author submitted comments drawing the issue to the attention of the working group.[253] As already discussed, the preamble, which regulates the temporal application of the SCC Rules and provides that the rules applicable at the time of the initiation of the (emergency) arbitration, was ultimately not altered, and thus emergency arbitration remains available under the 2017 Rules, also in cases where the investment treaty in question predates the 2010 introduction of emergency arbitration.

By way of comparison, the issue of temporal application was discussed also when the 1976 UNCITRAL Arbitration Rules were updated in 2010. The outcome of that discussion, which largely centred on the difference between contract-based and treaty-based arbitration, was to distinguish treaty-based cases from those in which the parties agree directly to arbitration in a contract. Under the headline "Scope of application," Article 1(2) now provides:

> The parties to an arbitration agreement concluded after 15 August 2010 shall be presumed to have referred to the Rules in effect on the date of commencement of the arbitration, unless the parties have agreed to apply a particular version of the Rules. That presumption does not apply where the arbitration agreement has been concluded by accepting after 15 August 2010 an offer made before that date.

This approach to temporal application establishes a presumption that the Rules in force at the commencement of the arbitration shall be applied, if the arbitration agreement is based on the acceptance of an offer made before the entry into force of the new Rules (which is typically the case in treaty-based arbitration). This presumption, although not binding on the parties or the tribunal,[254] "proceeds on a theory of consent and avoids retroactive application of the 2010 Rules where both parties could not have reasonably assented to their application."[255] By establishing a presumption, which can be deviated from if found appropriate in the individual case, the UNCITRAL approach to temporal application strikes a compromise between the SCC approach (which allows for the initiation of arbitration to be determinative also in treaty-based cases) and the ICC approach (which seemingly requires both disputing parties to opt in for emergency arbitration to be available). By way of comparison, the

253 J Dahlquist, *Comment on the Draft SCC Arbitration Rules 2017*, 13 May, 2016, available at https://www.linkedin.com/pulse/comment-draft-scc-arbitration-rules-2017-joel-dahlquist/, visited 11 January, 2019.

254 Caron & Caplan, p. 21.

255 Ibid., p. 22 with further references.

SIAC Rules provide that emergency arbitral relief is only available where the parties "expressly agree."[256]

The different approaches are relevant because, as pointed out above, the vast majority of investment treaties predate the introduction of emergency arbitration (in 2012 at the ICC and 2010 at the SCC).[257] The issue thus becomes a live one: should a state who entered into an investment treaty many years, sometimes even decades, ago be deemed to have consented to emergency arbitration which was introduced in the Rules only recently? Here the two institutions have opted for different approaches, at least if one subscribes to what seems to be the prevailing reading of Article 29 of the ICC Rules, as it was seemingly interpreted by the ICC Court the only time it so far has had to deal with the issue.

There might of course be similarly old *contracts* with arbitration clauses, where the parties could not have envisioned the development of emergency arbitration. A similar argument against "retroactive" application of emergency arbitration could of course be made in these instances too. However, in those cases both parties are direct signatories to the clause, whereas a state in a treaty gives an open, irrevocable consent to a wide class of potential claimants. Simply put, with the current SCC solution the investor has a much larger ability to analyse the currently applicable Rules before "consenting" to use them, than did the state when it consented (most commonly) decades ago.

It is submitted that some flexibility is called for in the application of emergency arbitration in the investment treaty arbitration context. The temporal approach used in the 2010 version of the UNCITRAL Rules would have been preferable over that adopted by both the ICC and the SCC. Under the UNCITRAL approach, each emergency arbitrator would have the discretion to interpret the instrument(s) relied upon in the application, in order to determine whether the disputing parties did in fact consent to emergency arbitration. For example, in the SCC context, if the treaty relied upon was concluded after 2010 but before 2017, the UNCITRAL solution would allow for an application of the 2010 SCC Rules – and thereby emergency arbitration – even if it would not be the default. It would also be possible for the 2017 Rules to apply to disputes based on a treaty concluded in the 20th century. The point is that such an application would not be presumed but rather left to the EA to decide, in accordance with the facts and legal grounds as presented in the individual case.

256 SIAC Investment Arbitration Rules, Rule 27(4); SIAC Investment Arbitration Rules, Schedule 1 Rule 1.

257 See Chapter 2 for an overview of 20th century treaties referring to the ICC Rules and the SCC Rules.

The approach of the ICC Rules is also less than satisfactory. Although seemingly close to the UNCITRAL solution, the wording is not clear, as it requires both disputing parties to be "signatories" to the same agreement. As discussed above, this wording is presumably based on an assumption that parties to a contract are signatories to an agreement, whereas an investor and a state in a typical treaty arbitration are not. Here again, the UNCITRAL solution is more open, in that it would not rule out application of emergency arbitration altogether, if the EA in question interprets the treaty in a way that, for example, provides that the parties wish for the latest version of the arbitration rules to be applicable.

In addition to the temporal application of the respective Rules, the use of emergency arbitration raises several other jurisdictional questions. A running theme in this text is that investment treaty arbitration typically involves complex jurisdictional questions.[258] Admittedly, this sometimes happens also in commercial cases[259] – where the use of emergency arbitration is less controversial – but to a much smaller extent.

The surveyed cases demonstrate that emergency arbitration is generally ill-suited to grapple with complex jurisdictional questions. It bears repeating that the SCC Rules afford an EA five days to render a decision; during this time both parties are to be given the opportunity to present their arguments, and the EA must not only be convinced that there is jurisdiction, but also decide the often-pointed issues of the application's merits. In every case to date, the emphasis has been on the latter aspects; all but one of the seven EAs have found that they have jurisdiction, without much discussion, and then spent the vast majority of the decision on the test for ordering interim measures. To a certain extent, the limited jurisdictional consideration by EAs is of limited concern given the *prima facie* nature of emergency arbitration. However, an order for emergency relief is more than a tool to bring into a subsequent arbitration; it is potentially an instrument of self-standing importance. Thus, it is submitted that "emergency arbitration jurisdiction" in the investment treaty context is deserving of more extensive analysis than what the procedure typically allows for when a case is being arbitrated. Below, a number of these issues are therefore discussed.

258 This is the premise of Chapter 3, in which it is demonstrated that domestic courts regularly engage in jurisdictional analyses that differ from those in international commercial arbitration.

259 A Carlevaris in C Giorgetti (ed.), p. 204.

4.4.4.2 Jurisdictional Issues – Emergency Arbitration without Privity?

All EAs have expressly discussed their jurisdiction on a *prima facie* basis,[260] in line with a general assumption that a more comprehensive jurisdictional determination is reserved for a potential "ordinary" tribunal. The exact scope of this prima facie determination is not laid down in the SCC Rules, nor is much guidance to be found in the relatively short EA decisions subject to this study.

The shared assumption, however, is that the test for an emergency arbitrator's jurisdiction is different from that of a "regular tribunal."[261] This is presumably motivated not only by legal reasoning according to which the result of the EA's determination is temporary and subject to review by a subsequent tribunal, but also by practical constraints: a five-day process is simply not conducive to a comprehensive review of complex jurisdictional issues. This notwithstanding, an important feature of the SCC Rules must be recognized in this context: the Rules allow for emergency arbitration even before a request for arbitration has been filed. It is therefore conceivable that no arbitration is initiated subsequent to an emergency arbitration decision, or even at all.[262] In these circumstances, under the SCC Rules, an emergency arbitrator's order expires within 30 days of the rendering of the order.[263] For 30 days, thus, a self-standing order (albeit one whose enforceability is doubtful) based on a relatively rudimentary jurisdictional analysis might be valid.

Most EAs were faced with an emergency application without a request for arbitration having been brought. In fact, SCC Case No. 183/2014 is the only case in which a request for arbitration was filed at the SCC prior to the application for emergency arbitration. In all other cases, there was no request for arbitration when the EA was asked to review its jurisdiction. The fact that emergency arbitration can be initiated prior to an investor's request for arbitration raises a fundamental question for the purposes of investment arbitration. Simply put: when an investor relies on a treaty to request an order for interim measures from an EA, but has not initiated an arbitration, is there an arbitration

260 *TSIKInvest v. Moldova*, Emergency Decision, para. 61; *Evrobalt v. Moldova*, Emergency Decision, para. 17; *Kompozit v. Moldova*, Emergency Decision, paras. 47 and 50; *Munshi v. Mongolia*, Emergency Decision, para. 33. The three remaining confidential awards contain similar discussions.

261 As put most clearly by the EA in SCC Case No. 092/2017, who employed a distinction between an emergency arbitrator and "the tribunal proper," stating that "[e]mergency measures do not seek to resolve a dispute or result in the final disposition of a dispute; they seek to preserve the status quo or to provide other temporary relief," see above at 4.4.2.6.

262 Although *TSIKInvest* and *Munshi* appear to be the only cases where a subsequent arbitration was not yet requested at the time this text was written.

263 SCC Rules, Appendix II, Article 9(4)(iii).

agreement, as we understand it in the investment treaty context? All EAs to date have seemingly assumed that the answer is yes. In particular, the EAs in SCC Case No. 002/2015 and SCC 092/2017 both stated that the investor had accepted the state's offer: in the 2017 by requesting emergency arbitration,[264] and in the 2015 in its letter initiating attempts to settle the dispute amicably (two months before requesting emergency arbitration).[265] Similarly, the SCC Rules, while not specifying expressly that an application for emergency arbitrator entails the completion of an arbitration agreement in the treaty-based context, provide in their preamble that

> [...] the parties shall be deemed to have agreed that the following rules, or such amended rules, in force on the date of the commencement of the arbitration, *or the filing of an application for the appointment of an Emergency Arbitrator*, shall be applied [...] (emphasis added)

With this construction, an arbitration agreement is at least implicitly understood to have been completed when an investor applies for emergency arbitration. Further to this point, both the SCC and the ICC have made emergency arbitration an integral part of their respective Rules.[266] For the SCC Rules, this has always been the case. In the ICC context, the choice could be contrasted with the earlier "Referee Rules," which pre-dated emergency arbitration and were contained in a separate set of rules.[267] Therefore, an argument could be made that requesting emergency arbitration is functionally equivalent to requesting arbitration, as both types of dispute resolution are seamlessly regulated by the arbitration rules to which the parties have agreed. As a general matter, the validity of this argument is doubtful, since emergency arbitration is different from the "regular" arbitration otherwise envisioned by the arbitration rules, in several important ways.

According to one commentator, emergency arbitration is not arbitration but rather best characterized as "a *sui generis* contractual mechanism,"[268] of a pre-arbitral nature. Supporting this argument is, *inter alia*, (i) the assumption that the parties would not have intended for two separate bodies with identical jurisdiction to order interim measures,[269] (ii) that the tribunal may freely review the EA's order (which would not be the case if the tribunal and

264 SCC Case No. 092/2017, Emergency Decision, para. 14.
265 SCC Case No. 002/2015, Emergency Decision, para. 18
266 P Shaughnessy, pp. 347–348; B Baigel, p. 16.
267 B Baigel, p. 16.
268 B Baigel, p. 9.
269 Ibid.

the EA were equated),[270] and (iii) the fact that an EA is never appointed by the parties.[271] According to this commentator, without a formal request for arbitration, there is no arbitral jurisdiction.[272] A similar analysis, but with a different outcome, is advocated by another commentator, writing in the context of the introduction of emergency arbitration in the SCC Rules.[273] According to her, it is not clear whether emergency arbitration is "arbitration," and as such within the scope of the Swedish Arbitration Act.[274] Regardless of this, she argues, the procedure is anchored in party autonomy:

> If parties are able to empower arbitrators to make final decisions regarding the entire dispute, and are able to empower arbitrators to make decisions on interim measures, what principle or interest would be served by limiting the parties' ability to empower emergency arbitrators to issue interim relief? The same principles of party autonomy underlie emergency arbitrator proceedings.[275]

In the investment treaty context, there might in fact exist such "principles or interests," having to do with the jurisdiction of the EA. This jurisdiction is formed by way of a consent to arbitration which is different from that in contractual arbitration. Furthermore, unlike regular arbitration, the jurisdictional determination by an EA cannot be reviewed by a court; at least not in the case of the seven treaty-based emergency arbitrations, who have all been seated in a jurisdiction that does not allow challenges of emergency decisions, as discussed above.

There are good reasons to distinguish emergency arbitration from "regular arbitration." Both Rules allow for the filing of an application for emergency arbitration prior to the formal request of arbitration, but also during a pending arbitration. Furthermore, the resulting decision by an EA is not an award; while the SCC Rules consistently style it as a "decision,"[276] the ICC Rules refer to it as an "order."[277] Another commentator, who was involved in the drafting of the ICC emergency arbitration rules states that "the main purpose of this

270 Ibid., p. 12.
271 Ibid. p. 15.
272 Ibid., p. 10.
273 P Shaughnessy.
274 Ibid., pp. 355–357.
275 Ibid., p. 357.
276 Although allowing arbitrators to call it an "award," SCC Rules Article 37(3) and Appendix II, Article 1(2).
277 ICC Rules, Appendix V, Article 6.

denomination is to distinguish the decision of the emergency arbitrator from an award issued by an arbitral tribunal."[278] Further support for this idea is the fact that under the ICC Rules, an emergency arbitrator's order is not subject to the mandatory scrutiny that all awards must go through.[279]

That every treaty-based emergency arbitration has been legally seated in Sweden is an important fact, given that under Swedish law the result of a successful application is not an arbitral award and thus not reviewable by Swedish courts. Presumably, this also means that an EA decision lacks other legal characteristics associated with an award, such as *res judicata* effect, which would further support the notion that emergency arbitration is something different from "regular" arbitration. Another such factor is that, under both Rules, the enforceability of an emergency arbitration decision is doubtful, since such a decision is not "final and binding" and as such presumably not covered by the New York Convention (although, as discussed above, that decision is ultimately left to the court of the enforcing jurisdiction).[280] Under both the ICC Rules and the SCC Rules the parties undertake to comply with any emergency decision,[281] but the consequences of not respecting this obligation are not necessarily the same as not complying with a final award, which can be enforced under the New York Convention.

In summary, under both sets of Rules emergency arbitration seems to be different from "regular" arbitration. This accords well with the reasoning of the EAs faced with treaty-based applications, who have consistently relied on this very distinction to justify that the task of an EA is to make *prima facie* determinations, on both jurisdiction and merits, to be later addressed in full by a tribunal. An overlooked aspect of this distinction, however, is the consequences it may have for the formation of an arbitration agreement in investment treaty arbitration. Under the conventional reading of the ICC Rules, this is a non-issue, since there can seemingly be no emergency arbitration in such cases, on the assumption that disputing parties are not deemed to be "signatories" to the same agreement. In the SCC context, however, it is very much a live issue, as the SCC Rules assume that a standing treaty offer to arbitrate under the SCC Rules also includes emergency arbitration.

278 N Voser, *Overview of the Most Important Changes in the Revised ICC Arbitration Rules*, 29 ASA Bull. 83, 2011, p. 818.

279 Ibid.

280 For a contrary argument, claiming that emergency orders generally are "final and binding" with regards to the issues that they address, see A Yesilirmak, *Provisional Measures in International Commercial Arbitration*, Kluwer, 2005, para. 4 et seq.

281 ICC Rules, Article 29(2); SCC Rules, Appendix II, Article 9(3).

If emergency arbitration is not "arbitration," it has to be something else, and the question arises what, if anything, it is that the treaty states may have consented to. In only one case did the respondent state raise objections to the EA's jurisdiction, and then the EA's approach was that the treaty states must have assumed that the arbitration rules would evolve over time.[282] This type of jurisdictional objection, to the effect that the state consented to arbitration – with the objective jurisdictional requirements and conditions included in the treaty – but not to this other type of dispute resolution, which effectively sidesteps those conditions, seems reasonable for the reasons discussed above.

In addition to the general questions of consent just discussed, a number of other familiar jurisdictional issues have been brought up in emergency arbitrations. To the extent that they have been discussed by the EAs, it has been done in the framework of *prima facie* jurisdiction.

"Investor" Holding an "Investment"?

Every investment treaty relied upon contain conditions *ratione personae* and *ratione materiae*. These requirements were discussed, albeit briefly, in most of the cases. In one short paragraphs, the *TSIKInvest* EA reached "the initial conclusion" that the claimant had demonstrated, prima facie, that it qualified as an investor, and that its shares qualified as an "investment."[283] Similarly, the Evrobalt EA accepted the claimant's contentions, noting that Moldova had not disputed either jurisdictional assertion in its response to the notice of dispute (note: the notice was not part of the emergency proceedings).[284] The Kompozit EA,[285] as well as the EA in Case No. 092/2017 also accepted the claimant's allegation without discussion. In the Munshi v. Mongolia case, the claimant had asserted that he was an investor, which was seemingly accepted by the EA.[286] There was however no discussion in the decision concerning what investment, in the legal sense, that the claimant may have claimed to have in Mongolia.

In sum, the notions of "investor" and "investment," and their functions as objective jurisdictional requirements, have not been discussed in any meaningful way by EAs. To the extent that they have, the claimant's characterizations have been taken at face value as part of a *prima facie* determination.

282 SCC Case No. 183/2014.
283 *TSIKInvest v. Moldova*, Emergency Decision, para. 61.
284 *Evrobalt v. Moldova*, Emergency Decision, para. 19.
285 *Kompozit v. Moldova*, Emergency Decision, paras. 48–50
286 *Munshi v. Mongolia*, Emergency Decision, paras. 28–29; para. 33.

"Cooling-Off" Clauses

A repeated issue in the studied emergency arbitrations has been the relevance of so-called "cooling off"-clauses. Such clauses provide that the disputing parties must engage in efforts to resolve a dispute amicably, often for a specified amount of time, prior to resorting to international arbitration. The exact implications of these clauses are frequently at issue in investment treaty arbitrations, and were also at the centre of several set-aside cases in domestic courts discussed in Chapter 3. In the emergency arbitration context, the issue has arisen because investors have tried to access emergency measures without first having resort to negotiations, when negotiating in the opinion of the investors would undermine the very availability of emergency measures. Therefore, several EAs have had to grapple with a conflict between two opposing interests: on the hand the availability of emergency arbitration, as agreed to by the disputing parties by virtue of a reference to the SCC Rules, and on the other hand a treaty provision possibly requiring a cooling-off period to expire before initiation of arbitration.

Every treaty relied upon by applicants has included some version of a cooling-off clause. In no case was the clause held to bar the applicant from accessing emergency arbitration. However, the different EAs found, without much discussion, that the clauses did not prevent their jurisdiction. To the *TSIKInvest* EA, it would be "procedurally unfair to Claimant and contrary to the purpose of the Emergency Arbitrator procedure to apply the Cooling-Off Period to the appointment of an Emergency Arbitrator."[287] Both the *Evrobalt* and the *Kompozit* EA focused on the futility of expecting the investor to comply with the cooling-off period: the *Evrobalt* decision expressly states that the clause could be disregarded where insisting on compliance with it would be "manifestly futile,"[288] which the EA found was the case based on the facts presented to him by the claimant. The *Kompozit* reasoning is similar, although without mentioning futility expressly, stating instead that the clause was not "applicable"[289] due to the state's failure to engage in settlement discussions in the week following the receipt of the investor's notice of dispute. In *Munshi*, the EA did not discuss the cooling-off period in the ECT, although the investor had possibly not complied with it; the EA does mention that the investor sent the last letter in a negotiation attempt on 29 November 2017,[290] less than two months prior to the application for emergency arbitration. It is unclear when the

287 *TSIKinvest v. Moldova*, Emergency Decision, para. 66.
288 *Evrobalt v. Moldova*, Emergency Decision, para. 22.
289 *Kompozit v. Moldova*, Emergency Decision, para. 55.
290 *Munshi v. Mongoloa*, Emergency Decision, para. 31.

earlier letters were sent, and whether or not six months elapsed between the first such letter and the application for emergency arbitration.[291] In Case No. 2014/183 the respondent state participated and raised a number of objections against the EA's jurisdiction, but a failure to comply with the cooling off-period was not among them.[292]

Typically, the way to resolve the uncertainty about the application of a certain provision in a treaty to a new context would be by way of treaty interpretation. So far, this has generally not been the approach by EAs faced with the question. Instead, a tacit assumption for most EAs has, once again, been that a cooling-off clause is intended for "regular" arbitration, and not for emergency arbitration.

Most-Favoured Nation Clauses

Another potential issue, which unlike the cooling-off clause, has not (yet) been at issue before an EA, is the application of a most-favoured nation (MFN) clause to access emergency arbitration. Although the SCC Rules are available under a significant number of BITs, in addition to the much relied-upon ECT, the vast majority of investment treaties in force do not provide for arbitration under the SCC Rules. It is therefore conceivable that an investor might to rely upon the MFN clause in a treaty that does not include SCC arbitration to obtain access to emergency arbitration in a treaty that does, on the assumption that access to emergency arbitration would be more "favourable" to an investor.

The only time an MFN argument was brought by an investor was not in this context, however. In *TSIKInvest*, the applicant did not attempt to access emergency arbitration that would otherwise not have been available under the primary treaty; instead the investor wanted to utilize the MFN clause to circumvent the cooling-off period provided for in the primary treaty, presumably by instead accessing another (unspecified) Moldovan treaty which does not contain a cooling-off clause.[293] There was no need for the EA to address this argument, as he held that the cooling-off clause did not constitute a bar to the investor's access to emergency arbitration and that the claim could proceed.

4.4.4.3 Practical Issues

There are also a number of practical issues raised by the seven emergency arbitrations. These issues are barely discussed in the EA decisions – which, once

---

291 Ibid.

292 SCC Case No. 2014/183, para. 22.

293 *TSIKInvest v. Moldova*, Emergency Decision, para. 59.

again, are by nature restricted in scope, especially as it concerns the procedural background of the case – nor are they subject to much academic discussion. Nevertheless, they raise questions as to the application of emergency arbitration in the treaty context.

One such issue is the manner in which the notice is served on the respondent state. It is often said that the SCC Rules do not allow for emergency arbitration to be conducted *ex parte,* i.e. without the respondent having been properly served.[294] Strictly speaking, this proposition is not borne out by the Rules, which provide that "[a]s soon as an application for the appointment of an Emergency Arbitrator has been received, the Secretariat shall send the application to the other party."[295] The only requirement expressly in the Rules is that the application for emergency arbitration has been *sent,* but not necessarily that it has been *read* by the respondent. Given this open-ended language in the Rules, other norms might provide some guidance. Generally speaking, notification via email is widely accepted in international arbitration; in the Swedish context commentators seem to agree that an email meets the formal requirement that notifications be sent in a written form.[296] The more relevant question, however, is not the form of the notification, but rather whether and when a party is deemed to have been notified. Is it enough that an email has reached the party, or must the party also have been given a proper opportunity to read – and understand the implications of – the email in question?[297] Article 5 of the SCC Rules addresses this question more generally:

> (1) Any notice or other communication from the Secretariat or the Board shall be delivered to the last known address of the addressee.
> (2) Any notice or other communication shall be delivered by courier or registered mail, e-mail or any other means that records the sending of the communication.
> (3) A notice or communication sent in accordance with paragraph (2) shall be deemed to have been received by the addressee on the date it would normally have been received given the means of communication used [...]

294 See for example, P Shaughnessy, p. 339; A Håvedal-Ipp, Emergency Arbitration Practice Note, p. 3.

295 SCC Rules, Appendix II, Article 3.

296 See J Englund, "E-post vid underrättelser enligt lagen om skiljeförfarande," Juridisk Tidskrift 133, 2009, p. 134.

297 Ibid.

Thus, under the SCC Rules generally, there is no express requirement that the party has in fact read the email.[298] In every emergency arbitration studied in this text, emails have been used to serve the application to the respondent state. Here, it is once again important that every treaty-based emergency arbitration has been legally seated in Sweden, which means that Swedish arbitration law as the *lex loci arbitri* supplements the SCC Rules. In a judgment by the Swedish Supreme Court – which was rendered in the context of enforcement of a foreign arbitral award,[299] but whose holding can arguably be extended beyond the enforcement scenario[300] – the court found that, as a general matter, there is a requirement that the notice "has reached the opposing party."[301] Given this decision by the court, a commentator involved in the drafting of the SCC emergency rules has stated that "[a] cautious emergency arbitrator sitting in Sweden may be reluctant to issue decisions or awards unless there is some proof that the opposing party is aware of the EA proceedings,"[302] adding that "an emergency arbitrator sitting in Sweden may want to be mindful of the Supreme Court's approach to the notice issue."[303]

Formally, the task of notifying the respondent falls to the SCC Secretariat. This being said, the five-day time frame is not initiated when the notification reaches the respondent, but rather when the application is referred to the EA.[304] Furthermore, the ultimate legal determination as to whether the respondent has been properly served is for the emergency arbitrator to make.[305] Naturally, once the case file has been transmitted to EA, the EA also has to communicate with the parties, or at least try to do so, meaning that the notification of the respondent is of some practical interest to the EA.

The notification issue was discussed in some of the decisions. Most notably, the EAs in *Kompozit* and SCC Case No. 092/2017 both addressed the notification of the respective respondent states. In *Kompozit*, the EA stated that he had

---

298 Outside of the emergency arbitration sphere, this issue was discussed in passing in the challenge of the *Ascom Stati v. Kazakhstan* award, in which the respondent state questioned the method of notification used by the SCC, discussed below at 4.5.3.

299 The (lack of) notification of the respondent may arise as an issue in enforcement proceedings, as the New York Convention Article V(1)(b) requires that the party against whom an award is being enforced was given "proper notice of the appointment of the arbitrator or of the arbitration proceedings."

300 P Shaughnessy, p. 341.

301 *Lenmorniiprokt OAO v. Arne Larsson & Partner Leasing AB*, Swedish Supreme Court, Case Ö 13-09, 16 April 2010, para. 8.

302 P. Shaughnessy, p. 341.

303 Ibid.

304 Cf. P Shaughnessy, p. 340.

305 A Håvedal-Ipp, Emergency Arbitration Practice Note, p. 4.

sent communications to the respondent using the email addresses proposed by the claimant.[306] The respondent state did not reply or participate in the proceedings, nor did it make any other contact with the EA.[307] The EA pointed out, however, that none of the emails sent to the respondent were "rejected" by the recipient.[308]

Similarly, in Case No. 092/2017, the EA discussed the use of emails to communicate with the (non-responsive) state:

> The Emergency Arbitrator considers it important to underline that no one of the email addresses used to liaise with the Respondent (or the Applicant for that matter) in respect of any email message has generated an irregularity report. The Application, the Procedural Order No 1 and other materials in the emergency proceedings must therefore be considered to have been properly served with the Respondent, in particular in view of the fact that the email addresses have been obtained from the Respondent's Facebook page and website.[309]

This is the most extensive discussion on the topic; in the remaining cases in which the state did not participate,[310] the fact was not mentioned: the decision in *Munshi* contains no details on the attempts to serve or communicate with the state, while the states in *TSIKInvest*, *Evrobalt* and SCC Case No. 83/2014 were *de facto* served with the notice. Nevertheless, although not recounted in most of the EA decisions,[311] it is SCC policy to always send requests for arbitration as well as emergency applications by registered mail or courier. In addition to what is stated in the individual emergency decisions, in all of the seven cases did the Secretariat obtain proof of delivery of a physical copy of the application.[312]

306 *Kompozit v. Moldova*, Emergency Decision, para. 11. The SCC Secretariat encourages claimants to include respondent's known contact information in their applications, A Håvedal-Ipp, Emergency Arbitration Practice Note, p. 4.

307 *Kompozit v. Moldova*, Emergency Decision, para. 17. Confusingly, the EA twice – in paras 12 and 14 – refers to the respondent having submitted comments to the EA, but given the context these are both likely typographical errors and should be read as "claimant" rather than "respondent."

308 Ibid., para. 11.

309 SCC Case No. 092/2017, para. 12.

310 SCC Case No. 183/2014 seems to be the only case in which the state participated.

311 One exception is *TSIKInvest v. Moldova*, Emergency Decision, para. 8, noting the receipt of service of process by way of courier.

312 Based on information obtained from the SCC Secretariat.

As a matter of Swedish arbitration law, it is doubtful if the absence of a "bounced" email is sufficient to determine that the notice has been served on a party, as held by the EAs in *Kompozit* and SCC Case No. 092/2017. In any event, since it is generally not possible to challenge an EA decision under the Swedish Arbitration Act, the matter cannot be tried by a court at the place of arbitration.[313]

Another practical issue – which for self-evident reasons has not been discussed in any of the decisions – is the challenging task of finding and appointing an emergency arbitrator within 24 hours. This task is similarly burdensome for commercial cases, but arguably the pool of potential arbitrators is even smaller for treaty-based arbitrations. Not only must the SCC Secretariat find an arbitrator who fits the profile, taking into account the various factors considered by the Secretariat in such a scenario,[314] but the arbitrator in question must also be independent and impartial. Conducting a full conflict check within a few hours is probably challenging for most potential arbitrators, especially those who are employed by large international law firms. It might be interesting to note, therefore, that most appointed EAs have been either independent arbitrators,[315] or working for a "boutique" law firm.[316]

4.4.4.4 The Nature of the Measures Requested: Treaty-Based Emergency Arbitration in Context

Unlike the typical scenario in investment treaty arbitration, none of the emergency cases has involved a claim for monetary compensation. Instead, all claimants have asked for some kind of specific performance, generally a decision ordering the respondent state to refrain from doing something. In fact, all but one[317] application have concerned the preservation of *status quo,* pending full resolution of a dispute. These measures might be viewed as extra sensitive to state sovereignty concerns, as they principally interfere with public decision-making to a larger extent than does an order for monetary compensation.

---

313 As noted above, it might be tried by an enforcing court under the New York Convention.

314 See generally *SCC Policy – Appointment of Arbitrators*, adopted by the SCC Board on 12 June 2006, Amended by the SCC Board on 8 September 2017, https://sccinstitute.com/media/220131/scc-policy-appointment-of-arbitrators-2017.pdf, accessed on 12 December 2018 and on file with author.

315 *Kompozit v. Moldova,* Emergency Decision; SCC Case No. 002/2015.

316 *Evrobalt v. Moldova,* Emergency Decision; SCC Case 183/2014; Case 092/2017; *Munshi v. Mongolia,* Emergency Decision. In *TSIKInvest*, the EA was partner with a Swedish law firm at the time.

317 *Munshi v. Mongolia*, Emergency Decision.

Questions concerning the appropriateness of non-monetary remedies in investment treaty arbitration are not new.[318] What is different in the present context, however, is the time in which an EA under the SCC Rules has to consider this issue, together with other issues such as those pertaining to jurisdiction. Furthermore, in six out of seven cases there was no respondent present to mount a legal defence. Similar to the case with the general lack of jurisdictional objections, one can but wonder what the decisions would have looked like if the respective EA would have been faced with reasoned objections against the requested measures.

As to the standard for granting interim measures, the SCC Rules do not provide much guidance for the EAs. Therefore, an EA is generally in the same position as a full tribunal in an "ordinary" procedure,[319] leaving the EA considerable discretion.[320] The review of the SCC decisions also shows a wide divergence in approach to the standard to be applied, with several EAs reassuringly stating the broad scope of the EA discretion. Furthermore, and similar to the jurisdictional aspects discussed above, several EAs also stress the *prima facie* nature of the measures ordered, almost so as to justify the limited discussion.

It has been argued elsewhere that the interim protection of party rights is recognized as a general principle of law, recognized across a wide spectrum of different types of international adjudication.[321] This reasoning is partly based on an assumption that emergency arbitration embodies considerations of non-aggravation, or a general duty to abstain,[322] which should be extended also to the pre-tribunal stage. Be that as it may, it is worth recalling that there is nothing in the SCC Rules[323] that limits the nature of the requests: investors may very well ask for other measures, such as monetary damages arising out of

318 In *Liamco v. Libya* – a contractual case often cited as a forerunner to modern-day investment arbitration – the tribunal famously refused to grant specific performance, see *Libyan American Oil Co. v. Libya,* 17 I.L.M. 3 (1978), 4 Y.B. COM. ARB. 177 (1979). See also *BP Exploration Co Ltd v Government of the Libyan Arab Republic*, Award, 10 October 1973 (1979) 53 ILR 297. For an overview of modern-day investment arbitration practice in this respect, see *Nova Group Investments, B.V. v. Romania*, ICSID Case No. ARB/16/19, Procedural Order No. 7, 29 March 2017.

319 Cf. SCC Arbitration Rules, Appendix II, Article 1(2).

320 P Shaughnessy, p. 343.

321 K Chung, "Emergency Arbitrator Procedure in Investment Treaty Disputes: To Be or Not To Be," forthcoming, Journal of World Investment & Trade 20 (2019) 96–43, at Section 3.2 with further references.

322 Ibid.

323 Nor in the ICC Rules, for that matter.

an alleged treaty breach.[324] Although the underlying reason for interim measures generally is to preserve the integrity of the arbitral process and prevent parties from aggravating the dispute,[325] interim measures are by no means synonymous with a preservation of *status quo.* Hence, references to the non-intervening nature of (most) interim measures are of limited principal relevance. For example, it is notable that in the only case in which the applicant did *not* ask for an order preserving status quo,[326] but instead requested the state to perform certain actions, the EA mostly rejected the request, primarily on the ground that it would infringe too much on the state's sovereignty.[327]

Regardless of whether the order is aimed at preserving *status quo,* i.e. ordering the state to refrain from doing something, or ordering the state to actively do something, an argument could be made that emergency arbitration in the investment treaty context is challenging traditional notions of sovereignty. Emergency arbitration generally is by its very nature demanding on the respondent, for whom the application may come as a surprise, but who in any case has to present potential objections within a very limited time-frame. In commercial arbitration, both parties can generally expect to be put in this position, whereas in treaty-based cases the state is the only potential respondent. The specific character of an emergency proceeding highlights the matters discussed above concerning the scope of the state's consent, as the burden on the respondent can generally be justified with a reference to party autonomy: by agreeing to arbitrate disputes under a given set of arbitral rules, both parties have consented to those rules in their entirety. This doctrinal view of arbitration as created by the contracting parties is tested, however, when the consent is asymmetrical and the respondent has consented in a unilateral instrument, which typically predates innovations in arbitral rules, such as emergency arbitration. Towards the end of this Chapter,[328] a more general argument is made to the effect that references to arbitration as dispute resolution created by the parties is often illusory when it comes to non-ICSID institutional arbitration, because both parties are not able to effectively exercise their autonomy. Emergency arbitration is a good example of this.

324 The EA is authorized to "grant any interim measures it deems appropriate," SCC Rules Article 37(1).

325 L Malintoppi, "Provisional Measures in Recent ICSID Proceedings: What Parties Request and What Tribunals Order," in C Binder, U Kriebaum, A Reinisch, and S Wittich (eds.), *International Investment Law for the 21st Century: Essays in Honour of Christoph Schreuer*, Oxford University Press, 2009, pp. 157–158.

326 *Munshi v. Mongolia*, Emergency Decision.

327 Ibid., paras. 56–58.

328 At 6.5.1.

For a relevant comparison, consider the ICSID Convention. In order for a state to be the respondent in a treaty-based ICSID arbitration, it must consent twice: both by consenting to ICSID arbitration in the investment treaty, but also by ratifying the ICSID Convention itself. This "double-consent" requirement[329] means that any specific ICSID arbitration's procedural framework is always made up of the 1965 ICSID Convention, which can only be modified if every signatory state so agrees. By contrast, the commercial arbitration rules change regularly, evolving beyond what they looked like at the time when the investment treaty was concluded. Generally speaking, this is nothing unusual in international law: states often agree to treaties on the understanding that the exact meaning of individual provisions may evolve over time. What is unusual here is of course the potential of palpable consequences, be they in the form of an order that the state suspend a decision or in the form of an order to financially compensate an investor, both of which challenge notions of state sovereignty to an extent that is rare in other spheres of international law.

Furthermore, leaving the doctrinal aspects aside for a while, there is also the actual practice to consider: in the experience so far, one in seven respondent states *de facto* participated; in the remaining six cases the respondent state did not even respond during the proceeding in question. To a certain extent, this fact might be explained by the nature of states: even if somebody authorized to act for the state signs a proof of delivery of the service of notice, that person is not necessarily the proper person to initiate the state's procedural defence. The proper inter-departmental decision-making involved in representing a sovereign in international adjudication is not easily performed within the span of a few days.

In sum, the interim measures requested in treaty-based emergency arbitration raise different, and more complicated, questions than does "contractual" emergency arbitration. As discussed above, the same applies also to the jurisdiction of EAs. Nevertheless, every EA faced with a treaty-based application for emergency measures has had a five-day span to grapple with these issues, and the resulting decisions have for natural reasons been very limited.

So far, states have raised limited policy objections against the use of emergency arbitration in the investment treaty context. Emergency arbitration is mentioned briefly in the OECD Appointing Authority Paper, and as such a topic of conversation within the OECD Roundtable for which the Report was drafted.[330] Apart from this, emergency arbitration is probably too arcane a

---

329 See T St John, pp. 7–8 with further references for the background to this formulation of ICSID jurisdiction.

330 OECD Appointing Authority Paper, pp. 50–52.

procedural detail to capture the attention of reform efforts currently sweeping over investment treaty arbitration.

4.5 Discussion: The Scope of Institutional Decision-Making

So far, this chapter has described various aspects of investment treaty arbitration at the ICC and the SCC. The following sub-sections put the previous presentation in context by discussing various aspects of the institutional experience.

4.5.1 *The Limits of Party Autonomy*

In the world of commercial arbitration, the procedure emanates from the parties' agreement, the premier source from which not only arbitrators but also institutions derive their authority. Given how small a portion of their overall case-loads is treaty-based, it would be reasonable to expect that notions of party autonomy, drawn from contract-based arbitration, would be influential in ICC and SCC practice generally, including treaty-based cases. The institutions do not only administer contractual cases, however; together the institutions have administered over 100 treaty-based cases under the ICC Rules or the SCC Rules; no mean feat, even when compared to the equivalent ICSID figures. This dual case-load raises questions concerning the tension between private/commercial and public/treaty-based disputes, which is discussed in this sub-section.

In private law generally, courts typically develop the law by considering both the outcome of the specific case and the "systemic" effects, whereas in public law the analysis generally focuses primarily or exclusively on the latter.[331] As already mentioned, investment arbitration is characterized by a certain "hybridity," which does not fit nicely in categories of private and public. Nevertheless, the ICC and the SCC to a large degree epitomize a "commercial" way of solving disputes.

The institutions' focus is on the parties. As rules and practice have developed over time, it has not necessarily been because a need to change the "systemic" effects, such as strives to achieve more consistent substantive outcomes. It has instead been because the preferences of the parties/users have evolved. As disputes involving states and based on treaties have entered the picture, the commercial/private paradigm has been challenged, but only to a limited extent: the rules have been altered in minor ways (such as introduction

331 A Mills, pp. 10–11.

of certain limited transparency measures, or the exclusion of emergency arbitration at the ICC), but not in ways that change the nature of the procedure.

The notion of "party autonomy" is developed in a contractual sphere,[332] and embodied in commercial arbitration instruments such as the New York Convention and the UNCITRAL Model Law.[333] It is commonly held as one of the significant hallmarks of commercial arbitration.[334] In the context of investment treaty arbitration, this fact raises a fundamental question: who are the "parties," whose autonomy to shape the procedure is to guide the arbitration? Both the ICC Rules and the SCC Rules are generally drafted on the assumption that the identities of the contracting parties and the disputing parties are the same.[335] However, in investment treaty arbitration that is not the case: in no case studied here was there a direct pre-dispute relationship between the disputing parties. This fact puts some strain on the principle of party autonomy, in the sense that the exercise of the "autonomy" is limited.

One example which illustrates the limitations in the concept of party autonomy is treaty-based emergency arbitration. In the above discussion of the SCC emergency cases, it was emphasized that emergency arbitration is an instrument developed primarily for commercial arbitration, which is applicable also in treaty cases by virtue of the "opt-out" structure chosen by the SCC. The availability of emergency arbitration generally can be justified by party autonomy. As put by Shaughnessy in her article discussing the introduction of emergency arbitration in the SCC Rules:

> If parties are able to empower arbitrators to make final decisions regarding the entire dispute, and are able to empower arbitrators to make decisions on interim measures, what principle or interest would be served by limiting the parties' ability to empower emergency arbitrators to issue interim relief? The same principles of party autonomy underlie emergency arbitrator proceedings.[336]

This reference to party autonomy as an outer justification for EA jurisdiction to order interim measures, while perfectly reasonable in the contractual context,

332 Stone Sweet and Grisel, Chapter 3.

333 J Karton, *The Culture of International Arbitration and the Evolution of Contract Law*, Oxford University Press, 2013 p. 79.

334 This fact is also a frequent premise for the discussions in UNCITRAL Working Group III.

335 There are exceptions to this. Most relevant in the present circumstances is the emergency arbitration provisions in the ICC Rules discussed above, but there are other examples involving multi-party proceedings under both Rules.

336 P Shaughnessy, p. 357.

is not necessarily satisfactory in the treaty context. The respondent did not expressly agree to the EA rules, and practice has shown that respondent states generally had very limited opportunity to participate in the resulting proceedings. Furthermore, the reviewed treaty cases demonstrate that the jurisdiction of an emergency arbitrator is far from clear-cut. A very fast procedure tailored for efficient interim relief is not well-suited for complex jurisdictional debate. In addition, the reviewability of an EA's decision is doubtful, as already discussed. Taken together, the jurisdiction of an EA to award interim relief in the treaty context raises different questions than in the contractual context for which the mechanism was primarily developed. This is further complicated by the fact that the fast and outcome-driven process does not lend itself to analysis of these questions.

In light of these concerns, mere references to "states having agreed to it" are not helpful. In fact, what most states agreed to was to arbitrate under the SCC Rules and/or to have arbitrations administered by the SCC. Of course, an argument could be made that this consent should be construed as evolving, i.e. as encompassing the SCC Rules as they develop over time.[337] However, this evolving consent arguably has an outer limit, and it is submitted that the creation of new types of dispute resolution is very close to that outer limit. In SCC Case No. 183/2014, the respondent state argued that emergency arbitration is a "qualitative change"[338] of the SCC Rules. The EA did not grapple with this objection, however, as it found that the SCC Rules in force at the time of the treaty's conclusion supported an "evolving" interpretation. In light of the above discussion about the nature of emergency arbitration, it is tempting to sympathize with the respondent state's objection. Several factors suggest that emergency arbitration is something different from "standard" arbitration, and as such not necessarily within the scope of the state's consent to arbitration.

By contrast, it would seem that at least part of the explanation for the ICC choice to exclude treaty-based cases from the emergency arbitration provisions has to do with the limited ability for states to actively agree to them in treaties already in force. The result of the "opt-in" model chosen by the ICC is that states, as disputing parties, would have to agree to the application of emergency arbitration separately for it to be applicable.

Another example of the limited exercise of autonomy is that in no treaty-based case at either institution was the place of arbitration specified by the treaty states. In commercial arbitration, a legal seat for the proceedings is among the standard features of an arbitration clause negotiated in a contract.

---

337 As discussed most extensively by the EA in SCC Case No. 183/2014, Emergency Decision.
338 See above at 4.4.2.4.

In treaty arbitration this is not the case. By agreeing to ICC or SCC arbitration, states instead consent to the institutions' designations, absent any party agreement, thereby indirectly vesting the institutions with authority to determine the legal framework governing the arbitration.

Institutional activities such as these examples are normally justified by party autonomy: even if the disputing parties did not *specifically* provide for emergency arbitration, or for a place of arbitration, they have indirectly allowed for it, by agreeing to arbitration under rules administered by institutions. If a state agrees, in an investment treaty, to ICC or SCC arbitration, this choice entails involving the ICC and the SCC in their dispute. This fact is generally an uncontroversial basic tenant of institutional arbitration. The point here, however, is that treaties are different from contracts. Taking the party autonomy justification for institutional authority to its logical conclusion, a commercial arbitration institution could introduce – formally, in the shape of an updated rule provision, or informally in the shape of developed institutional practice – more or less any new norm, and still be within the mandate given to it by states who consented to their arbitration rules. If the innovation was strange enough – extreme versions of emergency arbitration, or an unexpected mandatory place of arbitration, to go with the examples given above – commercial parties would in all likelihood opt for other types of arbitration agreements: they would, in essence, exercise their party autonomy. The situation is not the same for states and investment treaties, given that modifications and/or revocations of treaties are not done as easily. Most investment treaties are in force for a specified period of time, and also typically contain so-called sunset clauses which provide that the treaty is still in force for a number of years after it has been terminated.[339] The same can be said for ICSID, which is otherwise often the alternative to commercial institutions; there are a number of political and practical obstacles to renegotiating or terminating both the ICSID Convention and individual investment treaties.[340] Moreover, in order to take advantage of the avenues available under international law to react to institutional developments, states would have to be aware of both their existing investment treaties and the arbitral implications associated with those treaties, which has rarely been the case, at least historically.[341]

---

339 See generally T Voon and A D Mitchell, "Denunciation, Termination and Survival: The Interplay of Treaty Law and International Investment Law," ICSID Review - Foreign Investment Law Journal, Volume 31, Issue 2, 1 May 2016, pp. 413–433.

340 As discussed by T St John, p. 238.

341 See generally L Poulsen, *Bounded Rationality*. Recently, some state attention has been shifting towards institutional administration of treaty-based cases, as manifested by the

The commercial arbitration institutions can therefore, in theory, act relatively unconstrained by slow-moving treaty states. By agreeing to ICC or SCC arbitration in an investment treaty, states allow the institutions to develop their own practices. The scenario where an arbitral institution acts in the hypothetical manner described here and introduces some radical feature is of course unthinkable – the consequences on the arbitral "market place" would probably be felt promptly – but it illustrates a crucial point: one of the two disputing parties in a treaty arbitration is severely restricted in the exercise of its "autonomy." Actual party participation, as opposed to a theoretical possibility to participate, is often limited, both in the drafting of arbitration agreements and in the arbitral proceedings, and this empowers the arbitral institutions to act. In fact, both the ICC Rules and the SCC Rules are drafted in a way that leaves considerable margin to the disputing parties to shape the procedure, but if they do not, there are procedural defaults in place to ensure that the arbitration still proceeds.

4.5.2 *Procedural Defaults*

Both the ICC Rules and the SCC Rules are drafted with the expectation that the parties, and the tribunal, customize the proceeding in accordance with their own preferences.[342] However, as argued by Stone Sweet and Grisel, institutions overwhelmingly have moved from a "contractual model" to a "judicial model," reducing the space which is for parties to freely decide, and instead engaging in institutional legislating.[343] This general tendency is often discussed in the context of "judicialization," a theory according to which dispute resolvers increasingly act as agents of a larger community, and not only in the interest of the disputing parties,[344] with increasing procedural complexity as the result.[345]

The treaty-based experience studied in this text adds a nuance to the judicialization discussion, because the "legislative" tendencies in question are primarily based on notions of commercial arbitration. When the institutions develop their practice, they do so in close discussion with the users of their services. This has the benefit of allowing the institutions to develop their rules and work so that they reflect the users' expectations, which is part of the institutions' legitimacy. The desire to tailor best practice to user expectations touches upon a fundamental question, which becomes even more relevant in

---

OECD work on the issue, see OECD Appointing Authority Working Paper, and the discussions in UNCITRAL Working Group III.

342 A Stone Sweet and F Grisel, p. 83.

343 A Stone Sweet and F Grisel, p. 83 et seq.

344 A Stone Sweet and F Grisel, p. 7.

345 R Gerbay, pp. 51–52 with further references.

the treaty-based context: there is a certain circularity in the references to parties' expectations and the frequent references to the autonomy of the parties to shape their disputes as they see fit. The commercial arbitration rules do not only reflect expectations of its users, they also simultaneously shape them.

Arbitration agreements generally are sparse on procedural detail. For example, both recommended "model clauses," which the institutions market as the best default arbitration clause, are short on procedural specifics. Yet, in a commercial arbitration sphere characterized by party autonomy, contracting parties often tailor their disputes in various ways. Not so in investment treaty arbitration, where clauses have historically been light on detail.[346]

This fact highlights the relevance of the non-mandatory defaults which are common features of the ICC Rules and the SCC Rules. What happens if the (state or disputing) parties do nothing; what is the default position under the rules? Specifically for jurisdictional issues, several such defaults have regularly been activated in investment treaty cases. There are examples of both (i) default rules which allow for the institution to make certain decisions, but also (ii) other default rules which operate so as to ensure the administration of the procedure without active decisions having to be made.

In the first category, for example, the decision to designate the place of arbitration is made by the ICC Court and the SCC Board respectively, if neither the treaty parties nor the disputing parties agree to one. It has been argued above that there seems to exist a *de facto* default place of arbitration at both institutions when exercising this function.[347]

In the second category, i.e. defaults that do not require any active decision-making by the institution, several mechanisms are in place to shape the nature of the proceedings. One example is the question of which rules apply.[348] Both the temporal version of the arbitration rules, as well as the exact set of rules – such as expedited, emergency or "standard" arbitration rules – is regulated within the rules themselves. This level of specificity is not handled by the state parties to the treaty, but is rather solved through institutional defaults. The same applies to the size of the tribunal, i.e. whether the arbitration should be heard by one or three arbitrators, and to the question of *prima facie* jurisdiction of the institution, where no decision is made at either institution unless the respondent objects.

346 This is true primarily for the older generation of treaties which have formed the basis for the arbitrations studied in this text. In recent years, more elaborate clauses have been suggested, largely in response to earlier practice, as discussed in the final chapter of this text.

347 See above at 4.3.2.

348 See above at 4.2.1.

The most significant example of default regulation discussed in this chapter is emergency arbitration, which applies by default in the SCC Rules, but has been excluded in the ICC Rules. Once an emergency arbitrator has been appointed by the SCC – i.e. once the default has "kicked in" – an emergency arbitration proceeds quickly, according to the SCC Rules. Despite the fact that all treaties relied upon to access emergency arbitration predated the introduction of emergency arbitration, and despite the fact that the state participated in only one case, emergency decisions were rendered within days of the application.

The use of defaults in commercial arbitration rules bears similarities to what behavioural economists call "choice architecture."[349] In behavioural economics, choice architecture is used to explain how setting up default options steer individuals into making, or not making, certain decision.[350] In order to illustrate the mechanisms of choice architecture, simple examples are often used. For example, Ksenia Polonskaya uses a "coffee shop analogy," in which the owner of the coffee shop arranges the shop's food and beverages:

> There are several ways the owner of the coffee shop can approach such an arrangement. The owner may decide to display the goods with high-added sugar upfront to make it easier for the customers to access. Alternatively, the owner can choose to locate the low sugar goods at the front stand where they are easily accessible. The owner can also place all goods with the high level of added sugar at the second floor of the cafeteria to force customers to climb the stairs to get a chocolate chip cookie. Finally, the owner may make an absolutely random choice in displaying goods without taking into account the preferences or interests of the customers. In any scenario, whatever choice the owner makes, s/he in fact creates the architecture of choice.[351]

A similar dynamic arguably applies also in the case of commercial arbitration institutions, which provide services to their users. The manner in which the

---

349 The concept of "architecture of choice" in the context of institutional investment arbitration is borrowed from K Polonskaya, "Arbitral Institutions' Response to Perceived Legitimacy Deficits - Promoting Diversity, Transparency and Expedition in Investor-State Arbitration" in F Baetens (ed.), Legitimacy of Unseen Actors.

350 Ibid. See also R Thaler and C Sunstein, *Nudge: Improving Decisions About Health, Wealth, and Happiness*, Yale University Press, 2009.

351 K Polonskaya in F Baetens (ed.), Legitimacy of Unseen Actors, pp. 386–387.

rules are drafted create options which limit, shape and design the choices of the user. In this respect, Polonskaya writes that arbitration institutions:

> may play the role of 'choice architects' by establishing the defaults and changing arbitration rules in a way that "steer" other participants into making certain choices [...][352]

Defaults are often activated in investment arbitration, due to the nature of the arbitration agreement. The less detailed the arbitration agreement (i.e. the less "informed" the user's choices), the more important default rules become. This is an important aspect of understanding how arbitral institutions shape jurisdiction of tribunals. Commercial arbitration is characterized by a certain choice architecture, which ensures that arbitrations can proceed even in the absence of decisions by the parties, and even in the absence of participation by one party.

As already mentioned, institutional default rules arguably shape not only the individual case but, on aggregate, the expectations that states and parties come to have of the nature of investment treaty arbitration. For example, in discussing the 2010 introduction of emergency arbitration in the SCC Rules, Patricia Shaughnessy argues that the "opt-out" nature of that mechanism was the result of feedback from users, which generally favoured this default solution:

> In making emergency relief part of parties' agreement to arbitrate by "default," the rules are promoting a new procedure that is expected to serve the needs of the parties. Thus, the SCC EA Rules are proactive and may encourage future behaviour of parties. It will take time to determine whether the EA Rules are positively received and effectively used by SCC users. Based upon the comments received by the SCC when the proposed rules were circulated for review, the new procedure will be welcomed by users and an "opt-out" approach was generally favoured. Theoretically, parties who do not want their agreement to arbitrate to include the EA procedures can opt out when drafting the arbitration agreement. However, based on the very assumption that underlies the "opt-out" provision, namely that parties are unlikely to consider EA procedures at all when entering into arbitration agreements, parties are not likely to make an active choice to opt out.[353]

352 Ibid.

353 P Shaughnessy, p. 351.

This is a good illustration of the fact that default rules tend to "stick,"[354] as parties get used to them. Thereby the needle is moved for what expectations parties have on the arbitral procedure.[355]

4.5.3 *On Institutional Decision-Making and Due Process*

Both the ICC Rules and the SCC Rules make expressly clear that the respective institution does not decide disputes.[356] This fact has been repeatedly stressed by authors,[357] as well as domestic courts.[358] Instead, the conventional understanding is that institutions administer disputes that are then decided by others. This notwithstanding, both Rules repeatedly use the phrase "decide" in reference to decisions by the institutions.[359] The SCC Rules also expressly enumerate the decisions to be taken by the Board.[360] As demonstrated by the preceding description of institutional experience of treaty-based cases, it is beyond doubt that the institutions do decide *some* things, if not necessarily "disputes." The nature of the institutional activities matters, as it might affect the possibilities for parties to react to the decisions made.

The present inquiry has been focused on jurisdictional aspects. As discussed in Chapter 3, tribunals' jurisdictional decisions have often been subject to scrutiny by domestic courts. Decisions by institutions – jurisdictional or

---

354 K Polonskaya in F Baetens (ed.), Legitimacy of Unseen Actors, p. 388. See also O Ben-Shahar and J Pottow, "On the Stickiness of Default Rules" (2006) 33 Florida State University Law Review 651, 652.

355 See also T St John, at p. 247, arguing that commercial arbitration norms have acted as "stabilizers" in the investment arbitration context.

356 ICC Rules Article 1(2); SCC Rules, Appendix I, Article 2.

357 K P Berger, *Private Dispute Resolution in International Business: Negotiation, Meditation, Arbitration*, Kluwer, 2015, p. 363, stating that no arbitral institution "is allowed to or does in fact decide the dispute between the parties." See also R Gerbay, pp. 122, 164–165 with further references.

358 For example, this was emphasized by the Paris Court of Appeal in two different cases. In the later of the two, *Société Cubic Defense Systems Inc. v. Chambre de Commerce Internationale*, Cour de Cassation, 1ere Chambre Civile, 20 February 2001 the Cour de Cassation subsequently embraced the lower court's finding that "the ICC arbitration rules maintained a distinction between the function of organizing the arbitration, notably through the intermediary of the Court of International Arbitration, and the adjudicative function, which has been left solely to the arbitrators, the "Court" having no adjudicative power," as cited by Y Derains and E A. Schwartz, *A Guide to the ICC Rules of Arbitration*, Kluwer, 2005, pp. 18–19. The same authors also cite the older case, *Société Techni-Import Professionnel v. Société Electro Scientific Industries*, Paris Court of Appeal, 17 May 1983.

359 R Gerbay, p. 162, counts fifteen such examples in the ICC Rules. The present author similarly counts 15 such references to SCC Board decisions in the SCC Rules.

360 SCC Rules, Article 9.

otherwise – are, on the other hand, not subject to the same due process expectations. In fact, institutional decisions are rarely given reasons, and there are no direct avenues for judicial review. The limited possibilities for parties to challenge institutional decisions are likely motivated by the traditional assumption that institutions do not exercise decision-making functions. For example, there are a number of court cases in France, related to commercial arbitrations, in which various institutional decisions have been challenged directly. These judgements share the characteristic that French courts employed a different level of scrutiny to institutional decisions compared to arbitral tribunal decisions, on the assumption that the institutions exercise administrative, rather than judicial, functions.[361]

It has been argued here, however, that in certain scenarios institutions *do* act in ways that influence the scope of tribunal jurisdiction. This view has been advanced, in a more general sense, by Remy Gerbay. For Gerbay, the appropriate focus is on the materiality of the decision, rather than the identity of the decision-maker. He argues for a more flexible understanding of institutional activities, and characterizes institutions as "ancillary participants in the adjudicative process."[362] Gerbay defines "decision-making" as involving two elements: (i) determining among several potential outcomes with (ii) binding effect.[363] This relatively wide definition of decision-making is at odds with the ones advanced by others who argue that institutions do not make decisions because they do not typically adjudicate cases where differing opinions have been advanced by the parties. In the words of Fauchald: "when [the institution] designates an arbitrator, chooses a procedural venue, or fixes or extends deadlines, an institution is not confronted with any disagreement, it is not called upon to pass a judgement on conflicting arguments."[364]

However, as the present study has shown, the ICC and the SCC often decide issues where there are conflicting views, for example when designating the seat following party disagreement, or when the institution decides whether there is *prima facie* jurisdiction upon an objection by the respondent. In these cases, the institutions arguably engage in something beyond administration.[365]

361 See R Gerbay. pp. 126–142 for a discussion on these cases.

362 R Gerbay, Chapter 5.

363 R Gerbay, pp. 176–177.

364 R Gerbay's translation, at footnote 704.

365 It should also be noted that *arbitral tribunals* do not only adjudicate issues where there are differing views: a typical Procedural Order No. 1, for example, sets out a number of procedural issues without the parties having argued these points. Furthermore, there is a general debate in arbitration as to the scope of what tribunals may decide *sua sponte*.

Another area of institutional engagement in adjudication-like activities is the ICC Court scrutiny.[366] This process is a mandatory feature of the ICC Rules, which not only cannot be deviated from by the parties, but also takes place with limited party insight. In fact, even tribunals seem to have limited means of reacting to the Court scrutiny. It is a process which takes place largely outside of what is expressly regulated in the Rules. Article 33 of the ICC Rules provides that "[t]he Court may lay down modifications as to the form of the award and, without affecting the arbitral tribunal's liberty of decision, may also draw its attention to points of substance." As discussed above, in a few cases the ICC Court suggested changes to draft awards, in particular on complex jurisdictional issues. This practice is seemingly in compliance with the ICC Rules[367] – as agreed to by the parties – but might raise due process questions from the perspective of a state, which has exercised its sovereignty in allowing for investor access to arbitration under certain specific conditions as specified in a treaty. The extent to which the analysis of the scope of these conditions is conducted by anonymous business lawyers on the ICC Court is not clear for parties, who cannot react to what they do not know.[368]

One interesting counterpoint would be to compare the decisions made by institutions to an *ad hoc* situation. In the latter scenario, all decisions would instead be made by the arbitral tribunal – or, in certain cases, a domestic court[369] – and thus characterized differently (and, in some cases, be reviewable). Does the mere fact that it is an institution making the decision necessarily mean that different due process criteria should apply?

To illustrate, this issue might be a live one in the several pending intra-EU arbitrations currently seated in Stockholm and heard under the SCC Rules.[370]

366 Stone Sweet and Grisel argue that this process is "significantly judicialized," p. 105.

367 As stated by Fry, Greenberg & Mazza in their commentary to the ICC Rules: "While the scrutiny process may lead an arbitral tribunal to modify a substantive aspect of its decision, this will result from the Court's identifying a problem such as missing elements in the decision, weaknesses in the reasoning, inconsistencies, the failure to deal with certain issues or claims," para. 3-1207.

368 It should be noted that in 2016, the ICC issued a new practice in which parties and tribunals are informed about whether awards under scrutiny have been approved, or are subject to further scrutiny at a future Court session, see https://iccwbo.org/media-wall/news-speeches/icc-augments-transparency-in-scrutiny-process/. This new practice is incorporated in the ICC Note to Parties and Arbitral Tribunals on the Conduct of the Arbitration Under the ICC Rules of Arbitration, 2019, paras. 131–133.

369 Depending on the applicable *lex loci arbitri*, domestic courts may rule on the tribunal's jurisdiction when the arbitration is still pending, for example.

370 See the introduction to the present text. Other publicly known pending intra-EU cases include *Triodos SICAV II v. Spain; Sun Reserve Luxco Holdings SRL v. Italy; CEF Energia BV vs. Italy and Alten Renewable Energy Developments BV v. Spain* (all listed at the web page

Following the Court of Justice of the European Union's decision in the *Achmea* case, a prudent investor might consider attempting to remove the legal seat outside of the European Union. In the *ad hoc* scenario, both the initial decision on the seat, and a potential subsequent decision to reconsider and move the seat elsewhere would be for the arbitral tribunal to make. In fact, such a move of the seat been done in at least one intra-EU case heard under the UNCITRAL Rules. In *Antaris v. Czech Republic*, the tribunal initially designated The Hague as the seat.[371] Later in the proceedings, the tribunal issued a procedural order in which it allowed the EU Commission to file an amicus brief, and in that same procedural order also changed the seat from The Hague to Geneva.[372] If this case had instead been governed by the SCC Rules, it would have been the SCC Board that initially designated the seat. Presumably, therefore, the decision to *change* the seat must also be made the Board, rather than by the tribunal. Designating and re-designating the legal seat is part of the tasks given to the arbitral institutions under their rules, which are the primary source of authority for the institutions.[373] Neither rule set provides that institutional decisions must be accompanied by either a requirement to give reasons, for the opportunity for parties to submit opinion, nor for any remedies against the decisions. This raises the question posed already in 1990 by Jan Paulsson: should someone "police the police"?[374] Paulsson asked his question against a background of increasingly prolific institutional arbitration, stating that "there is no reason […] to consider institutional practices and procedures as immune from criticism."[375]

While procedural decisions by tribunals can be challenged, at least indirectly, at the post-award stage, there is no judicial review of institutional decisions.[376] It is, however, possible to indirectly advance arguments against an institution's decision-making, within the framework of a set-aside application. This was done by the Republic of Kazakhstan in the challenge of the SCC award *Ascom Stati et al v. Kazakhstan*, with respect to the appointment of

of the Energy Charter. https://energycharter.org/what-we-do/dispute-settlement/investment-dispute-settlement-cases/, visited 24 January 2020).

371 *Antaris Solar GmbH and Dr. Michael Göde v. Czech Republic*, PCA Case No. 2014-01, UNCITRAL, Award 2 May 2018, para. 31.

372 Ibid., para. 38.

373 Two different French courts have pointed this out in the case of the ICC see R Gerbay p. 158 et seq, with further references.

374 J Paulsson, "Vicarious Hypochondria," p. 226.

375 Ibid.

376 R Gerbay, pp. 207–208.

an arbitrator on behalf of the respondent state.[377] However, turning *directly* to a supervisory court, asking it to review a decision by an arbitral institution seems to be rare,[378] and has not happened in the cases studied here. In theory, it would be possible to challenge institutions' negative *prima facie* jurisdiction decisions. As discussed above, however, the competent court in such cases is not easily specified when the arbitration is based on a treaty.

Finally, there is the question of who makes jurisdiction-related decisions at the institutions. Under both Rules, the formal authority is primarily vested with the ICC Court and the SCC Board respectively.[379] Nevertheless, the studied material indicates that both secretariats informally influence the decisions to a certain degree. In this respect, one counter-perspective to that of commercial arbitration is that of dispute settlement in international law more widely.

In an article on WTO adjudication, Joseph Weiler argues that although the WTO Secretariat lawyers are meant to be "not even players, but facilitators of the play of others,"[380] the Secretariat inevitably becomes a "repository of

377 Kazakhstan v. Ascom/Stati, Svea Court of Appeal. Kazakhstan argued, unsuccessfully, that the SCC had appointed an arbitrator on behalf of Kazakhstan in a manner that violated both the SCC Rules, and fundamental procedural rights embodied in Swedish arbitration law.

378 Outside the sphere of jurisdictional issues, Argentina turned to Argentinian courts in an effort to "appeal" an ICC Court decision to not remove an arbitrator in the *National Grid* case, see Argentina Federal Administrative Chamber of Appeals, Causa 2.660/2006 En Procuracion Del Tesoro v. Cámara De Comercia Internacional (DECI 15-XII-05), 3 July 2007. The National Grid case was legally seated in Washington, presumably giving Washington courts jurisdiction over ancillary proceedings, as discussed in Chapter 3. This notwithstanding, Argentina turned to its own courts to "appeal" the ICC Court's decision to reject the state's challenge against the tribunal chair. Argentina also asked the court to notify the tribunal of its decision, so that the arbitration be halted and a new arbitrator appointed. The state argued that circumstances arising out of the arbitrator's involvement in two other cases against the state undermined his independence. The court ordered the tribunal to halt the proceedings, and the investor to refrain from advancing the arbitration. However, the arbitration proceeded without taking the Argentinian court decision into account; the tribunal ultimately proceeded to rendering an award. As a consequence of the arbitral award, the Federal Administrative Chamber of Appeals declared the matter moot in a decision on 19 March 2009, dismissing the state's case, see Argentina Federal Administrative Chamber of Appeals, Causa 2.660/2006 En Procuracion Del Tesoro v. Cámara De Comercia Internacional (DECI 15-XII-05), 19 March 2009.

379 It should be noted that ICC Secretary General generally has more tasks specified in the Rules than does the SCC equivalent, see for example the *prima facie* decisions concerning the arbitration agreement discussed above at 4.3.1. Presumably, this is because the SCC is a smaller operation, with fewer people and more informal points of contacts, whereas the ICC has a significantly larger Secretariat and decision-making body, thereby needing more formalized structures of decision-making.

380 J Weiler, "The Rule of Lawyers," p. 205.

institutional memory, of horizontal and temporal coherence, of long term hermeneutic strategy."[381] The consequence of this that the individual panels, who similar to investment arbitration tribunals, are established for one specific case, resorts to the Secretariat's expertise. Weiler even mentions that in discussions with a number of panellists, he was told that when it came to points of law they "did not feel they could meaningfully challenge the legal secretary."[382] Although it is difficult based on the documentation studied here to determine to what extent this latter situation is frequent in SCC and ICC arbitration,[383] it is worth noting that while WTO panellists are often not legal specialist, the opposite is true for investment arbitrators.[384] Nevertheless, the basic underlying premise is the same: the Secretariats are permanent, whereas arbitral tribunals are not. Nor is the ICC Court or the SCC Board permanent; the members are regularly changed. This creates a dynamic in which the Secretariats are the only constant in institutional arbitration. Decisions are put to the ICC Court and the SCC Board after having been prepared by the respective Secretariats. Both Secretariats seem to rely on institutional practice in their recommendations; information that is not readily available to the disputing parties, not to mention the treaty states that originally included the Rules in their treaty. What types of cases are heard by a sole arbitrator, as opposed to three arbitrators? Under what circumstances do the institutions designate non-EU seats? What is the extent of jurisdictional scrutiny which can be expected by the ICC Court? These are all examples of questions where there is a degree of "insider premium" and an asymmetry in the access to information; sometimes what is not in the rules is more important than what is in the rules. This information is part of the "product" that the institutions are selling: you need the ICC and the SCC in order to properly administer cases under their respective Rules, as the institutions have access to their own case-load and thereby to guiding previous experience. To illustrate, in the ICC Guide[385] arbitrators are encouraged to use the Secretariat as a "sounding board" and a "source of knowledge and practice."[386]

381 Ibid.

382 Ibid.

383 Although as discussed above, it seems the scrutiny exercised by the ICC *Court,* supported by the Secretariat, may have occasionally influenced the decision-making.

384 Cf. J Pauwelyn, "The Rule of Law Without the Rule of Lawyers? Why Investment Arbitrators Are from Mars, Trade Adjudicators from Venus," American Journal of International Law, 109(4), 761–805, 2015.

385 Which the ICC Secretariat often uses as support in their communication with tribunals, as repeatedly showed by Sweet Stone and Grisel, chapter 3.

386 Fry, Greenberg & Mazza, para. 3-1198.

At both institutions, the decision-making is collegial. Both Secretariats, as well as both formal decision-making bodies, consist of a number of individuals, who typically exercise their work collectively and go unnamed. By contrast, much of the work done by both ICSID and the PCA is at least formally identifiable and connected to an individual: one clear example is that the secretariat lawyer in charge of a specific case is regularly named on the decisions and awards, which is not the practice at the ICC or SCC Secretariats.

The collective decision-making of the ICC Court has been used by the ICC as a justification not to give reasons for the Court's decisions on challenges against arbitrators: it would not be possible to explain the basis of a decision that has been made, sometimes, by over 100 members.[387] A similar argument could be made for the SCC Board, which is smaller but nevertheless makes decisions on a collective basis.

Finally, unlike decisions made by the ICSID or the PCA, the collegial decision-making at the ICC Court and the SCC Board is performed primarily by private arbitration lawyers, as both bodies consist mostly of lawyers in private practice. From a state's perspective, this may raise concerns as to the perspectives represented among the decision-makers.[388] The commercial arbitration institutions are just that: commercial.

4.5.4 *The "Commercial" Context*

Whereas many public international lawyers view investment arbitration as part of general international law, and approach the disputes accordingly, in the world of commercial arbitration, investment arbitration is generally seen as a subset of international (commercial) arbitration.[389] This rings true also for the two commercial arbitration institutions studied here, for which investment disputes are anchored in the context of commercial arbitration, which make up the vast majority of the activities at the institutions.

International commercial arbitration institutions as "competitors" on a "market" have been the subject of extensive academic study.[390] Arbitration

387 C Rogers, Transparency in Arbitrator Selection (Working Paper), available at https://papers.ssrn.com/sol3/papers.cfm?abstract_id=2705878 visited 13 January 2019, p. 4.

388 In the 2012 update of the ICC Rules, the National Committees' role in ICC arbitrator appointments was restrained for the very reason that states felt that the committees were felt to disproportionately represent business interests, see ICC Task Force Report, para. 38. See also OECD Appointing Authority Paper, paras. 21–25.

389 S Schill, "W(h)ither Fragmentation?," p. 888 with further references.

390 For two prominent examples, see J Karton, *The Culture of International Arbitration and The Evolution of Contract Law*, OUP 2013, Chapter 3; Stone Sweet and Grisel, in particular pp. 44–60. See also B Warwas.

institutions respond to the need of users of the system. These are primarily corporate entities involved in commercial disputes. As of late, there has been some unofficial state input, at least at the ICC, manifested by the 2012 Paper, where some concerns were expressed by states. At the SCC, which updated its Rules in 2017, there does not seem to have been any involvement of states in the drafting process, although the process involved consultations that were open to the public.

States are not the principals of the ICC or the SCC.[391] Whereas ICSID is governed by its member states, and for example has a Convention-based duty to assure "representation [...] of the principal legal systems of the world" in their arbitrator appointments,[392] neither commercial institution owes any allegiance to states.

So, what does this mean for the content of the rules? The material analyzed above indicate that many aspects of the institutions' work in both drafting the arbitration rules and in administering disputes are characterized by what might be deemed, for lack of a better phrase, as "pro-arbitration" notions. This generally means a focus on giving effects to arbitration agreements, and a focus on the ultimate enforceability of awards. Such notions have influenced, *inter alia,* the designation of legal seats,[393] and the early-stage review of arbitration agreements.[394]

Similar concerns also motivate the introduction of emergency arbitration, which was the result of a need to "fill a void" in cases where interim measures were needed to protect the integrity of an arbitration prior to the appointment of a tribunal. When the SCC introduced emergency arbitration in 2010, it was alone among arbitral institutions in providing such a service;[395] now, it is a feature of many other commercial arbitration rules. However, emergency arbitration has also been discussed, but ultimately rejected, in the context of updated ICSID rules.[396]

---

391 Cf. T St. John, p. 246.

392 ICSID Convention Article 14(2). See also E de Brabandere, Investment Treaty Arbitration as Public International Law, pp. 78–79.

393 See above at 4.3.2.

394 See above at 4.3.1.

395 D Sabharwal and R Zaman, "Vive La Difference? Convergence and Conformity in the Rules Reforms of Arbitral Institutions: The Case of the LCIA Rules 2014," Journal of International Arbitration 31:6, 2014, p. 704.

396 The initial list of topics for potential reform included "Provisions on Provisional Measures," but no such reforms have been included in the final proposal, see https://icsid.worldbank.org/en/Documents/about/List%20of%20Topics%20for%20Potential%20ICSID%20Rule%20Amendment-ENG.pdf, visited 14 January 2019.

Although activities relating to arbitrator appointments are left out of this study, there is an important aspect to these activities which further highlights the role played by commercial arbitration at the ICC and the SCC: for prospective arbitrators in investment disputes, commercial cases are often the "way in." The smaller commercial cases are the "ground-floor" of the field and the way most arbitrators get their early appointments. Anecdotally, in the treaty-based cases studied in this chapter, very few arbitrators appointed by the ICC and the SCC were appointed for the first time. Instead, they are already experienced arbitrators and that experience has to come from somewhere, if not from the treaty-based sphere, where the bar for entry is relatively high. Many, if not most, arbitrators hearing treaty-based cases at the ICC and the SCC are also simultaneously involved in commercial cases governed by the same rules.

Finally, it should be noted that both institutions make decisions during arbitrations that may arguably also have consequences for other, more "public" functions. In particular, both institutions serve as anchors to the arbitration community in their respective city. By consistently designating Paris and Stockholm as the legal place of arbitration in large treaty-based cases, the two institutions in practice ensure that the two metropolitan communities remain centres of international arbitration. For example, as discussed in Chapter 3, the Paris Court of Appeal and Svea Court of Appeal are two of the most experienced courts in handling set-aside proceedings in investment cases. To a large degree, this is by virtue of institutional designations of the place of arbitration. A regular docket of treaty-based challenges not only serves to develop the respective domestic courts' experience and competence, it also ensures that local arbitration lawyers in Paris and Stockholm respectively are retained to argue such cases to a much larger extent than cities of similar size and arbitration community where there is no ICC or SCC equivalent. Furthermore, the fact that most cases are seated in the institutions' "home town" arguably contributes to the greater economy in those cities. In early 2018, a report[397] was released by the Stockholm Chamber of Commerce,[398] in which it was argued that the economic impact of the SCC's combined activity represented the equivalent of 0.21% of the Swedish economy. This number was arrived at by combining direct effects (such as the fees paid to Swedish arbitrators and counsel by foreign parties), as well as indirect effects (such as secondary service-providers like hotels, caterers and general retail), and other effects

397 Stockholm Chamber of Commerce, *Tvister säljer Sverige: Stockholm – ett internationellt skiljedomscenter,* Rapport 2018:1 (in Swedish with an English summary).

398 Note that the report was published by the larger body of which the SCC forms an independent part, and not solely by the arbitration institution.

the SCC's international case load has on factors such as attraction of foreign capital and corporate headquarters located in Stockholm. Admittedly, some of these consequences are not directly tied to the legal place of arbitration being in Stockholm, and the numbers were calculated by an institution with an incentive to ensure that more international arbitrations are conducted in Stockholm, but it provides some context to the indirect influence exercised by the SCC Board.

CHAPTER 5

Conclusions

5.1 Introduction

Many treaties allow for both ICSID and non-ICSID arbitration, at the discretion of the claimant-investor. The introductory chapter of this book described the emergence of treaties which offer investors this choice, but it did not provide a satisfactory explanation as to why states initially opted for commercial arbitration rules in investment treaties. The subsequent chapters, however, have shown that the choice matters.

Domestic courts and commercial arbitration institutions have often been involved in the adjudication of non-ICSID investment disputes. The present inquiry has focused on the scope of arbitral jurisdiction, and the extent to which it is affected, either directly (in the case of domestic courts) or indirectly (usually in the case of the commercial arbitration institutions).

Generally speaking, the involvement of both domestic courts and arbitral institutions in investment arbitration, it is submitted, is often justified. In the case of courts, investment arbitration depends on procedural safeguards for its legitimacy, both during and after the proceedings. The role of courts is traditionally to ensure the integrity of the arbitration, by acting as a check on the procedure. Furthermore, in the case of institutions, the nature of most investment treaty disputes makes them ill-suited for pure *ad hoc* arbitration. Arbitration institutions act as initial gatekeepers, and also ensure that the dispute is not disrupted by recalcitrant parties. Furthermore, the institutions update the arbitration rules, usually incrementally, thereby ensuring that the procedural framework is modernized over time.

The result of the study so far has discussed the experience of courts and institutions. This final chapter will now examine these findings, which should motivate reflection for anyone wishing to better understand investment treaty arbitration, including – most crucially – states, who through treaty-making determine its normative framework. This final chapter aims to contribute to this understanding by putting the findings from the text so far into context, concluding with a discussion on the future use of non-ICSID rules in investment treaty disputes.

 | DOI:10.1163/9789004413689_006

5.2 *Lex Loci Arbitri* – the Domestic Anchor

In international commercial arbitration literature, it is common to assume that the place of arbitration is increasingly unimportant.[1] Rather than relying on domestic norms – which was common in earlier practice – international arbitration is increasingly held to be autonomous, created by party agreement and independent of any domestic legal order.[2] As a general matter, this is accurate. However, while the seat of arbitration might be less relevant than before, it is by no means unimportant. As shown in this study, the place of arbitration matters. This is particularly true for investment treaty arbitration, for several reasons.

The place of arbitration provides a treaty-based dispute with a domestic anchor. Unlike treaty arbitrations conducted under the ICSID Convention, where the tribunal's jurisdiction is governed exclusively by international law, non-ICSID cases must maintain a link to a specified domestic jurisdiction. The parties' consent to arbitration in treaty cases is asymmetric and generally sparse on detail: this is true both for the offer included in the treaty, and for the subsequent agreement formed between the disputing parties, who tend to have a limited direct relationship and thus rarely specify procedural details. In fact, the respondent occasionally does not even participate in the dispute; this has especially been the case in emergency arbitration. Given these circumstances, the complimentary norms such as the domestic *lex loci arbitri* take on a larger importance.

In addition to providing the dispute with its normative framework when the arbitration is pending, the post-award review of the arbitral tribunal's jurisdictional decisions may vary, depending on the domestic jurisdiction in question. In these scenarios, domestic courts have approached the fundamental matter of standard of review, as well as the interpretation associated with most such review, differently. Compared to other grounds for challenging an arbitral award, domestic courts have tended to treat jurisdictional issues with a smaller degree of deference. In fact, many if not most courts have reviewed such issues anew.

As of yet, the ramifications of the choice of legal seat have not been equalled in input from treaty parties. It is rare that the seat is spelled out by treaty parties, even in recent treaties. With the exception of NAFTA's open-ended guidance – providing that the legal seat must be in a NAFTA state that is also party

1 See generally E Gaillard, Legal Theory of International Arbitration, Brill, 2010.

2 Stone Sweet and Grisel describe this tendency under the heading "The Decline of the Seat and the Rise of Transnational Freedom of Contract," p. 81. See also G Born, 2nd ed., p. 715.

to the New York Convention – no set-aside has been concluded before a court that was designated even indirectly by the state parties. The first treaties referring to a future multilateral body are no different on this point, as they both allow for UNCITRAL arbitration, while leaving the seat unspecified, as discussed below at 5.4.1.

Treaty parties could do a better job in designating the legal place of arbitration, in order to avoid legal unpredictability. In making this choice, states could be assisted by a growing caseload of treaty-specific challenge proceedings. Depending on the issues expected to arise, the (much more extensive) jurisprudence with respect to challenges of commercial awards might also be of assistance, but this text has demonstrated that there are several considerations which are specific to investment treaty arbitration, as challenges of tribunal jurisdiction generally raise different types of questions in such cases than in commercial cases. For many of the older treaties still in force, no jurisprudential guidance from domestic courts was to be found at the time of their conclusion, simply because the treaties were concluded before domestic courts were ever seized with challenges against treaty-based awards. The court practice only first developed in the first decade of the 21st century, and has escalated in the last handful of years.

Irrespective of the future of non-ICSID arbitration rules in investment treaty arbitration there is already – as discussed in Chapter 2 – a significant amount of treaties in force which allow for such procedures, meaning that the number of treaty-based challenges is set to increase further. At the time of writing, there are already many further such cases pending. Furthermore, as the number of arbitrations keeps rising more generally, it is reasonable to expect the number of challenges to rise as well (at least if the ratio of challenged awards so far is any indication). In essence, court decisions in set-aside proceedings constitute a growing body of case law in investment treaty arbitration, especially on frequent jurisdictional questions. Thus, treaty parties and disputing parties are able to familiarize themselves with a potential legal seat. In more recent court practice, arguments supported by decisions from international courts and tribunals have resonated with domestic courts, and there are no formal reasons why the same should not apply to jurisprudence from other domestic courts, which have been faced with similar questions of interpretation. Ultimately, the extent to which such jurisprudence is convincing is to be evaluated by the court seized. However, speaking generally, domestic courts are unfamiliar with both international sources, and with those from comparative domestic jurisdictions. Even the most frequently used courts seem to approach these issues with limited reference to the practice of other courts in similar positions. No dialogue or co-ordination between courts can be expected, as discussed further below at 5.3.2.2. In the individual cases, therefore, the responsibility rests primarily with the disputing parties, who may bring relevant case law from other seats to the attention of the court seized.

There is a connection between the activities by domestic courts and arbitral institutions, as the identity of the former is often determined by the latter. Most ICC and SCC cases have been seated in Paris and Stockholm respectively, turning courts in these jurisdictions into frequent arbiters of tribunal jurisdiction. Nevertheless, as the previous account has shown, far from all non-ICSID treaty cases are governed by French or Swedish arbitration law. Sometimes the seat in ICC and SCC proceedings has been located elsewhere, but more crucially, there is also a large amount of UNCITRAL or ICSID AF cases that are not administered by these two institutions, and where the default role of the ICC Court and the SCC Board does not apply.

In fact, the studied set-asides cover ten different jurisdictions. By extension, at least ten different *leges loci arbitri* have governed non-ICSID arbitration. In theory, the only restriction on how many different domestic laws may govern treaty-based cases is the number of states in the world. In practice, only a limited number of jurisdictions are chosen. This preference among the "choosers" of legal seats – primarily tribunals and institutions, more rarely disputing parties, but seemingly never treaty states – limits the potential wide range of different seats to those familiar from commercial arbitration practice. This containing force has meant that there is a convergence around formally relatively similar legal seats, with legislation based on, or at least similar to, the UNCITRAL Model Law. The present study has shown, however, that issues that are *not* so easily captured in a legislative act – such as the precise extent of review of jurisdictional issues, or the approach to treaty interpretation – have differed considerably among jurisdictions.

Hypothetically, as part of efforts to institutionalize the current *ad hoc* character of investment arbitration, a multilateral solution could be sought on a single place of arbitration that could provide the *lex loci arbitri* in every non-ICSID case. Although not unprecedented,[3] this does not seem likely, for several reasons. First, practically speaking, there are simply too many separate treaties already providing for the use of non-ICSID Rules. Secondly, a pre-determined place of arbitration is likely not to be attractive to many stakeholders, as it would limit the scope of the disputing parties' autonomy,[4] and face issues of

3 Both the Iran-United States Claims Tribunal (The Hague) and the Court of Arbitration for Sport (Lausanne) might provide some guidance.

4 Although, it must be repeated, despite the fact that most treaties already leave the choice of seat to the disputing parties, this right seems only rarely to have been exercised.

neutrality; there simply is no one single jurisdiction which could be deemed as "neutral" enough. Instead, therefore, despite the institutional bias in favour of Paris and Stockholm, we are left with many different *leges loci arbitri,* as demonstrated by the ten different domestic jurisdictions featured in Chapter 3. This brings the discussion to how the use of non-ICSID arbitration has contributed to the internal fragmentation of international investment law.

5.3 Internal Fragmentation

In investment treaty arbitration, unlike in commercial arbitration, jurisdiction is frequently a major point of contention. The investor's access to arbitration depends on the scope of consent, set down in a treaty. The present study has shown that the scope of this consent has frequently been the subject of "disputes within the disputes," not only during the arbitration itself, but often also at the post-award stage.

Similar to commercial arbitration, however, when treaty-based disputes are governed by non-ICSID rules there are several different actors potentially involved, applying legal frameworks primarily developed for contract-based arbitration. Before and during disputes, the ICC and the SCC have often made decisions that shape the scope of tribunal jurisdiction, both through updates to their arbitration rules (such as introducing emergency arbitration), and through decisions made by the institutions in the course of administering the dispute (such as *prima facie* jurisdictional determinations, designations of place of arbitration, or ICC Court scrutiny). After the award has been rendered, the mandate of the administering institution – similar to that of the tribunal itself – is extinguished. At that stage, another type of actor may still weigh in on the tribunal's jurisdiction: the domestic courts at the place of arbitration. Treaty-based awards have regularly been challenged in court, and these challenges haven often centred on the tribunal's jurisdiction. Domestic courts have approached this task differently, in particular with respect to standard of review and issues of interpretation.

A significant share of investment disputes is governed by rules which are drafted and interpreted by commercial arbitration institutions. In an even bigger share of the cases – including also the UNCITRAL Rules and the ICSID AF Rules – any challenge against the resulting awards must be brought to a domestic court. The precise nature of these activities has been discussed in the previous two chapters, but it should be pointed out that together they paint a fragmented picture of how tribunal jurisdiction is shaped by a large number of different actors. This matters, because the rights and obligations of international legal subjects depend on which body is seized with them.[5] For example, domestic courts function differently from international bodies, and commercial arbitration institutions function differently from international organizations.

Below, the more precise nature of the activities by courts and institutions are discussed, in order to get a better picture of the way in which they contribute to internal fragmentation. At this stage, the discussion focuses primarily on what this fragmentation looks like. Based on the studied material, some thoughts are also offered on how fragmenting effects may be mitigated. The more over-arching question of the desirability of the use of non-ICSID rules in investment arbitration is then addressed in Section 5.4.

5.3.1 *Commercial Arbitration Institutions*

The two commercial arbitration institutions studied here are arguably increasingly becoming autonomous actors, rather than mere "facilitators" of disputes decided by others. In terms of arbitral jurisdiction, commercial arbitration institutions, for example, decide the involvement of other actors (domestic courts, by virtue of their designations of the legal seat), and sometimes also, through their rule-making, create new ones (such as emergency arbitrators). More fundamentally, institutions are also, at least in theory, able to determine the conditions for investor access to treaty-based arbitration, by altering their arbitration rules. However, with the sole exception of the SCC introduction of emergency arbitration, there is little in the studied experience so far which would suggest any inclination to use their rule-making power in ways that alter the scope of the treaty states' consent to arbitration.

In the day-to-day administration of disputes, the influence of the institutional administration on tribunal jurisdiction seems to be limited, at least from what can be deduced from the studied awards and decisions. Instead, the most notable institutional role is that of drafting, amending and interpreting the arbitration rules. Since it is rare for arbitration clauses in investment treaties to specify procedural details, the institutions in practice fill out open-ended treaties. Emergency arbitration is the primary example of this, where the two institutions have opted for different approaches. Both institutions' rules also bestow the decision-making bodies of the respective institution with the authority to designate the place of arbitration, a decision which potentially is of crucial relevance for the individual dispute, and in some instances also beyond that, as many domestic courts review the tribunal's jurisdiction anew.

5 O K Fauchald and A Nollkaemper (eds.), p. 5. See also J Karton, The Culture of International Arbitration and the Evolution of Contract Law, Oxford University Press, 2013, Chapter 3.

Furthermore, although the present study does not support any unduly exercise of it, both institutions have the authority to reject a treaty-based case at the early stages, a decision which reviewability is doubtful.

For the present purposes, the appropriate question is not whether the ICC and the SCC "make decisions," but rather to what extent their involvement in the adjudication contribute to internal fragmentation. In this regard, the institutions contribute to fragmentation not primarily through the resolution of the individual arbitrations, but rather by the way they determine the mandates for the disputes. This is different from domestic courts, which respond to a given framework in individual disputes. Institutions engage in what is best described as "gap-filling" of the sparsely formulated investment treaties which indirectly authorize them with this power.

"Evolving" treaty standards are not uncommon in international treaty-making. Many treaties contain provisions that allow for "unratified" amendments – i.e. procedures to amend the treaty without seeking the express approval of each contracting state. Sometimes they allow for amendments or updates that become binding upon states that do not object, so-called "tacit acceptance,"[6] but in some treaties amendments may be introduced even over the objection of states.[7] In the context of investment law, another recent trend is to set up interpretative "commissions" that may issue binding and authoritative interpretations.[8]

---

6 Most notably, such a procedure is envisioned by many international instruments negotiated under the auspices of the International Maritime Organization, which on its web page describes this practice of "tacit acceptance" in the following way: "Instead of requiring that an amendment shall enter into force after being accepted by, for example, two thirds of the Parties, the "tacit acceptance" procedure provides that an amendment shall enter into force at a particular time unless before that date, objections to the amendment are received from a specified number of Parties.", see http://www.imo.org/en/About/Conventions/Pages/Home.aspx, visited 13 January 2019. See also the 1946 International Convention for the Regulation of Whaling, Article III, which establishes a Commission authorized to amend key issues of the treaty with binding effect, unless states object.

7 See for example, the 1987 Montreal Protocol on Substances that Deplete the Ozone Layer, whose annexes may be amended for all state parties, provided that two-thirds agree, Article 9.4.

8 In the context of investment law, the most well-known is arguably the one established by NAFTA. Furthermore, several recent treaties concluded by the EU set up such commissions, although their exact mandate differs. See H Lenk "Bilateral committees in EU trade and investment agreements: platforms for the reassertion of State control over investor-State adjudication?" in F Baetens (ed.), Legitimacy of Unseen Actors. See also A van Aaken, "Delegating Interpretative Authority in Investment Treaties: The Case of Joint Administrative Commissions," in J E Kalicki and A Joubin-Bret (eds.), Reshaping the Investor-State Dispute Settlement System: Journeys for the 21st Century, Brill, 2015.

The difference between such treaties and the investment treaties that indirectly bestow arbitral institutions with the power to develop the content of the treaty is that both the "tacit acceptance" procedure and the function of the "joint commissions" are expressly provided for in the relevant treaty. Furthermore, the procedure is generally used for technical issues, where the slower process of obtaining individual state consent would not be sufficiently responsive to faster real-world developments.[9] By contrast, nothing prevents arbitral institutions from introducing new features to their rules, which in theory may include rather drastic alterations of the scope of arbitral decision-making. Emergency arbitration, where the two institutions have opted for different approaches, is the clearest example of a development that significantly affects the scope of arbitral mandate. But the question is in principle larger. As discussed above at 4.5.1, there are no (legal) impediments for the two institutions to update their arbitration rules in a manner that would further modify the scope of arbitral tribunal jurisdiction. Potential examples of such changes include adding a default place of arbitration, changing the standard of review for a *prima facie* rejection of a case, or involving its decision-making bodies in more extensive review of draft jurisdictional awards. In short, the *potential* of institutional impact on fragmentation is larger than has been the experience to date.

5.3.2 *Domestic Courts*

Domestic courts are, at least theoretically, anchored within their own respective jurisdictions. However, the UNCITRAL Model Law provides that

> (1) In the interpretation of this Law, regard is to be had to its international origin and to the need to promote uniformity in its application and the observance of good faith.
> (2) Questions concerning matters governed by this Law which are not expressly settled in it are to be settled in conformity with the general principles on which this Law is based.[10]

This provision, which was inserted in the redrafted 2006 version of the Model Law, does not seem to have been expressly cited in any challenge proceeding

---

9 This is the explanation given by IMO for the introduction of "tacit acceptance" in IMO treaties, see http://www.imo.org/en/About/Conventions/Pages/Home.aspx, visited 13 January 2020.

10 UNCITRAL Model Law, Article 2(a).

subject to this study, although at least one courts has emphasized the international nature of the dispute before it.[11] Such statements notwithstanding, as discussed above, domestic courts primarily apply the law of their own jurisdiction, at least for questions that do not go to the tribunal's jurisdiction. Thus, a great number of courts, applying a great number of domestic norms, have been faced with ruling on the validity of treaty-based awards.

Therefore, it must be repeated, when discussing arbitration within the framework of the internal fragmentation of international investment law, one must distinguish ICSID from non-ICSID arbitration. While "international investment arbitration" is often referred to as one cohesive field, there are in fact (at least) two different sub-sets. When commercial arbitration rules are used to solve a treaty dispute, the process is potentially exposed to domestic law.

Furthermore, the fact that there is no distinct institutional centre is a well-known characteristic of investment treaty arbitration,[12] and rarely is this more salient than when it comes to the use of non-ICSID rules. There is now a substantial body of cases in which different domestic courts interpret key provisions of investment treaties, which conforms to a general trend of an increasing role of domestic courts in interpreting treaties.[13] The intention of the present text is not primarily to evaluate the desirability of this tendency, but rather to note that there is a benefit to keeping in mind the difference between ICSID and non-ICSID regimes when studying investment treaty arbitration. Non-ICSID arbitration is, by its very nature, prone to larger fragmenting characteristics (at least to the extent that one accepts that having various bodies deciding on the same, or similar, norms is in and of itself a sign of internal fragmentation).

In theory, the many potential domestic courts could lead to a multiplicity of divergent interpretations. While divergent outcomes in decision-making are signs of internal fragmentation, they could be mitigated to a certain extent, by at least two factors.

---

11 See for example the discussion on the Metalclad v. Mexico judgement above at 3.2.2, in which the Supreme Court of British Columbia relied on Article 6 of the ICAA which authorizes courts to look at the UNCITRAL Model Law when interpreting the ICAA.

12 J Pauwelyn, "Rational Design or Accidental Evolution? The Emergence of International Investment Law," in Z Douglas, J Pauwelyn, J E. Viñuales (eds.), The Foundations of International Investment Law – Bringing Theory Into Practice, Oxford University Press, 2014, pp. 14–15 with further references.

13 See generally W Burke-White and AM Slaughter, "The Future of International Law is Domestic (or, The European Way of Law)," (2006) 47 Harv Intl LJ 327.

5.3.2.1 Mitigating Internal Fragmentation I: The Vienna Principles

Consistent use of the same interpretative tools may work as unifying force to moderate a situation in which various domestic courts approach similar or identical jurisdictional standards in diverse ways. As Michael Waibel puts it, in a more general context:

> Theoretically, the growing role of national courts could herald more consistent interpretation of treaties across multiple jurisdictions, or exactly the opposite [footnote omitted]. An important factor for whether national courts are part of the problem or part of the solution is the interpretive methodology that they apply.[14]

In international law, there is one recognized approach to treaty interpretation: the Vienna Principles. However, the Vienna Principles are not a "catch-all" shibboleth, which can be pronounced and then magically solve interpretative problems. The Principles are much too general for that. In fact, paying lip service to the Vienna Principles can provide convenient cover even in cases for interpretative methodologies that in fact deviate from those inscribed in Articles 31–32 of the VCLT.[15] In this respect, the situation in domestic courts is not different from that in international courts and tribunals generally.[16] Hersch Lauterpacht remarked already in 1949 that rules of interpretation "are not the determining cause of judicial decision, but the form in which the judge cloaks a result arrived at by other means."[17] Against this background, is it even desirable that domestic courts follow a uniform approach to treaty interpretation?[18] Does it matter how domestic courts interpret treaties when faced with the question of an arbitral award's validity? Since interpretation is not an exact

---

14 M Waibel, Uniformity versus Specialization, p. 23

15 M Waibel, p. 6.

16 See A Bjorklund, BG Group, at 617, citing W M Reisman & M H.Arsanjani, "Interpreting Treaties for the Benefit of Third Parties: The 'Salvors' Doctrine' and the Use of Legislative History in Investment Treaties," 104 AM. J. INT'L L. 597, 598–99 (2010), that the Vienna principles "have become something of a clause de style in international judgments and arbitral awards; whether routinely and briefly referred to or solemnly reproduced verbatim, they are not always systematically applied."

17 H Lauterpacht, "Restrictive Interpretation and the Principle of Effectiveness in the Interpretation of Treaties," (1949) 26 BYIL 48, p. 53.

18 This question was posed as part of a large research project conducted at several universities, which culminated in the publication edited by H P. Aust and G Nolte. In the introduction to this publication, Nolte states that the point of departure must be "the assumption that treaties and other rules of international law must be interpreted in a uniform way by different domestic courts," G Nolte, "Introduction," in Aust & Nolte (eds.), p. 3.

science – especially not according to the Vienna Principles – why should we care how domestic courts come to their results?

Generally speaking, it is submitted that we should. Most investment treaties are bilateral, and the challenges are (again, with the exception of NAFTA) heard in a court in a third state, which the contracting states normally did not foresee at the time the treaty was negotiated and entered into. As mentioned above in Chapter 3, none of the courts that have ultimately decided on a challenged investment arbitration award did so by virtue of a direct mandate in the treaty. Instead, the place of arbitration – and by extension the competent court – was chosen by somebody other than the treaty states. This pattern is likely to be sustained for the foreseeable future, given how exceedingly rare it is for investment treaties to clearly spell out the place of arbitration.

The frequent use of domestic courts in this context could foster more consistent interpretation of treaties across multiple jurisdictions; it could also lead to exactly the opposite. An important factor for whether national courts contribute to, or mitigate, the internal fragmentation is the interpretive methodology that they apply.[19] Given this, it is submitted that the least a domestic court could do is to subscribe to some sort of common interpretative rules.[20] Those rules exist, and they are "treaty-blind," i.e. intended to be applied consistently irrespective of which treaty is being interpreted.[21] Their use minimize the fragmenting effects otherwise inherent in a regime consisting of thousands of predominantly bilateral treaties, in which the domestic court is designated in an indirect manner without direct involvement of the treaty states. Furthermore, applying the Vienna Principles makes the outcome most likely to accord with the treaty obligations in question;[22] international obligations ought to be given the meaning ascribed to them by the system of law in which they originated.[23]

It must also be pointed out that there are other, less dogmatic benefits of applying the Vienna Principles. By employing international law methodologies, domestic courts safeguard a certain respect for the outcome of their ruling among other actors in the international sphere. Even if the outcome can never be guaranteed, it would at least be harder to question a decision that is

19 Cf. M Waibel, Uniformity versus Specialisation, p. 15.

20 See also O K Fauchald and A Nollkaemper, "Conclusions," in O K Fauchald and A Nollkaemper (eds.), p. 355.

21 M Waibel, Uniformity versus Specialisation, p. 15.

22 R Gardiner, Treaty Interpretation, p. 142.

23 O K Fauchald and A Nollkaemper, "Conclusions," in O K Fauchald and A Nollkaemper (eds.), p. 356.

motivated in accordance with established customary international law.[24] Furthermore, and perhaps more relevant to the field of investment arbitration, a consistent application of the Vienna Principles demonstrates to other states, as well as to investors, a level of sophistication and comfort with international law, which might lead to more arbitrations being legally seated in the jurisdiction in question.

With this in mind, the practice of domestic courts – at least in recent times – is encouraging, as it generally demonstrates a keener awareness of investment treaties' role in a wider, international legal framework. Most later judgments demonstrate a use of the Vienna Principles which might limit concerns associated with various different decision-makers expressing themselves on similar treaty-based jurisdictional standards. If the trend of increasing use of the Vienna Principles continues, the fact that multiple domestic courts are asked to interpret similar treaty-based jurisdictional standards might not contribute to as large an internal fragmentation as one might otherwise assume.

5.3.2.2 Mitigating Internal Fragmentation II: The Potential of Judicial "Dialogue"

One further way to mitigate the effects of fragmentation – generally speaking as well as within the field of investment arbitration – is for domestic courts and tribunals to "communicate" with international courts and tribunals, as well as with other domestic courts.[25] This communication can take the form of citation, discussion, application or rejection of decisions of other courts.[26] Although frequently referred to as judicial dialogue,[27] it is rare that two courts communicate directly with each other; a better way of characterizing the practice would be as an exchange of views or reactions to other courts' decision.[28] For the present study, both the potential of engagement among domestic courts (which could be characterized as horizontal),[29] and between domestic

24 Aust, Rodiles, Staubach, Unity or Uniformity?, pp. 83–84; A Nollkaemper, "Grounds for the Application of International Rules of Interpretation in National Courts," in Aust & Nolte (eds.), p. 45 et seq.

25 O K Fauchald and A Nollkaemper, "Conclusions," in O K Fauchald and A Nollkaemper (eds.), p. 357 et seq, with further references.

26 Ibid., p. 359.

27 P Webb, "Immunities and Human Rights: Dissecting the Dialouge in National and International Courts," in O K. Fauchald and A Nollkaemper (eds.), p. 245 with further references.

28 A Tzanakopolus, "Judicial Dialouge as a Means of Interpretation," in Aust & Nolte (eds.), p. 75.

29 Ibid.

courts and international bodies such as the ICJ or investment treaty arbitration tribunals (which could be characterized as vertical)[30] are relevant.

In the field of investment treaty arbitration, the potential for such communication is especially evident, given the fact that similar provisions and object and purpose are present in most treaties.[31] Specifically for domestic courts in non-ICSID cases, one could add that many cases arise out of treaties to which the state of the court seized with the question is not a party, which might invite the court in question to look outside of its own domestic context as part of the interpretative exercise. In addition, domestic courts are part of a multilateral structure of arbitration-related norms, primarily the New York Convention, but to a certain extent also the UNCITRAL Model Law, which constitute a common, international framework to which domestic courts have to relate.

Given this, there is a good general case to be made that inspiration can be drawn from other domestic courts even if those judgments often formally deal with different treaties.[32] The case is even stronger if the treaty in question is not a bilateral investment treaty, but rather the multilateral NAFTA or ECT. In those cases, not only is the court's home state generally a party to the treaty, but it is also likely that another domestic court (or, for that matter, an ICSID annulment committee) has been faced with the exact same provision in the exact same treaty, as part of another challenge proceeding.

As of yet, the practice of such judicial dialogue is limited, although not unheard of. References to court practice from within the relevant jurisdiction – including those specific to treaty arbitration[33] – is common. Engagement with jurisprudence from *other* domestic courts, however, is rarer. One exception is the High Court of Singapore in *Sanum*, which found the English decision in the *Occidental* case to be both applicable and instructive.[34] The doctrine of "justiciability" exists in both English and Singaporean law and it is likely that the similarities between the two jurisdictions influenced the latter court's reliance on the former's decision. Furthermore – as pointed out by the Singapore High Court[35] – although the two treaties were different, the question facing both

---

30 Ibid.

31 Ibid, p.82.

32 Ibid.

33 In *Czech Republic v. EMV*, High Court, the Occidental set-aside was discussed, and in *Kazakhstan v. Ascom/Stati* et al, Svea Court of Appeal, the Petrobart set-aside was discussed. Furthermore, most Canadian courts have engaged with prior Canadian practice, as discussed at 3.2.2.3, and the second set-aside case in Singapore, *Lesotho v. Swissbourgh*, cited repeatedly from the first, *Laos v. Sanum*.

34 *Laos v. Sanum*, Singapore High Court, para. 30.

35 Ibid.

courts was the same: would a review of the tribunal's jurisdiction by a third country state violate the sovereign interests of the treaty states?

With this sole exception, it seems that domestic courts have not cited other domestic courts as part of their decisions in set-aside proceedings. To a certain extent, the limited "interaction" with other domestic courts might be a viewed as a function of a provincial mind-set, but it should be emphasized that later cases show a considerable engagement with arbitral jurisprudence. That being said, domestic courts have not been particularly inclined to engage in systemic reasoning, instead focusing primarily on the disputing parties and the jurisdictional scope of the individual arbitration agreement put before them. This is not surprising, as domestic courts have an allegiance to their own domestic legal system. The *BG Group* judgment is perhaps the most evident example of this rather provincial outlook.[36]

It should be noted that it is largely unknown to what extent parties have brought such cases to the attention of the court seized with the question,[37] but there have been examples of when the court in question was undoubtedly aware of the existence of potentially relevant jurisprudence from other courts.

One example is that the Svea Court of Appeal in *Ascom* came to essentially the same conclusion with the respect to the ECT's local litigation requirement as the United States Supreme Court in the *BG Group* challenge, although cloaked in different terminology. In his expert opinion submitted by the investors, Gary Born cited the US Supreme Court's finding in BG Group,[38] but this did not find its way into the reasoning of the Svea Court of Appeal. Although some of the other authorities advanced by the investors and Mr. Born resonated with the court, these were scholarly writings and international arbitral awards[39] – not the *BG Group* decision.[40]

Here it should also be noted that the Paris Court of Appeal in the *Rusoro* challenge came to essentially the same conclusion as both the US Supreme Court and the Svea Court of Appeal with respect to the nature of the cooling off-period. Although with typically French short reasoning, the Paris court found this issue to be a matter of admissibility which the court could

36 The same could arguably said for the CJEU's judgment in Achmea, which is not subject to this study but is an expression of the court's lack of interest in systemic, international law implications of its decision.

37 As discussed at 3.4.3.2 most jurisdictions do not make such pleadings available to the public.

38 See footnote 538, p. 191.

39 Kazakhstan v. Ascom/Stati et al, Svea Court of Appeal, pp. 48–50.

40 However, both courts relied on the same treatise by Born to support their findings that a cooling-off period does not constitute a jurisdictional requirement, see Ascom/Stati p. 41; BG Group, p. 16.

not review, without any mention of either of the two earlier cases in different jurisdictions.[41]

A different but related question is domestic courts' "dialogue" with *international* courts or tribunals, which might be useful when interpreting a treaty that has been under the competence of an international tribunal,[42] but arguably also when the tribunal in question was faced with a similar but formally different treaty.[43] In the present context, similar issues tend to be adjudicated irrespective of whether the arbitration is governed by the ICSID Convention or a domestic *lex loci arbitri*. An arbitral tribunal's alleged jurisdictional error might be challenged either before an international body, in the form of an ICSID annulment committee, or before a domestic court. The choice between the two, as shown above at 3.1.2.2, is rarely, if ever, made by the treaty states. With this in mind, it is interesting to see the extent to which ICSID jurisprudence is utilized by parties and domestic courts in the non-ICSID context.

There are several examples of domestic courts referencing international courts and tribunals in their judgments. ICSID awards seem to be particularly prevalent. For example, the Court of Appeal in the *Sanum* challenge engaged extensively with ICSID case law, both when discussing the possibility to allow the states' interpretative notes as evidence,[44] and when analysing the jurisdictional scope of the arbitration clause. This latter question had been dealt with by the (ICSID) *Tza Yap Shum v. Peru*[45] tribunal, based on a similarly worded clause in the China – Peru BIT. It seems that the investor had advanced this award as support for its wide reading of the arbitration clause, which resonated with the court. Laos, by contrast, had referred to a number of other arbitral awards, from both the ICSID and non-ICSID context, which were all distinguished by the court and found not to be relevant.

In English court practice, the (ICSID) *SGS v. Philippines* award[46] was relied upon by the Court of Appeal in *Occidental* to support that the object and purpose of investment treaties is to provide effective protection for investors.[47] Therefore, uncertainties in interpretation should be resolved in favour of the investor; a statement which was supported by reference to the ICSID tribunal's

41 Venezuela v. Rusoro, p. 4.

42 O K Fauchald and A Nollkaemper, "Conclusions," in O K Fauchald and A Nollkaemper, p. 357, with further references.

43 Cf. A Tzanakopolus, "Judicial Dialouge as a Means of Interpretation," in Aust & Nolte (eds.).

44 Sanum v. Laos, Singapore Court of Appeal, paras. 61; 105; 117.

45 Tza Yap Shum v. The Republic of Peru, ICSID Case No. ARB/07/6, Award, 7 July 2011.

46 SGS Société Générale de Surveillance S.A. v. Republic of the Philippines, ICSID Case No. ARB/02/6, Decision of the Tribunal on Objections to Jurisdiction, 29 January 2004.

47 Ecuador v. Occidental, Court of Appeal, para. 28.

finding on this point. In the later *EMV* challenge, the High Court found that this contention "goes rather further than appears to be justified in International law."[48] It is probably not a co-incidence that in both these two cases, the investors were represented by the same legal counsel: in the *Occidental* case, the *SGS v. Philippines* award was advanced by the investor's counsel,[49] and in the later *EMV* case the *Occidental* court's embrace of the same ICSID case was also invoked by the investor.[50]

Other examples of ICSID jurisprudence finding its way into court judgements are the challenges against the *Cargill*,[51] *SwemBalt*,[52] *Ascom/Stati*[53] and *Swissbourgh*[54] awards. However, jurisprudence from ICSID annulment committees – as opposed to arbitral awards – has not been utilized often in court practice, contrary to what might be expected given the parallel functions filled by courts and annulment committees in reviewing awards. One major exception seems to be the 2001 *Metalclad* challenge, in which the Supreme Court of British Columbia was faced with an argument by counsel from Mexico based on three well-known early ICSID annulment cases.[55] Mexico argued that the *Metalclad* tribunal had failed to address all questions put before it, which would be grounds for setting aside the award. Although the three annulment committees had based their interpretation on the ICSID Convention, Mexico claimed that the fact that the ICSID Additional Facility Rules – which were the rules governing the arbitration and similar to the ICSID Convention require the award to "deal with every question submitted to the Tribunal"[56] – would make ICSID annulment jurisprudence relevant for the Canadian court's determination. The court pointed out – quite correctly – that this provision of the

48 *Czech Republic v. EMV*, High Court, para. 23.

49 *Ecuador v. Occidental*, Court of Appeal, para. 28.

50 *Czech Republic v. EMV*, High Court, para. 21.

51 *Mexico v. Cargill*, Court of Appeal for Ontario, paras. 20–22, in which the court noted the *ADM v. Mexico* arbitration (which was an ICSID AF case) also concerned the question facing the *Cargill* tribunal, i.e. whether damages could be awarded for losses sustained outside of Mexico.

52 *Latvia v. SwemBalt*, Maritime and Commercial Court of Copenhagen, p. 19, in which the investor cited the 1997 *American Manufacture and Trading Inv. v. Zaire* ICSID award to support its finding that the Swedish parent company was a protected investor, even if the investment was performed through a wholly-owned Latvian subsidiary. Although this argument was included by the court in its recitals, it seems not to have made its way into the reasoning of the court.

53 As discussed above at 3.2.3.2, the court in Ascom/Stati did not expressly cite specific cases but referred to the parties' respective expert reports and the awards cited there.

54 *Lesoto v. Swissbourg et al*, High Court, paras. 121–161.

55 The *Klöckner, Amco* and *MINE* annulment decisions are discussed further in Chapter 2.4.2.

56 ICSID Convention, Article 53(1).

ICSID AF Rules does not concern grounds for annulment, which are to be found exclusively in either the ICSID Convention (as in the case of the three decisions relied upon) or in domestic arbitration legislation (as in this case, the ICAA).[57] The court was therefore not convinced by Mexico's reference to the three annulment decisions, which it nevertheless found to be "overly broad"[58] and "not universally accepted."[59]

The relatively frequent use of decisions by international courts and tribunals seems to be in line with the many references to international law scholars[60] and even review of other, similar investment treaties.[61] Domestic courts more frequently rely on sources that may be deemed "international," than decisions from their counterparts in other domestic jurisdictions, which may be deemed "foreign" (in more than one sense of the word). This is so despite the fact that there is great potential in "outgoing" communication from domestic courts – i.e. the reference in one domestic court proceeding to the findings or reasoning of another court – given the relevance and similarities in the issues adjudicated. In fact, both international tribunals and other domestic courts might be assisted by domestic courts' findings on the scope of investment treaty provisions.

In the studied court judgments, many questions of fundamental nature have been adjudicated. These judgments have a potential relevance for investment arbitration jurisprudence beyond their respective domestic jurisdictions. They include the scope of the well-known narrow arbitration clauses referring to compensation for expropriation,[62] taxation exceptions,[63] the definitions of 'investor'[64] and 'investment',[65] the territorial scope of a treaty,[66] the possibility to bring an arbitration against a state of which you are a citizen,[67]

57 Mexico v. Metalclad, Supreme Court of British Columbia., para. 125.

58 Ibid., para. 121.

59 Ibid., para. 124.

60 For some of the clearest examples, see Sanum v. Laos, Singapore Court of Appeal, Kazakhstan v. Ascom/Stati et al, Svea Court of Appeal; Hungary v. *EDF*, Swiss Federal Tribunal.

61 Czech Republic v. Saluka, Swiss Federal Tribunal; *BG* Group v. Argentina, United States Supreme Court; Kazakhstan v. Ascom/Stati et al, Svea Court of Appeal.

62 Czech Republic v. *EMV*, High Court; Sanum v. Laos, Singapore Court of Appeal.

63 Ecuador v. Occidental, High Court; Poland v. Schooner Capital, Paris Court of Appeal.

64 Canada v. S.D. Myers, Federal Court of Canada; Ukraine v. Tatneft, Paris Court of Appeal.

65 *RECOFI* v. Vietnam, Swiss Federal Tribunal; Latvia v. SwemBalt, Maritime and Commercial Court of Copenhagen; Czech Republic v. Pren Nreka, Paris Court of Appeal; Moldova v. Energoalians, Paris Court of Appeal.

66 Laos v. Sanum, Russia v. Stabil and Ukrnafta.

67 Cem Uzan v. Turkey, Svea Court of Appeal, Venezuela v. Garcia Armas, Paris Court of Appeal.

and the consequences of not complying with cooling-off periods,[68] to name a few notable examples.

One clear example of the similarities of the adjudicated issues is the different outcomes in the Paris-seated challenges against the *Pren Nreka* and *Energoalians* awards. In both proceedings, the challenging state relied on the *Salini* test, established in ICSID jurisprudence, to argue that rights under commercial contracts do not meet the definition of investment. In *Energoalians*, the treaty in question was the ECT, while in *Pren Nreka* it was the BIT between Czech Republic and Croatia. Both states seemingly emphasized in particular one element of the *Salini* test, *viz.* the condition of contribution to the host state economy, which both states prevented protection for claims to money under a contract.

Several ECT tribunals have been faced with a similar question to that at issue in these challenges; so far none has declined jurisdiction on the ground that claims to money under a contract does not constitute an investment.[69] In *Pren Nreka*, the underlying bilateral investment treaty defines, similar to the ECT, an investment as "any kind of asset invested in connection with economic activities by an investor."[70] The Paris court found that Mr. Pren. Nreka's right to a 15-year lease contract was covered by these "broad terms." By contrast, the same court found that Energoalians' right to recover compensation for electricity that was not paid for by a state-owned electricity company was not covered by the ECT. Notably the ECT is recognized as having an unusually wide definition of investment;[71] for example, the tribunal in *Plama v. Bulgaria* found it to "encompass virtually any right, property or interest in money or money's worth."[72] This notwithstanding, the Paris Court of Appeal found that an investment needs to make some sort of contribution to the host state's economy, relying partly on the treaty provision's language that an investment must be "associated with an economic activity in the energy sector."[73]

---

68 Kazakhsan v. Ascom/Stati et al, Svea Court of Appeal, *BG* Group v. Argentina, United States Supreme Court; Venezuela v. Rusoro, Paris Court of Appeal.

69 For example Petrobart Limited v. The Kyrgyz Republic, SCC Case No. 126/2003, Award, 29 March 2005; Mohammad Ammar Al-Bahloul v. The Republic of Tajikistan, SCC Case No. 064/2008, Final Award, 8 June 2010; Electrabel S.A. v. Republic of Hungary, ICSID Case No. ARB/07/19, Decision on Jurisdiction, Applicable Law and Liability, 20 November 2012.

70 Croatia – Czech Republic BIT (1996), Article 1(2).

71 T Roe, M Happold, J Dingemans, Settlement of Investment Disputes under the Energy Charter Treaty, Cambridge University Press, 2011, pp. 44–45.

72 Plama Consortium Limited v. Republic of Bulgaria, ICSID Case No. ARB/03/24 Decision on Jurisdiction, 8 February 2005, para. 125.

73 Moldova v. Energoalians, Paris Court of Appeal, p. 5.

The Court of Appeal's review of the *Energoalians* award thus constitutes a break with not only the tribunal majority's reasoning on the same question,[74] but with the same court's determination in an earlier, similar case based on a different treaty and with different factual background. It also stands as the only example to date where an alleged investment was found not to be covered by the ECT.[75]

Tor the present purposes, it is relevant that the Paris court's two decisions on this point are seemingly not consistent with each other. The earlier decision – which did not expressly rely on the Vienna Principles – found that no "contribution" was necessary, while the later decision – which did refer to the Vienna Principles – stated that the challenging state was correct in relying on this very condition as constituting element of an investment.[76] Yet again: if the Paris court had relied on the Vienna Principles in both cases, that might have made it easier to analyse the differing outcomes.

In any event, these judgements address the overarching question already raised, as to their normative legal value in subsequent cases, in particular in arbitrations. Would it be advisable for an international tribunal to rely upon any of these judgments, if faced with a similar question?

Generally speaking, there is nothing controversial in international tribunals drawing from domestic jurisprudence when identifying and applying norms of international law.[77] In investment arbitration, many of the studied challenges (including the examples *Pren Nera* and *Energoalians*) involve independent, *de novo* determinations of issues that have been subjected to new pleadings by the parties, which advanced their arguments based on jurisprudence by international arbitration tribunals. This means that courts are deciding on these matters almost as if they were the original tribunal, unlike ICSID annulment committees, which tend to refrain from engaging with the merits of jurisdictional determinations.

Needless to say, an arbitral tribunal cannot treat these resulting court decisions as formal authority, in the sense of binding precedents. Then again, the same goes for earlier awards by other arbitral tribunals and such decisions are in fact often relied upon in arbitral jurisprudence.[78] Therefore, it is possible to

74 Which, it must be pointed out, was critized by the dissenting chairman (!).

75 As mentioned in the introduction to this dissertation, the Court of Appeal's decision was subsequently overturned by the French Court of Cassation.

76 Moldova v. Energoalians, Paris Court of Appeal, p. 6.

77 H E Kjos, "International Law through the National Prism: the Role of Domestic Law and Jurisprudence in Shaping International Investment Law," Select proceedings of the European Society of International Law, Vol. 5, 2016, pp. 87–88. See also ICJ Statute Article 38(1).

78 E De Brabandere, Arbitral Decisions as a Source of International Investment Law, Section 2.2.

view domestic court practice as a largely untapped potential source of legal decisions, for other courts as well as for arbitral tribunals. At the same time, if this contention is true, what could explain this lack of reference to domestic court judgments? Perhaps there are good reasons why parties and decision-making bodies generally refrain from citing these sources.

In any event, it is submitted that at least part of the explanation can be explained by a lack of awareness of their utility: domestic actors often approach issues of international law without appreciation of the fact that actors in other jurisdictions have been put in similar positions before. This certainly seems to hold true for challenges of treaty-based arbitral awards.

5.4 Future Outlooks – on the Desirability of Non-ICSID Rules in Investment Arbitration

From a formal point of view, commercial arbitration institutions and domestic courts are involved in investment treaty arbitration for a reason: states have authorized them to be.[79] Having examined and analysed some of the consequences of this choice, the text now turns to lessons learnt for the purpose of future treaty-drafting: are commercial arbitration institutions and domestic courts well suited to exercise the functions entrusted to them by states?

In international law, states are used to controlling the agenda. Historically, states have been less "in control" of the development of international investment law than of other fields of international law. Instead, dispute resolution has arguably been the primary driver of normative development in the field. Now there are signs that things might be changing; states are re-asserting control. For the first time since the explosion of investment arbitrations in the period around the turn of the 20th century, there are broad multilateral reform discussions taking place. Furthermore, many states have indicated a wish to reform treaties currently in force, and drafted new "model BITs."[80] Within the European Union, the last five years have seen considerable pressure on member states to change the current system in the "intra-EU" context, as well as active EU-wide efforts to conclude new and different treaties in the "extra-EU" context. As these broader reform discussions are pending, 2017 marked the

79 Already in 1927, Hersch Lauterpacht wrote that "there is no better evidence of the legal conviction of governments than those international acts and agreements in which States formulate the law to be followed by international judicial tribunals," H Lauterpacht, Private Law Sources and Analogies of International Law, Longmans, Green & Co, 1927, p. 60.

80 See above Chapter 1, footnote 26.

year in which the lowest number of new investment treaties was concluded since 1983, and effective treaty terminations exceeded the number of new treaty conclusions for the first time.[81]

In the context of these discussions on what, if anything, will replace or alter the current regime, there has been considerable discussion on how to reconcile future solutions with the ICSID Convention.[82] Less attention has been paid to the non-ICSID rules and their role in a reformed future resolution of investment disputes, which is the focus of this sub-section.

5.4.1 *ICSID or Non-ICSID in Future Treaties?*

Initially, it's worth emphasizing that a noteworthy number of states participate in global investment flows without ever having been party to the ICSID Convention. This list of countries includes significant economies such as Brazil, India, Poland, Russia, South Africa and Thailand. For disputes involving these states (or investors from those states), ICSID arbitration is not available.[83] As explained above, the ICSID Additional Facility was created partly with such disputes in mind and has indeed been utilized for disputes involving these countries; particularly Mexico and Canada have been frequent users of the Additional Facility under the NAFTA.[84]

While some of the states staying outside of the ICSID system, particularly Brazil and South Africa, have also been restrictive in ratifying investment treaties generally, the fact still remains that many countries with extensive BIT programs are by definition referred to non-ICSID rules for settling their treaty disputes. Furthermore, three former ratifying states have denounced the ICSID Convention: Bolivia (on May 2, 2007), Ecuador (on July 6, 2009) and Venezuela (on January 24, 2012).[85] It has been debated to what extent the states'

---

81 UNCTAD, World Investment Report 2018, p. xiii.

82 For example, this was the topic of a special issue of ICSID Review Foreign Investment Law Journal (Volume 32, Issue 3, Fall 2017, pp. 457–728). See also N Jansen Calamita, "The (In)Compatibility of Appellate Mechanisms with Existing Instruments of the Investment Treaty Regime," The Journal of World Investment & Trade, 18(4), 585–627, extensively discussing the relationship between future mechanisms and the ICSID Convention (but not domestic law).

83 ICSID Convention Article 25(1) presupposes that the dispute is between a "Contracting State [...] and a national of another Contracting State."

84 Canada and Mexico joined the ranks of ICSID states in 2013 and 2018 respectively, see ICSID List of Contracting States and Other Signatories of the Convention (as of June 27, 2018), https://icsid.worldbank.org/en/Pages/icsiddocs/List-of-Member-States.aspx, last accessed 30 March 2020.

85 Ibid.

denunciations prevent further ICSID cases to be brought against them,[86] but all three still have bilateral investment treaties in force, providing for non-ICSID arbitration.

Furthermore, consent to arbitration by way of a treaty is different from arbitration agreements in contracts: a single treaty can be relied upon by an indefinite number of potential claimants. Thereby, each individual treaty that refers to the ICC Rules, the SCC Rules or the UNCITRAL Rules might be the source of multiple arbitrations. For example, at the SCC, the majority of the cases studied have been based on either the ECT or one specific bilateral investment treaty, whereas at the ICC, a small number of states together make up the vast majority of respondents.[87] This fact has implications for the future role of the ICC and the SCC in investment treaty disputes; a small number of treaty references may ensure a large number of future disputes.

In short, as long as a significant number of states remain non-signatories to the ICSID Convention, and the procedural landscape stays the same, i.e. the many treaties currently in force are not terminated *en masse*, it is likely we will see a continually fragmented scene of arbitration options. This is so irrespective of the choices made by investors and host states that have access to ICSID arbitration. As long as investors bring treaty cases under the current regime of treaties, a certain number of them will be heard outside of the system set up by ICSID Convention.

Moving from treaties already in force, which have formed the basis for the study so far, to future treaties, it seems that neither the ICC Rules nor the SCC Rules have been part of the public discussions so far. In the various model BITs – as well as the discussion in UNCITRAL Working Group III – the assumption largely seems to be that future investment arbitration is to be governed by either, on the one hand the ICSID Convention and/or the UNCITRAL Rules, or, on the other hand, something completely new. This means that the previous discussion in this text might be instructive in at least one respect: the

86 See for example C Schreuer, "Denunciation of the ICSID Convention and Consent to Arbitration," in M Waibel, A Kaushal, K-H Liz Chung and C Balchin (eds), The Backlash against Investment Arbitration: Perceptions and Reality, Kluwer, 2010; O M Garibaldi, "On the Denunciation of the ICSID Convention, Consent to ICSID Jurisdiction, and the Limits of the Contract Analogy," in C Binder, U Kriebaum, A Reinisch & S Wittich (eds.), International Investment Law for the 21st Century – Essays in Honour of Christoph Schreuer, Oxford University Press, 2009, pp. 251–277; C Tietje, K Nowrot & C Wackernagel, Once and Forever? The Legal Effect of a Denunciation of *ICSID*, Transnat'l Disp. Mgmt. 2008.

87 It might be worth noting that at the time of writing, very few cases under institutional rules have been administered – at either the ICC or the SCC – where both treaty states involved were ICSID signatories.

continuing appetite for UNCITRAL Rules most likely ensures that domestic courts will be involved also in future investment arbitration.[88]

However, the purpose here is not to consult the tea leaves about states' preferences but rather to discuss how and to what extent the studied past practice may be of assistance for future treaty-making.

5.4.2 *Future Challenges in Using non-ICSID Arbitration Rules – The Roles of Domestic Courts and* Lex Loci Arbitri

Given that the UNCITRAL Rules, unlike the ICC Rules and SCC Rules, seem to be an attractive option for drafters of future treaties, the studied material gives rise to a few suggestions, which might be relevant to the reform proposals currently being debated.

The future roles of domestic courts and domestic *leges loci arbitri* are perhaps most evident in connection with one of the most discussed reform proposals: a standing multilateral body for investment disputes and/or an appellate mechanism, which are both currently part of the UNCITRAL work in the field. In a report prepared for UNCITRAL Working Group III, Kaufmann-Kohler and Potestà analyse the potential for such multilateral reforms.[89] They discuss the relevance of the surrounding legal framework for such a body, stating that this framework "has important consequences for the possible supervisory competence of domestic courts, for annulment/appeal, and for enforcement.".[90] In this respect, the report discusses two possible avenues, one based on non-ICSID rules and one based on the ICSID Convention, seemingly preferring the latter.[91] The main advantage of opting for the ICSID, the authors argue, is the regime's self-contained nature, which would avoid a difficult choice of place(s) of arbitration.[92]

Three investment treaties have already been concluded containing a reference to such a future, as of yet unspecified, body, both concluded by the European Union.[93] As long as no such body has come to fruition, however, in the

---

88 Not only the already-mentioned treaties concluded by the EU refer to the UNCITRAL Rules, but many "new generation" BITs provide for it, see for example also the 2017 Israel – Japan BIT, Article 24; 2016 Morocco – Nigeria BIT Article 27; 2016 Argentina – Qatar BIT, Article 14; 2016 Rwanda – Turkey BIT, Article 10; India – Belarus BIT, 2018, Article 16.

89 Kaufmann-Kohler & Potestà.

90 Ibid., paras. 100–101.

91 Ibid. This may present a number of challenges with respect to the compatibility with the multilateral ICSID Convention, see N J Calamita, "The Challenge of Establishing a Multilateral Investment Tribunal at ICSID," in ICSID Review Foreign Investment Law Journal, Volume 32, Issue 3, Fall 2017, pp. 611–623.

92 Kaufmann-Kohler & Potestà, paras. 100–101.

93 Vietnam, Article 15; CETA Article 8.29.

meantime the three treaties set up novel arbitration regimes. At the time of writing, only the EU-Singapore Free Trade Agreement has entered into force, while neither the Comprehensive Economic and Trade Agreement (CETA), nor the EU-Vietnam Free Trade Agreement is fully ratified. Interestingly, they all allow for a claimant to submit a claim under the UNCITRAL Rules, the ICSID Convention, the ICSID AF Rules or any other rules agreed upon by the (disputing) parties.[94] Consequently, similar to many earlier treaties, the decision between ICSID and non-ICSID is not made in the treaty, but rather left to the investor. In the event that the investor opts for any of the non-ICSID alternatives, neither treaty makes a mention of the place of arbitration. This approach is also similar to most investment treaties in force, in that it allows the investor to decide the framework for the arbitration from several available options, and in that the place of arbitration is unspecified.

Less traditional in the CETA and the EU-Vietnam treaty are the novel openings for multilateral reform. CETA has been ratified and most parts of it, albeit not the investment chapter, has entered into force provisionally.[95] The treaty establishes a semi-standing tribunal, whose awards may be appealed to an appeals body.[96] The same structure is found in the EU-Vietnam treaty, which has not yet entered into force at the time of writing.[97] Furthermore, both treaties open up for the possibility of a multilateral investment tribunal. The treaty parties undertake to pursue such a solution, and should it become reality the respective treaties' investment dispute resolution mechanisms are to be replaced by those provided for in the multilateral instrument.[98]

In all of these scenarios, the place of arbitration is an open question. If the aim is to ensure a predictable and consistent case law,[99] the uncertainty with respect to the place(s) of arbitration risks contravening that aim, especially since many domestic courts to date have reviewed key investment treaty standards *de novo*.

With respect to a novel, multilateral permanent tribunal or appellate body, the need for clarity is especially imperative; there are simply too many

---

94 CETA Article 8(23); EU-Vietnam Free Trade Agreement, Chapter 8, Sub-Section 3, Article 7; EU-Singapore Investment Protection Agreement Article 3.6.

95 European Commission - Press release, EU-Canada trade agreement enters into force, 20 September 2017, http://europa.eu/rapid/press-release_IP-17-3121_en.htm, visited 15 January 2020.

96 CETA Articles 8.27–8.28.

97 EU-Vietnam Free Trade Agreement, Chapter 8, Sub-Section 4, Articles 12–13.

98 Ibid.

99 Which has been identified by UNCITRAL Working Group III as concern which needs to be addressed.

unknowns for an ambitious multilateral instrument to be silent on the matter.[100] If no legal seat is indicated in the treaty, it would be up to some other entity to make that designation. Under the UNCITRAL Rules as they currently stand, the disputing parties in each case would be able to agree to the seat, and if they do not, the tribunal/appellate body itself would presumably be authorized to designate it.[101] In a worst case scenario, therefore, different *leges loci arbitri* may be selected in different disputes under a future permanent body, which would also result in different domestic courts exercising supervisory jurisdiction over what the EU Commission has declared is intended to be "predictable [...] consistent case-law."[102]

With respect to the recent efforts to establish standing tribunals, there is also the possibility that the tribunal itself will determine the place of arbitration once and for all; both CETA and EU-Vietnam treaty authorize the tribunal to "draw up its own working procedures."[103] The scope of this power is unclear, but it is not unreasonable to assume that it includes determining the legal seat (especially not where one is required and has not been otherwise designated).

Furthermore, and more specific to a future appellate body, it is unclear to what extent such a mechanism is compatible with domestic laws. As discussed above at 3.2.4.1, only a limited number of jurisdictions expressly allow for the parties to opt out of the exclusive jurisdiction of domestic courts to rule on the ultimate validity of an arbitral award, while most other arbitration statutes, including the Model Law, are silent on the matter. Any treaty attempting to combine an appellate mechanism with non-ICSID arbitration rules would therefore have to be worded carefully in order to ensure that the two are compatible. By way of comparison, the Code for the Court of Arbitration for Sports (CAS), which is legally seated in Lausanne, Switzerland,[104] contains language restricting the possibility to challenge the award before Swiss courts. It provides that challenges of awards are prevented

> [...] to the extent that the parties have no domicile, habitual residence, or business establishment in Switzerland[105] and that they have expressly excluded all setting aside proceedings in the arbitration agreement or in a subsequent agreement, in particular at the outset of the arbitration

100 Cf. Kaufmann-Kohler and Podesta, para. 102.
101 2010 UNCITRAL Rules, Article 18.
102 COM(2017) 493, p.2.
103 CETA Article 8.27(10); EU-Vietnam Art 12(10).
104 Court of Arbitration for Sport, Code R28.
105 If both parties have either of these connections to Switzerland, an exclusion agreement is not valid under Swiss law, see PILA 192(1).

Another version of utilizing non-ICSID rules in conjunction with a future reformed option of dispute resolution would be to change the nature of non-ICSID arbitration as it has been known to date. Speaking specifically for the UNCITRAL Rules, it is theoretically possible – although complicated – for states to agree to only certain parts of the Rules. An instructive example is the US-Iran Claims Tribunal, where the Tribunal modified certain aspects of the 1976 UNCITRAL Rules, as discussed in Chapter 2. One way to avoid the identified uncertainties associated with the legal seat for a future dispute resolution system would be to "de-localize" the arbitration. Article 18 of the 2010 UNCITRAL Rules provides for a place of arbitration, and the Rules also contain one reference to pending jurisdictional determinations by a court.[106] However, the Rules are an instrument that does not contain any mandatory norms. In a treaty, states could agree to modify the UNCITRAL Rules and replace these provisions with something else, or remove them altogether. Similar to the way the ICSID Convention works as the "*lex loci arbitri*" in ICSID cases, the treaty in question would then supplement the arbitration rules as the outer framework for the procedure. One major point of controversy in this scenario would be the enforcement of the awards rendered under the auspices of such a treaty: the availability of the New York Convention is doubtful for awards with "no nationality."[107] This option does not seem to have been contemplated to date, at least not publicly. On the contrary, discussions seem to assume a wholesale use of the UNCITRAL Rules.[108]

In institutional practice so far, when designating the legal seat for treaty-based disputes the ICC and the SCC have favoured their respective home jurisdictions, seemingly on an assumption which involves a mix of the robust arbitration experience and "pro-arbitration" courts in Stockholm and Paris, combined with an estimation of what the disputing parties view as sufficiently "neutral" (in the sense that neither party is connected to the jurisdiction in question). This is essentially the way that the place of arbitration is designated in commercial arbitration. Based on the present study's finding, however, there might be reasons to view treaty-based cases differently. Given that most such challenges involve jurisdictional challenges, institutions might benefit from also considering different jurisdictions' approach to issues that are more specific to treaty-based arbitrations, such as the standard of review, and approach

106 UNCITRAL Rules, Article 23(3).

107 The ICSID Convention circumvents this problem by establishing its own enforcement mechanism.

108 See for example CETA Article 8.23; EU-Vietnam Investment Protection Agreement Article 3.33(2); 2018 Dutch Model BIT Article 19(1)(b); 2018 Indian Model BIT Article 16.1(c).

to treaty interpretation. For example, a challenge against an "English," "Singaporean" or "Swedish" award will likely involve a *de novo* trial, largely argued along lines of international law, whereas a "Canadian" or an "American" award will not necessarily be treated the same way. Furthermore, each jurisdiction is characterized by procedural particularities that are not necessarily discernible simply from that state's arbitration legislation. These particularities may affect how, when and by whom the jurisdiction of an arbitral tribunal is reviewed at the post-award stage. The experience of challenged non-ICSID awards so far ought to inspire reflection for treaty drafters.

5.5 Concluding Remarks

Although the competence to determine the jurisdictional scope of an investment treaty rests with the arbitral tribunal faced with the dispute, this text has shown that there are qualifications to this assumption. Both domestic courts and international commercial arbitration institutions have affected the scope of arbitral jurisdiction in individual treaty-based cases, to an extent that is arguably of relevance beyond the individual disputes.

For domestic courts, perhaps the clearest example is most courts' *de novo* review, when they have been asked to determine the scope of arbitral tribunals' jurisdiction within the frames of challenge proceedings. Similar to most norms in investment treaties, arbitral tribunal jurisdiction is generally sparsely formulated. The distance between norm and interpretation leaves room for domestic courts to construe the scope of the tribunal's mandate.[109] This is especially true in the many cases where courts have allowed for a new assessment of the legal points argued before the tribunal: in this scenario, the court has considerable margin to construe the scope of jurisdiction. The frequently repeated mantra that set-aside proceedings are concerned solely with the "integrity and fairness" of the proceedings[110] therefore deserves to be modified somewhat, at least as far as matters of arbitral jurisdiction are concerned. There are numerous examples of domestic courts engaging substantively with jurisdictional issues, without regard to the earlier arbitral procedure.

---

109 Cf. J E Viñuales, "Sources of International Investment Law: Conceptual Foundations of Unruly Practices," in S Besson and J d'Aspremont (eds.), The Oxford Handbook of the Sources of International Law, Oxford University Press, 2017. p. 1080.

110 Especially in the context of UNCITRAL Working Group III, see A/CN.9/WG.III/WP.149, para. 10.

For the ICC and the SCC, the clearest example of their influence over tribunal jurisdiction is the indirect authority vested in the institutions in their capacity as drafters of the arbitration rules referred to in investment treaties. One illustration of this is the relatively new emergency arbitration mechanism, which is available in treaty cases under the SCC Rules but seemingly excluded from the ICC Rules. The practical impact of institutional rule-making in some cases goes beyond the limited role assigned to them by an axiomatic insistence that they facilitate separate disputes between two parties; while responding to users' expectations, the institutions simultaneously shape those expectations. The effective introduction, by the SCC, of emergency arbitration in over hundreds of investment treaties is the clearest example of this.

In the case of institutional *administration* – as opposed to rule-making – the evidence is more limited that the institutions have used their treaty mandate in ways that have affected jurisdiction. One exception is the regular designations of the *lex loci arbitri*, with the often-essential consequences this has for tribunal jurisdiction, as demonstrated by the court practice discussed in Chapter 3. In order to satisfactorily study the extent of the case administration's effect on tribunal jurisdiction, a different type of study is required, going beyond the dogmatic analysis of awards and decisions made here. It is possible that a more sociologically-focused study would come to a different conclusion, in particular with respect to the nature of the permanent secretariats.

Paradoxically, commercial institutions seem readier to accept that they are part of a larger system than do domestic courts. Generally speaking, commercial institutions are responsive to concerns and seemingly mindful of their role in the architecture of investment arbitration. Both institutions studied here expressly considered treaty-based arbitration in the most recent version of their respective rules. Furthermore, when updating the rules, but also in external communication, the institutions recognize that they contribute to a procedural best practice. It has also been argued in this book that institutions also engage in a certain degree of treaty "gap-filling" by updating their arbitration rules. It is not as clear that the institutions fully appreciate the consequences of this role. In practice, the content of many treaties' arbitration clauses has been developed by the ICC and the SCC.

A premise for this study has been that investment treaty arbitration is characterized by internal fragmentation, in the sense that there are several different actors overseeing the adjudication of disputes. This is relevant, as the number of non-ICSID cases appear to grow, while at the same time there is multilateral pressure to reconsider the way investment disputes have been adjudicated to date. As part of any overhaul of legal principles, it is beneficial to know what is being reformed. In UNCITRAL Working Group III, states have agreed by consensus that concerns associated with arbitral tribunal decision-making justify reform. Taking this consensus on its words, it would be helpful to recognize that not only arbitral tribunals make decisions in investment treaty arbitration. The present text has shown that domestic courts in particular, but in an indirect manner also commercial arbitration institutions, have impacted the scope of jurisdiction. Depending on the applicable legal framework, what and how an arbitral tribunal decides disputes may differ, and often in fact has differed, from case to case. If states' preferences are indeed to address inconsistent decision-making through treaty drafting, states ought to recognize that also domestic courts and commercial arbitrations have played a role in determining the jurisdictional scope of disputes.

This book has not primarily employed a normative lens, but rather attempted to depict the nature of investment arbitration's internal fragmentation. It has explained, for example, that different approaches in different domestic courts can be explained by variances in domestic legal frameworks, or by different jurisdictions' approach to international law generally. Furthermore, the ICC and the SCC are institutions that are influenced by commercial arbitration, as manifested, for example, by both institutions' preference for "arbitration-friendly" jurisdictions as places of arbitration and (at least in the SCC case) the introduction of emergency arbitration in treaty-based cases. In short, there is nothing surprising or unexpected about different disputes being arbitrated in different manners. It should be noted, therefore, that the mere presence of several different types of decision-makers is not inherently undesirable. English courts approach the review of jurisdictional standards in a manner that differs from Canadian courts. The ICC Rules regulate emergency arbitration differently from the SCC Rules or, for that matter, from the ICSID Convention.

The multitude of potential decision-making bodies and the associated risk for diverging procedures and outcomes – which has been called internal fragmentation in this book – might rather be viewed as pluralism, which increases legitimacy and political acceptability of the international norms enshrined in investment treaties.[111] For example, an argument could be made that domestic courts are more accountable review bodies than are international organizations. Similarly, commercial arbitration institutions could be viewed as an expression of disputing party preference – both of states, who refer to the institutions and/or their rules in treaties, and of investors, who request arbitration relying on this state consent even when other avenues are available.

---

111 Cf. WW Burke-White, "International Legal Pluralism," (2005) 25 Mich J Int'l L 963, at 978.

The point here is not that the varying jurisdictional consequences of applying non-ICSID arbitration rules to treaty disputes somehow ought to be avoided. Rather, the argument advanced is that these varying consequences ideally should be the result of an educated choice by the states that authorize them in treaties. This has most likely not often been the case so far; by agreeing to non-ICSID arbitration in a treaty clause that does not specify further procedural details, states have in practice authorized other actors to provide those procedural details at a later stage. Given the expressed state concerns with unpredictability, a good case can be made that an examination this practice to date is valuable.

More generally, the presence of non-ICSID arbitration on the investment treaty map significantly contributes to the lack of a "deliberative hub" in investment arbitration. If, in theory, ICSID had remained the only arbitral forum provided for in investment treaties, ICSID could have been this hub, where states could meet in a single multilateral setting to discuss and share information about investment treaties and arbitration. To a certain extent these discussions were always bound to take place in several different fora at the same time – such as UNCITRAL, OECD and UNCTAD, to mention three platforms where discussions are currently taking place – but the fact that arbitrations are governed by a number of different rules complicates matters. Had ICSID remained the exclusively available arbitration forum, it would have been the natural meeting place for states and other stakeholders, presumably including also non-ICSID states.

In the more general fragmentation discussion in international law, fears were initially expressed about the threats posed by the increasing divergence into separate specialized fields. However, as put by the editors of Comparative International Law, "the international system has learned to live with some degree of divergence without descending into crisis."[112] This seems to ring true also for investment arbitration, where internal fragmentation has so far not been perceived as a problem.[113] The findings in this book, while emphasizing differences in approaches to arbitral tribunal jurisdiction in various ways, does not seem to immediately undermine the legitimacy or existence of investment treaty arbitration.

That being said, the fragmenting implications of involving a multitude of (different types of) actors have not previously been part of any conversation

---

112 A Roberts et al in A Roberts et al (eds.), p. 28. See also generally M Andenas and E Bjorge (eds.), A Farewell to Fragmentation – Reassertion and Convergence in International Law, Cambridge University Press, 2015.

113 S Schill, "W(h)ither Fragmentation," p. 893

concerning the future legitimacy of investment treaty arbitration. While there is plenty of critical discussion about many aspects of this particular type of dispute resolution, little emphasis has been placed on the distinction between ICSID and other arbitration rules. On the contrary, most reform discussions seem to take place on the assumption that both ICSID and non-ICSID rules will co-exist also in future treaty-making, without recognizing that there are differences between the two.

For the future, it is up to states to draft investment treaties that identify the involvement of domestic courts (and, by extension, domestic law), as well as commercial arbitration institutions, in the adjudication of investment disputes. So far, there is little evidence that this will happen in the near future, but hopefully the findings in this book can contribute to furthering the understanding of the implications of consenting to treaty-based non-ICSID arbitration.

Bibliography

Articles, Book Chapters, Monographs etc

S Abercrombie Baker & MD Davis, *The UNCITRAL Arbitration Rules in Practice – The Experience of the Iran-United States Claims Tribunal,* Kluwer Law and Taxation Publishers, 1992.

G Aksen, "The Iran-U.S. Claims Tribunal and the UNCITRAL Arbitration Rules – An Early Comment," in J Schultsz and A. van den Berg (eds), *The Art of Arbitration: Essays on International Arbitration,* Liber Amicorum Pieter Sanders, Kluwer, 1982.

W Alschner and Dmitriy Skougarevskiy, "Mapping the Universe of International Investment Agreements," *Journal of International Economic Law*, Vol. 19, No. 3, 2016

J Alvarez, "A BIT on Custom," (2009) 42 NYUJ Intl L & Poly 17.

J Alvarez, *International Organizations as Law-makers,* Oxford University Press, 2010.

J Alvarez, *The Public International Law Regime Governing International Investment,* Recueil des cours, Vol. 344 (2009).

K.H Ameli, "The Application of the Rules of the Iran-United States Claims Tribunal," in W.P. Heere (ed.), *International Law and The Hague's 750th Anniversary*, Asser Press, 1999.

A Amissah, "The ACP/EEC Conciliation and Arbitration Rules," 8 Arb. Int'l, 167 (1992). Cited as "A Amissah."

A Anghie, "International Financial Institutions," in C Reus-Smit (ed.), *The Politics of International Law,* Cambridge University Press, 2004.

H P Aust and G Nolte (eds.), *The Interpretation of International Law by Domestic Courts: Uniformity, Diversity, Convergence,* Oxford University Press, 2016. Cited as "Aust & Nolte (eds.)."

F Baetens, "Enforcement of Arbitral Awards: 'to ICSID or Not to ICSID" is Not the Question', in T Weiler and I Laird, (eds.) *Investment Treaty Arbitration and International Law.* New York: Juris, 2012, pp. 211–228. Cited as: "F Baetens, To ICSID or Not to ICSID."

F Baetens (ed.), *Legitimacy of Unseen Actors in International Adjudication*, Cambridge University Press, forthcoming 2019.

H Bagner, "Enforcement of International Commercial Contracts by Arbitration: Recent Developments," (1982) 14 Case Western Reserve J Intl L 573.

C Balchin, L K-H Chung, et al. (eds), *The Backlash against Investment Arbitration*, Kluwer Law International, 2010.

M N Barnett and M Finnemore, "The Politics, Power, and Pathologies of International Organizations," International Organization, Vol. 53, No. 4 (Autumn, 1999), 699–732

P Bernardini, "International Commercial Arbitration and Investment Treaty Arbitration: Analogies and Differences," in D D Caron, S W Schill, A Cohen S Mutny and E E Triantafilou, *Practising Virtue: Inside International Arbitration,* Oxford University Press, 2015.

A K Bjorklund, "Sovereign Immunity as a Barrier to the Enforcement of Investor-State Arbitral Awards: The Re-Politicization of International Investment Disputes," in D Bray, H L Bray, *International Arbitration and the Courts,* Juris, 2015.

G Blum, "Bilateralism, Multilateralism and the Architecture of International Law," (2008) 49 Harv Int'l LJ 32.

G Born, International Commercial Arbitration, Second Edition, Kluwer Law International, 2014. Cited as: "G Born."

E de Brabandere, *Investment Treaty Arbitration as Public International Law: Procdeural Aspects and Implications,* Cambridge University Press, 2014. Cited as "E de Brabandere, Investment Treaty Arbitration as Public International Law."

E De Brabandere, "Arbitral Decisions As a Source of International Investment Law", in: T Gazzini. and E De Brabandere, (eds.) *International Investment Law. The Sources of Rights and Obligations,* Martinus Nijhoff Publishers, 2012. Cited as "E de Brabandere, Arbitral Decisions as a Source of International Investment Law."

A Broches, *Observations on the Finality of ICSID Awards* (1991), reprinted in A Broches, *Selected Essays – World Bank, ICSID, and Other Subjects of Public and Private International Law,* Martinus Nijhoff (1995).

K Bondar, "Annulment of ICSID and Non-ICSID Investment Awards: Differences in the Extent of Review" (2015) 32 Journal of International Arbitration, Issue 6, pp. 621–675.

A Boyle and C Chinkin, *The Making of International Law,* Oxford University Press, 2007.

C Brower, "Ibrahim Shihata and the Resolution of International Investment Disputes: The Masterful Missionary", ICSID Review - Foreign Investment Law Journal, Volume 15, Issue 2.

C N. Brower & J D. Drueschke, *The Iran-United States Claims Tribunal,* Martinus Nijhoff Publishers, 1998. Cited as "Brower & Drueschke."

KH Böckstiegel, "States in the International Arbitral Process", 2 ARB.INT'L 22 (1986).

KH Böckstiegel, "A Special Arbitration Convention – The Algiers Declarations Creating the Iran-United States Claims Tribunal and Their Application," in Euro-Arab Arbitration Conference, Port el Kantaoui, 1987.

KH Böckstiegel, *The Iran - United States Claims Tribunal - A Unique Example of Arbitrating for Peace,* in J Dahlquist, U Franke and A Magnusson (eds.), *Arbitrating for Peace,* Kluwer, 2016.

K-H Böckstiegel, "Commercial and Investment Arbitration: How Different Are They Today? The Lalive Lecture 2012" (2012) 28(4) Arb Int'l 577.

A Carlevaris, "Preliminary Matters: Objections, Bi-furcation, Request for Provisional Measures," in C Giorgetti (ed.), *Litigating International Investment Disputes: A Practitioner's Guide,* Brill, 2014

D Caron, "The Nature of the Iran-United States Claims Tribunal and the Evolving Structure of International Dispute Resolution," 84 Am. J. Int'l L. (1990). Cited as "D Caron, The Nature of the Iran-United States Claims Tribunal."

D Caron and L Caplan, *The UNCITRAL Arbitration Rules - A Commentary,* Oxford University Press 2013. Cited as "Caron & Caplan."

D Caron and M Pellonpää, *The UNCITRAL Arbitration Rules as Interpreted and Applied by the Iran-U.S. Claims Tribunal,* Finnish Lawyer's Publishing, 1995, p. 21.

J Castello, "Unveiling the 2010 UNCITRAL Arbitration Rules," 65 Dispute Journal, Issue 2/3.

W Christopher (ed.), *American Hostages in Iran – The Conduct of a Crisis,* Yale University Press, 1985.

B W Daly and F C Smith, "Comment on the Differing Legal Frameworks of Investment Treaty Arbitration and Commercial Arbitration as Seen Through Precedent, Annulment, and Procedural Rules," in A J van den Berg (ed.), *50 Years of the New York Convention: ICCA International Arbitration Conference, ICCA Congress Series, Volume 14,* Kluwer Law International, 2009, pp. 151–164.

G R Delaume, "ICSID Arbitration and the Courts," The American Journal of International Law, Vol. 77, No. 4 (Oct., 1983), pp. 784–803.

G R Delaume, "The Finality of Arbitration Involving States: Recent Developments," 5 ARB. INT'L 21 (1989)

D A Desierto, "Contract, Governance, or a "Public-Private Partnership Lens? Methodological Consequences in International Investment Law," in A Reinisch, M E Footer and C Binder (eds.), *Select Proceedings of the European Society of International Law,* Volume 5, 2016.

R Dolzer and M Stevens, *Bilateral Investment Treaties,* Martinus Nijhoff Publishers, 1995. Cited as "Dolzer & Stevens."

R Dolzer and C Schreuer, *Principles of International Investment Law,* Oxford University Press, 2nd ed., 2012. Cited as "Dolzer & Schreuer."

Z Douglas, "The Hybrid Foundations of Investment Treaty Arbitration," British Yearbook of International Law, 2003; 74:1 151–289. Cited as: "Z Douglas, 'The Hybrid Foundations'."

Z Douglas, *The International Law of Investment Claims,* Cambridge University Press, 2009.

O K Fauchald and A Nollkaemper (eds.), *The Practice of International and National Coruts and the (De-)Fragmentation of International Law,* Bloomsbury, 2012. Cited as "O K Fauchald and A Nollkaemper (eds.)."

M B Feldman, "The Annulment Proceedings and the Finality of ICSID Arbitral Awards," 2 ICSID Rev – FILJ 85.

J Fernandez-Armesto, "Different Systems for the Annulment of Investment Awards," ICSID Review Foreign Investment Law Journal, Volume 26, Issue 1, 1 March 2011, pp 128–146.

J Fry, S Greenberg and F Mazza, *The Secretariat's Guide to ICC Arbitration - A Practical Commentary on the 2012 ICC Rules of Arbitration from the Secretariat of the ICC International Court of Arbitration,* International Chamber of Commerce (ICC), 2012. Cited as "Fry, Greenberg & Mazza."

E Gaillard, "CIRDI: Chronique des sentences arbitrales," 114 Journal du Droit International 135 (1987).

N Gallagher and W Shan, *Chinese Investment Treaties – Policies and Practice,* Oxford University Press, 2009.

R Gerbay, *The Function of Arbitral Institutions,* Kluwer, 2016. Cited as: "R Gerbay."

CS Gibson & CR Drahozal, "Iran-United States Claims Tribunal Precedent in Investor-State Arbitration," Journal of International Arbitration 23(6): 521–546, 2006.

L Gouiffès and L Chatelain, "L'Annulation En France des Sentences Arbitrales Rendues Sur Le Fondement de Traités D'Investissement," Revue de l'arbitrage, 2017, no. 3, pp. 839 et seq

G-R de Groot, "Legal Translation," in J M. Smits (ed.), *Elgar Encyclopedia of Comparative Law,* 2nd ed., Edward Elgar, 2012.

G van Harten, *Investment Treaty Arbitration and Public Law,* Oxford University Press, 2008, pp. 54–56.

R Higgins, "Policy Considerations and the International Judicial Process," International and Comparative Law Quarterly 17(1) 58–84.

R Higgins, *Problems and Process: International Law and How We Use It,* Clarendon, 1994.

K Hobér, *Selected Writings on Investment Treaty Arbitration,* Studentlitteratur, 2013.

K Hobér and N Eliasson, "Review of non-ICSID Awards by Municipal Courts" in K Yannaca-Small (ed.), *Arbitration Under International Investment Agreements: A Guide to the Key Issues,* 2nd ed., Oxford University Press, 2018. Cited as: "K Hobér & N Eliasson."

K Hobér with J Dahlquist Cullborg, *Investment Treaty Arbitration – Problems and Exercises,* Edward Elgar, 2018.

K Hobér, A Magnusson and M Öhrström (eds), *Between East and West: Essays in Honour of Ulf Franke,* Juris, 2010.

U Holmbäck (ed.), *Arbitration in Sweden,* Stockholm Chamber of Commerce, 1977.

J J van Hof, *Commentary on the UNCITRAL Arbitration Rules – The Application by the Iran-U.S. Claims Tribunal,* Kluwer Law and Taxation Publishers, 1991. Cited as "J J van Hof."

N Horn, "Current Use of the UNCITRAL Arbitration Rules in the Context of Investment Arbitration, Arbitration International," Vol. 24, No. 4.

J Husa, "Functional Method in Comparative Law – Much Ado About Nothing?," European Property Law Journal, 2 (1), 4–21.

A Håvedal-Ipp, "A Historical Perspective on the China-Sweden Arbitration Connection," China Business Law Journal, September 2015.

DL Jones, "The Iran-United States Claims Tribunal: Private Rights and State Responsbility," (1984) 24(2) Virg. J. Int'l L.

J Karton, *The Culture of International Arbitration and the Evolution of Contract Law*, Oxford University Press, 2013.

G Kaufmann-Kohler, "Arbitral Precedent: Dream, Necessity or Excuse," Arbitration International, Vol. 23(3) pp. 357 – 378.

C R Kelly, "The Politics of Legitimacy in the UNCITRAL Working Methods," in T Brude, M L. Busch, A Porges (eds.), *The Politics of International Economic Law,* Cambridge University Press, 2011.

R Khan, *The Iran-United States Claims Tribunal – Controversies, Cases and Contribution,* Martinus Nijhoff Publishers 1990.

M Kinnear and F Grob, "Asian Agricultural Products Limited v. Sri Lanka: 25 Years Later," in A Magnusson, U Franke and J Dahlquist, *Arbitrating for Peace*, Kluwer, 2016.

A Kjeldgaard-Pedersen, *The International Legal Personality of the Individual,* Oxford University Press, 2018.

HE Kjos, *Applicable Law in Investor-State Arbitration,* Oxford University Press, 2013.

K Knop, "Here and There: International Law in Domestic Courts," (2000) 32 New York University JILP 501.

A Kulick and J Dahlquist Cullborg, "International Investment Law and Arbitration Before Domestic Courts," in A Nollkaemper, Y Shany and A Tzanakopoulos, *Engagement of Domestic Courts with International Law,* Oxford University Press, (forthcoming 2019). Cited as "A Kulick and J Dahlquist Cullborg in Nollkamper, Shany and Tzanakopoulos (eds.)."

H Lauterpacht, "Decisions of Municipal Courts as a Source of International Law," 10 BRIT Y.B INT'L L 65, 95 (1929).

K Lemmens, "Comparative law as an act of modesty: a pragmatic and realistic approach to comparative legal scholarship," in. M Adams and J Bomhoff, *Practice and Theory in Comparative Law,* Cambridge, 2012, pp. 321–322.

B Leon and L Karimi, "The Canadian Position: Can Parties to an Arbitration Agreement Vary the Statutory Scope of Judicial Review of the Award," ILSA Journal of International & Comparative Law, Vol. 14:2.

JD M Lew, LA Mistelis, and S Kröll, *Comparative International Commercial Arbitration*, Kluwer 2003. Cited as "Lew, Mistelis and Kröll."

R Lillich (ed.), *The Iran-United States Claims Tribunal 1981–1983* (*Seventh Sokol Colloquium*), Virginia Legal Studies, 1984. Cited as "R Lillich (ed.)."

A F Lowenfeld, "The ICSID Convention: Origins and Transformation," 38 Ga. J. Int'l & Comp. L. 51 (2009). Cited as "A Lowenfeld."

J A Maupin, "Public and Private in International Investment Law: An Integrated Systems Approach, 54 Va. J. Int'l L. 367 (2014)." Cited as: "J A Maupin, Public and Private in International Investment Law."

C McLachlan, L Shore and M Weininger, *International Investment Arbitration: Substantive Principles*, Oxford University Press, 2007.

J Merrills, "The Means of Dispute Settlement," in M D Evans (ed.), *International Law*, 4th ed, Oxford University Press, 2014.

J A. Maupin, "Public and Private in International Investment Law: An Integrated Systems Approach," 54 Va. J. Int'l L. 367 (2014) at 372. Cited as "J A Maupin, Public and Private."

A Mills, *The Confluence of Public and Private International Law: Justice, Pluralism and Subsidiarity in the International Constitutional Ordering of Private Law*, Cambridge University Press, 2010. Cited as: A Mills.

M Moser, "Ulf Franke, Stockholm Arbitration and the Bridge to China," in K Hobér, A Magnusson, M Öhrström (eds), *Between East and West: Essays in Honour of Ulf Franke*, Juris 2010. Cited as "M Moser."

M Norton, "The Role of Precedent in the Development of International Investment Law", ICSID Review - Foreign Investment Law Journal, Volume 33, Issue 1, pp. 280–301.

K Partlett, *The Individual in the International Legal System. Continuity and Change in International Law*, Cambridge University Press, 2010.

M Paparinskis, "Investment Treaty Arbitration as Public International Law: Procedural Aspects and Implications. By Eric De Brabandere," The Cambridge Law Journal, 75(1), 2016 (book review).

A R Parra, *The History of ICSID*, Oxford University Press, 2012. Cited as "A Parra."

J Paulsson, "Arbitration Without Privity", Foreign Investment Law Journal, Vol. 10, No. 2 (1995). Cited as "J Paulsson, 'Arbitration Without Privity'."

J Paulsson, "The Role of Precedent in Investment Arbitration", in K Yannaca-Small (ed.), *Arbitration under International Investment Agreements. A Guide to Key Issues*, Oxford, 2010.

A Paulus, "International Adjudication", in S Besson and J Tasioulas (eds.), *The Philosophy of International Law*, Oxford University Press, 2010.

J Pauwelyn, "At the Edge of Chaos? Foreign Investment Law as a Complex Adaptive System, How It Emerged and How It Can Be Reformed," ICSID Review – Foreign Investment Law Journal 29. Cited as "J Pauwelyn, At the Edge of Chaos."

T Piiparinen, "Secretariats," in J K Cogan, I Hurd and I Johnstone (eds.), *The Oxford Handbook of International Organizations,* Oxford University Press, 2016.

S Puig, "Emergence & Dynamism in International Organizations: ICSID, Investor-State Arbitration, and International Investment Law," 44 Geo. J. Int'l L. 531 (2013). Cited as "S Puig, Emergence & Dynamism."

A Redfern and M Hunter, *Redfern and Hunter on International Arbitration – Student Version,* Oxford University Press, 2009. Cited as "Redfern & Hunter."

A Redfern, "ICSID – Losing its Appeal?," 3 ARB. INT'L 98 (1987), 116–117.

M Reimann, "Comparative Law and Neighbouring Disciplines," in M Bussani and U Mattei (eds.), *The Cambridge Companion to Comparative Law,* Cambridge, 2012.

A Reinisch, "The Proliferation of International Dispute Settlement Mechanisms: The Threat of Fragmentation vs. the Promise of a More Effective System? Some Reflections From the Perspective of Investment Arbitration," in I Buffard, J Crawford, A Pellet and S Wittich (eds.), *International Law between Universalism and Fragmentation. Festschrift in Honour of Gerhard Hafner,* Brill, 2008.

M Reisman, "Canute Confronts the Tide: States vs Tribunals and the Evolution of the Minimum Standard in Customary International Law," (2015) 30(3) ICSID Review, Foreign Investment Law Journal 616.

J C Reitz, "How to do Comparative Law," 46 AM. J. COMP.L. 617.

A Roberts, "Clash of Paradigms: Actors and Analogies Shaping the Investment Treaty System," The American Journal of International Law, Vol. 107, No. 1 (January 2013), pp. 45–94. Cited as: "A Roberts, 'Clash of Paradigms'."

A Roberts, "Power and Persuasion in Investment Treaty Arbitration: The Dual Role of States," 104 Am. J. Int'l L. 179 2010. Cited as "A Roberts, Power and Persuasion."

A Roberts, P B Stephan, P-H Verdier and M Versteeg (eds.), Comparative International Law, Oxford University Press, 2018. Cited as "A Roberts et al, Comparative International Law."

A Roberts, P B Stephan, P-H Verdier and M Versteeg, "Conceptualizing Comparative International Law" in A Roberts et al.

A Roberts, "Comparative International Law ? The Role of National Courts in Creating and Enforcing International Law, ICLQ vol 60, January 2011 pp 57–92. Cited as "A Roberts, ICLQ."

J W. Salacuse, *The Law of Investment Treaties,* Oxford, 2010.

P Sanders, "Has the Moment Come to Revise the UNCITRAL Rules of Arbitration?," (2004) 20 Arb Intl 243.

M Scherer, V Heiskanen and S Moss, "Domestic Review of Investment Treaty Arbitrations: The Swiss Experience," 27 ASA Bulletin 2/2009, pp. 256–277.

S W Schill, "Sources of international investment law," in S Besson and J d'Aspremont (eds.), *The Oxford Handbook of the Sources of International Law,* Oxford University Press, 2017. Cited as "S Schill, Sources of international investment law."

S W Schill, *The Multilateralization of International Investment Law*, Cambridge University Press, 2009. Cited as "S Schill, Multilateralization."

S W Schill, "W(h)ither Fragmentation: On the Literature and Sociology of International Investment Law," European Journal of International Law 22(3):875–908, 2011. Citesd as: "S Schill, W(h)ither Fragmentation."

S W Schill, C. J. Tams and R. Hofmann (eds.), *International Investment Law and History*, Cheltenham, 2018.

S W Schill, 'From Sources to Discourse: Investment Treaty Jurisprudence as the New Custom?' BIICL 16th Investment Treaty Forum Public Conference: Is There an Evolving Customary International Law on Investment?, 2011, www.biicl.org/files/5630_stephan_schill.pdf, visited 13 June 2018.

C Schreuer, "Calvo's Grandchildren: The Return of Local Remedies in Investment Arbitration," in The Law and Practice of International Courts and Tribunals 4: 1–17, Brill, 2005.

C Schreuer, "Three Generations of ICSID Annulment Proceedings," in E Gaillard and Y Banifatemi (eds.), *Annulment of ICSID Awards*, IAI Series on International Arbitration, No. 1, Juris, 2004.

A-V Schlaepfer, 'The Role of the Institution at the Commencement of the Proceedings', in *Arbitral Institutions Under Scrutiny: ASA Special Series No. 40*, p. 60.

S Schwebel, "Foreword," in A Broches, *Selected Essays – World Bank, ICSID, and Other Subjects of Public and Private International Law*, Martinus Nijhoff (1995).

J M Selby & D P Stewart, "Practical and Legal Aspects of Arbitrating Claims before the Iran-United States Claims Tribunal," 18 Va. Int'l L. 211 (1984).

L N Skovgaard Poulsen, *Bounded Rationality and Economic Diplomacy: The Politics of Investment Treaties in Developing Countries*, Cambridge University Press, 2015. Cited as "L Poulsen, Bounded Rationality."

J M Smits, *What is Legal Doctrine? On the Aims and Methods of Legal-Dogmatic Research*, Maastricht European Private Law Institute Working Paper No. 2015/06, available at https://papers.ssrn.com/sol3/papers.cfm?abstract_id=2644088, visited 19 June 2018. The paper was subsequently included as a chapter in R van Gestel, H-W Micklitz & E L. Rubin (eds.), *Rethinking Legal Scholarship: A Transatlantic Dialogue*, Cambridge University Press, 2017, pp. 207–228.

A M Steingruber, *Consent in International Arbitration*, Oxford University Press, 2012. Cited as: "A M Steingruber."

DP Stewart & LB Sherman, "Developments at the Iran-United States Claims Tribunal: 1981–1983," in R Lillich (ed.), *The Iran-United States Claims Tribunal 1981–1983* (*Seventh Sokol Colloquium*), Virginia Legal Studies, 1984.

A Stone Sweet and F Grisel, *The Evolution of International Arbitration: Judicialization, Governance, Legitimacy*, Oxford University Press, 2017. Cited as: "Stone Sweet and Grisel."

B Simma, "Foreword," in A von Bogdany and I Venzke (eds.), *International Judicial Lawmaking – On Public Authority and Democratic Legitimation in Global Governance*, Springer, 2012.

T St John, *The Rise of Investor-State Arbitration: Politics, Law and Unintended Consequences,* Oxford University Press, 2018. Cited as: "T St John."

AR Sureda, "Precedent in Investment Treaty Arbitration," in C Binder, U Kriebaum, A Reinisch and S Wittich (eds.), *International Investment Law for the 21st Century: Essays in Honour of Christoph Schreuer*, Oxford University Press, 2009.

R Teitelbaum, "Challenges of Arbitrators at the Iran-United States Claims Tribunal Defining the Role of the Appointing Authority," Journal of International Arbitration 23(6): 547–562, 2006.

H Thirway, "The Sources of International Law," in M D Evans (ed.), *International Law,* 4th ed., Oxford, 2010.

S J. Toope, *Mixed International Arbitration,* Cambridge University Press, 1990. Cited as "S Toope, Mixed International Arbitration."

K J. Vandevelde, *Bilateral Investment Treaties – History, Policy and Interpretation,* Oxford University Press, 2010. Cited as "K Vandevelde."

J Viñuales, "Sources of International Investment Law: Conceptual Foundations of Unruly Practices," in S Besson and J d'Aspremont (eds.), *The Oxford Handbook of the Sources of International Law*, Oxford University Press, 2017.

G Wang, "Consent in Investor-State Arbitration: A Critical Analysis" (2014) 13 Chinese Journal of International Law 335.

B A Warwas, *The Liability of Arbitral Institutions: Legitimacy Challenges and Functional Responses,* Springer, 2017. Cited as: "B Warwas."

J H H Weiler, "The Rule of Lawyers and the Ethos of Diplomats: Reflections on the Internal and External Legitimacy of WTO Dispute Settlement," Journal of World Trade 35(2):191–207, 2001.

I Venzke, *How Interpretation Makes International Law – On Semantic Change and Normative Twists,* Oxford University Press, 2012.

G Verhoosel, "Annulment and Enforcement Review of Treaty Awards: To ICSID or Not to ICSID," ICSID Review - Foreign Investment Law Journal, Volume 23, Issue 1, 1 March 2008, pp. 119–154. Cited as "G Verhoosel, To ICSID or Not to ICSID."

G Wang, "Consent in Investor-State Arbitration: A Critical Analysis", Chinese Journal of International Law, 2014, pp. 335–361.

G Wetter, "The Iran-United States Claims Tribunal," SvJT 1982 p. 193.

G Wetter, *The International Arbitral Process: public and private,* Oceana Publications, 1979.

JW Yackee and J Wong, "The 2006 Procedural and Transparency Related Amendments to the ICSID Arbitration Rules: Model Intentions, Moderate Proposals, and Modest Returns," in KP Sauvant (ed.), *The Yearbook on International Investment Law & Policy*, Oxford University Press, 2010.

K Zweigert and H Köts, "The Method of Comparative Law," in *An Introduction to Comparative Law,* 3rd ed., Oxford University Press, 1998.

Arbitral Awards and International Judgments

AAPL v. Sri Lanka, ICSID Case No. ARB/87/3, Final Award 27 June 1990.

Amco Asia Corp, Pan American Development, Ltd and PT Amco Indonesia v. Republic of Indonesia (ICSID Case No. ARB/81/1), Decision on the Application for Annulment, 16 May, 1986, 1 ICSID Reports 509. Cited as "Amco I Annulment Decision."

Arbitration between the Republic of Croatia and the Republic of Slovenia, Croatia v Slovenia, Partial Award, PCA Case No 2012-04, ICGJ 509 (PCA 2016), 30th June 2016, Permanent Court of Arbitration.

Bilcon of Delaware et al v. Government of Canada, PCA Case No. 2009-04, Award on Jurisdiction and Liability, 17 March, 2015.

ECE Projektmanagement & Kommanditgesellschaft Panta Achtundsechzigste Grundstücksgesellschaft MBH & Co v. The Czech Republic, UNCITRAL, PCA Case No 2010-5, Award, 19 September, 2013.

EnCana Corporation v. Republic of Ecuador, UNCITRAL, LCIA Case No. UN3481.

Enkev Beheer B.V. v. Republic of Poland, PCA Case No. 2013-01, First Partial Award 29 April 2014.

Energoalians TOB v. Republic of Moldova, UNCITRAL, Award, 23 October 2013.

Glamis Gold, Ltd. v. The United States of America, UNCITRAL

Grand River Enterprises Six Nations, Ltd., et al. v. United States of America, UNCITRAL.

GPF GP S.à.r.l v. Republic of Poland, SCC Case No. V 2014/168, Award on Jurisdiction, 1 February 2017. Cited as: "Griffin Group v. Poland."

Himpurna California Energy Ltd. v. Republic of Indonesia, Final Award, October 16, 2009.

Iran-United Claims Tribunal, American Bell International Inc. v. Iran, Award No. ITL 41-48-3, 6 Iran-US CTR at 83.

Iran-United States Claims Tribunal, Award No. 264-264-1. 13 Iran-US CTR at 130.

Iran v United States, Case A/15 (Award No 63-Al15-FT), reprinted in 2 Iran-US C. T.R. 40, at p.43.

Iran-United States Claims Tribunal, E-Systems Inc. V. Islamic Republic of Iran, award No ITM 13-388-FT (4 February, 1983), 2 Iran-US CTR 5.

Iran-United States Claims Tribunal, George W Drucker JR v. Foreign Transaction CO, Case No 121, Chamber Two, Order of 2 May, 1986, as reprinted in Caron & Caplan, p.70.

Klöckner Industrie-Anlagen GmbH and others v. United Republic of Cameroon and Société Camerounaise des Engrais, ICSID Case No. ARB/81/2, Award 21 October, 1983.

Klöckner v. Cameroon, Ad Hoc Committee Decision, 3 May, 1985, 2 ICSID Rep. Cited as "Klöckner I Annulment Decision."

Larsen v. Hawaiian Kingdom, PCA Case 1999-01, Final Award 5 February, 2001.

Maritime International Nominees Establishment (MINE) v. Government of Guinea (Guinea), ICSID Case ARB/84/4, Decision on the Application by Guinea for Partial Annulment of the Arbitral Award, 6 January 1988. Cited as "MINE Annulment Decision."

Methanex Corp v. United States of America, Decisions on Petitions from Third Persons to Intervene as *Amici Curiae,* 15 Jan 2001, UNCITRAL.

Methanex Corp v. United States of America, Partial Award, 7 August 2002 UNCITRAL.

Mohammed Munshi v. Mongolia, SCC Case No. 2018/007, Award on Emergency Measures, 5 February 2018.

Novenergia II - Energy & Environment (SCA) (Grand Duchy of Luxembourg), SICAR v. The Kingdom of Spain, SCC Case No. 2015/063, Final Award, 15 February 2018. Cited as "Novenergia v. Spain."

Occidental Exploration and Production Company v. The Republic of Ecuador, LCIA Case No. UN3467.

PL Holdings S.a.r.l. v. Poland, SCC Case No. 2014/163, Partial Award dated 28 June 2017. Cited as "PL Holdings v. Poland."

Saar Papier Vertriebs GmbH v. Republic of Poland, Interim Award of the Arbitral Tribunal, August 17, 1994.

Saluka Investments B.V. v. Czech Republic, UNCITRAL, Partial Award, March 17, 2006.

SCC Case No. 97/1996.

SCC Case No. 010/2000.

SCC Case No. 093/2004.

SCC Case No. 096/2008.

SCC Case No. 086/2010.

SCC Case No. 067/2012.

SCC Case No. 094/2013.

SCC Case No. 023/2014.

SCC Case No. 183/2014, Emergency Decision.

SCC Case No. 002/2015, Emergency Decision.

Société Générale in respect of DR Energy Holdings Limited and Empresa Distribuidora de Electricidad del Este, S. A.v. The Dominican Republic, UNCITRAL, LCIA Case No. UN 7927.

Slowakische Republik v. Achmea BV , European Court of Justice, C-284/16, Judgment of the Court (Grand Chamber) of 6 March 2018. Cited as: "Achmea."

SPP v. Egypt, ICSID Case No. ARB/84/3, Final Award, 20 May 1992.

ST-AD GmbH v. Republic of Bulgaria, UNCITRAL, PCA Case No. 2011-06, Award on Jurisdiction, 18 July 2013.

United Parcel Service of America Inc. v. Government of Canada, Decision of the Tribunal on Petitions for Intervention and Participation as Amici Curiae, Oct 17th 2001, UNCITRAL.

US. Steel Global Holdings v. The Slovak Republic, PCA Case No. 2013-6.

Windstream Energy LLC v. Government of Canada, UNCITRAL, PCA Case No. 2013-22, Award, 27 September, 2016.

Domestic Court Judgements

Adria v. Croatia, The Hague District Court, HAZ10-4097, Judgement, 15 August 2012. Cited as "Adria v. Croatia, The Hague District Court."

Argentina v. AWG Group Ltd., United States District Court for the District of Columbia, Civil Action No. 15-1057 (BAH), Judgement, 30 September 2016.

Argentina v. AWG Group, United States Court of Appeal for the District of Columbia, Judgement, 3 July 2018.

Argentina v. National Grid PLC, United States District Court for the District of Columbia, Civil Action No. 09-248 (RBW), 28 November 2011.

Argentina v. BG Group, United States Court of Appeals, 17 January 2012. Attorney General of Canada v. William Ralph Clayton, William Richard Clayton.

Douglas Clayton, Daniel Clayton and Bilcoin Delaware, Inc., 2017 FC 214, Federal Court of Canada, Judgement, 22 February 2017.

Auto Connect Sweden AB v. Consafe IT AB, Svea Court of Appeal, T 754-09, 18 May 2009.

Bayview Irrigation District #11 and ors v. Mexico, Ontario Superior Court, Judicial Review 07-CV-340139-PD2, Judgment, 5 May, 2008. Cited as "Bayview v. Mexico, Ontario Superior Court."

BG Group v. Argentina, United States Supreme Court, Case No. 12–138, Judgement, 7 June 2010. Cited as "BG Group v. Argentina, United States Supreme Court."

BG Group v. Argentina, United States Supreme Court, Case No. 12–138, Dissenting Opinion by Chief Justice Roberts, with Justice Kennedy joining, 7 June 2010. Cited as "BG Group v. Argentina, United States Supreme Court, Dissenting Opinion."

Canada v. Mobil Investments Canada Inc. and Murphy Oil Corporation, Superior Court of Justice Ontario, Court File No CV-15-11079-00CL, Judgement, 29 January 2016. Cited as "Canada v. Mobil/Murphy Oil, Superior Court of Justice Ontario."

Canada v. S.D. Myers, Inc, Federal Court of Canada, 2004 FC 38, Judgement, 13 January 2004. Cited as "Canada v. S.D. Myers, Federal Court of Canada."

Cem Uzan v. Turkey, Svea Court of Appeal, T 6582-16, Judgement, 26 February 2018. Cited as "Cem Uzan v. Turkey, Svea Court of Appeal."

Croatia v. MOL, Swiss Federal Tribunal, Case No. 4A_53/2017, Judgement, 17 October 2017.

Czech Republic v. CME, Svea Court of Appeal, T 8735-01, Judgement, 15 May 2003. Cited as "Czech Republic v. CME, Svea Court of Appeal."

Czech Republic v. EMV, High Court of Justice, Queen's Bench Division, Commercial Court, Ventures, 2007 EWHC 2851 (Comm), Judgement, 5 December 2007. Cited as "Czech Republic v. EMV, High Court."

Czech Republic v. Pren Nreka, Paris Court of Appeal, 07/04675, Judgement, 28 September 2008. Cited as "Czech Republic v. Pren Nreka, Paris Court of Appeal."

Czech Republic v. Rupert Joseph Binder, District Court of Prague 1, 21 C 174/2007-78, 22 June 2009.

Czech Republic v. Saluka, Swiss Federal Tribunal, Case No. 4P. 114/2006 /bie, Judgement, 7 September 2006. Cited as "Czech Republic v. Saluka, Swiss Federal Tribunal."

Dames & Moore v. Regan, 453 U.S. 654 (1981), United States Supreme Court. Ecuador v. Occidental Exploration and Production Company, England, High Court, Queen's Bench Division, ([2005] EWHC 774 (Comm)), Judgement, 29 April 2005. Cited as "Ecuador v. Occidental, High Court."

Ecuador v. Occidental Exploration and Production Company, Court of Appeal (England and Wales), ([2005] EWCA Civ 1116), Judgement, 9 September 2005, reported in 138 ILR 92. Cited as "Ecuador v. Occidental, Court of Appeal."

Ecuador v. Chevron Corporation and Texaco Petroleum Company, Hague District Court, 386943/HA ZA and 408948/HA ZA4.4, Judgement, 2 May 2012. Cited as "Ecuador v. Chevron, The Hague District Court."

Ecuador v. Chevron Corporation (USA) & Texaco Petroleum Company, Supreme Court of the Netherlands, ECLI:NL:HR:2014:2837, Judgement, 26 November 2014. Cited as "Ecuador v. Chevron, Supreme Court of the Netherlands."

Energoalians SARL (Komstroy) v Moldova, Cour de cassation, Chambre civile 1, 16-16568, 28 March 2018.

Federal Administrative Chamber of Appeals Buenos Aires, Causa 2.660/2006, 3 July 2007.

French Court of Cassation, 16-16568, Judgement, 28 March 2018.

Government of the Lao People's Democratic Republic v. Sanum Investments, Singapore High Court, [2015] SGHC 15, 20 January 2015. Cited as "Laos v. Sanum, Singapore High Court."

Government of the Lao People's Democratic Republic v. Sanum Investments, The Court of Appeal of the Republic of Singapore, [2016] SGCA 57, 29 September 2016. Cited as "Sanum v. Laos, Singapore Court of Appeal."

GPF GP S.a.r.l v. The Republic of Poland, [2018] EWHC 409 (Comm), Judgement, 2 March 2018, Cited as "Griffin v. Poland, High Court."

Hungary v. EDF, Swiss Federal Tribunal, 4A_34/2015, Judgement, 6 October 2015. Cited as "Hungary v. EDF, Swiss Federal Tribunal."

International Thunderbird Gaming Operations v. United Mexican States, United States District Court for the District of Columbia, Civil Action 06-00748 (HHK), Judgement 14 February, 2007.

Kaliningrad Region v. Lithuania, Paris Court of Appeal, Case No. 09/1953, Judgement, 8 November 2010.

Kazakhstan v. Ascom/Stati et al, Svea Court of Appeal, T 2675-14, Judgement, 9 December 2017. Cited as "Kazakhstan v. Ascom/Stati et al, Svea Court of Appeal."

Kyrgyz Republic v. Petrobart, Svea Court of Appeal, T-5208-05, Judgement, 19 January 2007. Cited as "Kyrgyz Republic v. Petrobart, Svea Court of Appeal."

Latvia v. SwemBalt, Maritime and Commercial Court of Copenhagen, S-22-01, Judgement, 7 January 2003. Cited as "Latvia v. SwemBalt, Maritime and Commercial Court of Copenhagen."

Lebanon v. France Telecom Mobiles, Swiss Federal Tribunal, Judgement, 10 November 2015. Cited as "Lebanon v. France Telecom, Swiss Federal Tribunal."

Lee John Beck and Central Asian Development Corporation v. Kyrgyz Republic, Moscow Arbitrazh Court, Judgement, 5 June 2015.

Lenmorniiprokt OAO v. Arne Larsson & Partner Leasing AB, Swedish Supreme Court, Case Ö 13-09, 16 April 2010.

Mexico v. Metalclad, Supreme Court of British Columbia, 2001 BCSC 664, Judgement, 5 August 2001. Cited as "Mexico v. Metalclad, Supreme Court of British Columbia."

Mexico v. Marvin Roy Feldman Karpa, Court of Appeal for Ontario, 11 January 2005

Mexico v. Cargill, Court of Appeal for Ontario, 2011 ONCA 622, Judgement, 4 October 2011. Cited as "Mexico v. Cargill, Court of Appeal for Ontario."

Moldova v. Energoalians, Paris Court of Appeal, Case No. 13/22531, Judgement, 12 April 2016. Cited as "Moldova v. Energoalians, Paris Court of Appeal."

Pakistani Supreme Court in Societe Generale de Surveillance SA v Pakistan, Secretary, Minister of Finance, Revenue Division and Islamabad, Appeal to Supreme Court, Civil Appeal No 459/2002, Civil Appeal No 460/2002, 2002 SCMR 1694, ILDC 82 (PK 2002).

Poland v. Saar Papier, Swiss Federal Tribunal, Judgement, 20 September 2000. Cited as "Poland v. Saar Papier, Swiss Federal Tribunal."

Saar Papier v. Poland, Swiss Federal Tribunal, 1 March 2002. Cited as "Saar Papier v. Poland, Swiss Federal Tribunal."

Peter and Kristof de Sutter and others v. Madagascar, Paris Court of Appeal, 14/19164, 15 March 2016. Cited as "de Sutter et al v. Madagascar, Paris Court of Appeal."

Poland v. Horthel, Swiss Federal Tribunal, Case No. 4A_157/2017, Judgement, 14 December 2017.

PT Putrabali Adyamulia v. Est Epices, French Court de Cassation, Judgement, 29 June 2007.

Raymond L. Loewen v. United States, United States District Court for the District of Columbia, Civil Action No. 04-2151 (RWR), Judgement, 31 October 2005.

RECOFI v. Vietnam, Swiss Federal Tribunal, 4A_616/2015, Judgement, 20 September 20, 2016. Cited as "RECOFI v. Vietnam, Swiss Federal Tribunal."

Republique de Moldavie v. Société Komstroy (venant aux droits de la société Energoalians), Paris Court of Appeal, 13/22531, Judgement, 12 April 2016.

Russian Federation v. PJSC Ukrnafta and Russia v. Stabil LLC, Swiss Federal Tribunal, 4A_396/2017 and 4A_398/2017, Judgements, 16 October 2018.

Russian Federation v. Franz J. Sedelmayer, Stockholm District Court, T 6-583-98, Judgement, 18 December 2002.

Russian Federation v. RosInvestCo, Stockholm District Court, T 24891-07, 9 November 2011.

Russian Federation v. Yukos, The Hague Court of Appeal, Case No. 200.197.079/01, Judgement, 25 September 2018.

Slovakia v. Achmea, German Federal Supreme Court, Judgement 31 October 2018.

Stans Energy v. Kyrgyz Republic, Moscow Arbitrazh Court Judgement 25 May 2015.

Stockholm District Court T 24891-07, Judgement, 17 November 2008.

Stockholm District Court, T 24891-07, Judgement, 9 November 2011.

Svea Court of Appeal, Ö 9773-08, Judgement, 3 April 2009.

Svea Court of Appeal, T 10060-10, Judgement, 5 September 2013.

Swedish Supreme Court, NJA 2015, p. 991, Judgement, 21 December 2015.

Swedish Supreme Court, Ö 2301-09, Judgement, 12 November 2010.

Swedish Supreme Court, T 778-16, Judgement, 14 December 2016.

Swissborough et al v. Lesotho, Court of Appeal of the Republic of Singapore, Civil Appeal No 149 of 2017, Judgement, 27 November 2018.

Tembec Inc. et al v. United States, United States District Court for the District of Columbia, Civil Action No. 07-1905 (RMC), 14 August 2008.

UK High Court of Justice, [2018] EWHC 409 (Comm), GPF GP S.à.r.l v. The Republic of Poland, Judgement, 2 March 2018.

Ukraine v. Tatneft, Paris Court of Appeal, Case No. 14/17964, Judgement, 29 November 2016. Cited as "Ukraine v. Tatneft, Paris Court of Appeal."

Venezuela v. Garcia Armas and Gracia Gruber, Paris Court of Appeal, Case No. 15/01040, Judgement 25 April 2017.

Y and S, English Commercial Court, [2015] EWHC 612, 13 March 2015.

Reports, Working Papers, etc

2015 International Arbitration Survey: Improvements and Innovations in International Arbitration, by Queen Mary University of London and White & Case Law firm.

Center for International Environmental Law and International Institute for Sustainable Development, *Revising the UNCITAL Arbitration Rules to Address State Arbitrations*, available at http://www.iisd.org/pdf/2007/investment_revising_uncitral_arbitration .pdf., visited 6 January 2019.

Dutch Model BIT, available at https://www.internetconsultatie.nl/investeringsakkoorden, visited 5 January 2019.

J Harrison, *Recent Developments to Promote Transparency and Public Participation in Investment Treaty Arbitration*, University of Edinburgh School of Law Working Paper No. 2011/01.

ICSID, *Backgrounder on Proposals for Amendment of the ICSID Rules*, https://icsid.worldbank.org/en/Documents/Amendment_Backgrounder.pdf, visited 5 January 2019.

ICSID, *The ICSID Caseload – Statistics* (*Issue 2018-2*).

International Law Commission, *Fragmentation of International Law: Difficulties Arising from the Diversification and Expansion of International Law*, UN Doc A/CN.4/682 (2006).

J Paulsson and G Petrochilos, *Revision of the UNCITRAL Arbitration Rules*, September 2006, available at http://www.uncitral.org/uncitral/uncitral_texts/arbitration/2010Arbitration_rules_travaux.html and on file with author. Cited as "Paulsson & Petrochilos."

J Pohl, K Mashigo and A Nohen, *Dispute Settlement Provisions in International Investment Agreements: A Large Sample Survey*, OECD Working Papers on International Investment, 2012/02, OECD Publishing. Cited as "J Pohl, K Mashigo & A Nohen."

M A Raouf, *UNCITRAL Arbitration Rules and the settlement of investment disputes: The experience of CRCICA*. Available at http://www.crcica.org.eg/newsletters/nl201203/UNCITRAL_ARBITRATION_RULES_AND_THE_SETTLEMENT_OF_INVESTMENT_DISPUTES_%20THE%20EXPERIENCE_OF_CRCICA.pdf, visited 7 January 2019 and on file with author.

Model Text for the Indian Bilateral Investment Treaty (available at http://investmentpolicyhub.unctad.org/Download/TreatyFile/3560, visited 5 January 2019).

OECD Freedom of Investment Roundtable 27, *Appointing Authorities and the Selection of Arbitrators in Investor-State Arbitration: An Overview*, Working Paper, DAF/INV/WD(2017)16, 17 October 2017. Cited as "OECD Appointing Authority Paper."

Organization of American States Foreign Trade Information System, Guide to Commercial Arbitration and Other Alternative Dispute Resolution Methods, available at http://www.sice.oas.org/dispute/comarb/icsid/icsid3.asp. Visited 5 January 2019.

UNCTAD IIA Issues Note No. 1, February 2015. Available at http://unctad.org/en/PublicationsLibrary/webdiaepcb2015d1_en.pdf.

UNCTAD, *Recent Developments in Investor-State Dispute Settlement* (*ISDS*) (UNCTAD/WEB/DIAE/PCB/2013/3).

UNCTAD, *Recent developments in the international investment regime* [IIA Issue Note, No. 1, 2018] (UNCTAD/DIAE/PCB/INF/2018/1), 1 May 2018, Issue Note.

Online sources

N Bernasconi-Osterwalder & M Brauch, *Comparative commentary to Brazil's cooperation and investment facilitation agreements* (*CIFAs*) *with Mozambique, Angola, Mexico, and Malawi*, September 2015. Available at http://www.iisd.org/library/

comparative-commentary-brazil-cooperation-and-investment-facilitation-agreements-cifas, visited 5 January 2019.

D Charlotin and L E Peterson, *As Miculas and Romania Spar over Whether Award Has Been Satisfied, a UK Court Orders State to Post Security; UK Enforcement Efforts Remain Stayed Until EU Courts Rule on European Commission's State Aid Determination, https://www.iareporter.com/articles/as-miculas-and-romania-continue-to-spar-over-whether-icsid-award-has-been-satisfied-a-uk-court-orders-state-to-post-security-uk-enforcement-efforts-remain-stayed-until-eu-courts-rule-on-european-com/,* Investment Arbitration Reporter, 31 July, 2018.

IAReporter, *Serbia Disputes: Mytilineos Files a New Arbitration Claim in Long-running Fight, While Solar Park Investor Adds Treaty Claim to Threat of Contract Arbitration,* 10 December 2013, at http://www.iareporter.com/articles/serbia-disputes-mytilineos-files-a-new-bit-claim-in-long-running-fight-while-solar-park-investor-adds-treaty-claim-to-threat-of-contract-arbitration/, Investment Arbitration Reporter.

J Hepburn and L E Peterson, Emergency Arbitrator Bernardo Cremades Orders Mongolian State to Ensure Businessman Has "Reasonable Access" to Counsel, but Declines to Order State to Free Him from Prison," 3 April 2018, https://www.iareporter.com/articles/emergency-arbitrator-bernardo-cremades-orders-state-to-ensure-businessman-has-reasonable-access-to-counsel-but-declines-to-order-state-to-free-him-from-prison/, Investment Arbitration Reporter.

L E Peterson, *Poland Liable for Breach of Germany-Poland BIT; Arbitrators Grappling with Damages in UNCITRAL Proceeding*, 29 June, 2009, available at http://www.iareporter.com/articles/poland-liable-for-breach-of-germany-poland-bit-arbitrators-grappling-with-damages-in-uncitral-proceeding.

L E Peterson, *Cypriot Energy Trader Files Claim Against Poland Under Energy Charter Treaty; Poland has Faced At Least Eight Other Treaty Arbitrations*, 26 August, 2008, available at http://www.iareporter.com/articles/cypriot-energy-trader-files-claim-against-poland-under-energy-charter-treaty-poland-has-faced-at-least-eight-other-treaty-arbitrations/.

L E Peterson, *Kazakhstan seeks to annul \$125 Million ICSID Award in Telecoms dispute; we review earlier Kazakh arbitrations,* http://www.iareporter.com/articles/kazakhstan-seeks-to-annul-125-million-icsid-award-in-telecoms-dispute-we-review-earlier-kazakh-arbitrations/, Investment Arbitration Reporter, 12 November 2008.

A Roberts, *UNCITRAL and ISDS Reforms: Moving to Reform Options … the Process,* EJIL: Talk!, Blog of the European Journal of International Law, 7 November 2018, https://www.ejiltalk.org/uncitral-and-isds-reforms-moving-to-reform-options-the-process/, visited 5 January 2019.

UNCITRAL, Archive of Working Group Audio Recordings, U.N. COMM'N ON INT'L TRADE LAW, http://www.uncitral.org/uncitral/audio/meetings.jsp, 28 November 2017.

Travaux Preparatoire, Historical Documents etc

Address by Aron Broches to the Second Annual Meeting. September 30, 1968.

Concluding Document of the Ministerial ("The Hague II") Conference on the International Energy Charter, available at http://www.energycharter.org/fileadmin/DocumentsMedia/Legal/ECTC-en.pdf, visited 6 January, 2019.

Documents Exchanged January 12, 1977 between American Arbitration Association, USSR Chamber of Commerce and Industry and Stockholm Chamber of Commerce, on file with author.

Email from Mark B Feldman, 9 February 2015, on file with author.

Email from Arthur W. Rovine, 16 Dec 2014, on file with author.

ICSID Doc. AC/67/18, Administrative Council Proceedings, First Annual Meeting, 25 September, 1967.

ICSID Doc. AC/83/3, Additional Facility: Note of the Secretary-General, 27 July, 1983.

ICSID Doc. ICSID/16, *Model Clauses Relating to the Convention on the Settlement of Investment Disputes Designed for Bilateral Investment Treaties.* Available in International Legal Materials, Vol. 8, No. 6, 1969, pp. 1341–1352.

ICSID First Ann. Rep. 1966/1967.

ICSID Rules and Regulation Amendment Process are gathered at https://icsid.worldbank.org/en/amendments, visited 5 January 2019.

ICSID Seventh Annual Report, 1972/1973

ICSID Sixth Annual Report 1971/1972.

Interview with Ulf Franke, 26 October 2015. Transcript on file with author. Cited as "Franke Interview".

Interview with Nils-Urban Allard, 29 May 2015. Transcript on file with author. Cited as "Allard Interview".

History of the ICSID Convention, Documents Concerning the Origin and the Formulation of the Convention, Volumes I–IV (1968–1970).

Letter from Ulf Franke to Professor S. Lebedev (CC Professor Pozdniakov), on file with author.

Letter from Professor S. Lebedev to Ulf Franke, 14 March, 1986, on file with author.

Report of UNCITRAL Committee of the Whole II, Annex II to Report on the Work of its 9th Session, UN Doc A/31/17, (1976).

Report of the Working Group on Arbitration and Conciliation on the Work of its Forty-Fifth Session, UN Doc A/CN.9/614.

Report of the Executive Directors on the ICSID Convention, available at the ICSID Web Page, https://icsid.worldbank.org/ICSID/StaticFiles/basicdoc/partB.htm.

Statement by Eugene J. McAllister in Hearing before the Committee on Foreign Relations of the United States Senate 18 September 1990.

Stockholm Chamber of Commerce, Press Release, *Soviet-US Arbitration Meeting on May 5, 1986 at the Swedish Consulate-General in New York*, on file with author.

The World Bank/IFC Archives, Transcript of interview with Aron Broches, May 23 1984.

UNCITRAL Doc A/72/17, Report of the United Nations Commission on International Trade Law Fiftieth session.

UNCITRAL Report of the Working Group on Arbitration and Conciliation on the work of its forty-sixth session (A/CN.9/619).

UNCITRAL Report of the Working Group on Arbitration and Conciliation on the work of its forty-eighth session (A/CN.9/646).

Index